Annual Editions:
Education, 41e

by Rebecca B. Evers
Winthrop University

http://create.mcgraw-hill.com

ISBN-10: 0078136229   ISBN-13: 9780078136221

Contents

Preface

The public conversation on the purposes and future direction of education is as lively as ever. Alternative visions and voices regarding the broad social aims of schools and the preparation of teachers continue to be presented. *Annual Editions: Education, 41/e* attempts to reflect current mainstream as well as alternative visions as to what education ought to be. This year's edition contains articles on important issues facing educators such as educational reforms; effective teaching practices for reading and mathematics; teaching all students in communities of caring learners, with an emphasis on students who live in poverty; and effectively using technology to teach all students.

We face a myriad of quandaries in our schools today, not unfamiliar to our history as a nation, which are not easily resolved. Issues regarding the purposes of education, as well as the appropriate methods of educating, have been debated throughout the generations of literate human culture. Today, we are asking ourselves and others to provide our children a *quality education* for the twenty-first century. But first we must answer the questions: What is a quality education? How do we provide such an education for all children?

There will always be debates over the purposes and the ends of "education," as it depends on what the term means at a given place or time and as each generation constructs its definition of "education" based on its understanding of "justice," "fairness," and "equity" in human relations. Each generation must establish its understanding of social justice and personal responsibility for our children and youth.

All of this is occurring as the United States continues to experience important demographic shifts in its cultural makeup. Furthermore, our ability to absorb children from many cultures into our schools has become a challenge in troubled economic times. Teachers in large cities have worked with immigrant populations since this nation began, but now schools in mid-sized cities and rural towns are experiencing increasing numbers of children who speak a language other than English. Several articles in this edition address teaching methods for English Language Learners throughout the units on diversity, caring communities, and managing student behavior. Further, we address the larger issues of literacy, which includes reading, writing, and mathematics. There are issues surrounding the use of technology in teaching,

such as what to do with the increasing presence of cell phones. Technological breakthroughs in information sciences have an impact on how people learn. Can teachers and schools keep up? Does the technology come at such a fast pace that we are overwhelmed with finding the time to keep up? The articles in this section address how technology can change the fundamental delivery of content and expand options for personalizing learning.

There are those who demand increased collaboration among teachers across grades and content areas as well as with families and the communities that are served by the schools. Are we preparing our teacher candidates for that work? Issues surround how students who are in the sexual minority are treated and educated in public schools. This is an extremely personal hot button issue that educators must face. These articles are presented not to inflame, but to begin the conversation about our responsibilities and the decisions we must make. Finally, bullying, it just does not go away. The problems of bullying are still as difficult for schools to address as they were when I was a preteen. The last two units cover bullying and the students most likely to be bullied, those who are different in some way from an unclear standard regarding gender identity, sexual orientation, ability, or race and ethnicity.

In assembling this volume, we make every effort to stay in touch with movements in educational studies and with the social forces at work in schools. Members of the advisory board contribute valuable insights, and the production and editorial staffs at the publisher, McGraw-Hill Contemporary Learning Series, coordinate our efforts.

The readings in *Annual Editions: Education, 41/e* explore the social and academic goals of education, the current conditions of the nation's educational system, the teaching profession, and the future of American education. In addition, these selections address the issues of change and the moral and ethical foundations of schooling.

[signature]

Rebecca B. Evers
Editor

Correlation Guide

The *Annual Editions* series provides students with convenient, inexpensive access to current, carefully selected articles from the public press. **Annual Editions: Education, 41/e** is an easy-to-use reader that presents articles on important topics such as *school reform, literacy, technology,* and many more. For more information on *Annual Editions* and other *McGraw-Hill Contemporary Learning Series* titles visit www.mhhe.com/cls.

This convenient guide matches the units in **Annual Editions: Education, 41/e** with the corresponding chapters in two of our best-selling McGraw-Hill Education textbooks by Sadker/Zittleman and Spring.

Annual Editions: Education	Teachers, Schools, and Society, 10/e by Sadker/Zittleman/Sadker	American Education, 15/e, by Spring
Unit : School Reform in the Twenty-first Century	**Chapter 5:** Purposes of America's Schools and the Current Reform Movement	**Chapter 1:** The History and Goals of Public Schooling **Chapter 4:** The Economic Goals of Schooling: Human Capital, Global Economy, and Preschool **Chapter 8:** Local Control, Choice, Charter Schools, and Home Schooling
Unit : Understanding Poverty	**Chapter 4:** Student Life in School and at Home	**Chapter 2:** The Social Goals of Schooling **Chapter 4:** The Economic Goals of Schooling: Human Capital, Global Economy and Preschool **Chapter 5:** Equality of Educational Opportunity: Race, Gender and Special Needs
Unit : Literacy Is the Cornerstone of Learning	**Chapter 4:** Student Life in School and at Home **Chapter 6:** Curriculum, Standards, Testng	**Chapter 2:** The Social Goals of Schooling **Chapter 4:** The Economic Goals of Schooling: Human Capital, Global Economy and Preschool
Unit : Improve School Climate to Improve Student Performance	**Chapter 8:** Philosophy of Education **Chapter 11:** Teacher Effectiveness	**Chapter 1:** The History and Goals of Public Schooling **Chapter 9:** Power and Control at State and National Levels: Political Party Platforms and High-stakes Testing
Unit : Teaching English Language Learners	**Chapter 3:** Teaching your Diverse Students	**Chapter 7:** Multicultural and Multilingual Education
Unit : Technology Supports Learning	**Chapter 4:** Student Life in School and at Home **Chapter 9:** Financing and Governing America's Schools	**Chapter 2:** The Social Goals of Schooling **Chapter 11:** Globalization of Education
Unit : Collaboration	**Chapter 4:** Student Life in School and at Home	**Chapter 2:** The Social Goals of Schooling
Unit : Sexual Minority Students	**Chapter 3:** Teaching your Diverse Students **Chapter 4:** Student Life in School and at Home	**Chapter 2:** The Social Goals of Schooling **Chapter 3:** Education and Equality of Opportunity
Unit : Bullying Continues to Be a Serious Problem	**Chapter 4:** Student Life in School and at Home	**Chapter 2:** The Social Goals of Schooling

Topic Guide

This topic guide suggests how the selections in this book relate to the subjecs in your course.

All articles that relate to each topic are listed below the bold-faced term.

Unit 1

UNIT

Prepared by: Rebecca B. Evers, *Winthrop University*

School Reform in the Twenty-first Century

We are a democratic society, committed to the free education of all our children, but are we accomplishing that goal? There has been a deep divide about this question which has resulted in much discussion of school reform and several attempts to find the perfect reform solution for our schools.

In an attempt to give direction to the reform movement, the Clinton administration established Goals 2000 under the *Educate America Act.* One of these goals continues to be important to the discussion of what constitutes a well-educated citizen.

Goal 2 states that "The high school graduation rate will increase to at least 90%." (U.S. Department of Education, n.d.) To date, data indicate that we have not reached this goal and are far from achieving it. Educators have acknowledged that high school graduates get more satisfactory jobs, are happier in their job choices, and earn higher salaries than non-graduates. Heckman and LaFontaine (2010) note the decline in high school graduation since 1970 (for cohorts born after 1950) has flattened growth in the skill level of the U.S. workforce. We must confront the drop-out problem to increase the skill levels of the future workforce. We must also consider how high schools that respond only to higher education demands may be ignoring the needs of the nation at-large for a skilled workforce that can compete in a global market. Bridgeland, Dilulio, and Morrison (2006) found in a survey of dropouts that 47 percent reported a major reason why they left school was the classes were not interesting and did not prepare them for their adulthood goals and the life they wished. We should consider that by simply preparing students to attend traditional four-year institutions, we may be ignoring their interests and desires, thus alienating them.

Next we had the No Child Left Behind legislation which placed emphasis on the specific student subgroups—requiring schools to be accountable for the progress of minority students and students with disbilities and quantifying achievement gaps. The fundamental philosophy underlying the legislation is that all children can learn and schools must demonstrate that their students have made progress. Schools are issued annual report cards based on standardized assessments and must demonstrate *adequate yearly progress* (AYP). In their latest report, the Center on Educational Policy (2012) stated

> An estimated 48% of the nation's public schools failed to make adequate yearly progress based on 2010–11 test results. This marks the highest national percentage of schools ever to fall short and an increase of 9 percentage points from the previous year (p. 9).

In 2009, the Secretary of Education issued a call to action by stating that education is the civil rights issue of this generation and the fight for education is about much more than just education; it is about social justice (Duncan, 2009). In 2009, President Obama's *Race to the Top* was passed and established new goals for schools, teachers, and students. However, is it realistic to expect that schools will make greater strides now than in the past? Boyle and Burns ask an important question: "Why do we ask citizens rather than education professionals to govern public schools?" Their concerns are centered on the responsibility of schools to socialize children into society. We transmit our collective knowledge and shared values via the public schools. Therefore, we must have public debate about the purpose of public education. Part of that debate may well include discussion of trust and accountability. Can we trust our teachers to do what they should or must we regulate every topic in the curriculum and hold them accountable via standardized assessments? Levin discusses the two theories put forward by Douglas McGregor some 60 years ago and the implications for establishing educational policies today.

Among the efforts to improve the educational outcomes is a move to adapt national Common Core State Standards (CCSS). Yatvin expresses concerns that, as written, the CCSS in English/Language Arts present an unreachable and harmful set of goals for students in elementary grades. In response to his critics' claim that he has no research data to support his dislike of the CCSS, he retorts that the critics have no evidence to validate the use of the CCSS. This should continue an already lively debate about the adoption of CCSS. In the second article about the Common Core, Bell and Thatcher examine the actions that will be needed to enact and find funding for the Common Core. Finally, in *The International Experience,* the authors look at what is working in other countries and discuss what we can and cannot learn from those countries. However, they also suggest that we not look only at the highest performing countries, but also at the countries that have failed. There is something to be learned from both.

As we consider the educational system of the United States, we must engage in an intensively reflective and analytical effort. Further, we must give considerable contemplation and forethought to the consequences, because our actions will shape not only the students' futures, but also the future of our country in the global community. Prospective teachers are encouraged to question their own individual educational experiences as they read the articles presented in this section. All of us must acknowledge that our values affect both our ideas about curriculum and what we believe is the purpose of educating others. The economic and demographic changes in the last decade and those that will occur in the future necessitate a fundamental reconceptualization of how schools ought to respond to the social and economic environments in which they are located. There are additional articles in the next unit on poverty that, with the articles in this unit, will offer practical ideas to help answer the following question. How can schools reflect the needs of, and respond to, the diverse group of students they serve while meeting the needs of our democratic society?

References

Bridgeland, J. M., Dilulio, J. J., & Morrison, K. B. 2006. "The Silent Epidemic: Perspectives of High School Dropouts." Bill & Melinda Gates Foundation. Retrieved on 28 May 2008 from www.gatesfoundation.org/Pages/home.aspx.

Center on Educational Policy, (2012). AYP results for 2010–11 – November 2012 update. Author. Retrieved on June 26, 2013 from www.cep-dc.org/displayDocument.cfm?DocumentID=5414

Ducan, A. (2009). Partners in Reform. Address to the National Education Association. Retrieved on 13 May 2012 @ www2.ed.gov/news/speeches/2009/07/07022009.html

Heckman, J. J. & LaFontaine, P. A. (2010). The American high school graduation rate: Trends and levels. *The Review of Economics and Statistics,* 92(2).

U.S. Department of Education. Summary of Goals 2000: Educate America Act. Author. Retrieved on 28 May 2008 from www.ed.gov/legislation/GOALS2000/TheAct/sec 102.html

Article   Prepared by: Rebecca B. Evers, *Winthrop University*

Keeping the Public in Public Schools

Why do we ask citizens rather than education professionals to govern public schools? Democracy demands self-government for the public good.

PHIL BOYLE AND DEL BURNS

Learning Outcomes

After reading this article, you will be able to:

- Discuss the effects of the education policy known as Race to the Top.
- Create the questions you would ask about the Race to the Top.

U.S. public schools serve a variety of purposes. They conserve contemporary values, attitudes, and social mores. They provide economic opportunity and social mobility to children of less advantaged families and thereby promote a dynamic society. They ensure a supply of educated workers. They help take care of and raise children whose parents carry out economic lives away from home. And they make a growing body of knowledge—which is increasingly difficult to collect, organize, and learn individually—accessible to all children.

Consider the public aspect of our schools. What is *public* about public education other than its funding? Why should we ask citizens rather than education professionals to govern public schools? For what purpose, and toward what ends, do we invest in educating the next generation of Americans? We educate children for a number of reasons, but ultimately to preserve our democratic republic.

Public education and our democratic republic have evolved over time together. In spite of the efforts of some reformers, they cannot be separated. In the Founding Fathers' view of a classical republic, government is inextricably linked with society. There can be no absolute separation of state or government from society.

Similarly, there can be no absolute separation of public from schools, no absolute separation of the educational from the political. This lack of separation can be troubling, particularly to dedicated public school leaders and professionals who very much want public schools to be about children rather than

politics. However, we say that such a separation is neither possible nor desirable.

Public schools carry out a public role in socializing children into society, preparing the next generation to take their place as Americans in what is today the oldest republic in the world. All other socialization is a private responsibility—carried out by and through parents, families, and church and community institutions. Public schools are the way we transmit our collective knowledge and shared values to each succeeding generation. If we are serious about tasking public schools with such a purpose, then we must be willing to engage in an equally serious conversation about the public purposes of public schools.

Four Big Things

Our contemporary debate and discussion about public education focuses more on education as a private, economic good than as a public, democratic good. This focus encourages us to see public education as an economic investment. We emphasize individual student achievement. We think of ways to privatize public schools, to operate schools and classrooms in accord with market principles, and to give education a competitive edge.

Public education certainly has important economic considerations and benefits, but this by no means makes it only or even primarily an economic enterprise. Our capacity to discover and exploit the economic benefits of all sorts of human endeavors does not limit the potential of those endeavors to economic outcomes.

The *public* in public schools is about four big things. First, it's about how we preserve liberty, personal freedom, and individual differences yet still maintain a *United* States of America. Second, it's about how we forge a sense of connection and belonging in a nation of individuals predicated on the principle of self-interest. Third, it's about how we grapple with issues of justice, fairness, and equality in a nation less homogeneous than any other. And fourth, it's about the role we expect a market economy to play in our lives, an economy central to the nation's founding as a commercial republic.

To uncover the full sense of the public in public schools, we must ask, as did Aristotle, what kind of human character our society aims at and intends to form. In asking this question we discover that the goals of public education, the goals that make education public, are the goals of human potential, of the human spirit, and of the possibilities of human character. Public education serves to shape human character and develop human potential by satisfying the core public values of liberty, equality, community, and prosperity.

In terms of liberty, public schools help create and perpetuate a nation of free individuals dedicated to self-government and capable of exercising rights, freedoms, and choice responsibly. They preserve and pass on knowledge about what it means to be an American. Through public participation and engagement, public schools provide opportunities for citizens to learn and practice the arts and skills of democracy.

In terms of community, public schools extend the boundaries of home and help socialize children and teens to assume roles and responsibilities as adults, citizens, neighbors, spouses, parents, and members. They transmit the values of American society to ensure adequate social and moral order to preserve the republic. Public schools help weave and maintain the social fabric of the nation by providing for a common democratic experience for all children.

In terms of equality, public schools serve as the great equalizer in our society. They include everyone, equalize educational opportunity, teach children tolerance and fair play, model fairness and treating people justly, and cultivate an acceptance of differences in preparing students for life in an increasingly diverse society. Public schools serve as the primary public means by which we mitigate the effects of socioeconomic inequality.

In terms of prosperity, public schools prepare each individual to be economically self-sufficient in a competitive national and global market economy in whatever form that self-sufficiency might take. Schools teach future producers, employers and consumers to balance individual self-interest with concern for and contribution to the general welfare.

Five Reasons Why Schools are Public

First, schools are not so much about children as they are about what kind of society we wish to develop and maintain. Because public schools are populated with children, we tend to think of them only as institutions that serve children. They are not. At their core, they are political and ideological institutions in which each adult generation battles among itself for supremacy in determining the purposes, goals, and direction of public education.

Second, there are no new arguments or solutions in the battles over the direction and future of public schools. Generations, technology, and politicians change, but the arguments do not. From battles over school lunch to school dress to school prayer, each generation reinterprets what it means to be an American and recapitulates the political and ideological arguments of the Founding Fathers and framers of the Constitution.

Third, there are no permanent solutions to the seemingly endless set of issues and challenges facing public schools. More than two centuries after the American Revolution, public schools continue to serve as political battlefields for debates on freedom. What does freedom mean? How much freedom should we have? Can we have too much freedom? These are timeless questions with no definite answers.

Fourth, the governing processes and policy tools we use to decide how to educate the next generation, what to teach them, how to distribute educational opportunity, who should go to school where and with whom, and how to pay for public schools reflect the social, political, and economic character of America. We have not been able to design a form of public school governance separate from the fundamental political principles of our democratic republic. As the numerous alternative governance proposals that fill the skies like hot air balloons attest, this is not for lack of trying. Changing these principles requires changing the essence and character of America, a process which the Founding Fathers made very difficult on purpose.

Fifth, unless public schools operate at the level of a public or political community, they cannot satisfy the purposes we have invested them with or achieve the goals we ask of them. As Martin Diamond wrote in an essay titled "Ethics and Politics: The American Way," Aristotle argued that human society must rise to the level of a political community because the other human groups—the family, tribe, village, corporation—do not suffice for the fulfillment of human nature.

Societies based on alliances for the sake of commerce may have a thriving economy, but they would lack a concern for the development of a common character among citizens. Focusing public schools on the advancement of economic interests may help promote a thriving commerce, but it will not develop excellent human beings. Public schools are public, then, because any lesser form of education cannot come to terms with the challenges of the human condition.

Moral, Ethical, and Political Enterprise

Despite its technical and professional clothing, public education at its core consists of moral, ethical, and political beliefs about the meaning of the good life and a vision of society and of the future. Consider these examples drawn from public schools:

- A first-grader was so excited about joining the Cub Scouts that he brought a camping utensil to school to use at lunch. School officials decided he violated the district's zero-tolerance policy on weapons and sentenced him to 45 days in the district's reform school. After its 80-page code of conduct received national attention, the district rescinded the sentence.

- A state legislature passed a bill permitting school districts to promote "critical thinking" and "objective discussion" about evolution, the origins of life, and global warming by allowing teachers to use supplementary materials to critique the standard textbook.

- Football cheerleaders at a public high school painted messages like "Commit to the Lord" on giant paper banners that the players charged through onto the field. After the school was cautioned about the risk of a constitutional challenge due to an insufficient separation of church and state in school-sponsored activities, the school board struck down the tradition.

These examples raise several big questions for public schools. First, why do we educate children, and what do we want and expect from public schools? Second, what should we teach children and what is the best way to educate them? Third, who should educate children? Fourth, how do our communities benefit from public schools, and how might they be different without public schools? And fifth, why do public schools give rise to so many controversial issues, and what should citizens and public school leaders do about these issues?

Notice that these questions are about the *public* in public schools. They involve our understanding of the public good. They are not technical questions about how we teach arithmetic or about whether state history should precede U.S. history in the curriculum. They are value-based questions about the social and political context of public schools and about our vision for the future. Public values are the values of public education, because public schools comprise the public institution by which we prepare each generation of Americans to become Americans.

If our democratic experiment is to survive, we must teach our children the moral, ethical, and political obligations of living in a free society. What good does it do, for example, to promote anti-bullying campaigns in schools only to have students and parents observe board members bullying each other?

We cannot preserve our republic without preserving the democratic virtues that make our republic possible in the first place. And we cannot preserve the public in public schools without taking responsibility as citizens for governing public schools. For as Alexis de Tocqueville noted, in the habit and practice of self-government, American character reaches up toward the republican virtues. Should we fail in this task, our republic will edge ever closer to the precipice of political extinction. If public schools serve no other purpose, they should serve this one.

Critical Thinking

1. Select one of the five reasons why schools are public. Develop an argument for or against that reason.

2. The authors provide three examples of school boards' reaction to incidents in their schools. Do you believe the boards of education in these districts responded appropriately? Offer justification for your opinion.

3. Choose one of the questions posed by the authors in the paragraph following the examples. Compose a response to the question to share in class discussion.

Create Central

www.mhhe.com/createcentral

Internet References

U.S. Department of Education: Race to the Top
www2.ed.gov/programs/racetothetop/index.html

American School Board Journal
www.asbj.com

PHIL BOYLE (pboyle@leadingandgoverning.com) is president of Leading and Governing Associates, a public leadership education and consulting practice. Del Burns (dburns@gmka.com) is GMK Associates' director of education services and the former superintendent of North Carolina's Wake County Public Schools. This article is excerpted from the authors' book, *Preserving the Public in Public Schools: Visions, Values, Conflicts and Choices*, Rowman & Littlefield Press.

Article   Prepared by: Rebecca B. Evers, *Winthrop University*

Balance Trust and Accountability

Education reformers want more accountability even though the evidence suggests better outcomes result from fewer rules.

BEN LEVIN

Learning Outcomes

After reading this article, you will be able to:

- Discuss McGregor's theory of human nature.

- Review the impact those outside of the system on establishing the balance between trust and accountability.

"Trust but verify," Ronald Reagan famously said about nuclear arms reduction proposals in the 1980s. Exactly this same dilemma is at the forefront of education policy debates today around the world as education systems struggle to balance trust and regulation. How much do school systems need to be controlled by rules, and how much can we trust the judgment of those working in the system?

These two contrasting approaches were the subject of discussion at a recent meeting in Jerusalem of representatives from 17 countries, sponsored by the Van Leer Institute and several other Israeli organizations. Each country brought a team of three—a teacher, a principal, and a government leader. The theme of the meeting was "Trust and Regulation" as understood and experienced by people in these different roles.

In practice, as was clear from the discussions at this event, every education system has a mix of trust and regulation. Of necessity, some things must be regulated—the school year and day, and graduation requirements, for example—but everything about school can't possibly be regulated. Still, the situations in these countries—mostly European but also Canadian, American, and Japanese—are very different. Some see their systems as heavily based on trust, with relatively little regulation. That would be the case in Finland, but also in most Asian countries. In other countries, extensive regulation suggests a climate of distrust, leaving educators feeling beleaguered and unmotivated.

These two ideas about human nature are not new: Some 60 years ago, Douglas McGregor wrote about them as Theory X and Theory Y. Theory X holds that people can't be trusted; that, unless they're watched closely, they'll take advantage of any situation for their own benefit. Policy and management therefore must develop incentives, accountability measures, and penalties to prevent misbehavior. This view underlies quite a few recent policy efforts in education—for example, increased inspection, testing, or evaluation linked to various consequences, whether for students, teachers, or schools. It's also behind more traditional centralized approaches, including systems that believe every school should be doing the same things in the same way at the same time.

A second position, Theory Y, starts with the assumption that most people know what they are doing and are reasonably well intentioned, at least most of the time. In this view, organizations benefit by putting more trust in people to do their jobs and building organization cultures that encourage such an attitude. Proponents of this position tend to opt for fewer rules and weaker accountability measures. Proposals for greater autonomy for individual schools are one instance of this attitude, as is the position of many teacher organizations that individual teachers should determine their own practice.

Unsurprisingly, those outside the system tend to favor policies with more regulation, while insiders tend to favor more trust. Most of us think we're trustworthy while others are often, in our view, less reliable, and so they need more controls. As one wag put it, it's human nature to want more autonomy for ourselves and more predictability—and therefore less autonomy—from everyone else. So, in the same way, teachers may want more autonomy in their work, but they often want more rules for students; the same is true of principals with teachers, and policy makers with schools. The double standard is alive and well!

More Regulation

The pressure for increased regulation is not confined to education; the same dynamic is at work in other fields. It's evident in nurses who feel they spend more time documenting than caring for patients, or government agencies that must check and recheck even the smallest expenditure or have highly restrictive procedures for hiring or procurement. And the private sector also complains about increased requirements related to health and safety, audits, or antidiscrimination.

In most cases, as these examples imply, regulations have reasons behind them. The danger of being sued for wrongdoing certainly encourages more adherence to rules and careful record keeping. In many other cases, rules arise from perceived abuses of trust, many of which make good media stories. When there is public outrage about some particular breach, new regulations are often the result. For example, only a very few cases of child abuse are necessary to generate a requirement for background checks on all employees and volunteers.

In some cases, though, the perceived problems may be few in number and small in effect while the cost of new regulation is quite high. For example, a few cases of misspending, even of relatively small amounts, can lead to new reporting rules that can be quite costly to implement; indeed, prevention can cost more than the problem while not fully preventing further occurrences. Yet, if the public clamor is sufficient, resisting the call for greater regulation is virtually impossible. As a result, there can be much more scrutiny in many organizations of very small items, such as employee travel expenses than there is of whether the bulk of the budget is helping to meet the organization's goals. What gets noticed gets attended to, but the most important things aren't always the ones to get noticed.

There is good evidence that too much regulation can be counterproductive, as people tend to reduce effort and initiative when they feel they're distrusted, and too many rules can lead to lots of stupid behavior. As Dee Hock, founder of the Visa credit system put it, "Simple, clear purpose and principles give rise to complex, intelligent behaviors. Complex rules and regulations give rise to simple, stupid behaviors" (2010). Anyone who has worked in a large organization can attest to this reality!

Distrust of professions and institutions is fed not only by media attention but also by a better educated public that's increasingly disinclined to believe in the altruism and beneficence of professionals, as witnessed by concerns about levels of public confidence in virtually all institutions and professions around the world. Ironically, one result of education may be to make people less trustful of large institutions, including schools.

Participants at the Jerusalem meeting struggled with these questions. Not surprisingly, each group felt that it merited more trust and less regulation. On the other hand, everyone recognized that both elements were important at every level of the system. But, in most cases, the balance was seen as being tilted too much toward regulation. Teachers especially felt that they weren't respected by the system as a whole.

Most importantly, it was clear that higher performing education systems tended to have less regulation and to rely more on strategies that involved not simply trust of individuals but building professional cultures that supported intelligent behavior directed toward organizational goals.

Indeed, this would seem to be the desired direction based on what we're learning about effective education systems. These rely neither on leaving it up to individuals to determine what they do, nor on trying to control practice through detailed regulation. Instead, effective systems build organizational and professional cultures in which there is strong collective pressure to improve performance and achieve goals, but also lots of support for people to improve their skills so they can contribute more effectively.

As is so often the case, good education policy mirrors good classroom practice. In effective classrooms, students feel a sense of autonomy and independence within a system that's carefully structured and organized to encourage the right kinds of actions. The desired practices and beliefs are nurtured not only by the organization of the classroom but also by social relationships built among participants.

These examples bring home the point that in any endeavor, strong teams display this same combination of individuals feeling important coupled with powerful group norms around performance. The rules, if they're intelligent ones, provide a vital framework that encourages the right behavior. Good regulations play a key role in building trust. The wrong rules will have the opposite effect. The issue isn't whether to have rules or autonomy, but how to create regulations that help schools do the work we want them to do.

On this point, it was clear in Jerusalem, no country has it just right. There is always a tension between regulation and autonomy, and ongoing differences of opinion on the right balance are inevitable, perhaps even desirable. On the whole, though, there seems too much confidence in education policy that we can get where we want primarily with a rulebook even though the evidence suggests otherwise.

Reference

Hock, D. (2010, February 17). Dee Hock on complex rules (web log post). http://builtforchange.blogspot.ca/2010/02/dee-hock-on-complex-rules.html

Critical Thinking

1. Levin quotes McGregor's theory of human nature: Theory X and Theory Y. Which of these theories do you believe hold true for most of the humans you know? Offer an example that supports your decision.
2. It is commonly asserted that schools should serve a public good and in this article Levin describes what happens when the public wants accountability and the schools want trust. Are these two ideas conflicting thoughts or can a middle ground be found?
3. Where do you stand on the issues of trust and accountability? Should those outside the system be allowed to impose their educational philosophy or should those inside the system be trusted to do what is best for children in the schools?

Create Central

www.mhhe.com/createcentral

Internet References

American School Board Journal
www.asbj.com

The Center for Comprehensive School Reform and Improvement
www.centerforcsri.org

BEN LEVIN (ben.levin@utoronto.ca) is a professor and Canada research chair in education leadership and policy at the Ontario Institute for Studies in Education, University of Toronto. His current research interests are in large-scale change, poverty and inequity, improving high schools, and finding better ways to connect research to policy and practice in education. He has been deputy minister (chief civil servant) for education for the province of Ontario and deputy minister of advanced education and deputy minister of education, training, and youth for the province of Manitoba. He is the author of seven books, including *How to Change 5,000 Schools* (Harvard Education Press, 2008) and *More High School Graduates* (Corwin Press, 2011).

Article   Prepared by: Rebecca B. Evers, *Winthrop University*

Warning: the Common Core Standards May Be Harmful to Children

The language arts standards of the Common Core in too many places are simply too difficult and/or irrelevant for elementary grade students.

JOANNE YATVIN

Learning Outcomes

After reading this article, you will be able to:

- Analyze the data presented about student achievement in your state as it measures up to the rest of the United States.

When I first read the Common Core English/language arts standards for grades K-5, my visceral reaction was that they represented an unrealistic view of what young children should know and be able to do. As an elementary teacher and principal for most of my life, I could not imagine children between the ages of 5 and 11 responding meaningfully to the standards' expectations. But clearly I was in the minority. Forty-five states have adopted the standards without a murmur of complaint; writers and publishers are racing to produce materials for teaching them, and the teachers quoted in news articles or advertisements speak of the standards as if they are the silver bullet they have been waiting for.

Since then, I have read the English/language arts (ELA) standards many times; each time, they are more troubling. Some standards call on young children to behave like high school seniors, making fine distinctions between words or literary devices, carrying on multiple processes simultaneously, and expressing their understandings in precise academic language. Others expect them to have a strong literary background after only two or three years of schooling. Some standards are so blind to the diversity in American classrooms that they require children of different abilities, backgrounds, and native languages to manipulate linguistic forms and concepts before they have full control of their own home language. And, sadly, a few standards serve only to massage the egos of education elitists, but are of no use in college courses, careers, or everyday life.

To give you just an inkling of the problems in applying the ELA standards to young children, I offer a scenario of what might happen in a 1st-grade classroom when the following language standard is approached:

> **(L.1.1)** *Use the most frequently occurring inflections and affixes (e.g., -ed, -s, re-, un-, pre-, -ful, -less) as a clue to the meaning of an unknown word.*

While reading aloud from a 1st-grade book, Zach stumbled over the word "recheck" and, although he eventually pronounced it correctly, his teacher felt that he did not fully grasp its meaning in the sentence. It seemed like a good time to make the class aware of the prefix "re" and how it works. So, she stopped the lesson and wrote these words on the white board: remake, rewrite, and retell. Then she asked the children to explain what each word meant. Several students raised their hands and answered correctly.

"What does the 're' part of each word tell us?" she then asked. The first student called on said "re" means to do something again. Nodding in approval, the teacher wrote "recheck" on the board leaving a space between "re" and "check." Then she asked, "So, what does 'recheck' mean?"

"To check something again," answered the class in chorus.

Since things were going well, the teacher decided to continue by asking students to name other words that worked the same way. Various class members confidently suggested, re-eat, re-dance, re-sleep, re-win, and others were waving their hands when she stopped them.

"Those aren't real words," she said. "We don't say, 'I'm going to resleep tonight.' Let's try to think of real words or look for them in our books." After giving the class a few minutes, she asked again for examples.

This time, the words were real enough: repeat, renew, reason, remove, return, read, and reveal, but none of them fit the principle being taught. Since it seemed futile to explain all that to 1st graders, the teacher did the best thing she could think of: "You reminded (uh-oh) me of 'recess,'" she said. "So, let's go out right now."

As they left the room, the children chatted happily among themselves: "We're going to 'cess' again!" "We'll 're-see' our friends." "I want to 're-play' dodge ball."

"Next time," thought the teacher, "I'd better try a different prefix." But then "un-smart" and "un-listen" popped into her head, and she decided to leave that particular standard for later in the year.

Although I could write scenarios for several other standards, they would make this paper much longer and not be as amusing as this one. Instead, I will present just a few standards that I find inappropriate for K-5 students along with brief explanations of their problems.

A Reading/Literature standard for 4th grade calls on students to:

> **(RL.4.4)** *Determine the meaning of words and phrases as they are used in a text, including those that allude to significant characters found in mythology (e.g., Herculean).*

I can't help wondering how 9- and 10-year-olds are supposed to do their "determining." Competent, engaged readers of any age do not stop to puzzle out unknown words in a text. Mostly, they rely on the surrounding context to explain them. But, if that doesn't work, they skip them, figuring that somewhere down the page they will be made clear.

Should students regularly consult a dictionary or thesaurus while reading? I don't think so. That's a surefire way to destroy the continuity of meaning. Nor would I expect them to recall an explanatory reference from the field of classic literature at this early stage of their education. Moreover, for each "Herculean" word that matches a literary character, there would be several like "cupidity" and "pander" that have strayed far from their original meanings.

In the Reading/Information category, I quickly found a standard with expectations far beyond the knowledge backgrounds of the children for whom it is intended:

> **(RI.2.3)** *Describe the connection between a series of historical events, scientific ideas or concepts, or steps in technical procedures in a text.*

Just assuming that 2nd graders are familiar with "a series" of historical events, etc., is simply unrealistic. But expecting them to "describe the connection between (sic) them" is delusional. Is there only one simple connection among a series of "scientific ideas"? How would you, as an adult, describe the connections among the steps in building a robot or even baking a pie?

In most of the Reading/Information standards, the same expectations for describing complex relationships among multiple items appear:

> **(RI.5.5)** *Compare and contrast the overall structure (e.g., chronology, comparison, cause/effect, problem/solution) of events, ideas, concepts, or information in two or more texts.*

For 5th graders, this standard would be even more difficult to meet than the previous one because it asks them to carry out two different operations on two or more texts that almost certainly differ in content, style, and organization

In the Writing and Speaking/Listening categories, there are fewer standards altogether. Yet, some of these standards also make unrealistic demands. One asks 1st graders to:

> **(W.1.7)** *Participate in shared research and writing projects (e.g., explore a number of "how-to" books on a given topic and use them to write a sequence of instructions).*

Since this standard does not mention "adult guidance and support," as many others do, I assume that a group of 1st graders is expected to work on its own to digest the content of several books, prune it to the essentials, and then devise a well-ordered list of instructions. This would be a complicated assignment even for students much older, requiring not only analysis and synthesis, but also self-regulation and compromise. I cannot see 1st graders carrying it out without a teacher guiding them every step of the way.

Of all the ELA standards, the ones in the Language (i.e., grammar) category are the most unrealistic. I could cite almost all of them as unreasonable for the grades designated and a few as pointless for any grade. Here is part of a kindergarten standard that fits both descriptions:

> **(L.K.1).** *(When speaking) Produce and expand complete sentences in shared language activities.*

Most of the kindergartners I know have no idea what the term "complete sentence" means. Children and adults commonly speak short phrases and single words to each other. I can't imagine any kindergarten teacher insisting during a group language activity that children speak in "complete sentences" or that they "expand" their sentences. Those directions would in all likelihood end the activity quickly as most children fell silent.

Here is another unrealistic standard, this time designated for 3rd grade:

> **(L.3.1)** *Explain the function of nouns, pronouns, verbs, adjectives, and adverbs in general and their functions in particular sentences.*

Aside from the unreasonableness of expecting 7- and 8-year-olds to explain the use of grammatical terms, this standard has no applications in reading, speaking, or writing. Research has shown unequivocally that being able to name parts of speech or diagram sentences has no positive effect on students' writing. This standard wastes instructional time on a useless skill.

I cannot leave this critique of the ELA Standards without taking one more swipe at the Language category. Standard **(L.4.1)** asks 4th graders to:

> *Use relative pronouns (who, whose, whom, which, that) and correctly use frequently confused words (e.g., to, too, two; there, their) in speech and writing.*

Several of these words are ones that many educated adults use incorrectly all the time. In fact "who" is so often used in place of "whom" that it is widely recognized as correct. Why not hold adults accountable for meeting this standard before expecting 4th graders to do so?

In finding fault with so many of the K-5 ELA standards, my familiarity with children's abilities and educational needs have guided me. Standards advocates may well argue that I have offered no evidence and scant research to support my views. In rebuttal, I would argue that they are in the same position and that much of what they propose for children flies in the face of established learning theory and brain development research. The reality is that the standards' creators have laid out a set of expectations for America's children that are grounded only in an antiquated conception of education and their personal preferences. And their followers, bedazzled by the standards length and breadth, illusion of depth, and elitist aura, have fallen into line as if lured by the Pied Piper of Hamelin.

Critical Thinking

1. Yatvin presents examples of Common Core State Standards (CCSS) that she believes to be inappropriate for the developmental level of the students in elementary school grades. Do you agree with her? Are you able to recall research or educational psychology theories that would support her ideas? If you disagree with her, are you able to recall research or educational psychology theories that would refute her ideas?

2. If you are a middle-level or high school teacher, do you believe that here are problems with the CCSS at your grade level? Which standards trouble you?

3. If you believe that the CCSS are harmful to students, how do we account for the fact that so many states have adopted these standards? Think back to the first two articles in this unit. How might the ideas in them apply to the issues discussed by Yatvin?

Create Central

www.mhhe.com/createcentral

Internet References

What Works Clearinghouse
   www.ies.ed.gov/ncee/wwc

The Center for Comprehensive School Reform and Improvement
   www.centerforcsri.org

JOANNE YATVIN (jyatvin@comcast.net) is an adjunct professor and supervisor of student teachers at the Portland State University Graduate School of Education, Portland, Ore., and is a past president of the National Council of Teachers of English (NCTE).

Yatvin, Joanne. From *Phi Delta Kappan*, March 2013, pp. 42–44. Reprinted with permission of Phi Delta Kappa International. All rights reserved. www.pdkintl.org

Article   Prepared by: Rebecca B. Evers, *Winthrop University*

Challenged to the Core

Lawmakers face the daunting task of enacting the laws and coming up with the funds needed to bring the Common Core State Standards to life.

JULIE DAVIS BELL AND DANIEL THATCHER

Learning Outcomes

After reading this article, you will be able to:

- Explain the pros and cons of adopting the Common Core Curriculum

I t is either one of the most significant state education reforms ever or just another short-term fix, depending on who you ask. But one thing is for sure, most lawmakers would say they are tackling some of the most sweeping and complicated reforms for grades K-12 they've ever attempted. The Common Core State Standards (CCSS)—fully adopted by 45 states between 2010 and 2011—now place legislatures squarely in the middle of the most important next step. They must decide which reforms and laws are necessary to meet the initiatives' requirements.

A Movement Begins

The notion of having national academic standards has been bandied about for years. But it wasn't until 2009 when the National Governors Association's Center on Best Practices and the Council of Chief State School Officers coalesced their members' support around an initiative to develop voluntary, state-led standards that the idea took root. Minus the participation of Alaska and Texas, 48 states committed to the idea of the Common Core State Standards and began deliberations in 2010 over whether to adopt them.

Advocates argued that in this era of increased global competitiveness and family mobility, the country needed common academic metrics and goals that all students—whether living in Las Alamos or the Bronx—must measure up to and master.

"We must insist on standards that will prepare our high-school graduates for the demanding challenges they will face," wrote former Florida Governor Jeb Bush and former New York Schools Chancellor Joel Klein in an op-ed for *The Wall Street Journal* in 2011. "Recognizing our great need for more rigorous academics, state leaders and educators have come together to create model content standards."

The Basics on the Standards

Academic standards define the knowledge and skills students should have at various grade levels. The common core standards initiative is an attempt by states to correlate their previously inconsistent academic goals—so that what Sarah in Sacramento is expected to know in third grade is the same as what Sara in St. Petersburg is learning.

The new standards were built upon the strengths of current state standards, and were written with the goals of measuring up against international standards, being rigorous in content and capable of preparing all students for a career or college, specifically,

- Math and English standards have been developed for each grade from kindergarten to eight and for every two years in high school.
- Science standards are being developed now and will be added later.
- There are no plans to develop standards in any other subjects, so states may continue using their own in these areas.
- States may augment the common standards with up to 15 percent of their own state-specific standards.

A Standard Example

To illustrate one common core standard in reading, third-grade students, under the "Phonics and Word Recognition" category, must be able to:

- Identify and know the meaning of the most common prefixes and derivational suffixes.
- Decode words with common Latin suffixes.
- Decode multi-syllable words.
- Read grade-appropriate irregularly spelled words.

Soon, business leaders joined the chorus of supporters. "Fifty different sets of standards make no sense," Craig Barrett, former CEO of Intel Corp., argued in *The Wall Street Journal*. "Common education standards are essential for producing the educated work force America needs to remain globally competitive."

To date, all but Alaska, Nebraska, Texas and Virginia have adopted the new standards.

Cautious Optimism

Today, the core standards movement enjoys wide bipartisan support. "This is the right thing to do, to recognize that we as a country need to do better—and the action is happening in the states," says Delaware Senator Dave P. Sokola (D). Members of NCSL's bipartisan Education Committee voted to support adoption of the standards as long as they remain voluntary and state-led.

Other lawmakers aren't so optimistic, voicing a concern that the legislative branch has been left in the dark on the pace and progress of the standards. "I am not getting any information about this from our state education department," Wisconsin Senator Luther Olsen (R) says. "Legislators are not getting briefed by our state commissioners about what is happening and what is going to be needed."

Even though the standards were developed at the state level, some policymakers are concerned the federal government will insert its influence into the project, causing states and localities to lose some control over education and their state standards.

Minnesota Representative Sondra Erickson (R) is among the skeptical. "Mostly I am concerned about state authority," she says. "We may be disappointed in the end that we all agreed to do the same thing."

The U.S. Department of Education has encouraged states' efforts to establish standards by awarding additional points to those applying for Race to the Top grants and No Child Left Behind waivers if they have adopted and are working on the common core standards. The federal department also has awarded $330 million to two groups developing assessments based on the standards: the Partnership for Assessment of Readiness in College and Careers (PARCC) and the SMARTER Balanced Assessment Consortium.

"I feel better about the common standards than I did at first," says West Virginia Senator Robert H. Plymale (D). "We're making them work for West Virginia. I am less concerned about federal intrusion now, and it is forcing some very good conversations in the states about what we have to do to improve student achievement."

A Colossal Task

Although 26 of the current governors and 22 current chief state school officers were not in office when their states agreed to the standards, they—along with school leaders, teachers and state legislators—still must get involved in the specific nuts and bolts of getting them established. Like conductors of an orchestra, states will need to direct myriad moving policy parts—from curriculum and textbooks to teaching and assessments to fit together, work and harmonize.

"I'm concerned that by trying to do everything at once we are going to implode, especially when state legislators have not been party to this from the beginning," says Wisconsin Senator Olsen. "It's overwhelming," agrees Idaho Senator John W. Goedde (R).

The Timeline

2012 to 2013

States have a lot to do to prepare their school systems for the Common Core Standards. In the next two years, state legislatures will:

1. Decide whether to participate in one or both consortia developing assessments.
2. Review statutes and regulations and amend or adopt new laws if needed.
3. Support the development of new curricula, professional development programs, models to track student progress, interactive reporting of test results and teacher evaluation systems.
4. Procure the technology needed for the assessments.

Higher education officials will:

1. Align admission requirements to the standards.
2. Correlate freshmen year core curriculum to the standards.
3. Review teacher preparation programs.

School districts will:

1. Begin developing curriculum and designing instruction based on the standards.

2014

School districts will:

1. Finish writing curriculum and designing class instruction.
2. Pilot individual test items.
3. Phase in course assessments.

2015

1. Teachers must administer the new end-of-year assessments in the spring.
2. Schools must report the results of the end-of year assessments.

If done correctly, advocates say, harmonizing existing policies with the standards will equip teachers with the tools they need to guide students to reach the new standards, which in most states are tougher than any previous state ones. But do states have the resources to provide teachers with the professional development they'll need to teach the new standards? Senator Sokola says this is a huge "capacity building" challenge for states. "You hear that 90 percent of teachers think the standards are a good idea, but only 25 percent feel they are ready for them."

The standards present lawmakers with a variety of challenges and opportunities in adapting the program statewide, and usually require changes to a number of policies or statutes. Legislators want to make sure the new assessments fit within their states' existing frameworks while they:

• Set high benchmarks for new curricula aligned to the standards.

• Support ongoing professional development for teachers and school leaders.

- Require rigorous teacher preparation programs in state colleges.

- Participate in one of the state consortia developing assessments to ensure they align with specific state needs.

- Adapt teacher evaluations to the new, tougher assessments, which might require revisiting recently enacted changes that include student performance in teacher accountability measures.

- Connect K-12 assessments to higher education entrance standards.

- Establish and fund an adequate statewide collection and analyses of test score data.

- Ensure state-of-the-art technology is available as needed to teach and test the standards.

Cost Concerns

But by far the biggest concern lawmakers have, according to a recent NCSL survey, is costs.

"My biggest concern is how much all this is going to cost," says Oklahoma Senator John W. Ford (R). "We know we have to pay for things. Where do we take the money from?"

Others are concerned that the costly technology necessary—from broadband access to updated software—is far from adequate in many of their schools and school districts.

With all the pieces that must fall into place before student testing begins in 2015, the timetable is vexing. "To pass anything I need 50 percent of all members to vote for it and the governor to sign it and we don't meet again until January," says Iowa Representative Greg Forristall (R). "We just did major education reform last session and it is really hard."

Despite the challenges, some states are forging ahead. "We were one of the first states to adopt the common core standards," says West Virginia Delegate Mary M. Poling (D). "We've been informed by our superintendent that West Virginia standards had already been revised and are more rigorous than the common core standards."

Professional development opportunities for adopting the common core standards into classroom teaching and customizing the standards for West Virginia were part of legislation passed last year. "West Virginia's Next Generation Content Standards and Assessment are well underway," Poling says.

The Last Detail

The final challenge will be garnering support from students and parents. Clear and ongoing communication will be key. Explaining the goals of the program—as well as why the state and nation need a new, common set of standards—is vital.

The going could be rough. When the new program's first round of test scores are released, many policymakers are preparing for a significant public backlash. The tougher standards and more sophisticated assessments will likely result in significantly lower student scores, at least at first. Teachers, principals, legislators and governors will have their hands full explaining the test results, and why, by setting the bar higher, students appear less prepared for college or a career than they did before.

Critical Thinking

1. Restate and explain the challenges faced by the states that have adopted the Common Core State Standards.
2. In the final paragraph, Bell and Thatcher appear to have concerns about the assessment data and student learning outcomes under these new standards. Do you think they are being realistic, pessimistic, or display a lack of trust that teachers and student can measure up under tougher standards? Be prepared to support your answer.

Create Central

www.mhhe.com/createcentral

Internet References

American Research Institute
   http://www.air.org/focus-area/education/index.cfm?fa=viewContent&content_id=1673&id=2
Education Week on the Web
   www.edweek.org

JULIE DAVIS BELL is group director of and Daniel Thatcher is a policy specialist in education at NCSL.

Bell, Julie Davis; Thatcher, Daniel. From *State Legislatures*, September 2012, pp. 13–17. Copyright © 2012 by Phi Delta Kappan. Reprinted by permission.

Article   Prepared by: Rebecca B. Evers, *Winthrop University*

The International Experience

CARLOS X. LASTRA-ANADÓN AND PAUL E. PETERSON

Learning Outcomes

After reading this article, you will be able to:

- Predict which practices from other counties might be successful in the United States.
- Reflect on the cultural differences that may influence accountability and autonomy within the education system.

Undoubtedly, the United States has much to learn from education systems in other countries. Once the world's education leader, the U.S. has seen the percentage of its high-school students who are proficient trail that of 31 other countries in math and 16 countries in reading, according to a recent study by Harvard's Program on Education Policy and Governance (PEPG). Whereas only 32% of United States 8th graders are proficient in math, 50% of Canadian students and nearly 60% of Korean and Finnish students perform at that level. It may be misleading to point out that 75% of Shanghai's students are proficient, as that Chinese province is the nation's most advanced, but in Massachusetts, the highest-achieving of the states, only 51% of the students are proficient in math.

Given these performance disparities, it is only natural to think that there is something to be learned from practices elsewhere. Yet it is not easy to figure out what institutions and practices will translate into a different cultural milieu or how to do it. In the larger world of governmental constitutions, efforts to insert United States arrangements into distant political cultures have failed more often than not. Much the same could happen in reverse if the United States attempted to fix its schools simply by copying something that seems to work elsewhere.

It is tempting to undertake an in-depth study of those places that are performing at the highest levels—China's Shanghai province, Korea, Finland, Singapore, Japan, the Netherlands, and Canada, for example. But a proper comparison requires that one contrast what successful countries do with the mistakes made by the less successful ones. International comparisons should look at information from all countries and adjust for factors that affect student performance, even though such rigorous studies typically face their own challenges, including collecting the requisite data. Moreover, countries are different across so many dimensions (from the political system to the cultural

prestige of the teaching profession) that it is typically difficult to attribute differences between countries to any specific factors.

For these reasons, learning from international experience can be a bit like reading tea leaves: People are tempted to see in the patterns whatever they think they should see. But for all the hazards associated with drawing on international experience, the greatest risk lies in ignoring such information altogether. Steadfastly insisting that the United States is unique and that nothing is to be learned from other lands might appeal to those on the campaign trail. But it is a perilous course of action for those who wish to understand—and improve—the state of American education. If nothing else, reflection on international experience encourages one to think more carefully about practices and proposals at home. It is not so much specific answers that come from conversing with educators from around the world, as it is gaining some intellectual humility. Such conversations provide opportunities to learn the multiple ways in which common questions are posed and answered, and to consider how policies that have proved successful elsewhere might be adapted to the unique context of United States education.

That, perhaps, is the signal contribution of the August 2011 conference on "Learning from the International Experience," sponsored by Harvard's Program on Education Policy and Governance. Many who attended said the conference had sparked conversations well beyond the usual boundaries on thinking about United States education policy, whether the issue was teacher reforms, school choice, the development of common standards and school accountability, or the promise of learning online.

Need to Take Action

The conference opened with an urgent call from United States Deputy Secretary of Education Anthony Miller that action be taken. He highlighted two aspects of Harvard's PEPG study in his remarks. First, by showing the dismal performance of students from families in which a parent has a college education, "the findings . . . debunk the myth that the mediocre performance of United States students on international tests is due simply to the presence of large numbers of disadvantaged students." Indeed, the study shows that the percent proficient among United States students whose parents are college-educated or who are white is significantly less than the percent proficient among all students in countries such as Korea,

Singapore, and Finland. Second, by breaking out results for every state, it shows that "the United States education system is comprised of 50 state systems, and therefore we must look at our performance on a state-by-state basis."

Hoover Institution scholar Eric Hanushek built on Miller's remarks by reporting that, according to work he did with University of Munich economist Ludger Woessmann, the United States could boost its annual GDP growth rate by more than 1 percentage point annually by raising student math performance to levels currently attained in countries such as Canada and Korea. That kind of increase in economic productivity could, over the long run, boost the United States economy by trillions of dollars. According to Hanushek, "the impact of the current recession on the economy is dwarfed" by the magnitude of the loss in wealth that has at its root subpar United States education performance.

Hanushek was careful to state that the goal was not to strengthen United States performance at the expense of other nations: The creation of well-educated citizens does not constitute a "a zero-sum game that countries or states are playing against each other," but one in which every country and state can become more productive, and create more wealth for one another by boosting and sharing their talents. The United States can welcome the higher Canadian, Finnish, Korean, and Chinese performances even as those accomplishments make a compelling case for "changing the direction the United States is going."

Further developing the case for reform, University of Arkansas scholars Jay P. Greene and Josh P. McGee provided conference participants with a glimpse of their new report, which identifies the international standing of nearly every school district in the United States. "People tend to think their own districts are OK," even when the United States as a whole appears to be doing badly, Greene said. "But they really are not." Even in expensive suburbs, student performance does not look very good from an international perspective, they said. "There is no refuge for 'elite' families in this country." Greene and McGee reported that in 17 states they were unable to find a single district that performed at levels comparable to those reached by students in the world's leading countries.

Teachers and Teaching

Offering hope that urgent action can be taken, Mona Mourshed told the conference that she and her colleagues at McKinsey & Company have shown that "systems can achieve significant gains in as short a time as six years." Mediocre systems can become much better, and "those that are good can become great." In her view, there are "clusters of interventions" that are appropriate for each stage of system development, and for each one, the key driver of change is teachers. The most important factor for every system's journey of transformation, she said, is to develop teachers' capabilities to their full potential. And others agreed. As New Jersey's chief education officer Christopher Cerf put it, "The single greatest in-school variable driving [learning] outcomes is the quality of the teacher."

But how can we ensure high-quality instruction? According to Mourshed, much depends on the stage a school system has reached. If a system is mediocre and has only low-performing teachers, then it can make the most progress through strong administrative actions that identify clear expectations for teachers and are fairly prescriptive. This may involve scripted teaching materials, monitoring of the time teachers devote to each task, and regular visits by master teachers or school inspectors. But, as the performance of the system rises and the teaching force reaches a higher level of quality, it can move "from good to great" by giving those teachers both greater autonomy and support. Among other things, great school systems decentralize pedagogical methods to schools and teachers, and put in place incentives for frontline educators to share innovative practices across schools. "Teacher teams" collaborate to push the quality and customization of classroom materials even further, and the educators rotate throughout the system, spreading peer learning and enriching mentorship opportunities.

Fernando Reimers of Harvard's Graduate School of Education said that most teachers are trained in academic programs that have low prestige and are far removed from the activities of the classroom. Students in these programs are asked to think about sociological, psychological, and policy issues rather than to discuss what it takes to teach a particular lesson effectively. In this regard, schools of education are unlike other professional schools. He gave the example of business schools, which are increasingly asked to link instruction directly to the work future managers will be expected to do. Reimers urged that education-training programs combine mastery of the subject matter, needed especially today in math and science, with the ability to adapt teaching to different learners, to use technology effectively, and to enable project-based learning and teamwork.

In making these points, Reimers built on the presentation on Finnish training programs given by Jari Lavonen of the University of Helsinki. Advanced training at an education school in Finland is "more popular than medical school," Lavonen told conference participants. Those admitted are a select group, and acceptance virtually guarantees a well-compensated and prestigious career. Rigorous training programs expect future teachers to demonstrate content knowledge in both a major and a minor subject, research competence, and classroom effectiveness. He admitted that the pedagogical research component was often contested by students ("we are teachers, not researchers"), but, he says, alumni later tell him that it was one of the most valuable parts of their educational experience. In his view, it is this component that enables them to tackle complex classrooms situations effectively later on. But, Lavonen cautioned, the system works in Finland only because the political situation was stable enough that the country was able to make "consistent decisions over the course of 40 years."

Gwang-Jo Kim, former education vice-minister in Korea and current head of UNESCO in Thailand, also stressed the quality of those entering the teaching profession. Koreans are known for their "high regard for teachers and for the teaching profession." Primary-school teacher-training programs receive many more applicants than there are spaces. There are multiple routes to certification as a secondary-school teacher, but the chances of getting a job are as low as 5%, as positions are avidly sought. Similarly, in Singapore, applicants to teacher-training programs are carefully selected, with a large proportion coming from the top 30% of the college population.

Kim said the Korean and Singapore success stories could not be understood apart from deep-seated cultural factors. The demand for teacher excellence comes from parents, who want their children to do well on national examinations that determine future education and occupational opportunities. As a result, teachers are under a lot of pressure. With unionization of the teaching profession in Korea, Kim wonders whether the current model can be sustained.

Building on these insights, White House education adviser Roberto Rodríguez reported that the Obama administration is developing models of teacher mentorship and induction that will support new recruits into the profession and renew teacher-preparation programs. "We don't have a system that recruits talent. There is not a high bar for ed schools," Rodríguez said. In addition, he emphasized the current lack of high-quality professional development for teachers and adequate mentorship for new teachers. Rodríguez confirmed the administration's intention to create differentiated tracks for master teachers, administrators, and specialist teachers, in which teacher compensation is tied to progress on those tracks. Currently, he stated, "we lose too many good teachers to administration." Underlining a point made by Deputy Secretary Miller, Rodríguez reminded the conference that, to be effective, change must come not only from the federal government but from "high levels of energy at the state and local level."

Agreeing that state action is vital, New Jersey's Christopher Cerf told conference participants that successful education systems do the same thing high-quality businesses strive to do: recruit from the very best, maximize the productivity of employees, evaluate responsibly and helpfully, deploy its workforce where it can be most helpful, and have a clear talent-retention strategy. But in the United States, he said, "We do all of these things badly in education. We recruit from whatever the ed schools give us, there is no productivity angle and no pay for results. We have taken the view that doing teacher evaluations is so hard that we should do nothing at all, and our retention strategy amounts to saying to high-performing teachers, 'please stay.'" To change that system and lift the quality of the teaching force to international levels won't be easy, cautioned Gerard Robinson, Florida's chief education officer. "It is all about brute political force; the rest is a rounding error."

Jason Glass, director of the Department of Education for the state of Iowa, reminded the audience that "we cannot take the challenges one at a time if they refuse to stay in line." Glass said his priority is to alter the "one-minute interviews" used to make decisions on teacher hiring in too many school districts. He also seeks to improve the mentorship that teachers receive in their first year of teaching, which he says is virtually nonexistent in parts of his state. He plans to introduce more sophisticated systems that will identify—and retrain or remove—the state's least-capable teachers. In reforming Iowa's public school system, he intends to get beyond the prevalent false dichotomies, such as "cash for test scores versus step-and-lane

compensation" and "due process versus random firing." Performance measures able to identify the least capable teachers can and should be found. He concluded with a hopeful warning: "Watch out for Iowa over the next few years."

Choice and Autonomy

Hindering the conversation on school choice was the fact that the mechanisms for choice in the United States do not resemble the choice mechanisms elsewhere. In the United States, private schools receive little government aid (except for transportation, lunch programs, and, in a few places, school vouchers), whereas in most other countries governments fund private schools at levels close to those for state-run schools. Charter schools are privately operated schools that are funded by the government, but they may not teach religion, while government-funded private schools in most other countries may do so.

Avis Glaze, former superintendent of the Ontario education system, correctly observed that Canada does not have charter schools, but others mentioned that the large number of religious schools that are both government-funded and subject to state regulation give Canadians even more choice than exists in the United States.

The conversation was also shaped by the recent release of a study by the Program for International Student Assessment (PISA), the same agency that collected the international data on which the PEPG report was based. According to the PISA study, international experience suggests that nothing is to be gained from expanding the private sector in education. Students in private schools do no better than students in public schools, once differences in family background characteristics are taken into account.

That finding, said Martin West, assistant professor at Harvard's Graduate School of Education, is both misleading and, paradoxically, exactly what one should expect. When undertaking an international analysis of school choice, he argued, one should not compare the effectiveness of the public and private sectors but should instead look at the extent to which competition between the two sectors affects the achievement of all the students in the country, regardless of whether they go to public or private school. In countries such as high-achieving Netherlands, a large percentage of students attend private schools, with government paying the tuition. In countries such as low-performing Spain, only a few students attend private school. Other countries fall in between these two extremes. Using a sophisticated statistical technique, West showed that all students in a country learned more when the private sector was larger. Specifically, the study by West and his colleague found that an increase in the share of private school enrollment of 10 percentage points was associated with better than a quarter of a year's worth of learning in math, though somewhat less in reading. Moreover, this increase in performance takes place within school systems that spend 6% less overall.

A degree of choice can be introduced in the state sector if decisionmaking is shifted to the school level, as has been done in Ontario, Glaze said. The United States Department of Education should provide support and oversight to local decisions and push specific "nonnegotiable" programs, such as the literacy program Ontario implemented in the 2000s. Paul Pastorek, Louisiana's former chief education officer, agreed that the Ontario experiment had been successful but said the United States needed a different approach. The story of school reform has too often been one of a strong district or state leader driving reform until the end of her tenure, with stagnation afterward. Only the powers of competition embedded within a system can lead to sustained improvements. "The problem is that we don't know how to leverage competitive forces in the multibillion-dollar business that is education in this country," said Pastorek. "Our education system is a communist system; we don't have anything that relates what we pay for resources to the economic value they generate."

The introduction of competition in New Orleans, where 85% of the schools are now charter schools, said Pastorek, provided a foundation for continued reform and improvement. But choice works only if choice systems are equitable, schools are held accountable by the state or school district, and parents are given readily understandable information about school quality. In the view of many, a great system would be one in which through the power of competitive forces, as Pastorek described, states create a system that "self-corrects, self-challenges, and self-innovates" to achieve better results for children.

State Standards and Accountability

Common standards and tests that evaluate performance against those standards are to be found in most of the countries that are performing better than the United States, whether they be in Europe or Asia. Shengchang Tang, principal of the Shanghai High School (the leading high school in China), said that the standards and examinations in the Shanghai province are a powerful tool that parents use to exert pressure on their children as well as on teachers and principals. (These particular standards and exams do not extend to the whole of China, which is deemed too large to have a single set of exams.) In his view, that pressure focuses attention in schools and fuels the drivers of the successful Shanghai education system, including higher investments, a high-caliber teaching force, and a strategy tailored to the specific situation faced by each school.

Tang questioned whether common standards would be effective in the very different United States context. Specifically, he was skeptical that such standards would catalyze more effective parent pressure on United States schools, given parents' comparatively low expectations of their children and their schools. In contrast, in a recent poll in Shanghai, 85% of parents declared that they expected their children to be in the top 15% of their age cohort. Standardized exams, in Tang's view, serve as a necessary tool to measure reality against these high expectations. For Angus MacBeath, former school commissioner in Edmonton, Alberta, Canada, however, setting high standards in his home province allowed him to "tell the ugly truth," and it was the necessary first step toward Alberta's journey of educational

improvement. Common standards allow parents, educators, and policymakers to be clear about current achievement levels so they can act on that knowledge.

This is perhaps the reason the Obama administration has lent its support to the Common Core State Standards Initiative, which has been embraced as a reform solution by 44 states and the District of Columbia. Still, many wondered with James Stergios of the Pioneer Institute in Boston whether one can set standards capable of driving high performance nationwide in a country that has great regional disparities in student achievement and a decentralized governmental system (where schools are "radically local," as one panelist put it). Declaring himself "a massive opponent of common standards," Stergios argued that the excellence achieved by Massachusetts so far could not be sustained if nationwide standards were substituted for state ones.

Gerard Robinson began his comments by acknowledging that he was chief education officer in Virginia while that state was opposed to common standards and is now chief in Florida, which is committed to common standards. He offered two reasons for embracing common standards: 1) students must compete with those in other states and, indeed, with students all over the world, and 2) companies need common standards in order to compare job applicants. "The difficult part is not to have consensus on having common standards," he observed, "but on how to work on the political process to achieve them."

In the end, the standards issue seemed to turn on the questions raised by Shanghai's Shengchang Tang. Could the United States create common standards that were high enough to spur high achievement? While "having high state standards makes a big difference to underprivileged people," as Christopher Cerf put it, common standards might be set too low and so, contrary to what the PEPG report showed, may not serve to raise standards of achievement when United States students are compared to their peers in high-achieving countries. He reminded the group that the same political context exists today as existed when No Child Left Behind was crafted. As prescribed in that legislation, every child was supposed to be proficient, but to comply with federal expectations many states "dumbed down" their definition of student proficiency.

Digital Learning

In her opening remarks for the panel on digital learning, New Mexico's chief education officer Hanna Skandera stressed that the new technologies provided new opportunities to address together all the reforms under discussion. Digital learning that exploits online courses and broadband capabilities can expand choice for students, ensure transparency and accountability for courses offered online, and create opportunities for many more students to come into contact with the very best teachers. Further, it can serve as a catalyst for higher standards and can do all this without driving up the cost of education.

Shantanu Prakash, of Educomp Solutions, informed the audience about the business he started and now heads in India. Educomp serves more than 12 million students in India alone and operates in a number of other developing countries where traditional schools have limited resources and set low standards for instruction. Educomp targets schools with products it says are not only inexpensive but user-friendly and easily combined with traditional classroom instruction. "The whiteboard can be used with millions of modules that are very good, that will support any teacher," he noted. Prakesh expects the demand for his products to grow rapidly, as "the pressure of parents will make the introduction of digital materials into the learning of children in a meaningful way inevitable." It is an obvious means for parents with high expectations all over India to ensure that their children receive high-quality instruction, in a context of scarce resources and low teaching standards.

Susan Patrick, president and CEO of the International Association for K–12 Online Learning (iNACOL), agreed: "Education is no longer a cottage and local industry," but one in which true competition can thrive, improving standards and driving productivity gains. Digital learning can give students greater choice, even down to the specific instructor for a particular course. Digital learning is a growing reality in many other countries. Citing numerous references, Patrick told of its widespread adoption across the world. In Singapore, for example, all schools blend online learning with classroom instruction, and the country's schools of education have made online instructional techniques an integral part of the curriculum. South Korea is once again a leader, and virtual education has become a rapidly growing industry, partly to reduce the cost to parents of the "cram schools" that families expect their adolescent children to attend.

Also participating in the conference was Julie Young, president and CEO of the Florida Virtual School (FLVS), the leading example of digital learning in the United States. Since its beginnings in 1996, FLVS has grown steadily and currently has nearly 200,000 course enrollments. The reasons for its success, according to Young, include student access to teachers seven days a week and beyond the regular school day, choice in assignments, and a constantly improving curriculum and instruction that is transparent to administrators, parents, and outsiders.

The main barrier to the spread of digital learning in the United States, iNACOL's Patrick noted, are "policies that were created 30 to 40 years ago for a different world. Digital teachers cannot easily be qualified in multiple states, funding follows student and sometimes physical attendance, and there are no common standards across states that would reduce the costs of development." Only when those policies are upgraded purposefully to accommodate and encourage a different kind of classroom environment will digital learning become an integral part of the American education system.

Tea Leaves or Tea?

So what did the conference brew? No one can make the case that the conference provided secret bullets for school reform in the United States, and most every conference participant would agree that the particulars of the United States make it difficult to introduce wholesale many of the practices that have been successful abroad. Popular culture shows little appreciation for the educated citizen; a decentralized government arrangement with multiple veto points precludes rapid innovation; and education politics is marked by antipathy between teachers unions

and school reformers. But a nuanced assessment of the conversation allows for at least preliminary conclusions that go beyond a simple call for urgent action:

- Teacher selection, teacher training, teacher evaluation, and teacher retention in the United States can be done much better than it is being done today. While no country has exactly the right model for the United States, none of the successful systems leave good teaching simply to chance the way the United States does.
- School choice plays a bigger—and perhaps more successful—role in the world's educational experience than is usually recognized. It should not be seen as a threat but rather as an incentive for improvement for the public education system.
- Standards and testing systems that hold students accountable for their performance are part and parcel of most, if not all, of the world's top education systems. If the United States has a heterogeneity that precludes the adoption of a uniform examination system as those found in Korea, Singapore, and in many parts of Canada, that provides no reason not to set clearer, and higher, expectations for students than is commonly the case.
- Digital learning has yet to prove itself fully and to develop into an integrated paradigm-shifting approach, but early stories of success are promising, provided digital learning respects the principles of transparency, accountability, and choice for students.

More than reaching any specific conclusion, the conference was most successful in inspiring participants with a renewed understanding of and dedication to their common commitment to a better system of education. The commitment is now informed by the experience of other countries with similar challenges that have managed, through sustained and consistent policies (as the Finnish representative, Jari Lavonen, insisted) to find solutions.

Critical Thinking

1. Rodríguez, education advisor to the White House, asserts that "We don't have a system that recruits talent. There is not a high bar for ed schools." Do you agree with his assertion? What should be required to gain admission to a school of education?

2. Christopher Cerf, acting Commissioner of New Jersey's Department of Education, stated, "We have taken the view that doing teacher evaluations is so hard that we should do nothing at all. . . ." How do you think teachers should be evaluated? Suggest four or five actions administrators can take to ensure the best teachers are in our classrooms.

3. Select one of the four bullet points at the end of the article. Prepare a list of three questions you would ask the authors about their conclusions.

Create Central

www.mhhe.com/createcentral

Internet References

The Bill & Melinda Gates Foundation
    www.gatesfoundation.org/Pages/home.aspx

CARLOS X. LASTRA-ANADÓN is a research fellow at the Program on Education Policy and Governance. PAUL E. PETERSON is director of the Program on Education Policy and Governance at Harvard University and senior fellow at the Hoover Institution.

Unit 2

Understanding Poverty

UNIT

Prepared by: Rebecca B. Evers, *Winthrop University*

Understanding Poverty

The problem of high levels of poverty in our country is of great concern to American educators. One in four American children do not have all of his/her basic needs met and lives under conditions of poverty. Almost one in three lives in a single-parent home, which in itself is no disadvantage, but under conditions of poverty it may become one. Children living in poverty are in crisis if their basic health and social needs are not adequately met and their educational development can be affected by crises in their personal lives. We must teach and support these students and their families, even when it appears that they are not fully invested in their education. As a teacher, you may not have much control over the factors that shape the lives of our students, but hopefully with these readings you will begin to see how you can help students in other ways.

What is poverty? Jensen (2009) defines poverty as "a chronic and debilitating condition that results from multiple adverse synergistic risk factors and affects the mind, body and soul" (p. 6). Some of the risk factors frequently mentioned in the literature on poverty include 1) violence in the community, 2) stress and distress felt by the adults in the child's life, 3) a disorganized family situation, including physical and substance abuse, 4) negative interactions between parents and children, and 5) parents' lack of understanding of developmental needs. Rawlinson (2007) grew up in poverty and later wrote about her experiences in *A Mind Shaped by Poverty: Ten Things Educators Should Know*. These words give us a peek into the mind of the children we teach.

> When I entered school, I took all the pain, anger, frustration, resentment, shame, low self-esteem, debilitating worldview, and dehumanizing effects of poverty with me. I had a poverty mind-set (p. 1).

After looking at the list of risk factors and Rawlinson's admitted poverty mind-set, what are teachers to do? Can teachers ignore these concerns to treat and teach all students as NCLB requires? Smiley and Helfenbein (2011) found that how teachers see themselves, their students, and the larger community plays a powerful role in planning and instructing students from poverty. That study leaves us with new questions. So what can we do about our beliefs? If a majority of teachers in the United States are non-minority, middle-class, and female how do they relate to students who are so unlike themselves?

Children who live in poverty may attend schools in areas of high unemployment, high-minority population, or low-levels of funding. Further, during the last decade, homelessness of school-age children has risen; in 2009 41 percent of the homeless population was comprised of families. The McKinney-Vento Act which ensures the right to attend public school regardless of where a child may reside, includes children who may live in a homeless shelter outside the school's primary attendance area. This is important enough to say here that children and youth are considered homeless if they are

- sharing the housing of other persons due to loss of housing, economic hardship, or a similar reason (sometimes referred to as *doubled-up*);
- living in motels, hotels, trailer parks, or camping grounds due to lack of alternative adequate accommodations;
- living in emergency or transitional shelters; abandoned in hospitals; or awaiting foster care placement; have a primary nighttime residence that is a public or private place not designed for, or ordinarily used as, a regular sleeping accommodation for human beings;
- living in cars, parks, public spaces, abandoned buildings, substandard housing, bus or train stations, or similar settings; and
- migratory children who qualify as homeless because they are living in circumstances described above (U.S. Department of Education, p. 2).

Poverty plus homelessness can have devastating results for children in public schools, unless the teachers and school personnel are sensitive to and supportive of those children. Until we see a significant economic recovery from the current recession, we are likely to be confronted with the problems of poverty and homelessness. How educators respond to these children will have profound effects on the future of our nation.

The articles in this unit were selected so that the readers could begin that conversation about relating to the children born into or living in poverty. Further, the articles offer some new ideas about how to change the mind-set of both teachers and the children of poverty. And lastly, the articles will offer examples of schools and teachers who are making a difference for children, not just by raising test scores, but also by changing lives.

This unit begins with the article *Who Are America's Poor Children?: The Official Story* because it is important to understand what we mean by the phrase "living in poverty." This article will frame the issues and provide a context for the remaining articles in this section. Where are America's poor children? is another question we might ask. If you answered *in the inner city* you will be surprised to know that just over one-quarter (28%) of America's poor children live in urban settings. The majority live in small cities and rural areas (39%) and the second largest group are from the suburbs (33%). In *Struggling in Suburbia*, Wilson cautions readers to combat the "culture of poverty" often found in the work of Charles Murray and Ruby Payne. In this article you will learn about poverty in the middle land between inner city and rural countryside. Wilson also offers strategies for working with suburban families who live in poverty and homelessness.

The next two articles are about schools in areas of high poverty that are making a difference in the education of children. Chenoweth and Theokas suggest that principals in successful high-poverty schools share four common characteristics. If you are looking to place you child or find a job in a high-poverty school you may want to find a principal with these attributes. However, what if teachers with these beliefs taught in high-poverty schools? Perhaps we would find even greater success. Morgan advises that we look to the rest of the world as well as disadvantaged areas of the United States. He recommends that better schools and more successful academic programs would better serve students who live in poverty. However, he notes there are obstacles to raising the achievement gap and discusses what we can learn from top-ranked countries.

As you read the first two articles, you will learn who the poor are and where they live. In the next two articles you will learn that successful schools in high poverty areas have principals and teachers who have a set of common characteristics and are highly qualified educators. In the final article, Rosenshine reminds us that all teachers need to use a fundamental set of research-based teaching strategies regardless of who they teach. He reminds us that good teaching is essential for students to acquire basic skills and knowledge they can use. Further, he notes that the most effective teachers ensure that all students acquire, rehearse, and connect background knowledge while receiving sufficient instructional support. His ten principles of good teaching are supported by research in cognitive science and cognitive supports as well as observation of master teachers.

References

Jensen, E. 2009. *Teaching with Poverty in Mind: What Being Poor Does to Kid's Brains and What Schools Can Do About It.* Alexandria, VA: Association for Supervision and Curriculum Development.

National Coalition for the Homeless, 2009. Homeless Families with Children. Author. Retrieved on 14 May 2012 from www.nationalhomeless.org/factsheets/families.html

Rawlinson, R. M. 2007. *A Mind Shaped by Poverty: Ten Things Educators Should Know.* New York: Universe, Inc.

U. S. Department of Education (n.d.). Guidance for the Education for Homeless Children and Youth. Author. Retrieved on 12 May 2012 from www2.ed.gov/programs/homeless/guidance.pdf

Smiley, A. D., and R. J. Helfenbein. 2011. "Becoming Teachers: The Payne Effect." *Multicultural Perspectives, 13*(1): 5–15

Article Prepared by: Rebecca B. Evers, *Winthrop University*

Who Are America's Poor Children?
The Official Story

VANESSA R. WIGHT, MICHELLE CHAU, AND YUMIKO ARATANI

Learning Outcomes

After reading this article, you will be able to:

- Compare the data regarding students who live in poverty with data from your local schools.

- Discuss the needs and resources of persons living in poverty.

Over 15 million American children live in families with incomes below the federal poverty level, which is $22,050 a year for a family of four.[1] The number of children living in poverty increased by 33 percent between 2000 and 2009. There are 3.8 million more children living in poverty today than in 2000.

Not only are these numbers troubling, the official poverty measure tells only part of the story. Research consistently shows that, on average, families need an income of about twice the federal poverty level to make ends meet.[2] Children living in families with incomes below this level—for 2010, $44,100 for a family of four—are referred to as low income. Forty-two percent of the nation's children—more than 31 million in 2009—live in low-income families.[3]

Nonetheless, eligibility for many public benefits is based on the official poverty measure. This fact sheet describes some of the characteristics of American children who are considered poor by the official standard.[4]

How many children in America are officially poor?

The percentage of children living in poverty and extreme poverty (less than 50 percent of the federal poverty level) has increased since 2000.

- Twenty-one percent of children live in families that are considered officially poor (15.3 million children).
- Nine percent of children live in extreme poor families (6.8 million).

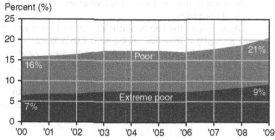

Children living in poor and extreme poor families, 2000–2009

Rates of official child poverty vary tremendously across the states.

- Across the states, child poverty rates range from 10 percent in New Hampshire to 30 percent in Mississippi.

What are some of the characteristics of children who are officially poor in America?

Black, American Indian, and Hispanic children are disproportionately poor.

- Twelve percent of white children live in poor families. Across the 10 most populated states,[5] rates of child poverty among white children do not vary dramatically; the range is nine percent in California and Texas to 16 percent in Ohio.
- Thirty-six percent of black children live in poor families. In the 10 most populated states, rates of child poverty among black children range from 30 percent in California and New York to 46 percent in Ohio and Michigan.
- Fifteen percent of Asian children, 34 percent of American Indian children, and 24 percent of children of some other race live in poor families (comparable state comparisons are not possible due to small sample sizes).[6]

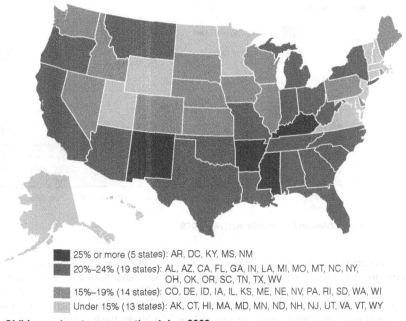

25% or more (5 states): AR, DC, KY, MS, NM

20%–24% (19 states): AL, AZ, CA, FL, GA, IN, LA, MI, MO, MT, NC, NY, OH, OK, OR, SC, TN, TX, WV

15%–19% (14 states): CO, DE, ID, IA, IL, KS, ME, NE, NV, PA, RI, SD, WA, WI

Under 15% (13 states): AK, CT, HI, MA, MD, MN, ND, NH, NJ, UT, VA, VT, WY

Child poverty rates across the states, 2009

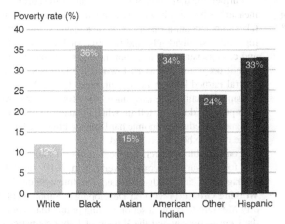

Child poverty rates by race/ethnicity, 2009

- Thirty-three percent of Hispanic children live in poor families. In the 10 most populated states, rates of child poverty among Hispanic children range from 25 percent in Florida and Illinois to 41 percent in North Carolina and Georgia.

Having immigrant parents can increase a child's chances of being poor.

- Twenty-seven percent of children in immigrant families are poor; 19 percent of children with native-born parents are poor.

- In the six states with the largest populations of immigrants —California, Florida, Illinois, New Jersey, New York, and Texas—the poverty rate among children in immigrant families ranges from 16 percent to 34 percent.

Official poverty rates are highest for young children.

- Twenty-four percent of children younger than age 6 live in poor families; 19 percent of children age 6 or older live in poor families.

- In about two-thirds of the states (35 states), 20 percent or more of children younger than age 6 are poor, whereas only about a half (24 states) have a poverty rate for all children (younger than age 18) that is as high.

What are some of the hardships faced by children in America?

Food insecurity, lack of affordable housing, and other hardships affect millions of American children, not just those who are officially poor.

- Twenty-one percent of households with children experience food insecurity. The share of households with children experiencing food insecurity was split with about half (10 percent) reporting food insecurity among adults, only, and the other half (about 11 percent) reporting low and very low food security among children.[7]

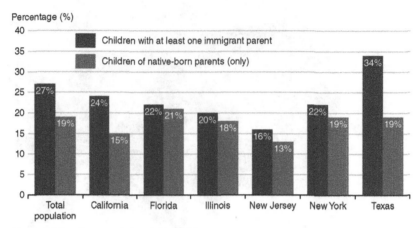

Poor children by parents' nativity, 2009

- Nearly 50 percent of tenants living in renter-occupied units spend more than 30 percent of their income on rent.[8]
- Although crowded housing is relatively uncommon, five percent of poor households and nearly two percent of all households are moderately crowded with 1.01–1.50 persons per room. Severe crowding with 1.51 or more persons per room characterizes about 1.1 percent of poor households and 0.3 percent of all households.[9]
- Compared to white families with children, black and Latino families with children are more than twice as likely to experience economic hardships, such as food insecurity.[10]

Many poor children lack health insurance.

- Sixteen percent of poor children lack health insurance, whereas 11 percent of all children (poor and non-poor) lack health insurance.[11]
- In the 10 most populated states, the percentage of poor children who lack health insurance ranges from 12 percent in New York to 38 percent in Texas.[12]

Measuring Poverty: Needs and Resources[13]

The official U.S. poverty rate is used as one of the nation's primary indicators of economic well-being. The measure of poverty, which was developed in the 1960s, is calculated by comparing a family's or person's resources to a set of thresholds that vary by family size and composition and are determined to represent the minimum amount of income it takes to support a family at a basic level.[14] Families or people with resources that fall below the threshold are considered poor.

The current poverty measure is widely acknowledged to be inadequate.[15] The method of calculating the poverty thresholds is outdated. Originally based on data from the 1950s, the poverty threshold was set at three times the cost of food and adjusted for family size. Since then, the measure has been updated only for inflation. Yet food now comprises only about one-seventh of an average family's expenses, while the costs of housing, child care, health care, and transportation have grown disproportionately. The result? Current poverty thresholds are too low, arguably arbitrary, and they do not adjust for differences in the cost of living within and across states.

Further, the definition of resources under the current poverty measure is based solely on cash income. So while the measure takes into account a variety of income sources, including earnings, interest, dividends, and benefits, such as Social Security and cash assistance, it does not include the value of the major benefit programs that assist low-income families, such as the federal Earned Income Tax Credit, food stamps, Medicaid, and housing and child care assistance. Therefore, the way we measure poverty does not tell us whether many of the programs designed to reduce economic hardship are effective because the value of these benefits is ignored.

Considerable research has been done on alternative methods for measuring income poverty.[16] In 2010, the Office of Management and Budget formed the Interagency Technical Working Group (ITWG) on Developing a Supplemental Poverty Measure to create a set of starting points that would allow the Census Bureau and the Bureau of Labor Statistics to produce a supplemental poverty measure for estimating poverty at the national level. The group targeted two main issues: 1) establishing a threshold and 2) estimating family resources.[17] First, the ITWG suggested that the poverty threshold represent a dollar amount that families need to purchase a basic bundle of commodities that include food, shelter, clothing and utilities (FSCU), along with a small amount for additional expenses. The threshold should be based on the expenditure data of families with two children and then adjusted to reflect different family types and geographic differences in housing. Finally, the threshold should be set to the 33rd percentile of the spending distribution for the basic bundle. Second, the ITWG suggested that family resources represent the sum of cash income from all sources along with near-cash benefits that families can use to purchase the basic FSCU bundle. In addition, expenses not included in the threshold, such as taxes, work and child care

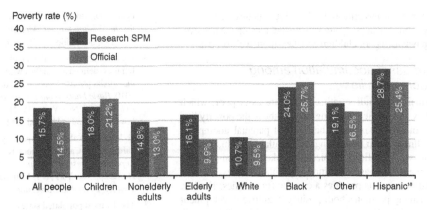

Poverty rate (%)

Percent of people in poverty by different poverty measures, 2009

Source: Short, K. S. 2010 "Who is Poor? A New Look with the Supplemental Poverty Measure." Paper presented at the 2011 Allied Social Science Associations, Society of Government Economists, Denver, CO.

expenses, and medical out of pocket expenses should be subtracted from the sum of cash income and near-cash benefits.

Recently, the Census Bureau released estimates of poverty based on the research SPM, a preliminary measure of poverty incorporating the ITWG recommendations.[18] In general, the findings in this report indicate that poverty is higher with the new measure when compared with the official measure. Approximately 14.5 percent[19] of the population is poor using the official measure compared with 15.7 percent using the research SPM (see figure). Children have lower poverty rates while adults, particularly the elderly, have higher rates using the new measure. Differences by race/ethnicity suggest higher poverty among most groups using the research SPM.

These differences are partly a function of the new measure's higher thresholds that consequently capture more people. However, some of the differences are explained by the new definition of resources, which subtracts medical out-of-pocket expenses from income—a large expenditure among the elderly population—as well as other work-related and child care expenditures.

What should be done about child poverty?

Research suggests that being poor during childhood is associated with being poor as an adult.[21] Yet, child poverty is not intractable. Policies and practices that increase family income and help families maintain their financial footing during hard economic times not only result in short-term economic security, but also have lasting effects by reducing the long-term consequences of poverty on children's lives. NCCP recommends a number of major policy strategies to improve the well-being of children and families living in poverty:

Make work pay

Since research is clear that poverty is the greatest threat to children's well being, strategies that help parents succeed in the labor force help children.[22] Increasing the minimum wage is important for working families with children because it helps them cover the high cost of basic necessities, such as child care and housing.[23] Further, policies aimed at expanding the Earned Income Tax Credit and other tax credits such as the Additional Child Tax Credit and the Making Work Pay Tax Credit are particularly instrumental in putting well-needed dollars back into the hands of low-earning workers. Finally, many low-wage workers need better access to benefits such as health insurance and paid sick days. Reducing the costs of basic needs for low-income families Medicaid/SCHIP not only increase access to health care, but also helps families defray often crippling health care costs by providing free or low-cost health insurance. The Patient Protection and Affordable Care Act signed into law by President Obama promises to provide more affordable coverage and to prevent families from bankruptcy or debt because of health care costs. Further, housing is known to be a major expense for families. However, current housing subsidy programs are available for a small percentage of eligible families due to inadequate funding.[24] Housing subsidies have been shown to be positively related to children's educational outcomes.[25] Thus, it is important to increase funding for housing subsidies for families with children.

Support parents and their young children in early care and learning

To thrive, children need nurturing families and high quality early care and learning experiences. Securing child care is particularly important for working parents with young children. Research has found that child care subsidies are positively associated with the long-term employment and financial well-being of parents.[26] Along with providing child care subsidies, policies and practices that ensure high-quality child care are also important. For example, programs that target families with infants and toddlers, such as Early Head Start, have been shown to improve children's social and cognitive development, as well as improve parenting skills.[27] Investments in preschool for 3- and

4-year-olds are just as critical. In short, high-quality early childhood experiences can go a long way toward closing the achievement gap between poor children and their more well-off peers.[28]

Support asset accumulation among low-income families

Many American families with children are asset poor, which means they lack sufficient savings to live above the poverty line for three months or more in the event of parental unemployment or illness when no earnings are available.[29] This type of economic vulnerability is typically masked by conventional poverty measures based on income. Unlike wages, income generated from assets provides a cushion for families. Further, parental saving promotes both positive cognitive development and subsequent college attendance among children.[30] There are two ways to support asset accumulation among low-income families. First, eliminating asset tests from major means-tested programs reduces the risk of running up large amounts of debt and increases the amount of financial resources parents have to invest in children. Second, there are programs that actively promote and encourage the development of saving habits among asset-poor families through matching funds incentives, such as the Individual Development Accounts (IDA) program and the Saving for Education, Entrepreneurship, and Down-payment (SEED) National Initiative programs.

Endnotes

1. Unless otherwise noted, national data were calculated from the U.S. Current Population Survey, Annual Social and Economic Supplement, March 2010, which represents information from calendar year 2009. State data were calculated by NCCP analysts from the 2009 American Community Survey, which represents information from 2009. Estimates include children living in households with at least one parent and most children living apart from both parents (for example, children being raised by grandparents). Children living independently, living with a spouse, or in group quarters are excluded from these data. Children ages 14 and under living with only unrelated adults were not included because data on their income status were not available. Among children who do not live with at least one parent, parental characteristics are those of the householder and/or the householder's spouse. In the most recent CPS and ACS, parents could report children's race as one or more of the following: "white," "black," "American Indian or Alaskan Native," or "Asian and/or Hawaiian/Pacific Islander." In a separate question, parents could report whether their children were of Hispanic origin. For the data reported, children whose parent reported their race as white, black, American Indian or Alaskan Native, or Asian and/or Hawaiian/Pacific Islander and their ethnicity as non-Hispanic are assigned their respective race. Children who were reported to be of more than one race were assigned as Other. Children whose parent identified them as Hispanic were categorized as Hispanic, regardless of their reported race.

2. Lin, J.; Bernstein, J. 2008. What We Need to Get By: A Basic Standard of Living Costs $48,779, and Nearly a Third of Families Fall Short. Washington, DC: Economic Policy Institute.

Pearce, D.; Brooks, J. 1999. *The Self-Sufficiency Standard for the Washington, DC Metropolitan Area.* Washington, DC: Wider Opportunities for Women.

3. For more information about children living in low-income families (defined as families with incomes below 200 percent of the official poverty level), see: Chau, M.; Thampi, K.; Wight, V.R. 2010. *Basic Facts About Low-income Children, Children Under Age 18, 2009.* New York, NY: National Center for Children in Poverty, Columbia University, Mailman School of Public Health.

4. To learn more about child poverty and family economic hardship, see Cauthen, Nancy K.; Fass, Sarah. 2008. *Ten Important Questions About Child Poverty and Family Economic Hardship.* New York, NY: National Center for Children in Poverty, Columbia University, Mailman School of Public Health.

5. The 10 most populated states in 2009 were California, Texas, New York, Florida, Illinois, Pennsylvania, Ohio, Michigan, Georgia, and North Carolina.

6. Data for Asian, American Indian, and children of some other race are unavailable due to small sample sizes.

7. Wight, V. R.; Thampi, K.; Briggs, J. 2010. *Who Are America's Poor Children?: Examining Food Insecurity Among Children in the United States.* National Center for Children in Poverty, Columbia University, Mailman School of Public Health.

8. American Community Survey. 2009. Table B25070: Gross Rent as a Percentage of Household Income in the Past 12 Months. American FactFinder. Washington, DC: U.S. Census Bureau. American Community Survey.

9. U.S. Census Bureau. 2008. American Housing Survey for the United States in 2009. Washington, DC: U.S. Government Printing Office.

10. Wight, V.R.; Thampi, K. 2010. *Basic Facts About Food Insecurity Among Children in the United States, 2008.* National Center for Children in Poverty, Columbia University, Mailman School of Public Health.

11. Chau, M.; Thampi, K.; Wight, V.R. 2010. *Basic Facts About Low-income Children, Children Under Age 18, 2009.* New York, NY: National Center for Children in Poverty, Columbia University, Mailman School of Public Health.

12. Authors' calculations from the 2009 American Community Survey.

13. For more information about the official poverty measure, see: Fass, Sarah. 2009. *Measuring Income and Poverty in the United States.* New York, NY: National Center for Children in Poverty, Columbia University, Mailman School of Public Health; Cauthen, Nancy K. 2007. Testimony before the House Subcommittee on Income Security and Family Support, Committee on Ways and Means. August 1, 2007; NYC Center for Economic Opportunity. 2008. The CEO Poverty Measure: A Working Paper by the New York City Center for Economic Opportunity. New York: New York City Center for Economic Opportunity.

14. Iceland, John. 2005. Measuring Poverty: Theoretical and Empirical Considerations. *Measurement* 3: 199–235.

15. See Iceland, John. 2003. *Poverty in America.* Berkeley: University of California Press.; Citro, Constance F., and Robert T. Michael (eds.), Measuring Poverty: A New Approach, Washington, DC: National Academy Press, 1995.; Ruggles, P. 1990. *Drawing the Line: Alternative Poverty Measures and their Implications for Public Policy.* Washington, DC: Urban Institute.

16. Citro, Constance F., and Robert T. Michael (eds.), Measuring Poverty: A New Approach. Washington, DC: National Academy Press, 1995.

17. ITWG. 2010. "Observations from the Interagency Technical Working Group on Developing a Supplemental Poverty Measure" available at: www.census.gov/hhes/www/poverty/SPM_TWGObservations.pdf.

18. Short, K. S. 2010. "Who is Poor? A New Look with the Supplemental Poverty Measure." Paper presented at the 2011 Allied Social Science Associations, Society of Government Economists. Denver, CO.

19. This estimate is slightly higher than the published poverty rate that appears in the Census publication, Income, Poverty, and Health Insurance Coverage in the United States: 2009 (P60-238) because it includes unrelated individuals under age 15 in the poverty universe.

20. People of Hispanic origin may be of any race. In this figure, persons of Hispanic origin, whatever their race, are shown by their origin but not by their race and persons not of Hispanic origin are shown by race.

21. Wagmiller, Robert L. Jr.; Adelman, Robert M. 2009. *Childhood and Intergenerational Poverty: The Long-term Consequences of Growing up Poor.* New York, NY: National Center for Children in Poverty, Columbia University, Mailman School of Public Health.

22. Duncan, Greg J.; Brooks-Gunn, Jeanne. 1997. *Consequences of Growing up Poor.* New York: Russell Sage Foundation.

23. Purmort, Jessica. 2010. *Making Work Supports Work: A Picture of Low-wage Workers in America.* New York, NY: National Center for Children in Poverty, Columbia University, Mailman School of Public Health.

24. Ibid.

25. Currie, J.; Yelowitz, A., 2000. Are Public Housing Projects Good for Kids? *Journal of Public Economics 75:* 99–124

26. Martinez-Beck, Ivelisse; George, Robert M. 2009. Employment Outcomes for Low-income Families Receiving Child Care Subsidies in Illinois, Maryland, and Texas. Final Report to U.S. Department of Health and Human Services Administration for Children and Families. Office of Planning, Research, and Evaluation. Chicago, Chapin Hall at the University of Chicago. Forry, Nicole D. 2008. The Impact of Child Care Subsidies on Low-income Single Parents: An Examination of Child Care Expenditures and Family Finances. *Journal of Family and Economic Issues* 30(1): 43–54.

27. Stebbins, Helene; Knitzer, Jane. 2007. *State Early Childhood Policies.* New York, NY: National Center for Children in Poverty, Columbia University, Mailman School of Public Health.

28. Knitzer, Jane. 2007. Testimony on the Economic and Societal Costs of Poverty. Testimony before the U.S. House of Representatives, Committee on Ways and Means. Jan. 24, 2007.

29. Aratani, Yumiko; Chau, Michelle. 2010. *Asset Poverty and Debt among Families with Children in the United States.* New York, NY: National Center for Children in Poverty, Columbia University, Mailman School of Public Health.

30. Conley, Dalton. 2001. Capital for College: Parental Assets and Postsecondary Schooling. Sociology of Education 74: 59–72. Yeung, W. Jean; Conley, Dalton. 2008. Black–white Achievement Gap and Family Wealth. *Child Development* 79(2): 303–324.

Critical Thinking

1. Does what you learned when reading this information support what you are hearing and seeing on the nightly news?

2. Why do we, as teachers, need to be concerned about the rising level of poverty in our country?

3. Based on this article, what are some actions you can take to support families in your school district and state?

4. How will what you have learned impact how you teach? Give specific actions with details.

5. Do you know the levels of poverty in your school district or the school district where you go to college? To know more about poverty in your area, you can go to the websites provided in this unit's section at the front of this edition, such as the National Center for Children in Poverty www.nccp.org or the U.S. Census Bureau www.census.gov/hhes/www/poverty/poverty.html.

Create Central

www.mhhe.com/createcentral

Internet References

National Center for Children in Poverty
www.nccp.org/
U.S. Census Bureau
www.census.gov/hhes/www/poverty/poverty.html.

Vanessa R. Wight, PhD, is senior research associate at the National Center for Children in Poverty. Her research focuses on the contribution of early childhood experiences and involved parenting to children's well-being. Michelle Chau is a research analyst on the Family Economic Security team at the National Center for Children in Poverty. Yumiko Aratani, PhD, is senior research associate and acting director of Family Economic Security at the National Center for Children in Poverty. Her research has focused on the role of housing in stratification processes, parental assets and children's well-being.

Acknowledgments—This research was supported by funding from Annie E. Casey Foundation. Special thanks to Morris Ardoin, Lee Kreader, Amy Palmisano, Curtis Skinner, and Telly Valdellon.

Article Prepared by: Rebecca B. Evers, *Winthrop University*

Struggling in Suburbia

Many suburban schools are facing what for them is a new problem—poverty.

David McKay Wilson

Learning Outcomes

After reading this article, you will be able to:

- Summarize the actions teachers and their schools can take to counteract their perceptions of students who are at-risk.

- Describe the socioeconomic context of schools.

In Denver's western suburbs, a social studies teacher thought up a novel approach to teaching her students the unsettling realities of urban homelessness. She assigned them the task of sleeping overnight in the backseat of the family car.

But the assignment held a surprise in store for the teacher—one that provides a glimpse into the reality of 21st-century poverty in America. The teacher did not realize that one of her students was homeless. The girl had already spent many nights in her parents' car.

"These days in suburbia, you never know who you will have in your class," says Sheree Conyers, homeless liaison for the Jeffco Public Schools of Jefferson County, Colorado. "These are hard times. So many of our families are in transition."

A decade ago, the Jeffco Schools had just 59 homeless students in a district that serves about 86,000 students. By 2012, there were close to 3,000, representing 3 percent of the district enrollments. At Parr Elementary School, 28 percent of the students were homeless, according to a 2012 report.

The increasing poverty in Jefferson County, where close to one in three students qualifies for free and reduced price lunch, reflects the explosion of poverty in suburbs nationwide. Throughout the 2000s, the suburbs were home to the largest and fastest-growing poor population in the nation, according to a 2011 analysis of U.S. Census data by the Brookings Institution. From 2000 to 2010, the report also says, poverty grew by 53 percent in the nation's suburbs.

This rapid change has left many educators behind. They are still teaching as if the suburbs have remained immune from the poverty that has long troubled urban areas, says M.J. Lechner, a University of Colorado-Denver professor who oversees seven student teachers at Parr. "Some teachers have been responsive [to the changes]," she says, "while others are still struggling to give up the notion that all kids are the same as they were 10 years ago."

A Poorly Defined Problem

The explosion in suburban poverty is part of a larger, more disturbing trend. Childhood poverty nationwide is at its highest point since 1993, with 16.5 million, or 22 percent of children ages 18 and under living in poor families, according to the 2010 U.S. Census. Race is still a factor. For African-American children, the poverty rate was 38 percent; for Latino children, it was 32 percent.

Being classified as "poor" means that a family of four earns no more than $22,314. However, the National Center for Children in Poverty at Columbia University estimates that families typically need twice that income to cover their basic needs. That looser definition puts 44 percent of American children in low-income families.

The growth in suburban poverty has had a major impact on suburban schools, like those near Denver. Without the safety net of social services that city governments provide for the urban poor, suburban schools have had to scramble to set up programs that address basic needs, such as adequate food and clothing, for their students from low-income families.

The Jeffco district has established school-based food banks and an emergency fund for health needs, such as eyeglasses or medication. It also has held clothing drives at schools with large homeless populations. Schools feed students free or low-cost meals during the week, but not on the weekends. So 13 Jeffco schools have partnered with community sponsors and local food banks to provide food for the weekends.

At Parr, school officials have even altered the curriculum to accommodate homeless students. But some teachers have not adjusted to the new reality. "If a student has neither the place nor the tools with which to complete tasks sent home, they are often reprimanded or punished by missing recess," Lechner says. "This makes our homeless population feel even more singled out and ostracized."

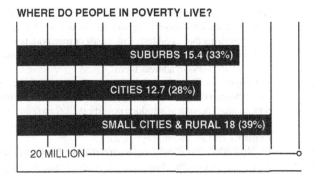

WHERE DO PEOPLE IN POVERTY LIVE?

SUBURBS 15.4 (33%)

CITIES 12.7 (28%)

SMALL CITIES & RURAL 18 (39%)

20 MILLION

Who Are the New Suburban Poor?

According to Scott Allard, an associate professor at the University of Chicago, the new suburban poor are a mix of old and new poverty. In more mature cities, like Chicago and New York, poverty has grown up around the inner-ring suburbs, where urban families have migrated from rundown city neighborhoods and the recession has deepened financial need. Many such communities experienced a spike in poverty during the economic downturn of the late 1980s.

The new suburban poverty, says Allard, has developed in the outer-ring suburbs, which underwent tremendous growth in the 1990s and 2000s. New immigration patterns have brought immigrants directly to the suburbs as well, unlike previous waves of newcomers who first settled in urban areas. In addition, Allard says, these outer-ring suburbs were hit hard by the recession, and by the subprime mortgage bust, which has led to foreclosure on more than 6 million homes.

"It's not unusual for immigrants now to go straight to the suburbs and become part of the working poor," says Allard. "The changes in the suburbs have been significant."

This means that the face of suburban poverty can be diverse. Impoverished immigrants may lack both language skills and job prospects. In addition, some who were once members of the suburban middle class have lost their jobs and their homes. A traditional view of America's underclass is that poverty is a cultural phenomenon that gets passed down from generation to generation. But the new suburban poverty, at least in part, comprises families descended from the middle class who find themselves suddenly poor.

How Educators Can Help

Teachers can help low-income students simply by knowing all their students better. A teacher who's aware that a student is sleeping in a car—or just struggling to stay in her house—will be more sensitive about approaching topics like homelessness. Teachers can also help by confronting biased attitudes against low-income neighbors. Jokes about "rednecks," "white trash" or dressing "ghetto" should be addressed as they come up in classrooms and hallways.

Combating the "Culture of Poverty"

Educators grappling with the new poverty in the suburbs often turn to popular writers such as Charles Murray and Ruby Payne. They will find themselves misled.

According to *The New York Times,* "The libertarian writer Charles Murray has probably done more than any other contemporary thinker to keep alive the idea of a 'culture of poverty,' the theory that poor people are trapped by distorted norms and aspirations and not merely material deprivation."

Murray reinforced that idea in his 2012 book, *Coming Apart: The State of White America, 1960–2010.* One of his long-held beliefs is that social programs make the problems of poverty worse, not better. But Murray's libertarian beliefs leave him little room to do more than call for less government. "I don't do solutions very well," he says.

Payne, an educational consultant, has had a more direct impact on schools. Her work is rooted in a long-held view that much of American poverty is generational, with children growing up in families that have been mired in the underclass for two or more generations. Although her outlook is popular, critics argue that her characterizations are overly simplistic, even bigoted, and harm relations between teachers and students.

According to Payne, children whose families have been poor for generations tend to value relationships over achievement, believe in physical fighting to resolve conflicts, view the world through a strictly local lens and value food for its quantity rather than quality.

Low-income children run into problems, says Payne, because their schools are run on the hidden rules of the middle class. These rules hold that work and achievement are the driving forces for decision-making, that fights are conducted with words rather than fists, the world is defined in national terms, and food is valued for its quality rather than quantity.

Paul Gorski, an assistant professor of integrated studies at George Mason University, says that Payne's approach—considered a "deficit" model because it focuses on what low-income children lack—doesn't hold up. The increasing diversity of the poor in the suburbs, he says, makes such an approach even harder to justify. "The suburban poor are diverse, and becoming even more diverse, so the stereotypical version of the poor, urban person just doesn't work anymore."

Gorski says that educators need to move away from a focus on the "culture of poverty." Instead, they should look at more structural issues, such as the lack of resources in some schools that teach the poorest children. Today, that includes suburban schools struggling to address the needs of a new wave of impoverished children.

"We talk about education being the great equalizer, yet our poorest students are in the least equipped schools," he says. "We don't need to fix poor people. We need to fix the system."

SUBURBAN POVERTY INDEX

5 MILLION	ONE THIRD	2.7 MILLION
number of suburban families added to poverty rolls since 2000	portion of the nation's poor who live in suburbs	the number by which suburban families outnumber urban families living in poverty

But much of the most important work needs to take place at the administrative level. Here are some tips for school administrators who might be seeing widespread poverty at school for the first time:

Watch for changes of address. Families facing sudden poverty may move a lot. In many cases, the parents are understandably afraid their children will be forced out of a desirable school or district. This puts great stress on the students—stress the school or district can ease in part by helping the parents understand their rights.

Work around the car culture. Gasoline and car maintenance can be huge expenses. Don't assume that parents can always shuttle their kids to and from school activities.

Become familiar with the McKinney-Vento Act. This federal law guarantees the rights of children and youth experiencing homelessness to a free and appropriate public education. It requires a local homeless education liaison in every school district. It also ensures enrollment, access to services, school stability and academic support.

Help with fees. Students who are suddenly impoverished usually avoid field trips and extracurricular activities that require fees. In some cases, they'll even misbehave right before a big event to be prohibited from going. Make sure teachers are on the lookout for this behavior, and make sure the school has a response. For example, see if the PTA can create a fund to keep these students from being marginalized.

Find out what's needed. Ask parents what's needed to help their children stay in school. Perhaps they need the library open late a few nights a week to have a place to go after school. Perhaps students need more computer access to complete assignments. Perhaps they need help with meals or transportation.

Provide services. After the problems have been identified, advocate for ways to address them.

Conyers, Jeffco's homeless liaison, says one of the simplest things educators and support staff can do is to simply remain alert. A student's sudden poverty is likely to show up in increased absences, exhaustion, mood changes, change in performance and an unkempt appearance.

Also, educators should understand that the families of these students now face the daunting task of navigating the labyrinthine social-service network—a disorienting and often embarrassing task. "These former middle-class families don't know how to apply for food stamps, they don't know where to begin," Conyers says. "There needs to be more hand-holding."

Critical Thinking

1. Why is it important to revisit the popular views of who is poor, why they are poor, and where they live?

2. How does this article change your perception about teaching in a suburban school district?

3. Look at the poverty levels in the largest city in the state where you are (or your home state) and compare that rate with the poverty levels found in at least two of the suburbs near that city. What do you find? Does it match the data in the article? If not, research or speculate what might be the reasons for the difference?

Create Central

www.mhhe.com/createcentral

Internet References

Brookings Institute
www.brookings.edu/research/books/2013/confrontingsuburbanpovertyinamerica

Wilson, David McKay. From *Teaching Tolerance*, Issue 43, Fall 2012, pp. 40–43. Copyright © 2012 by Southern Poverty Law Center. Reprinted by permission. www.tolerance.org/

Article

Prepared by: Rebecca B. Evers, *Winthrop University*

Homelessness Comes to School
How Homeless Children and Youths Can Succeed

Researchers and advocates have identified successful strategies for schools enrolling homeless students.

JOSEPH F. MURPHY AND KERRI J. TOBIN

Learning Outcomes

After reading this article, you will be able to:

- Design a plan for supporting students who are homeless.
- Understand the framework needed to support homeless children.

Analysts who investigate homelessness conclude that it's a national scandal, one that is pulling increasing numbers of children and unaccompanied youth into its gravitational force. Only half of the story of homelessness highlights what its victims are missing—a normal domicile. The other half of the narrative attends to where the homeless stay, defining the homeless by where they sleep at night. The "literal homeless" find themselves in shelters or on the streets. The others (the majority) are involuntarily "doubled up" with relatives or friends—or for some unaccompanied youths, it means staying in temporary homes sponsored by the state.

Researchers and advocates cut homelessness in a variety of ways—by the reasons people find themselves homeless, by how long they've been homeless, by the severity of the displacement, by the damage it does to them, and so forth. One well established taxonomy divides the homeless into two groups based on age: adults and young persons. The "young persons" category is also divided into two groups: accompanied "children" (from birth to age 18) with their family, or part thereof, and unaccompanied "youth" out on their own. Unaccompanied youth includes three types of homeless minors: "runaway" homeless, "throwaway" homeless, and "system" homeless. Those in the first group leave home of their own volition; those in the middle group have been asked to leave and are actively prevented from returning; the final group includes youngsters who have been in and out of government programs such as foster care.

The Damage to Children

Few events have the power to affect life in negative directions more than homelessness. And homelessness is especially damaging for children, their mothers, and unaccompanied youths: "Of all homeless people, homeless children are most vulnerable" (Burt et al., 2001). Figure 1 demonstrates the deleterious effects of homelessness. Of particular importance are the educational consequences of homelessness for America's youngsters. According to scholars who examine the issue, homelessness almost always translates into less opportunity to learn—time loss associated with "residency" transitions and with trying to connect to learning in the new school. That is, homeless children are disproportionately absent from school compared to housed peers (Rouse & Fantuzzo, 2009). This group of America's most deeply at-risk youngsters are also suspended and expelled from school at higher rates than domiciled counterparts (Better Homes, 1999).

Studies confirm that homeless children and youths perform worse than housed students on the full array of important measures of academic performance. To begin with, studies that contrast homeless children and youth with housed peers reveal that they're below grade level at much higher rates (Duffield & Lovell, 2008). These youngsters also have, in general, poor to average grades, scores categorized by Dworsky (2008, p. 43) as "alarming." Homelessness is also correlated with being left behind in grade (Masten et al., 1997). In addition, data from a series of investigations over the last quarter century document the persistent underachievement of homeless youngsters (Biggar, 2001), compared to housed youngsters in general and housed poor youngsters specifically (Dworsky, 2008). Finally, perhaps nowhere is the connection between homelessness and education bleaker than in high school graduation. The National Center on Family Homelessness (2009) reports that fewer than a quarter of the homeless children in the United States complete high school.

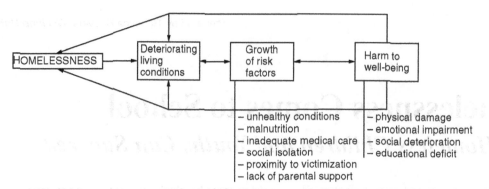

Homelessness (point 1) opens the door to conditions that often amplify problems already at play in the lives of children and youth (e.g., abuse at the hands of parents/guardians, struggles in school). More expansively, homelessness leads to living conditions (point 2) that fuel existing problems and power up new ones. Homeless minors generally enter a world of enhanced risks (point 3) (e.g., social isolation). At the same time, they often find themselves enveloped in environments marked by violence that encourages the formation of dysfunctional social relationships. The result is often severe physical, social, emotional, and educational damage (point 4).

Figure 1 The Homelessness Impact Model

How many youths are homeless?

Counting the number of homeless people is difficult. But we know that there are more homeless persons today than at any time since the Great Depression. Homeless families with children and unaccompanied youth represent the fastest growing category of homeless (National Center on Family Homelessness, 2009). While families with children were only a small percentage of the homeless population during the last homeless era (1950–1979), they're a major storyline in the modern (1980–2010) narrative. Estimates fluctuate, but an aggregation of results yields the following trend line: Homeless families grew from almost nothing in the 1950s and 1960s to about 25% of the total homeless population by the 1980s, to about 33% in the 1990s, and to about 40% in the 2000s, with perhaps as much as 50% in the nation's major urban centers (Burt et al., 2001; Better Homes Fund, 1999; National Alliance to End Homelessness, 2007).

According to various studies, children and youth comprise about a quarter of the total homeless population in the United States (Markward & Biros, 2001). Employing a different metric, analysts claim that about 2% to 3% of American children and youth are homeless in a given year. Alternatively, every year about one in every 50 children experiences homelessness (NCFH, 2009). Across a full year, estimates say that more than one million children and more than one million unaccompanied youth are homeless (Moore, 2007; NCFH, 2009).

Fewer than a quarter of the homeless children in the United States complete high school.

There is also consensus that these education deficits create serious handicaps for reintegrating homeless youngsters into society as they grow into adulthood. These poor education outcomes also have discernable consequences for the economic well-being of these youngsters. For example, they're much more likely than students who never experienced homelessness to be chronically unemployed as adults (Shane, 1996).

Schools can work proactively to ensure that all students have the basics of food, clothing, school supplies, hygiene items, and health services.

An Education Framework

While acknowledging that homelessness is a complex and layered phenomenon, schools must be a hallmark element in any attack on the homeless problem. Taking care of homeless children in school involves seven provisos: Developing awareness about homelessness and homeless children and youth; attending to basic needs; creating an effective instruction program; developing a stable and supportive environment; providing additional supports; collaborating with other agencies and organizations; and promoting parental involvement.

1. **Develop awareness.** Assistance for homeless children and youth should start by educating professional staff about how to work effectively with these highly vulnerable students. Educators need to learn more about the condition of homelessness and the problems displacement causes families and young persons. Training needs to center on sensitizing educators to the needs of homeless families and youngsters. Educators also need to learn about the McKinney-Vento Act and its legal protections for children and unaccompanied youth.

Teachers and administrators also must learn what they can do to help homeless students. Teachers, in particular, need to understand the impact of homelessness on the learning process. They need to know about resources and services that can help homeless students. Relatedly, they need to become knowledgeable about how they can advocate for homeless students in their community. They also have a special obligation to help their housed students understand what homelessness means for their displaced peers.

2. **Attend to basic needs.** Homelessness deprives youngsters of many of the necessities of life that most students take for granted—sufficient food, basic school supplies, health services, clean clothes, and routine items for personal hygiene. Because basic needs must be met before children can learn successfully, schools can work proactively to ensure that all students have the basics of food, clothing, school supplies, hygiene items, and health services.

3. **Provide effective instruction.** On the pedagogical side of the instruction ledger, research suggests that homeless children and youth may be advantaged by two instructional approaches. First, individualized instruction appears to help these highly vulnerable students. Second, cooperative learning platforms allow homeless students to master important academic content while developing much-needed social skills as they interact with peers from a range of economic and social backgrounds.

Evidence suggests that breaking assignments for homeless children and youth into discrete pieces of work is a good instruction strategy. Such an approach recognizes the likely transience of homeless youngsters and helps ensure completion before departure. Lessons should open and close on the same day, and individualized contracts should be established for short durations and renewed frequently.

Researchers and advocates alike routinely argue for a strength-based approach when planning instruction, as opposed to an overreliance on a problem-oriented perspective. Homeless adolescents need practical life skills and extra help to deepen often-underdeveloped interpersonal skills.

On the curricular side of the instruction ledger, scholars conclude that homeless youngsters don't need a different or separate curriculum. They need access to the same high-quality curriculum available to their peers. Because homeless students are almost always at a disadvantage in doing required schoolwork, schools should be willing to restructure schedules, social organization, and functions in order to best meet the needs of students who have no idea of place (Quint, 1994, p. 15). One important action is to accelerate students along with their peers while simultaneously addressing remedial needs. That is, homeless students should not be put into closed remediation loops in which they never catch up with peers. Schools that work well for homeless children

and youth accelerate and address deficiencies at the same time.

Homeless students will also benefit from more flexible ways to traverse the curriculum. Partial credit programs and credit recovery programs seem to be especially helpful. Credit recovery allows homeless students to fill in gaps in coursework. Partial credit programs allow them to gain credit for part of a course. Policies that provide flexibility for homeless youngsters to complete schoolwork and school projects at school are also helpful for ensuring the academic success of homeless adolescents.

4. **Create a supportive environment.** Ensuring "success" for homeless children and youth will require a robust instruction program. Success also depends on the staff's ability to create a caring and stable culture in classrooms and in the school as a whole. The aim, researchers assert, is to make school an oasis of stability and caring in what can often seem like a random, chaotic, and inhumane world to homeless children. To do so, staff must set objectives for the student and the school. On the student front, the primary goal is to offset stress and feelings of inadequacy by nurturing a sense of acceptance and belonging, and a sense of hope. Make sure the youngsters become part of the school community, thus replacing social isolation with social connections and support. On the school front, the goal is creating a climate in which homeless students feel welcomed.

For schools to work well for homeless children and youth, they'll need to extend their reach to address the full array of needs displaced minors bring with them to the schoolhouse—safety, health, education, nutrition, and so forth. At the same time, for homeless children and adolescents to flourish, schools must develop environments that are less institutional and less bureaucratic. As Quint (1994) argues, the school must "attempt to act more like a family than an institution" (p. 90) if education success for homeless children and adolescents is to become the norm.

5. **Provide additional supports.** Schools must provide more than basic services. Ensuring that homeless minors have a secure and safe place to be is essential. But supplemental services also are important for keeping children in school. If crafted well, these programs can enhance the social skills needed to survive in and out of school, build self-esteem, lengthen academic learning time, and deepen achievement. In short, crafting a system of additional supports will embed students in a safe environment with a dense web of interpersonal relationships and provide additional academic scaffolding. Together, these supports help offset the cognitive and social-emotional problems accompanying homelessness. They help keep these young people in school while ensuring maximum academic and social development. Advocates typically categorize additional services as basic needs supports (e.g., clothing, health services), special

academic services (e.g., tutoring), and nonacademic activities (e.g., clubs and recreational activities).

6. **Collaborate with other organizations.** The staggering complexity of problems associated with homelessness precludes any single agency from resolving matters. No single agency has the comprehensive authority, nor does any single agency have all the appropriate information and resources to meet the multiple needs of homeless children and youth.

The proposed solution will surprise no one: greater collaboration among agencies that work with homeless families and unaccompanied children and/or homeless adolescents. What's needed is an integrated system or a network of service providers to replace the current fragmented system of assistance (Tucker, 1999, p. 92).

Analysts and advocates regularly suggest that schools are critical to the success of interagency collaboration. Others go even further, holding that schools should be the hub of social service delivery for homeless children and youth. For a variety of reasons, educators may be best positioned to spearhead collaborative efforts. Scholars note, for example, that schools have a legal mandate to collaborate and coordinate with local service agencies or programs providing services to homeless children and youth and their families.

7. **Promote parental involvement.** Research on school improvement over the last 30 years has consistently documented that parent involvement is a critical variable in the school effects formula. More specifically, studies confirm the significant role that parents of at-risk students play in helping their children succeed in school and that parent involvement is linked to the academic advancement of homeless children. Advocates for children argue that schools must be more aggressive in enlisting parents as partners. Overall, the parent involvement narrative features three themes: the difficulty of creating meaningful parent involvement in the homeless community, the heightened importance of such connections for the well-being of homeless children, and an acknowledgement that schools can do more than they often have done to remove barriers to engagement and to garner the rewards of involvement.

Zeroing in on the third theme, educators must attend to both parent education and parent involvement. Few homeless parents know their rights and therefore don't know how to advocate for their children. Schools must be more proactive in educating parents about these rights. Schools can train homeless parents to be advocates for themselves and champions for their children, both in schools and in the larger service community. Schools should offer education that teaches homeless parents how they can connect to needed services. Many homeless parents also don't have a well-stocked toolbox of parenting skills. However, because improved parenting skills can help students learn, educators can and should do more to assist parents in deepening general skills. Through adult education programs, schools can help parents acquire the academic content they often missed when they were younger, such as basic language and literacy skills and high school completion.

Schools that work well for homeless children and their families also are places where parents have the opportunity to become partners in the education of their children and where they're included in meaningful ways in the life of the school. Such involvement has been linked to keeping children enrolled and attending school and to student academic achievement.

References

Better Homes Fund. (1999). *Homeless children: America's new outcasts.* Newton, MA: Author.

Biggar, H. (2001). Homeless children and education: An evaluation of the Stewart B. McKinney Homeless Assistance Act. *Children and Youth Services Review, 23* (12), 941–969.

Burt, M., Aron, L., Lee, E., & Valente, J. (2001). *Helping America's homeless: Emergency shelter or affordable housing?* Washington, DC: The Urban Institute.

Duffield, B. & Lovell, P. (2008). *The economic crisis hits home: The unfolding increase in child and youth homelessness.* Washington, DC: National Association for the Education of Homeless Children and Youth.

Dworsky, A. (2008). *Educating homeless children in Chicago: A case study of children in the family regeneration program.* Chicago, IL: University of Chicago Press.

Markward, M. & Biros, E. (2001). McKinney revisited: Implications for school social work. *Children and Schools, 23* (3), 182–187.

Masten, A., Sesma, A., Si-Asar, R., Lawrence, C., Miliotis, D., & Dionne, J.A. (1997). Educational risks for students experiencing homelessness. *Journal of School Psychology, 35* (1), 27–46.

Moore, J. (2007). *A look at child welfare from a homeless education perspective.* Greensboro, NC: National Center for Homeless Education at SERVE. www.serve.org/nche

National Alliance to End Homelessness. (2007). *Fact checker: Family homelessness.* Author.

National Center on Family Homelessness. (2009). *America's youngest outcasts: State report card on child homelessness.* Newton, MA: Author. www.homelesschildrenamerica.org/pdf/rc_full_report.pdf

Quint, S. (1994). *Schooling homeless children: A working model for America's public schools.* New York, NY: Teachers College Press.

Rouse, H. & Fantuzzo, J. (2009). Multiple risks and educational well-being: A population-based investigation of threats to early school success. *Early Childhood Research Quarterly, 24* (1), 1–14.

Shane, P. (1996). *What about America's homeless children?* Thousand Oaks, CA: Sage.

Tucker, P. (1999). Providing educational services to homeless students: A multifaceted response to a complex problem. *Journal for a Just and Caring Education, 5* (1), 88–107.

Critical Thinking

1. One of the provisos mentioned in this article is to collaborate with other organizations. Find out what organizations are available in the school district where you teach or go to college. Select one of the organizations and seek more information, for example, interview someone who works/ volunteers there, if possible.

2. Pick one of the other provisos that you would like to plan or implement. Make a plan to learn more and become involved. Explain why you selected this proviso.

3. Schools are being asked to take on more and more responsibility for the physical and emotional welfare of students. Is there a point at which schools should say no? Or do you think schools should do even more for children who have needs beyond instruction? Prepare a response for a class discussion.

Create Central

www.mhhe.com/createcentral

Internet References

Doing What Works
  http://dww.ed.gov

JOSEPH F. MURPHY is the Frank W. Mayborn Chair of Education and associate dean at Peabody College, Vanderbilt University, Nashville, Tenn. **KERRI J. TOBIN** is an assistant professor of education at Marywood University, Scranton, Penn. They are co-authors of *Homelessness Comes to School* (Corwin Press, 2011).

Murphy, Joseph F. and Tobin, Kerri J. From *Phi Delta Kappan*, November 2010, pp. 32–37. Reprinted with permission of Phi Delta Kappa International, www.pdkintl.org All rights reserved. www.kappanmagazine.org

Article   Prepared by: Rebecca B. Evers, *Winthrop University*

Poverty-Stricken Schools: What We Can Learn from the Rest of the World and from Successful Schools in Economically Disadvantaged Areas in the US

Hani Morgan

Learning Outcomes

After reading this article, you will be able to:

- Explain how teachers' beliefs about poverty may determine their teaching practices.

- Discuss if modeling successful schools in disadvantaged areas is an effective strategy.

In December of 2010, many Americans were shocked when the Organisation for Economic Co-operation and Development (OECD) announced the latest scores of the Program for International Student Assessment (PISA) tests. For the first time, China was in first place in math, reading, and science, and the US continued to score in the average range, failing to score as high as the top ten ranked countries in any subject. The announcement of the PISA scores was one of the leading stories on many national news shows and led some Americans to wonder if this was comparable to the "Sputnik" problem. Although many US students perform well on international tests such as the PISA, students who attend disadvantaged schools generally score poorly; consequently, national scores are lowered, and the US often lags behind the countries performing highest on international testing, such as Finland and South Korea (Baines, 2007).

One of the biggest problems in the US educational system is the inadequate condition of many schools located in economically disadvantaged areas. McGee (2004) describes this concern as the most crucial issue in the American educational system. Darling-Hammond and Sykes (2003) indicate that most schools in economically-disadvantaged areas in the US suffer from teachers who are underprepared and too often

work in schools with poor working conditions, high teacher-turnover rates, and low pay. As a result of attending inadequate schools, many students do very poorly on international achievement tests when compared with more advantaged students. This article discusses how the education of the poor can be improved by focusing on successful models in the US and abroad.

The Gap in Academic Achievement

Although the gap in academic achievement could be the result of many causes such as parental involvement, cultural attitude towards education, and the educational resources available at the home of a child, the school and its teachers can make a huge impact on a student's education. Unfortunately, even in 21st century America, severe inequalities in academic achievement persist. On a recent PISA test, for example, Brozo, Shiel and Topping (2007) indicate that white students in America were ranked second among the 32 countries that took the test, but that African American and Hispanic students were ranked 25th. On state testing, the situation is very similar. In 2001, for example, on the Illinois standards achievement test, only 40% of low-income third graders met the state's reading standards, compared with 75% of their classmates who were not considered disadvantaged students, and the reading results for grades 5 and 8 were similar (McGee, 2004).

McGee (2004) argues that the gap in achievement is not about students who are failing, but about a system that is not providing the educational opportunities that low-income students are entitled to. A description of many low-income schools does in fact support McGee's hypothesis.

The Need for Better Schools for the Poor

One of the biggest problems that schools in poor districts face is a shortage of qualified teachers. Experienced teachers often leave these schools, and many good teachers avoid them. Most teachers who teach in poor districts are likely to hold less educational credentials, teach a subject they do not specialize in, and graduate from less prestigious universities when compared with teachers who teach in more advantaged areas (Robinson, 2007). Very often teachers with little experience or credentials take positions in poor districts and then leave, once they have gotten the experience which makes them marketable for wealthier districts.

Frost (2007) refers to many inequalities between poor schools serving low-income students and those in wealthier areas, pointing out that in some advantaged districts, schools spend over twice as much per pupil than those in the poorest districts. In some inner-city schools, such as those in Chicago, children not only have teachers with inadequate training, but also have to deal with overcrowded classrooms, run-down buildings, and dilapidated textbooks. Although the federal *No Child Left Behind* program was designed to provide funds to help impoverished schools, children in these schools, who are predominantly students of color, are often found in classrooms that leave little opportunities for learning (Frost, 2007). New York City is another area that encountered severe teacher problems. Haycock and Crawford (2008) describe how teachers in this city were often not licensed or had failed the licensure exam on numerous occasions. Fortunately, the school system in New York stopped this practice and is now recruiting more qualified teachers.

Although Kozol (1991) documented many inequalities between the schools disadvantaged children attend and those of more fortunate students almost twenty years ago, authors such as Glickman and Scally (2008) offer evidence showing that little has changed in the 21st century. Noguera and Akom (2000) mention that many parents view inner city schools "as hopeless and unresponsive to their needs" (p. 29). In order for students who live in low-income areas to do well in school, they need competent teachers who understand their needs. Frost (2007) discusses that they need highly-qualified teachers more than students in wealthier districts.

Successful Academic Programs for Disadvantaged Youth

In contrast to the many inadequate schools serving the poor in the US, many school systems from around the world provide the poor with a better education. Students from low socioeconomic backgrounds in the OECD countries outscoring the US on international tests, such as South Korea and Singapore, perform better than their counterparts in the US, in part, because these students get a qualified teacher regardless of their socioeconomic background (Paine & Schleicher, 2011). Some countries do the opposite of the US with regard to the way the poor are educated. In contrast to the overcrowded schools in many poor districts in the US, approximately half of OECD countries tend to provide a lower teacher/student ratio for students from low socioeconomic backgrounds based on the logic that these students need better, and more, teachers. In Singapore for example, a country known for its high scores, the best teachers teach the students who have the most difficulty, which is the opposite of what usually occurs in the US (Paine & Schleicher, 2011).

Some schools in the US with large numbers of low-income students are achieving good results, and modeling what these schools are doing can reduce the gap in achievement. Chenoweth (2009) describes a few schools, consisting primarily of students coming from poor families, who are achieving at similar levels to students in wealthier districts. Some of the schools mentioned include George Hall Elementary in Mobile, Alabama, Graham Road Elementary in Falls Church, Virginia, and P.S./M.S. 124 Osmond A. Church School in Queens, New York. What is different about these schools is the way they are organized and their tremendous devotion to helping students learn.

Chenoweth (2009) mentions that successful schools in poverty-stricken areas assess students well by *accurately* evaluating what they know, and do not know. In one of these schools, for example, teachers review each test with each student to find out which questions or problems were most difficult. In another case, teachers discovered that students had weak vocabulary skills, a very common deficiency among low-income students. Some of these schools build vocabulary skills by taking students on field trips to places they have likely never been to, as a result of being poor. Other schools help students understand new vocabulary by showing short documentary videos.

In addition, Chenoweth (2009) discusses that many of the successful schools serving students from low-income families allow teachers to meet together, and this leads them to accurately assess the students. In many schools in the US today, teachers are isolated and spend little, if any, time interacting with each other. When teachers interact with each other, Chenoweth (2009) contends that students benefit from the broader knowledge of a school's faculty, but when they sit isolated, students are dependent only on the expertise and skills of one individual teacher.

McGee (2004) mentions that high-performing, high-poverty schools in Wisconsin tend to have certain common characteristics, including student-centered instruction, more interaction between teachers, parental involvement, small class size, project-based instruction, staff-initiated professional development, and proactive administrative leadership.

Learning from the Top-Ranked Countries

Some of the recommendations that McGee (2004) emphasizes to close the achievement gap in the US include improving teacher education and professional development, since many countries deal with these aspects of the educational system in a different manner than the US. Exploring teacher-education systems in the countries that outperform the US on international testing can yield important information. Teacher-education programs in these countries are superior to those in the US in many ways. The gap in achievement between advantaged and disadvantaged students will likely be reduced significantly if the policies towards education in the top-ranked countries in international testing are implemented in America, for several reasons. The most important of which is that these countries not only practice the methods that high-performing schools in low-income areas in the United States use, they also offer many more advantages to both teachers and students.

In Singapore, for example, mentor teachers guide beginning teachers, and novices in the teaching profession also collaborate with other teachers, and visit different classes for as long as 20 hours a week (Darling-Hammond, 2008). In addition, students get the best teachers possible because Singapore recruits teachers from the top one third of each high school class and offers them 100 hours per year of professional development which is paid by the government (Darling-Hammond, 2008). Teachers in Singapore also have opportunities to choose different career opportunities—master teacher, principal, or curriculum specialist (Schleicher & Stewart, 2008). In the United States, on the other hand, not only are the poorest teachers more likely to end up with students from low-income areas, but almost half of America's K-12 teachers come from the bottom one-third of their college classes, as measured by SAT scores (Kristof, 2011).

Obstacles for Reducing the Achievement Gap

One of the main issues in the public school system today is that administrators are reluctant to take action against teachers whose performance is unsatisfactory. Although many teachers in the public school system are hard working, others are not, and often do not get removed even when complaints of inadequate performance, or inappropriate conduct, are received.

Thomas, Wingert, Conant, and Register (2010) explain that teachers in most states receive tenure after two or three years and are very difficult to fire as a result of belonging to powerful unions. In New York, for example, in 2008, only three out of the 30,000 tenured teachers were dismissed. This problem has led many inner-city school teachers to develop apathetic attitudes blaming parents and students, and not themselves, for their students' poor academic performance (Thomas et al., 2010).

Medina (2010) explains how officials who want to remove ineffective teachers in big cities such as New York cannot do so because the teachers' union heavily influences laws making it difficult to fire teachers. In some cases teachers who are investigated for poor conduct or inadequate teaching receive their full salary as they wait for their cases to be resolved, which can take years. Medina (2010) discusses that in New York City, these teachers report to a "rubber room" until the investigation is over, and this process costs the educational system $30 million per year.

Although taking on the unions will not be easy, there is hope for a better future for several reasons. First, many high-performing inner-city schools in the US, which are not part of the public school system, but are charter schools, have been organized. Programs like KIPP (Knowledge Is Power Program) have organized successful inner-city schools that outperform the public schools. In addition, reformers are challenging the powerful unions. A good example of this is what happened recently at Central Falls High School in Rhode Island where the local superintendent threatened to fire 74 teachers for failing to lead the students in the school to perform well. The school had a very high dropout rate of almost 50%, and a 7% proficiency rate in math among 11th graders (Thomas et al., 2010). What is encouraging in this example is that Education Secretary Duncan and President Obama supported what the superintendent had done, and this could be a sign that the US is heading in the right direction. Many upper-middle-class parents send their children to expensive private institutions to avoid schools with similar problems, but for working-class families, this is not a feasible alternative.

Conclusion

An important step in reducing the achievement gap between low-income students and more privileged students is to acquire skillful teachers for all students. Unfortunately, in America, quality teachers are unevenly distributed (Darling-Hammond, 2008; Haycock and Crawford, 2008; Paine & Schleicher, 2011). The difference between good and poor teachers is a critical issue. Haycock and Crawford (2008) refer to a study showing that students with good teachers were found to make academic gains, whereas those taught by poor teachers fell behind.

Solving the achievement gap in American schools seems simple: place teachers who are properly trained with low-income students. The leading countries in international testing are already doing this. Countries whose students outperform others, such as Finland, Sweden, Singapore, and Japan prepare their teachers much more extensively than the US, pay their teachers well, and make sure qualified teachers are evenly distributed among schools (Darling-Hammond, 2008).

In some countries such as Sweden and Finland, teachers are able to finish graduate level work with a government stipend. Compared to the United States, where some teachers are allowed to teach through an "alternate route" program, without any teacher-training experience, this is a very important advantage. Public schools sometimes argue that alternative programs are necessary to deal with the shortage of teachers, but this is not necessarily good logic. If teachers were paid well, trained well, and supported well, chances are there would not be a problem with teacher shortages. In Europe, for example, where teachers have these advantages, schools do not have problems recruiting new teachers with strong academic backgrounds (Thomas et al., 2010). Another example showing how well teachers can be treated involves teacher salaries in Singapore; in that country first-year teachers make more than beginning doctors (Darling-Hammond, 2008).

In the US, there are high-performing schools that benefit working-class students tremendously, and modeling these schools can benefit the educational system. However, this is not enough. For sustained improvement towards closing the gap in achievement, American schools need a similar infrastructure and organization to those of the countries leading the world in international testing. Policy changes aimed at modeling the educational systems of these countries will likely offer a much better solution than merely imitating American schools with "best practices".

Lackluster scores on international tests should cause America to worry because there is a link between economic prosperity and educational achievement. Paine and Schleicher (2011) refer to a study done at Stanford University suggesting that an average increase of 25 points for the US on the PISA scores could lead to a $41 trillion increase for the US economy. If the US does not keep up with the rest of the world, it will likely lead to a gloomy future for education in America. The good news is that improving the educational system and raising test scores is possible. Some countries, such as South Korea, have made rapid progress, and were not among the leaders two generations ago, and in the US, some districts in Florida, North Carolina, and California have also made noticeable gains (Paine & Schleicher, 2011).

The US also has some very active reformers such as Michelle Rhee, who created a new program called Students First (Dillon, 2011). One of the main goals of this program is to gain back some power from teachers' unions and textbook manufacturers and to provide parents, teachers, students, and administrators with more opportunities to produce better results at both the local and national level. Rhee is also fighting a system known as Last In, First Out (LIFO).

Her referendum urges the cessation of the antiquated Last-In, First-Out policy used by US school districts for generations regarding teachers; it encourages a system where teachers are retained for good teaching in the classroom and discourages the complacency experienced by tenured teachers in too many cases. Changes of this kind can only bode well for a new and better future for American schools.

References

Baines, L. (2007). Learning from the world: Achieving more by doing less. *Phi Delta Kappan, 89*(2), 98–100.

Brozo, W. G., Shiel, G., & Topping, K. (2007). Engagement in reading: Lessons learned from three PISA countries. *Journal of Adolescent & Adult Literacy, 51*(5), 304–315.

Chenoweth, K. (2009). It can be done, it's being done, and here's how. *Phi Delta Kappan, 91*(1), 38–43.

Darling-Hammond, L., & Sykes, G. (2003). Wanted: A national teacher supply policy for education: The right way to meet the "highly qualified teacher" challenge. *Education Policy Analysis Archives, 11*(33), 1–55. Available at: http://epaa.asu.edu/ojs/article/view/261/38 7

Darling-Hammond, L. (2008, February 25). Educating teachers: How they do it abroad. *Time, 171*(8), 34. Available at: http://www.time.com/time/magazine/article/0,9171,1713557,00.html

Dillon, S. (2011, May 20). Former foes join forces for education reform. *The New York Times.* Retrieved on May 26, 2011 from http://www.nytimes.com/2011/05/21/education/21rhee.html?pagewanted=all

Frost, J. L. (2007). The changing culture of childhood: A perfect storm. *Childhood Education, 83*(4), 225–230.

Haycock, K., & Crawford, C. (2008). Closing the teacher quality gap. *Educational Leadership, 65*(7), 14–19.

Kozol, J. (1991). *Savage inequalities: Children in America's schools.* NY: Crown.

Kristof, N. D. (2011, March 12). Pay teachers more. *The New York Times.* Retrieved on February 2, 2012 from http://www.nytimes.com/2011/03/13/opinion/13kristof.html

McGee, G. W. (2004). Closing the achievement gap: Lessons from Illinois' golden spike high-poverty high-performing schools. *Journal of Education for Students Placed at Risk, 9*(2), 97–125.

Medina, J. (2010, February 23). Progress slow in city goal to fire bad teachers. *The New York Times.* Retrieved on February 2, 2012 from http://www.nytimes.com/2010/02/24/education/24teachers.html?ref=education

Noguera, P. A., & Akom, A. (2000). Disparities demystified. *The Nation, 270*(22), 29–31.

Paine, S. L., & Schleicher, A. (2011). What the U.S. can learn from the world's most successful education reform efforts. Retrieved on January 26, 2012, from http://www.mcgrawhillresearchfoundation.org/wp-content/uploads/pisa-intl-competitiveness.pdf

Robinson, J. (2007). Presence and persistence: Poverty ideology and inner-city teaching. *The Urban Review, 39*(5), 541–565.

Schleicher, A., & Stewart, V. (2008). Learning from world-class schools. *Educational Leadership, 66*(2), 44–51.

Thomas, E., Wingert, P., Conant, E., & Register, S. (2010, March 15). Why we can't get rid of failing teachers. *Newsweek, 155*(11), 24–27.

Critical Thinking

1. Review the state report cards for two schools in each of the richest and poorest school districts in your state (or home state). Does that data agree with the data in the article?

2. Select and critique two suggested actions from this article. Offer any alternative actions you might know about. Discuss these actions with your peers to reach consensus about actions that would work in the schools where you teach or plan to teach.

Create Central

www.mhhe.com/createcentral

Internet References

National Center for Children in Poverty
www.nccp.org

U.S. Census Bureau: Poverty
www.census.gov/hhes/www/poverty/

Hani Morgan is currently teaching and doing research for the University of Southern Mississippi.

Morgan, Hani. From *Education*, vol.133, no. 2, 2012, pp. 291–297. Copyright © 2012 by Education. Reprinted by permission.

Article   Prepared by: Rebecca B. Evers, *Winthrop University*

Principles of Instruction
Research-Based Strategies That All Teachers Should Know

BARAK ROSENSHINE

Learning Outcomes

After reading this article, you will be able to:

• Understand the principles of effective instruction.

This article presents 10 research-based principles of instruction, along with suggestions for classroom practice. These principles come from three sources: (a) research in cognitive science, (b) research on master teachers, and (c) research on cognitive supports. Each is briefly explained below.

A: *Research in cognitive science:* This research focuses on how our brains acquire and use information. This cognitive research also provides suggestions on how we might overcome the limitations of our working memory (i.e., the mental "space" in which thinking occurs) when learning new material.

B: *Research on the classroom practices of master teachers.* Master teachers are those teachers whose classrooms made the highest gains on achievement tests. In a series of studies, a wide range of teachers were observed as they taught, and the investigators coded how they presented new material, how and whether they checked for student understanding, the types of support they provided to their students, and a number of other instructional activities. By also gathering student achievement data, researchers were able to identify the ways in which the more and less effective teachers differed.

C: *Research on cognitive supports to help students learn complex tasks.* Effective instructional procedures—such as thinking aloud, providing students with scaffolds, and providing students with models—come from this research.

Even though these are three very different bodies of research, there is *no conflict at all* between the instructional suggestions that come from each of these three sources. In other words, these three sources supplement and complement each other. The fact that the instructional ideas from three different sources supplement and complement each other gives us faith in the validity of these findings.

Education involves helping a novice develop strong, readily accessible background knowledge. It's important that background knowledge be readily accessible, and this occurs when knowledge is well rehearsed and tied to other knowledge. The most effective teachers ensured that their students efficiently acquired, rehearsed, and connected background knowledge by providing a good deal of instructional support. They provided this support by teaching new material in manageable amounts, modeling, guiding student practice, helping students when they made errors, and providing for sufficient practice and review. Many of these teachers also went on to experiential, hands-on activities, but they always did the experiential activities after, not before, the basic material was learned.

> **The most effective teachers ensured that students efficiently acquired, rehearsed, and connected knowledge. Many went on to hands-on activities, but always after, not before, the basic material was learned.**

The following is a list of some of the instructional principles that have come from these three sources. These ideas will be described and discussed in this article:

• Begin a lesson with a short review of previous learning.[1]
• Present new material in small steps with student practice after each step.[2]
• Ask a large number of questions and check the responses of all students.[3]
• Provide models.[4]
• Guide student practice.[5]
• Check for student understanding.[6]
• Obtain a high success rate.[7]
• Provide scaffolds for difficult tasks.[8]
• Require and monitor independent practice.[9]
• Engage students in weekly and monthly review.[10]

1. Begin a lesson with a short review of previous learning: Daily review can strengthen previous learning and can lead to fluent recall.

Research findings

Daily review is an important component of instruction. Review can help us strengthen the connections among the material we have learned. The review of previous learning can help us recall words, concepts, and procedures effortlessly and automatically when we need this material to solve problems or to understand new material. The development of expertise requires thousands of hours of practice, and daily review is one component of this practice.

For example, daily review was part of a successful experiment in elementary school mathematics. Teachers in the experiment were taught to spend eight minutes every day on review. Teachers used this time to check the homework, go over problems where there were errors, and practice the concepts and skills that needed to become automatic. As a result, students in these classrooms had higher achievement scores than did students in other classrooms.

Daily practice of vocabulary can lead to seeing each practiced word as a unit (i.e., seeing the whole word automatically rather than as individual letters that have to be sounded out and blended). When students see words as units, they have more space available in their working memory, and this space can now be used for comprehension. Mathematical problem solving is also improved when the basic skills (addition, multiplication, etc.) are overlearned and become automatic, thus freeing working-memory capacity.

In the classroom

The most effective teachers in the studies of classroom instruction understood the importance of practice, and they began their lessons with a five- to eight-minute review of previously covered material. Some teachers reviewed vocabulary, formulae, events, or previously learned concepts. These teachers provided additional practice on facts and skills that were needed for recall to become automatic.

Effective teacher activities also included reviewing the concepts and skills that were necessary to do the homework, having students correct each others' papers, and asking about points on which the students had difficulty or made errors. These reviews ensured that the students had a firm grasp of the skills and concepts that would be needed for the day's lesson.

Effective teachers also reviewed the knowledge and concepts that were relevant for that day's lesson. It is important for a teacher to help students recall the concepts and vocabulary that will be relevant for the day's lesson because our working memory is very limited. If we do not review previous learning, then we will have to make a special effort to recall old material while learning new material, and this makes it difficult for us to learn the new material.

Daily review is particularly important for teaching material that will be used in subsequent learning. Examples include reading sight words (i.e., any word that is known by a reader automatically), grammar, math facts, math computation, math factoring, and chemical equations.

When planning for review, teachers might want to consider which words, math facts, procedures, and concepts need to become automatic, and which words, vocabulary or ideas need to be reviewed before the lesson begins.

In addition, teachers might consider doing the following during their daily review:

- Correct homework.
- Review the concepts and skills that were practiced as part of the homework.
- Ask students about points where they had difficulties or made errors.
- Review material where errors were made.
- Review material that needs overlearning (i.e., newly acquired skills should be practiced well beyond the point of initial mastery, leading to automaticity).

2. Present new material in small steps with student practice after each step: Only present small amounts of new material at any time, and then assist students as they practice this material.

Research findings

Our working memory, the place where we process information, is small. It can only handle a few bits of information at once—too much information swamps our working memory. Presenting too much material at once may confuse students because their working memory will be unable to process it.

Therefore, the more effective teachers do not overwhelm their students by presenting too much new material at once. Rather, these teachers only present small amounts of new material at any time, and then assist the students as they practice this material. Only after the students have mastered the first step do teachers proceed to the next step.

The procedure of first teaching in small steps and then guiding student practice represents an appropriate way of dealing with the limitation of our working memory.

In the classroom

The more successful teachers did not overwhelm their students by presenting too much new material at once. Rather, they presented only small amounts of new material at one time, and they taught in such a way that each point was mastered before the next point was introduced. They checked their students' understanding on each point and retaught material when necessary.

Some successful teachers taught by giving a series of short presentations using many examples. The examples provided concrete learning and elaboration that were useful for processing new material.

Teaching in small steps requires time, and the more effective teachers spent more time presenting new material and guiding student practice than did the less effective teachers. In a study of mathematics instruction, for instance, the most effective mathematics teachers spent about 23 minutes of a 40-minute period in lecture, demonstration, questioning, and working examples. In contrast, the least effective teachers spent only 11 minutes presenting new material. The more effective teachers used this extra time to provide additional explanations, give many examples, check for student understanding, and provide sufficient instruction so that the students could learn to work independently without difficulty. In one study, the least effective teachers asked only nine questions in a 40-minute period. Compared with the successful teachers, the less effective teachers gave much shorter presentations and explanations, and then passed out worksheets and told students to solve the problems. The less successful teachers were then observed going from student to student and having to explain the material again.

Similarly, when students were taught a strategy for summarizing a paragraph, an effective teacher taught the strategy using small steps. First, the teacher modeled and thought aloud as she identified the topic of a paragraph. Then, she led practice on identifying the topics of new paragraphs. Then, she taught students to identify the main idea of a paragraph. The teacher modeled this step and then supervised the students as they practiced both finding the topic and locating the main idea. Following this, the teacher taught the students to identify the supporting details in a paragraph. The teacher modeled and thought aloud, and then the students practiced. Finally, the students practiced carrying out all three steps of this strategy. Thus, the strategy of summarizing a paragraph was divided into smaller steps, and there was modeling and practice at each step.

3. Ask a large number of questions and check the responses of all students: Questions help students practice new information and connect new material to their prior learning.
Research findings
Students need to practice new material. The teacher's questions and student discussion are a major way of providing this necessary practice. The most successful teachers in these studies spent more than half of the class time lecturing, demonstrating, and asking questions.

Questions allow a teacher to determine how well the material has been learned and whether there is a need for additional instruction. The most effective teachers also ask students to explain the process they used to answer the question, to explain how the answer was found. Less successful teachers ask fewer questions and almost no process questions.

In the classroom
In one classroom-based experimental study, one group of teachers was taught to follow the presentation of new material with lots of questions.[11] They were taught to increase the number of factual questions and process questions they asked during this guided practice. Test results showed that their students achieved higher scores than did students whose teachers did not receive the training.

Imaginative teachers have found ways to involve all students in answering questions. Examples include having all students:

- Tell the answer to a neighbor.
- Summarize the main idea in one or two sentences, writing the summary on a piece of paper and sharing this with a neighbor, or repeating the procedures to a neighbor.
- Write the answer on a card and then hold it up.
- Raise their hands if they know the answer (thereby allowing the teacher to check the entire class).
- Raise their hands if they agree with the answer that someone else has given.

Across the classrooms that researchers observed, the purpose of all these procedures was to provide active participation for the students and also to allow the teacher to see how many students were correct and confident. The teacher may then reteach some material when it was considered necessary. An alternative was for students to write their answers and then trade papers with each other.

Other teachers used choral responses to provide sufficient practice when teaching new vocabulary or lists of items. This made the practice seem more like a game. To be effective, however, all students needed to start together, on a signal. When students did not start together, only the faster students answered.

In addition to asking questions, the more effective teachers facilitated their students' rehearsal by providing explanations, giving more examples, and supervising students as they practiced the new material.

The following is a series of stems[12] for questions that teachers might ask when teaching literature, social science content, or science content to their students. Sometimes, students may also develop questions from these stems to ask questions of each other.

How are _____ and _____ alike?
What is the main idea of _____ ?
What are the strengths and weaknesses of _____?
In what way is _____ related to _____?
Compare _____ and _____ with regard to _____ .
What do you think causes _____?
How does _____ tie in with what we have learned before?
Which one is the best _____, and why?
What are some possible solutions for the problem of _____?
Do you agree or disagree with this statement: _____?
What do you still not understand about _____?

4. Provide models: Providing students with models and worked examples can help them learn to solve problems faster.
Research findings
Students need cognitive support to help them learn to solve problems. The teacher modeling and thinking aloud while demonstrating how to solve a problem are examples of effective cognitive support. Worked examples (such as a math problem for which the teacher not only has provided the solution but has clearly laid out each step) are another form of modeling that has been developed by researchers. Worked examples allow students to focus on the specific steps to solve problems and thus reduce the cognitive load on their working memory. Modeling and worked examples have been used successfully in mathematics, science, writing, and reading comprehension.

In the classroom
Many of the skills that are taught in classrooms can be conveyed by providing prompts, modeling use of the prompt, and then guiding students as they develop independence. When teaching reading comprehension strategies, for example, effective teachers provided students with prompts that the students could use to ask themselves questions about a short passage. In one class, students were given words such as "who," "where," "why," and

"how" to help them begin a question. Then, everyone read a passage and the teacher modeled how to use these words to ask questions. Many examples were given.

Next, during guided practice, the teacher helped the students practice asking questions by helping them select a prompt and develop a question that began with that prompt. The students practiced this step many times with lots of support from the teacher.

Many of the skills taught in classrooms can be conveyed by providing prompts, modeling use of the prompt, and then guiding students as they develop independence.

Then, the students read new passages and practiced asking questions on their own, with support from the teacher when needed. Finally, students were given short passages followed by questions, and the teacher expressed an opinion about the quality of the students' questions.

This same procedure—providing a prompt, modeling, guiding practice, and supervising independent practice—can be used for many tasks. When teaching students to write an essay, for example, an effective teacher first modeled how to write each paragraph, then the students and teacher worked together on two or more new essays, and finally students worked on their own with supervision from the teacher.

Worked examples are another form of modeling that has been used to help students learn how to solve problems in mathematics and science. A worked example is a step-by-step demonstration of how to perform a task or how to solve a problem. The presentation of worked examples begins with the teacher modeling and explaining the steps that can be taken to solve a specific problem. The teacher also identifies and explains the underlying principles for these steps.

Usually, students are then given a series of problems to complete at their desks as independent practice. But, in research carried out in Australia, students were given a mixture of problems to solve and worked examples. So, during independent practice, students first studied a worked example, then they solved a problem; then they studied another worked example and solved another problem. In this way, the worked examples showed students how to focus on the essential parts of the problems. Of course, not all students studied the worked examples. To correct this problem, the Australian researchers also presented partially completed problems in which students had to complete the missing steps and thus pay more attention to the worked example.

5. Guide student practice: Successful teachers spend more time guiding students' practice of new material.
Research findings
It is not enough simply to present students with new material, because the material will be forgotten unless there is sufficient rehearsal. An important finding from information-processing research is that students need to spend additional time rephrasing, elaborating, and summarizing new material in order to store this material in their long-term memory. When there has been sufficient rehearsal, the students are able to retrieve this material easily and thus are able to make use of this material to foster new learning and aid in problem solving. But when the rehearsal time is too short, students are less able to store, remember, or use the material. As we know, it is relatively easy to place something in a filing cabinet, but it can be very difficult to recall where exactly we filed it. Rehearsal helps us remember where we filed it so we can access it with ease when needed.

A teacher can facilitate this rehearsal process by asking questions; good questions require students to process and rehearse the material. Rehearsal is also enhanced when students are asked to summarize the main points, and when they are supervised as they practice new steps in a skill. The quality of storage in long-term memory will be weak if students only skim the material and do not engage in it. It is also important that all students process the new material and receive feedback, so they do not inadvertently store partial information or a misconception in long-term memory.

In the classroom
In one study, the more successful teachers of mathematics spent more time presenting new material and guiding practice. The more successful teachers used this extra time to provide additional explanations, give many examples, check for student understanding and provide sufficient instruction so that the students could learn to work independently without difficulty. In contrast, the less successful teachers gave much shorter presentations and explanations, and then they passed out worksheets and told students to work on the problems. Under these conditions, the students made too many errors and had to be retaught the lesson.

The most successful teachers presented only small amounts of material at a time. After this short presentation, these teachers then guided student practice. This guidance often consisted of the teacher working the first problems at the blackboard and explaining the reason for each step, which served as a model for the students. The guidance also included asking students to come to the blackboard to work out problems and discuss their procedures. Through this process, the students seated in the classroom saw additional models.

Although most teachers provided some guided practice, the most successful teachers spent more time in guided practice, more time asking questions, more time checking for understanding, more time correcting errors, and more time having students work out problems with teacher guidance.

The most successful teachers spent more time in guided practice, more time asking questions, more time checking for understanding, and more time correcting errors.

Teachers who spent more time in guided practice and had higher success rates also had students who were more engaged during individual work at their desks. This finding suggests that, when teachers provided sufficient instruction during guided practice, the students were better prepared for the independent practice (e.g., seatwork and homework activities), but when the guided practice was too short, the students were not prepared for the seatwork and made more errors during independent practice.

6. Check for student understanding: Checking for student understanding at each point can help students learn the material with fewer errors.

Research findings

The more effective teachers frequently checked to see if all the students were learning the new material. These checks provided some of the processing needed to move new learning into long-term memory. These checks also let teachers know if students were developing misconceptions.

In the classroom

Effective teachers also stopped to check for student understanding. They checked for understanding by asking questions, by asking students to summarize the presentation up to that point or to repeat directions or procedures, or by asking students whether they agreed or disagreed with other students' answers. This checking has two purposes: (a) answering the questions might cause the students to elaborate on the material they have learned and augment connections to other learning in their long-term memory, and (b) alerting the teacher to when parts of the material need to be retaught.

In contrast, the less effective teachers simply asked, "Are there any questions?" and, if there were no questions, they assumed the students had learned the material and proceeded to pass out worksheets for students to complete on their own.

Another way to check for understanding is to ask students to think aloud as they work to solve mathematical problems, plan an essay, or identify the main idea in a paragraph. Yet another check is to ask students to explain or defend their position to others. Having to explain a position may help students integrate and elaborate their knowledge in new ways, or may help identify gaps in their understanding.

Another reason for the importance of teaching in small steps, guiding practice, and checking for understanding (as well as obtaining a high success rate, which we'll explore in principle 7) comes from the fact that we all construct and reconstruct knowledge as we learn and use what we have learned. We cannot simply repeat what we hear word for word. Rather, we connect our understanding of the new information to our existing concepts or "schema," and we then construct a mental summary (i. e., the gist of what we have heard). However, when left on their own, many students make errors in the process of constructing this mental summary. These errors occur, particularly when the information is new and the student does not have adequate or well-formed background knowledge. These constructions are not errors so much as attempts by the students to be logical in an area where their background knowledge is weak. These errors are so common that there is a research literature on the development and correction of student misconceptions in science. Providing guided practice after teaching small amounts of new material, and checking for student understanding, can help limit the development of misconceptions.

7. Obtain a high success rate: It is important for students to achieve a high success rate during classroom instruction.

Research findings

In two of the major studies on the impact of teachers, the investigators found that students in classrooms with more effective teachers had a higher success rate, as judged by the quality of their oral responses during guided practice and their individual work. In a study of fourth-grade mathematics, it was found that 82 percent of students' answers were correct in the classrooms of the most successful teachers, but the least successful teachers had a success rate of only 73 percent. A high success rate during guided practice also leads to a higher success rate when students are working on problems on their own.

The research also suggests that the optimal success rate for fostering student achievement appears to be about 80 percent. A success rate of 80 percent shows that students are learning the material, and it also shows that the students are challenged.

In the classroom

The most effective teachers obtained this success level by teaching in small steps (i.e., by combining short presentations with supervised student practice), and by giving sufficient practice on each part before proceeding to the next step. These teachers frequently checked for understanding and required responses from all students.

It is important that students achieve a high success rate during instruction and on their practice activities. Practice, we are told, makes perfect, but practice can be a disaster if students are practicing errors! If the practice does not have a high success level, there is a chance that students are practicing and learning errors. Once errors have been learned, they are very difficult to overcome.

As discussed in the previous section, when we learn new material, we construct a gist of this material in our long-term memory. However, many students make errors in the process of constructing this mental summary. But students are more likely to develop misconceptions if too much material is presented at once, and if teachers do not check for student understanding. Providing guided practice after teaching small amounts of new material, and checking for student understanding, can help limit the development of misconceptions.

I once observed a class where an effective teacher was going from desk to desk during independent practice and suddenly realized that the students were having difficulty. She stopped the work, told the students not to do the problems for homework, and said she would reteach this material the next day. She stopped the work because she did not want the students to practice errors.

Unless all students have mastered the first set of lessons, there is a danger that the slower students will fall further behind when the next set of lessons is taught. So there is a need for a high success rate for *all* students. "Mastery learning" is a form of instruction where lessons are organized into short units and all students are required to master one set of lessons before they proceed to the next set. In mastery learning, tutoring by other students or by teachers is provided to help students master each unit. Variations of this approach, particularly the tutoring, might be useful in many classroom settings.

8. Provide scaffolds for difficult tasks: The teacher provides students with temporary supports and scaffolds to assist them when they learn difficult tasks.

Research findings

Investigators have successfully provided students with scaffolds, or instructional supports, to help them learn difficult tasks. A scaffold is a temporary support that is used to assist a learner. These scaffolds are gradually withdrawn as learners become more competent, although students may continue to rely on scaffolds when they encounter particularly difficult problems. Providing scaffolds is a form of guided practice.

Scaffolds include modeling the steps by the teacher, or thinking aloud by the teacher as he or she solves the problem. Scaffolds also may be tools, such as cue cards or checklists, that complete part of the task for the students, or a model of the completed task against which students can compare their own work.

The process of helping students solve difficult problems by modeling and providing scaffolds has been called "cognitive apprenticeship." Students learn strategies and content during this apprenticeship that enable them to become competent readers, writers, and problem solvers. They are aided by a master who models, coaches, provides supports, and scaffolds them as they become independent.

In the classroom

One form of scaffolding is to give students prompts for steps they might use. Prompts such as "who," "why," and "how" have helped students learn to ask questions while they read. Teaching students to ask questions has been shown to help students' reading comprehension.

Similarly, one researcher developed the following prompt to help students organize material.[13]

1. Draw a central box and write the title of the article in it.
2. Skim the article to find four to six main ideas
3. Write each main idea in a box below the central box.
4. Find and write two to four important details to list under each main idea.

Another form of scaffolding is thinking aloud by the teacher. For example, teachers might think aloud as they try to summarize a paragraph. They would show the thought processes they go through as they determine the topic of the paragraph and then use the topic to generate a summary sentence. Teachers might think aloud while solving a scientific equation or writing an essay, and at the same time provide labels for their mental processes. Such thinking aloud provides novice learners with a way to observe "expert thinking" that is usually hidden from the student. Teachers also can study their students' thought processes by asking them to think aloud during problem solving.

One characteristic of effective teachers is their ability to anticipate students' errors and warn them about possible errors

some of them are likely to make. For example, a teacher might have students read a passage and then give them a poorly written topic sentence to correct. In teaching division or subtraction, the teacher may show and discuss with students the mistakes other students have frequently made.

One characteristic of effective teachers is their ability to anticipate students' errors and warn them about possible errors some of them are likely to make.

In some of the studies, students were given a checklist to evaluate their work. Checklist items included "Have I found the most important information that tells me more about the main idea?" and "Does every sentence start with a capital letter?" The teacher then modeled use of the checklist.

In some studies, students were provided with expert models with which they could compare their work. For example, when students were taught to generate questions, they could compare their questions with those generated by the teacher. Similarly, when learning to write summaries, students could compare their summaries on a passage with those generated by an expert.

9. Require and monitor independent practice: Students need extensive, successful, independent practice in order for skills and knowledge to become automatic.

Research findings

In a typical teacher-led classroom, guided practice is followed by independent practice—by students working alone and practicing the new material. This independent practice is necessary because a good deal of practice (overlearning) is needed in order to become fluent and automatic in a skill. When material is over-learned, it can be recalled automatically and doesn't take up any space in working memory. When students become automatic in an area, they can then devote more of their attention to comprehension and application.

Independent practice provides students with the additional review and elaboration they need to become fluent. This need for fluency applies to facts, concepts, and discriminations that must be used in subsequent learning. Fluency is also needed in operations, such as dividing decimals, conjugating a regular verb in a foreign language, or completing and balancing a chemical equation.

In the classroom

The more successful teachers provided for extensive and successful practice, both in the classroom and after class. Independent practice should involve the same material as the guided practice. If guided practice deals with identifying types of sentences, for example, then independent practice should deal with the same topic or, perhaps, with a slight variation, like creating individual compound and complex sentences. It would be inappropriate if the independent practice asked the students to do an activity such as "Write a paragraph using two compound and two complex sentences" however, because the students have not been adequately prepared for such an activity.

Students need to be fully prepared for their independent practice. Sometimes, it may be appropriate for a teacher to practice some of the seatwork problems with the entire class before students begin independent practice.

Research has found that students were more engaged when their teacher circulated around the room, and monitored and supervised their seatwork. The optimal time for these contacts was 30 seconds or less. Classrooms where the teachers had to stop at students' desks and provide a great deal of explanation during seatwork were the classrooms where students were making errors. These errors occurred because the guided practice was not sufficient for students to engage productively in independent practice. This reiterates the importance of adequately preparing students before they begin their independent practice.

Some investigators[14] have developed procedures, such as cooperative learning during which students help each other as they study. Research has shown that all students tend to achieve more in these settings than do students in regular settings. Presumably, some of the advantage comes from having to explain the material to someone else and/or having someone else (other than the teacher) explain the material to the student. Cooperative learning offers an opportunity for students to get feedback from their peers about correct as well as incorrect responses, which promotes both engagement and learning. These cooperative/competitive settings are also valuable for helping slower students in a class by providing extra instruction for them.

10. Engage students in weekly and monthly review: Students need to be involved in extensive practice in order to develop well-connected and automatic knowledge.

Research findings

Students need extensive and broad reading, and extensive practice in order to develop well-connected networks of ideas (schemas) in their long-term memory. When one's knowledge on a particular topic is large and well connected, it is easier to learn new information and prior knowledge is more readily available for use. The more one rehearses and reviews information, the stronger these interconnections become. It is also easier to solve new problems when one has a rich, well-connected body of knowledge and strong ties among the connections. One of the goals of education is to help students develop extensive and available background knowledge.

Knowledge (even very extensive knowledge) stored in long-term memory that is organized into patterns only occupies a tiny amount of space in our limited working memory. So having larger and better-connected patterns of knowledge frees up space in our working memory. This available space can be used for reflecting on new information and for problem solving. The development of well-connected patterns (also called "unitization" and "chunking") and the freeing of space in the working memory is one of the hallmarks of an expert in a field.

Thus, research on cognitive processing supports the need for a teacher to assist students by providing for extensive reading of a variety of materials, frequent review, and discussion and application activities. The research on cognitive processing suggests that these classroom activities help students increase the

number of pieces of information in their long-term memory and organize this information into patterns and chunks.

The more one rehearses and reviews information, the stronger the interconnections between the materials become. Review also helps students develop their new knowledge into patterns, and it helps them acquire the ability to recall past learning automatically.

The best way to become an expert is through practice—thousands of hours of practice. The more the practice, the better the performance.

The best way to become an expert is through practice—thousands of hours of practice. The more the practice, the better the performance.

In the classroom

Many successful programs, especially in the elementary grades, provided for extensive review. One way of achieving this goal is to review the previous week's work every Monday and the previous month's work every fourth Monday. Some effective teachers also gave tests after their reviews. Research has found

---

17 Principles of Effective Instruction

The following list of 17 principles emerges from the research discussed in the main article. It overlaps with, and offers slightly more detail than, the 10 principles used to organize that article.

- Begin a lesson with a short review of previous learning.
- Present new material in small steps with student practice after each step.
- Limit the amount of material students receive at one time.
- Give clear and detailed instructions and explanations.
- Ask a large number of questions and check for understanding.
- Provide a high level of active practice for all students.
- Guide students as they begin to practice.
- Think aloud and model steps.
- Provide models of worked-out problems.
- Ask students to explain what they have learned.
- Check the responses of all students.
- Provide systematic feedback and corrections.
- Use more time to provide explanations.
- Provide many examples.
- Reteach material when necessary.
- Prepare students for independent practice.
- Monitor students when they begin independent practice.

—B.R.

that even at the secondary level, classes that had weekly quizzes scored better on final exams than did classes with only one or two quizzes during the term. These reviews and tests provided the additional practice students needed to become skilled, successful performers who could apply their knowledge and skills in new areas.

Teachers face a difficult problem when they need to cover a lot of material and don't feel they have the time for sufficient review. But the research states (and we all know from personal experience) that material that is not adequately practiced and reviewed is easily forgotten.

The 10 principles in this article come from three different sources: research on how the mind acquires and uses information, the instructional procedures that are used by the most successful teachers, and the procedures invented by researchers to help students learn difficult tasks. The research from each of these three sources has implications for classroom instruction, and these implications are described in each of these 10 principles.

Even though these principles come from three different sources, the instructional procedures that are taken from one source do not conflict with the instructional procedures that are taken from another source. Instead, the ideas from each of the sources overlap and add to each other. This overlap gives us faith that we are developing a valid and research-based understanding of the art of teaching.

Critical Thinking

1. Rosenshine presents the research behind each of the principles of instruction. Review those parts of the article and then select up to three of the research findings that surprised, intrigued, or concerned you. Be prepared to share your thoughts in class discussion.
2. Find a lesson plan, either one you or a peer designed or one from an online source. If possible, use a lesson you have taught. Review the plan looking for each of the principles listed in the article. Make a list of missing principles.
3. Revise the lesson plan from #2 above by adding the missing elements. If possible, teach the lesson again to a different group of students. Did you see a difference in the results?

Create Central

www.mhhe.com/createcentral

Internet References

Edutopia
www.edutopia.org
Donors Choose
www.donorschoose.org

Endnotes

1. *Suggested readings:* George A. Miller, "The Magical Number Seven, Plus or Minus Two: Some Limits on Our Capacity for Processing Information," *Psychological Review* 63, no. 2 (1956): 81–97; and David LaBerge and S. Jay Samuels, "Toward a Theory of Automatic Information Processing in Reading," *Cognitive Psychology* 6, no. 2 (1974): 293–323.

2. *Suggested readings:* Carolyn M. Evertson, Charles W. Anderson, Linda M. Anderson, and Jere E. Brophy, "Relationships between Classroom Behaviors and Student Outcomes in Junior High Mathematics and English Classes," *American Educational Research Journal* 17, no. 1 (1980): 43–60; and Thomas L. Good and Jere E. Brophy. *Educational Psychology: A Realistic Approach,* 4th ed. (New York: Longman, 1990).

3. *Suggested readings.* Thomas L. Good and Douglas A. Grouws. "The Missouri Mathematics Effectiveness Project," *Journal of Educational Psychology* 71, no. 3 (1979): 355–362; and Alison King, "Guiding Knowledge Construction in the Classroom: Effects of Teaching Children How to Question and How to Explain," *American Educational Research Journal* 31, no. 2 (1994): 338–368.

4. *Suggested readings:* John Sweller, "Cognitive Load Theory, Learning Difficulty, and Instructional Design," *Learning and Instruction* 4, no. 4(1994): 295–312; Barak Rosenshine, Carla Meister, and Saul Chapman, "Teaching Students to Generate Questions: A Review of the Intervention Studies," *Review of Educational Research* 66, no. 2 (1996): 181–221; and Alan H. Schoenfeld, *Mathematical Problem Solving* (New York: Academic Press, 1985).

5. *Suggested readings:* Evertson et al., "Relationships between Classroom Behaviors and Student Outcomes"; and Paul A. Kirschner, John Sweller, and Richard L. Clark, "Why Minimal Guidance during Instruction Does Not Work: An Analysis of the Failure of Constructivist, Discovery, Problem-Based, Experiential, and Inquiry-Based Teaching," *Educational Psychologist* 41, no. 2 (2006): 75–86.

6. *Suggested readings:* Douglas Fisher and Nancy Frey, *Checking for Understanding: Formative Assessment Techniques for Your Classroom* (Alexandria, VA: Association for Supervision and Curriculum Development, 2007); and Michael J. Dunkin, "Student Characteristics, Classroom Processes, and Student Achievement," *Journal of Educational Psychology* 70, no. 6 (1978): 998–1009.

7. *Suggested readings:* Lorin W. Anderson and Robert B. Burns, "Values, Evidence, and Mastery Learning," *Review of Educational Research* 57, no. 2 (1987): 215–223; and Norman Frederiksen, "Implications of Cognitive Theory for Instruction in Problem Solving," *Review of Educational Research* 54, no. 3 (1984): 363–407.

8. *Suggested readings:* Michael Pressley and Vera Woloshyn, *Cognitive Strategy Instruction that Really Improves Children's Academic Performance,* 2nd ed. (Cambridge, MA: Brookline Books, 1995); and Barak Rosenshine and Carla Meister, "The Use of Scaffolds for Teaching Higher-Level Cognitive Strategies," *Educational Leadership* 49, no. 7 (April 1992): 26–33.

9. *Suggested readings:* Barak Rosenshine, "The Empirical Support for Direct Instruction," in *Constructivist Instruction: Success or Failure?* ed. Sigmund Tobias and Thomas M. Duffy (New York: Routledge, 2009), 201–220; and Robert E. Slavin, *Education for All* (Exton, PA: Swets and Zeitlinger, 1996).

10. *Suggested readings:* Good and Grouws, "The Missouri Mathematics Effectiveness Project"; and James A. Kulik

and Chen-Lin C. Kulik, "College Teaching," in *Research on Teaching: Concepts, Findings, and Implications*, ed. Penelope L. Peterson and Herbert J. Walberg (Berkeley, CA: McCutchan, 1979).

11. Good and Grouws, "The Missouri Mathematics Effectiveness Project."

12. These stems were developed by King, "Guiding Knowledge Construction in the Classroom."

13. Sandra J. Berkowitz, "Effects of Instruction in Text Organization on Sixth-Grade Students' Memory for Expository Reading," *Reading Research Quarterly* 21, no. 2 (1986): 161–178. For additional strategies to help students organize material, see Wisconsin Department of Public Instruction. *Strategic Learning in the Content Areas* (Madison, WI: Wisconsin Department of Public Instruction, 2005).

14. Slavin, *Education for All.*

BARAK ROSENSHINE is an emeritus professor of educational psychology in the College of Education at the University of Illinois at Urbana-Champaign. A distinguished researcher, he has spent much of the past four decades identifying the hallmarks of effective teaching. He began his career as a high school history teacher in the Chicago public schools. This article is adapted with permission from *Principles of Instruction* by Barak Rosenshine. Published by the International Academy of Education in 2010, the original report is available at www.ibe.unesco.org/fileadmin/user_upload/Publications/Educational_Practices/EdPractices_21.pdf.

Rosenshine, Barak. From *American Educator*, Spring 2012, pp. 12–19, 39. Copyright © 2012 by ASCD. Reprinted with permission from the Spring 2012 issue of *American Educator*, the quarterly journal of the American Federation of Teachers, AFL-CIO, and by permission of the author.

Unit 3

UNIT

Prepared by: Rebecca B. Evers, *Winthrop University*

Literacy Is the Cornerstone of Learning

In this unit of the Annual Edition, we focus on core literacy skills that are taught in all public schools: reading, writing, and math. We have selected this topic because these skills are fundamental skills acquired from printed materials that are a primary source of knowledge. Additionally, being able to read, write, and calculate are fundamental rights of all citizens in a democratic society. Many of us who read for both learning and pleasure cannot imagine a life without books or reading. Writing remains a primary source of communication, especially within the hallowed halls of public schools. Just as reading and writing are essential skills for learning and living a successful life, so are math skills. Imagine not being able to balance your checking account, keep a budget, or understand and check the deductions on your paycheck. Good math skills are even more important when you try to read the fine print on car and home mortgage loans or credit card bills. These issues are a reality for persons who lack basic math skills. In school, students may have the intellectual ability to attend college, but cannot pass those higher level math classes required in college prep programs. Often this lack of mathematical achievement may be linked to similar difficulties with language in reading and writing. Mathematics is a language; therefore, we have several articles about math in this unit on literacy.

Reading is the single skill every child must have to be successful in school, at work, and in life activities. However, limited access to books, poverty, and learning disabilities are just some of the factors that can have profound effects on learning to read. These factors alone can derail all that is done in classrooms. In the first article of the unit, Lester notes that rural education is simply not on the radar, that 19.65 percent of rural families live below the poverty level, that nation-wide 80 percent of rural counties have been rated as "low education," meaning that 25 percent or more adults in these counties do not have a high school diploma and finally, there is a strong compounding effect of these three issues. That paints a grim picture of rural education and the prospects of the children and youth who grow up in rural areas of the United States. But Lester is not without a vision of the possibilities: she has two primary suggestions. The first is Place-Based Education. By combining the academic curriculum with students' knowledge of their community, teachers can help students learn the basics as well as understand the rich cultural and historic life around them. Examples of PBE are available in the article. The second suggestion is that teachers use technology to provide students with information about the larger community outside their own. A list of resources for virtual field trips is provided.

One suggestion frequently given to teachers who are teaching struggling readers, is to use lower level books with levels of high interest for the student. However, caution is important here. Low level books can mean low vocabulary or abridged versions of required readings. These may not be in the best interest of the reader and may provide an unsatisfactory reading experience as important details may be excluded when books are abridged. So what is a teacher to do? Leko, Mundy, Kang, and Datar offer research on selecting appropriate texts and suggestions and resources for selecting independent reading materials for adolescents with Learning Disabilities.

Valerie and Foss-Swanson have taken "the backpack note home" to a higher level by making it more about family literacy than a teacher providing information. Getting the students involved in talking about the school day or what they learned in science class helps the student's writing skills as well as supporting family involvement. Imagine how that might help families who are new to this culture and/or living in homeless shelters to reinforce learning wherever home might be or to help the transition to a new way of schooling.

Burns explains that her passion for the Common Core State Standards for Mathematical Practice is because new standards will encourage teachers to teach their students not only numerical reasoning but also mental math skills. One night at dinner she asked a simple question of her son, J. D. His answer led her to consider that we should listen to how our students are thinking about problems rather than listening for the answer we expect or prefer. She has developed an inventory that teachers can use in one-on-one interviews with their students.

Graduation requirements for higher math can be a difficult hurdle for students who have learning disabilities as well as for some students without disabilities, such as those who are ELL or are not motivated to think about college requirements.

As noted in the first unit of this edition, the U.S. appears to be falling behind in math proficiency which may be a good reason to consider national core curriculum standards for all states and their public schools. To that end, a group of concerned educators and interested citizens have developed just such a document. According to the National Council of Teachers of Mathematics, *The Common Core State Standards* were developed to provide a consistent and clear understanding of what students are expected to learn. The primary aim is to provide greater focus and coherence across grade levels and to set a standard of mathematical practice. However, there is some concern that these standards take away the rights of states to determine what students in their states need to know or learn. Clearly, Main has some concerns about how these new standards will impact very young learners. Once you have read the article, you might want to return to the internet resources to learn more for yourself.

Article   Prepared by: Rebecca B. Evers, *Winthrop University.*

Putting Rural Readers on the Map

Strategies for Rural Literacy

This article presents two research-based strategies that have potential to enhance literacy instruction for all teachers, particularly those teaching in rural communities.

LAURA LESTER

Learning Outcomes

After reading this article, you will be able to:

- Explain how to support literacy for students in poverty in rural areas of the United States.

Having grown up in a small Virginia town of only 2,369 residents, I am a product of a rural community. As a child, I attended local schools, graduated from the only county high school, and attended a nearby university, where I studied education and obtained my teaching degree. I was drawn to teaching because of the close-knit community of family, friends, and teachers I had growing up. Although I had developed an appreciation for the small schools in the county and the feelings of safety, comfort, and familiarity they offered, like many natives of rural communities, I did not return to my hometown after graduating from college. Instead, I settled in a large suburban area and began teaching first grade.

After several years, personal commitments drew me home, where I took a job in a rural elementary school teaching kindergarten. I remember reflecting back on the many fond memories of my upbringing and becoming eager to return to the warmth I felt from my community; the strong support, links, and ties I had with local residents; and the comfort of knowing most everyone. As I prepared to return, I wondered how different my teaching career in the rural community would be from the suburban one I had become familiar with and comfortable in.

My romantic memories of growing up in a rural community actually match the perspectives of many. However, as I pondered the ways in which my teaching career was about to change, I realized that my expectations for teaching rural children had to quickly be readjusted. Having grown up in a rural middle-class family, I had a very positive experience in school

and was unaware of the stress, poverty, and isolation that many rural children face. It was eye opening to realize that many of the experiences of my suburban students were a far cry from the experiences of children growing up in rural poverty.

My fond memories of my school experiences were suddenly shattered as I witnessed the reality of the unkind features of rural life that many students bring to school with them each day. In my new role as a rural teacher, I rediscovered an appreciation for the uniqueness of rural communities and developed an understanding of the many ways in which rural students are advantaged. However, I also became acutely aware of community characteristics that have potential to place rural children at risk for academic difficulties and disadvantage.

First, rural issues are simply not on the radar screen, and the phenomena surrounding rurality are often not considered or are simply overlooked in educational policy and research (Howley, 1997). Over the past century and a half, improvements made in rural schools have been centered on "reshaping and redirecting them into a national system" (p. 2), rather than preserving and fostering their uniqueness. However, recent legislature has centered on helping rural schools meet achievement criteria of federal acts, such as No Child Left Behind (Arnold, Biscoe, Farmer, Robertson, & Shapley 2007). Until this recognition is shared by federal, state, and local governments, educational policy will likely continue to represent urban mindsets, providing a potential disservice to many rural students.

Second, statistics from 2006 show the prevalence of poverty in rural areas, as 19.65% of rural families and 11.45% of nonrural families are considered to be below the poverty line (Durham & Smith, 2006). Educational and familial resources, experiences, and opportunities may be significantly affected by poverty, especially in rural communities plagued with minimal educational revenue from low property taxes, stagnating economies, high unemployment rates, high numbers of low-wage labor and service sector jobs, and few public libraries, local colleges, and high-quality affordable preschools (Roscigno, 1995; Roscigno & Crowley, 2001).

Third, in 2009, more than 10.5 million children were reported attending rural schools, and 80% (499 of 622) of rural counties were deemed "low education" (U.S. Department of Agriculture [USDA], 2010). Statistics reveal that "low-education" counties have one in four adults, ranging in age from 25 to 64 years, without a high school degree and may be affected by resource inequalities and discrepancies (USDA, 2010). Hence educational resources provided at home may be hindered by the limited resources students receive at school, whereas the resources provided at school may be ineffective for students experiencing resource disparities at home (Roscigno & Crowley, 2001). High rates of poverty and minimal educational resources in rural communities can create and contribute to a perpetuation of high concentrations of poor students, making it difficult to bridge the gap between rural and urban/ suburban student achievement (Aikens & Barbarin, 2008; Roscigno & Crowly 2001).

Fourth and finally, the compounding of these issues can have vast effects on community residents, including rural "brain drain." This term reflects the relocation of educated individuals to suburban/urban areas, based on the pursuit of better economic, educational, and employment opportunities (McGranahan, 1991; McGranahan & Ghelfi, 1991; Roscigno & Crowley, 2001; Swaim & Teixeira, 1991). Although many educated rural residents do stay, brain drain reflects a lack of energy, progressivism and hopelessness for growth and development, while the most vulnerable residents are left behind. A recent article in the *Chronicle of Higher Education* (Carr & Kefalas, 2009) reported that non-college-bound students left behind in rural areas need heightened exposure to and awareness of their community's culture, environment, opportunities, and resources to develop interests in their community and contribute to its sustainability.

These four compelling reasons for why particular attention should be given to rural issues, serve as the driving force behind this article. Although it serves as a small first step toward creating awareness, I ask the question, "What strategies can teachers incorporate into their instruction to bolster literacy development, achievement, and success of students in rural schools?"

Strategies and Frameworks for Bolstering Literacy Instruction in Rural Communities

The remainder of this article is centered on the following research-based educational framework and strategy:

- Place-based education, which connects rural students' unique knowledge of their community to school curriculum.
- Virtual field trips, which provide students with exposure to places around the world and foster vocabulary growth and content knowledge acquisition.

Although these strategies are examples of general best practices and could benefit students in many geographical locations, they have potential to positively influence and supplement the literacy instruction taking place in rural schools based on unique rural needs. In each of the following two sections, the framework and strategy will be defined, rationalized, illustrated, and discussed using examples.

Bringing Together Home, School, and Community with Place-Based Education

Place-based education (PBE) is a framework for instruction that integrates traditional curriculum-based subject matter with students' knowledge of "place" (Shamah & McTavish, 2009). PBE is not a curriculum in and of itself, but provides a rich avenue for learning centered on helping students make connections between curriculum and their community's culture, environment, and history. Much recent state educational reform promotes and reflects a national agenda of learning standards, without highlighting the features of rural communities, which can often connect with learning standards (Kannapel & DeYoung, 1999; Seal & Harmon, 1995; Smith, 2003; Wallace & Boylan, 2009).

Having been a teacher in a rural school, I witnessed first-hand that features and characteristics of rural students' own surroundings are rarely featured in their school learning, creating disconnect. PBE provides a learning benefit because standards are taught through an environment, community, or culture that students know (The Rural School and Community Trust, 2000). The added benefit is that students have many opportunities to understand the value of their community and want to continue to be a part of it. The following quotation exemplifies the way in which one student lacked opportunities to develop an understanding of the value and importance of his rural hometown, resulting in relocation:

> Nothing in my education prepared me to believe, or encouraged me to expect, that there was any reason to be interested in my own place. If I had hoped to amount to anything, I understood, I had better take the first road east out of town as fast as I could. And, like so many of my classmates, I did. (Gruchow, 1995, as cited in Haas & Nachtigal, 1998, pp. 1–2)

The message embedded within this quote portrays the importance of helping students gain an understanding of and develop an appreciation for their own community.

How can teachers begin planning and teaching PBE lessons? Figure 1 provides a list of third-grade state standards; relevant characteristics of a rural, West Virginia community; and place-based activities that integrate literacy, social studies, and science standards.

The steps in planning and implementing the lessons in Figure 1 are to consider community characteristics and features, determine lesson objectives and corresponding standards, and plan activities that provide opportunities to investigate within the community, incorporate culturally relevant literature, and help students make connections. In the provided examples, the school is situated in a coal-mining community in the Appalachian

Third grade West Virginia social studies and literacy standards	Characteristics of community relevant to standard	Possible place-based education activities	Literacy links and benefits
Social Studies Standards: SS.0.3.3.7-Illustrate the path of a product from the raw material to the final product (e.g., cotton to sweater, coal to electricity). SS.0.3.5.3-Compare and contrast present cultures to the cultures of people of other historical times (e.g., sources of food, clothing, shelter, products used).	Appalachian Mountain Region: • Coal-mining and logging communities (e.g., Cass, West Virginia) • Historical small towns	• Read fiction and nonfiction stories about coal communities, • Research coal-mining communities and families in the early 20th century (possible website: www.msha.gov/CENTURY/LITTLE/PAGELasp) • Interview a community member about life during the coal-mining era. • Write a biography or report. • Present to the class or for parents.	Students have opportunities to • Comprehend information and text through exposure to a wide variety of culturally relevant books, such as *Coal Mining Peaches, In Coal Country,* and *When I Was Young in the Mountains* • Acquire novel vocabulary words through discussions and place-based activities• Conduct research, analyze data, and reflect on their learning through writing, such as biographies and reports.
S.S.O.3.5.10-Organize information from various reference sources to prepare short reports and presentations. RLA.S.3.1-Students will apply reading skills and strategies to inform, to perform a task and to read for literacy experience by selecting a wide variety of literature and diverse media to develop independence as readers. RLA.S.3.2-Students will apply writing skills and strategies to communicate effectively for different purposes by using the writing process, applying grammatical and mechanical properties in writing and selecting and evaluating information for research purposes.		Optional activities: • Present to the class or for parents. • Research maps of coal mines across the country and compare with local mines. • Write a report of how coal is used to produce electricity. • Create an ad about coal-mining safety. • Visit a coal mine and create a model of a mine • These examples illustrate how PBE can be embedded within curriculum standards. The list is by no means exhaustive.	• Make connections between concepts, experiences, personal life, and books

Third grade West Virginia social studies and literacy standards	Characteristics of community relevant to standard	Possible place-based education activities	Literacy links and benefits
Science Standards: SC.S.3.1-Students will demonstrate the ability to think and act as scientists by engaging in active inquiries and investigations, while incorporating hands-on activities. RLA.S.3.1-Students will apply reading skills and strategies to inform, to perform a task and to read for literacy experience by selecting a wide variety of literature and diverse media to develop independence as readers. RLA.S.3.2-Students will apply writing skills and strategies to communicate effectively for different purposes by using the writing process, applying grammatical and mechanical properties in writing and selecting and evaluating information for research purposes.	• Mountains • Forests and wooded areas • Rivers, streams, and lakes • Home to a variety of animals and wildlife	• Research the habitat zone of the Appalachian Mountain region. • Use nonfiction and information books with students, to learn about animals in their region. • Create a class book in which each student selects an animal to research. Each page should highlight a different animal. • Take students on a nature walk to investigate the wildlife present in the community after studying and researching animals in the Appalachian Mountains. • Keep a log of which animals are seen. Students will develop first-hand knowledge through inquiry and exploration of animals in their community. • Have students compare animals in other areas to those present in their own community.	Students have opportunities to • Comprehend information and text through exposure to a wide variety of culturally relevant books, such as *Wildlife, Wildflowers, and Wild Activities: Exploring Southern Appalachia* and *Voice of the Birds* • Acquire novel vocabulary words through discussions and place-based activities • Conduct research, analyze data, and reflect on their learning through writing, such as biographies and reports. • Make connections between concepts, experiences, personal lives, and books

Figure 1   A Place-Based Education Example

Note. This figure illustrates two third-grade place-based education lessons, one for each of social studies and science.

Mountains. The objective of the social studies lesson is to learn about the influence of the coal-mining industry on the local community over time, and in the science lesson, the objective is for students to become researchers and investigators in their own community to learn about animal habitats and characteristics. The following vignette exemplifies the way in which a portion of the science lesson was executed. (All student, teacher, and school names used within this article are pseudonyms.)

> For days students had used a variety of texts to each research a particular animal and created a class book on animals in the Appalachian Mountain Region. They were finally ready to explore and investigate the local environment. As Ms. Adams led the students onto the trail behind the school, students were prepared with their science journals, a log to record the animals they saw, and a list of the animals in their class book. Upon entering the wooded trail, James called out, "Hey, I think I see a wren! I read that they live in the temperate forest of the Appalachian region! Look, it has a small round body with a tail that turns up at the base of its back. It is light brown and spotted." Ms. Adams helped the other students spot the wren as they recorded the information in their science notebook and log.

> "I've never seen a wren before. Oh, I see a white-tailed deer over there." Chelsea called out as the students turned their heads to see. Although many students had never seen a wren, most had seen a deer. Quickly the discussion turned to deer hunting, to which many children were able to make connections. As the walk continued, students had opportunities to see and discuss a variety of animals, as well as tell stories about prior experiences seeing the animals. The exploration provided an authentic learning experience within the local community, which the students would never forget.

This vignette illustrates an example of a teacher who provided a learning experience that helped students realize the value of their surroundings, enhanced their knowledge of the community, and contributed to the development of reading, writing, and oral language skills.

In both examples, the overarching purpose is for students to engage in literacy-related activities that meet state standards and highlight community features and resources. Through PBE, students can make connections in their learning as they naturally investigate and expand their comprehension of information and text. Lessons should include culturally relevant books related to content and follow-up activities that require students to reflect orally or through writing on their experiences and knowledge. Students should also have time to discuss, explore, and apply novel words in a variety of contexts during PBE lessons.

As teachers strive to help their students become lifelong learners, it is essential to provide motivating and interesting learning opportunities while reading and writing about what is familiar to them. Children's roots are closely linked to their developing identities and become stronger with age; therefore, as they begin to conceptualize themselves in the world, their rural roots and identities will be reflected and they will see that their home and community are valued in school.

Providing Virtual Field Trips for Rural Students

Whether a school is located in the heart of New York City or the mountains of West Virginia, virtual field trips can provide exposure to a realm of places and resources for students in an unlimited number of geographical locales. Although rural students are often advantaged by their knowledge of the community and environment, they may be disadvantaged by limited accessibility to cultural resources and institutions. For example, many students have never visited an ocean, art museum, or zoo or traveled on an airplane, subway, or metro. The goal of virtual field trips is to connect curriculum to the real world and provide students with access to experiences and places they may not otherwise have, potentially expanding their understandings of the world (Gerzog & Haugland, 1999; Tuthill & Klemm, 2002).

There are three particular benefits of incorporating virtual field trips into rural classrooms. First, virtual field trips can provide students with opportunities to make cross-curricular connections, contribute to comprehension of reading material and standardized test content, and develop broad and sophisticated vocabularies (Christ & Wang, 2010). Second, according to the National Telecommunications and Information Administration (Fact Sheet: Rural Areas Magnify "Digital Divide," 1999), rural children at all socioeconomic levels have fewer computers at home and are less likely to have Internet connections than suburban and urban children, creating a need for greater technology exposure at school. This exposure is critical in helping students become independent learners in the current technological age (Malloy & Gambrell, 2006). Third, students in many rural communities, especially those plagued with transportation barriers, may spend hours in transit to and from school (Williams, 2010) and the additional time and funding needed for field trip travel is often too great a cost.

What must teachers understand about virtual field trips? Field trips should help students: connect curriculum to real-world information, events, and places; spark inquiry and questioning and activate the senses through exploration and discovery; contribute to the development of new ideas; and acquire sophisticated oral and written vocabularies (Blachowicz & Obrachta, 2005; Tuthill & Klemm, 2002). First, teachers must select lesson objectives, identify related standards, and consider whether the lesson warrants a field trip. Once it has been determined that learning would be enhanced by a field trip, the next step is to determine whether an actual trip is obtainable. If not, a virtual field trip may be an appropriate alternative.

Currently, the Federal Communications Commission is working on creating an Online Learning Registry of high-quality websites (White, 2010), which teachers could use to plan virtual field trips. Although under construction, teachers can find websites by searching Google Earth, Smithsonian National Museum of Natural History, Seven Wonders Panoramas, Colonial Williamsburg, United States Capitol Tour, and Virtual Journey into the Universe, for instance. The website www.field-trips.org also lists various curriculum-based topics, objectives, targeted vocabulary words, associated national standards, and website lists (Smedley & Higgins, 2005). The last step is to consider the logistics of how the field trip will be executed. Figure 2 provides an example of a virtual field trip to the National Zoo.

The teachers in the above example simulate an actual field trip in several ways. First, the book *My Great-Aunt Arizona* (Houston, 1997) is read to set the stage for the virtual experience. The book tells the tale of a woman living in the Appalachian Mountains who desires to travel outside her region. Her circumstances and location make travel impossible, so she becomes a teacher and imagines taking trips with her students. Second, to build student interest, the teachers collect permission forms, request bagged lunches, take a bus ride, and discuss expectations and rules. Third, the website nationalzoo.si.edu/ is displayed in each classroom with a different video clip highlighted from the National Zoo website. Throughout the day students rotate through three classrooms, exploring different components of the website, related to each of the three

parts of the learning standard: animal needs, physical characteristics, and wild/ tame characteristics. After the whole-class virtual field trip, students rotate through learning centers to explore additional zoo websites in small groups, an added benefit of virtual field trips.

Linking virtual field trips to literacy is important in helping students make connections between books, experiences, and information. Comparing and contrasting concepts and expressing views and opinions through oral discussions and writing activities can enhance learning and comprehension of content material. Teachers can debrief with students after the field trip by asking questions, encouraging students to ask questions and discuss answers, reviewing vocabulary words, completing written reflections, and reading books relating to the experiences from the field trip.

Features of virtual field trips to keep in mind are as follows:

First grade Virginia science standard	Life Processes: 1.5 The student will investigate and understand that animals, including people, have life needs and specific physical characteristics and can be classified according to certain characteristics. Key concepts include(a) life needs (air, food, water, and a suitable place to live), (b) physical characteristics (body coverings, body shape, appendages, and methods of movement), and (c) other characteristics (wild/tame, water homes/land homes)
Actual trip	Visit to the National Zoo in Washington, DC
Reason trip is unattainable	*Costs:* gas for school buses, compensation for school bus drivers *Distance:* Approximately 415 miles from Southwest Virainia *Travel Time:* 5–6 hours
Virtual field trip to the National Zoo	• Collect bagged lunches and permission slips. • Read *My Great-Aunt Arizona* to prepare for the virtual learning experience. • Board buses for pretend travel and review rules and expectations. • Exit buses and lead students to their individual classrooms. • Use the SMART board to display a different page of the website nationalzoo.si.edu in each classroom. Each classroom's activity should reflect one of the three components of the learning standard: • *Classroom 1*-Needs of animals around the world: Students visit animal habitats, such as the Amazonian or Asian Trail. Discuss and compare the needs of animals in regions around the world, address vocabulary, and make connections between animals around the word and in the local community. • *Classroom 2*-Physical Characteristics: Students compare the characteristics of animals from the "Kid Farm" webpage to animals from the Small Mammal House or the Reptile Discovery Center, for instance. Animal characteristics can be compared and contrasted as new vocabulary is discussed. • *Classroom 3*-Wild or Tame: Students explore, for instance. Beaver Valley. Elephant Trails, Bird House, Great Cats and Great Ape House. Read, discuss, and write about differences and similarities in wild versus tame animals and discuss examples within the local community.
Literacy links and benefits	Students have opportunities to • Learn content information while building reading and writing skills • Make connections between their own knowledge of rural animals and animals around the world • Comprehend related text and information • Activate background knowledge by listening to culturally relevant literature • Acquire novel vocabulary words through discussion, exploration, reading, and writing activities • Reflect on learning by writing and expressing views and opinions • Compare the similarities and differences between concepts

Figure 2   An Example of a Virtual Field Trip

Note. This figure illustrates how a virtual field trip is used to teach content in primary grades.

- Virtual field trips are not appropriate for all lessons and should enhance and supplement instruction, not replace it.
- Virtual field trips should reflect the curriculum and link to literacy.
- Some field trips may be best suited for a whole class, whereas others may be best suited for small groups.
- Students should be awarded time for individual/small group exploration.
- Post-field trip debriefing should provide students with opportunities to ask questions about concepts or vocabulary words and reflect on learning.

Table   Websites for Virtual Field Trips

Category	Websites
Art, literature, and music	• National Gallery of Art www.nga.gov/collection/ • Metropolitan Museum of Art www.metmuseum.org/Works_Of_Art/index.asp • Book Wink: Author/Book Talks www.bookwink.com/
Animals around the world	• Butterfly Conservatory www.amnh.org/exhibitions/butterflies/tour.html • National Zoo for kids nationalzoo.si.edu/Audiences/kids/ • Smithsonian Ocean Planet seawifs.gsfc.nasa.gov/ocean_planet.html • Sea World www.seaworld.org/animal-info/index.htm • National Geographic kids.nationalgeographic.com/kids/animals/
History and culture	• Natural History and Geology Museum unmuseum.mus.pa.us/unmuseum.htm • Colonial Williamsburg www.history.org/history/museums/online_exhibits.cfm • National Museum of Natural History www.mnh.si.edu/panoramas/ • The White House, Washington DC www.whitehouse.gov/about/tours-and-events/ • Oriental Institute Museum oi.uchicago.edu/museum/virtual/ • New York City tour www.tramline.com/tours/misc/nyc/_tourlaunch1.htm

To help teachers get started, the Table contains a list of websites that are particularly useful for rural students. The list is divided into three subsections: art, literature, and music; animals around the world; and history and culture, all of which include information rural students may not have exposure to. For example, The Book Wink website under "art, literature, and music," hosts interactive, kid-friendly book talks by librarians. Students are exposed to cultural music, various book genres, and topics representative of places and people around the world. This resource may be important for students residing in areas without public libraries or bookstores.

Finally, the need for providing exposure to cultural institutions and museums around the world for rural students is becoming a well-known, national incentive. A recent National Rural Education Technology Summit provided educators and technology experts an opportunity to discuss ways in which rural education could be enhanced, with virtual learning in the spotlight (Leithner, 2010).

Final Thoughts

As the goal of this article is to provide teachers in rural communities with simple and easy-to-implement strategies that can bolster content and literacy instruction in rural schools, I hope that it will also serve as a gateway into further exploration of rural literacy education. Recognizing the uniqueness of rural communities is the first step in moving forward in providing effective and culturally relevant instruction for students.

Critical Thinking

1. Why are rural schools different from urban or suburban schools?
2. How are the students in your classroom or local school district similar to or different from students in rural schools?
3. How might the strategies in this article support learning of students who are not in rural schools?

Create Central

www.mhhe.com/createcentral

Internet References

The Rural School and Community Trust
   www.ruraledu.org/

LAURA LESTER is a graduate teaching assistant at Virginia Tech, Blacksburg, USA: e-mail lalester@vt.edu

Article　　　　　　　　　　Prepared by: Rebecca B. Evers, *Winthrop University.*

If the Book Fits: Selecting Appropriate Texts for Adolescents with Learning Disabilities

Melinda M. Leko, et al.

Learning Outcomes

After reading this article, you will be able to:

- Develop a reading list for a tenth grade adolescent who is enrolled in your content area class.

Ensuring that adolescents are engaged in reading is important as time spent reading often separates good readers from struggling readers (Allington, 2001). Students who practice reading improve more quickly and are subsequently more motivated to continue reading, thus creating a cycle of increasing achievement. The opposite is true for students who struggle with reading and therefore avoid it, a phenomenon experts call the *Matthew effect* (Stanovich, 1986). Unfortunately the majority of adolescents with learning disabilities (LD) fall in the latter group and experience difficulties when reading. In fact, 62% of eighth grade students with disabilities read below a proficient level according to data from the National Assessment of Educational Progress (U.S. Department of Education, 2011).

The high percentage of adolescents with LD who do not read at proficient levels is concerning because these students are at greater risk of academic, social, emotional, and economic difficulties (National Joint Committee on Learning Disabilities [NJCLD], 2008). These students are more likely to be retained, feel isolated from the larger school community, and ultimately drop out of school (Daniel et al., 2006; National Center for Education Statistics, 2003). Without adequate reading skills they will not be well positioned to secure jobs in a competitive market in which the fastest growing jobs require greater literacy skills (Barton, 2000). Finally, adolescents with poor reading skills are more likely to be adjudicated (Kutner et al., 2007).

To help adolescents with LD improve their reading skills, experts recommend several practices. First, struggling readers benefit from explicit, systematic instruction in core skill areas such as word study, vocabulary, and comprehension (Biancarosa & Snow, 2006; Kamil et al., 2008; NJCLD, 2008; Scammacca et al., 2007). Second, reading instruction should be couched in content area materials and texts (Biancarosa & Snow, 2006; Faggella-Luby, Ware, & Capozzoli, 2009). Third, adolescents with LD may need reading instruction that is extended in duration, provides multiple opportunities to practice, and increases in intensity (Biancarosa & Snow, 2006; Faggella-Luby et al., 2009; Kamil et al., 2008). Finally, experts believe it is important to build adolescents' engagement and motivation for reading (Biancarosa & Snow, 2006; Kamil et al., 2008).

An important first step in building students' motivation for reading is incorporating appropriate texts into reading instruction. Appropriate texts for adolescents with disabilities are (a) written on a level commensurate with students' reading abilities, (b) aligned with adolescents' interests, and (c) diverse (Alvermann, 2002; Lenters, 2006). In the following sections strategies are presented that will assist teachers in identifying students' reading and interest levels, level of texts, and ways to incorporate diverse texts. In addition, links to resources and strategies are provided.

Select Texts at Students' Reading Level

To promote adolescent engagement in reading, texts must be written to match students' reading abilities. In other words, students will be motivated to read and spend time engaged in reading instruction when they are presented with texts that they are able to read without excessive difficulty. Reading texts at an appropriate level will help them improve their decoding, fluency, and comprehension skills, all of which are interconnected. When students can decode texts without excessive difficulty, they will be able to read more fluently, which often improves their comprehension (Marshall & Campbell, 2006; Tyner, 2009). In fact, students do not make the same reading fluency gains when they are instructed using materials that are matched based on their grade level as opposed to reading level (O'Connor et al., 2002).

To describe the appropriateness of a text for an individual student, experts often use a categorical system, labeling text levels as *independent, instructional,* or *frustration* (Tyner, 2009). Books at a student's independent level are those that can be read with 98% to 100% accuracy. Independent level texts are appropriate when students want to read by themselves without assistance. Instructional-level texts are those that students can read with 93% to 97% accuracy. For example, given a 100-word passage, a text would be considered instructional level if a student could read the passage with seven or fewer errors. These texts are too difficult for students to read independently but can be read with teacher support such as in differentiated small group instruction (Clay, 1991). For students to improve in their reading abilities, it is important for them to have plenty of opportunities to read texts at their instructional level. These texts provide students with the opportunity to "build an effective cueing [system]: does it look right, does it sound right, does it make sense?" (Tyner, 2009, p. 58). Finally, texts at students' frustration level are those that students struggle to read and result in an accuracy rate less than 93%. Texts that are at students' frustration level should never be used for independent or small group reading; however, these texts can be used for teacher read-alouds, modeling, and shared readings. Using these texts in this manner allows students to be exposed to rich story content and vocabulary without being frustrated by attempting to read a text that is simply too difficult (Reutzel & Cooter, 2012).

There are multiple ways to determine if a text is written on a level that is appropriate for an individual student. First, teachers can administer a running record, which provides information on a student's performance when reading a selected text. Running records are convenient to use because they are quick to administer (i.e., approximately 10 minutes or less per student) and can be conducted using any text. Figure 1 provides instructions on how to administer a running record.

Another useful reading assessment is an informal reading inventory (IRI), which can help teachers identify a student's reading level and ability (Reutzel & Cooter, 2012). An IRI measures reading rate (number of words read correctly per minute)

and comprehension. Like running records, IRIs are quick to administer, but they should be administered multiple times during the year to monitor student progress.

Once a student's reading level has been determined, it is important to select texts that match this level. A readability estimate is a quick method to identify the reading level of a text. There are several methods that can be used to calculate a readability estimate. Common readability estimates used in education include the Flesch-Kincaid (Kincaid, Fishburne, Rogers, & Chissom, 1975), Fry (1975), and Raygor (1977) methods.

Select Texts That Interest Adolescents

In addition to proper reading level, texts must also be of interest to students (Guthrie & Alao, 1997). This is particularly significant during adolescence, a time when the emerging independence and affective needs of students must be taken into consideration (Deshler, Ellis, & Lenz, 1996; Guthrie & Davis, 2003). Many secondary students disengage from reading because they are forced to read texts that neither interest them nor relate to their personal lives (Guthrie & Davis, 2003). To engage students with texts, teachers must pay attention to the connection between students' interests and texts that match those interests (Bean, Readence, & Baldwin, 2008). The top-ranking genres adolescents like to read include horror/scary books, comic books, magazines, mysteries, science fiction, fantasy, and series books. Adolescents' favorite topics include sports, animals, drawing, and cars/trucks (Ivey & Broaddus, 2001; Worthy, Moorman, & Turner, 1999). To determine student interest, a reading interest inventory can be administered.

Providing students with some choice regarding the texts they read is another effective way to peak students' interest and increase their motivation for reading (Ivey & Broaddus, 2001). Keeping school and classroom libraries stocked with high-interest texts that students helped select will provide adolescents with more enticing reading choices that they will be motivated to read.

High-Interest/Low-Readability Texts

Finding texts that match reading abilities and interests of adolescents with LD is often a challenge for teachers. Many times the books these students want to read are too difficult and the books that meet their instructional needs do not include appropriate content for their age group. For too long teachers have been trying to engage adolescent readers with texts that are either too difficult or not age appropriate simply because there were few other options available (Rog & Burton, 2001). In recent years publishing companies have responded to this concern by producing a greater number of books that meet older students' reading needs while also appealing to their interests. Such books are often referred to as *high-interest/low-readability* (Biancarosa & Snow, 2006). These texts are meant

---

Administering a Running Record

Step 1: Count the first 100 words in a text

Step 2: Ask the student to read aloud the 100 words and as the student reads aloud tally the number of errors made

Step 3: Once the student has finished reading, subtract the total number of errors from 100 and then divide by 100.

Step 4: Determine into which category the percentage falls:

Independent = 98%–100%

Instructional = 93%–97%

Frustration = below 93%

For example, if a student misses seven words, the calculation would be:

100 − 7 = 93 and 93/100 = 93%,

which indicates the text is at the student's instructional level.

Figure 1.   Administering a running record.

Table 1   Publishing Companies That Sell High-Interest/Low-Readability Texts.

Company	Web Site that Links to High-Interest/Low-Readability Books	Range of Products
Capstone Press	www.CapstonePub.com/category/LIB_F_FICFORMAT_NOVEL	Interest levels: 4–9, reading levels: 1–3
Carson-Dellosa Publishing	www.carsondellosa.com/cd2/SearchCatalog.aspx?k=high+interest+low1readability&CM_VC=10001	Interest levels: 7–12, reading levels: K–8
EDCON Publishing Group	www.edconpublishing.com/index.php?route=product/category&path=14	Interest levels: 3–12, reading levels: 1–6
High Noon	www.highnoonbooks.com/inside-readers.tpl?cart=132129406119729	Interest levels: 3–12, reading levels: 1–6
HIP Books	www.hip-books.com	Interest levels: 3–12, reading levels: 2–4
National Reading Styles Institute	store.nrsi.com/catalogsearch/result/?q=high+interest+books+for+struggling+readers&x=0&y=0	Interest levels: pre-K–10, reading levels: pre-K–7
PCI Education	www.pcieducation.com/search/default.aspx?keywords=high+interest+low+readability	Interest levels: 4–12, reading levels: 1–6
Perfection Learning	www.perfectionlearning.com/browse.php?categoryID=3929&level=2&parent=2543	Interest levels: 2–12; reading levels: 1–6
Remedia	www.rempub.com/reading/high-interest-reading	Interest levels: 3–12, reading levels: 1–5
Saddleback Educational	www.sdlback.com/estore/b/reading/?v=hilo_reading	Interest levels: 4–9, reading levels: 1–6
Scholastic	store.scholastic.com/webapp/wcs/stores/servlet/SearchEndecaCmd?storeId=10052&catalogId=10051&searchTerm=high+interest+low+readability	Interest levels: 4–12, reading levels: 1–12
Steck Vaughn/Houghton Mifflin/Harcourt	steckvaughn.hmhco.com/en/adolesliteracy.htm	Interest levels: 4–12, reading levels: 2–11
Sundance	www.sundancepub.com/c/@fr6bQVs_ZMevk/Pages/product.html?record@S3443	Interest levels: 2–8, reading levels: 1–8

to appeal to older students while being written at easier levels that struggling readers can read without excessive difficulty.

High-interest/low-readability books are labeled and marketed according to reading level and age appropriateness. For example, a high-interest/low-readability book might be on a fifth-grade reading level but have content that appeals to an eighth or ninth grader. Some of these texts have reading levels as low as first grade, enabling older students who are reading several years below grade level to participate successfully in reading instruction. These books often resemble the *chapter books* or novels that their typical peers might read. Thus, adolescents with LD may be more willing to participate in reading instruction because they are not embarrassed by having to read books that look like they are intended for younger students. High-interest/low-readability books span a variety of genres, including fiction, nonfiction, poetry, and graphic novels. The use of high-interest/low-readability nonfiction texts (also referred to as expository texts) can also help adolescents with disabilities access content standards addressed in the general education curriculum that would otherwise be too difficult with traditional grade level texts. Moreover, adolescents with LD should have adequate access to and practice with nonfiction texts. This is important since this type of text can be a large component of secondary curricula and can be especially difficult for students with LD to comprehend (Gajria, Jitendra,

Stood, & Sacks, 2007). Table 1 provides information about companies that publish high-interest/low-readability texts. Several of these companies produce accompanying lesson plans, activities, and online resources for teachers and students.

Select Diverse Texts

Incorporating diverse texts into reading instruction is an important way to address the needs and interests of adolescents with LD. Diverse texts address real-life problems and represent a variety of cultural, linguistic, and demographic groups (Guthrie & Davis, 2003). Diverse texts provide students with opportunities to identify with characters who are similar to them, which is an important element when planning reading instruction that will engage older struggling readers who are anxious to "see themselves" in texts. Simply including any text about individuals from diverse backgrounds, however, is not an effective practice. The texts should be evaluated for quality and authenticity. High quality diverse texts should (a) be accurate in their representation of historical events and settings, (b) provide reflections of accurate cultural norms, values, and language use, (c) be devoid of racial and cultural stereotypes, (d) ensure accuracy in their depiction of difficult social issues as complicated and multifaceted rather than as simple generalizations, and (e) represent diversity within a specific cultural group. The use of trade books, digital and web-based texts, and books that incorporate pop culture can be effective in introducing more diverse texts into reading instruction (Guthrie & Davis, 2003).

Text diversity also refers to texts from a variety of genres and print and media sources such as digital texts, hypermedia texts, web-based texts, and periodicals (Pitcher, Martinez, Dicembre, Fewster, & McCormick, 2010). The incorporation of digital and web-based texts is a promising way to engage adolescents and provide them with access to appropriate texts. Emerging research indicates that adolescents are particularly motivated to engage in literacy-related activities that incorporate digital technologies (e.g., text messaging, chat rooms, social networks, the Internet Alvermann, 2002). Digital and web-based texts also can support universal design for learning, a flexible approach to instruction that allows for the individualization of instructional goals, curriculum, and assessment (Rose & Meyer, 2002). Traditional textbooks and print materials are more difficult for teachers to adapt and individualize, but digital texts and web-based curricula offer more possibilities for customization and individualization (Edyburn & Edyburn, 2012; Pisha & Stahl, 2005). For example digital and web-based texts can (a) incorporate audio supports and text-to-speech features that will read text aloud, (b) be tiered to accommodate a range of student reading levels, (c) provide advanced organizers and summaries, (d) provide highlighting and note taking features, and (e) embed vocabulary and dictionary supports that provide word meanings when students click on unknown words (Boone & Higgins, 2003; Edyburn & Edyburn, 2012; Malmgren & Trezek, 2009). In addition, digital texts can include video clips that build students' background knowledge on a topic and can provide links to additional resources that students might find interesting or helpful.

Publishing companies such as those found in Table 1 often include online and digital materials that accompany their print materials. Another source for digital texts (also known as ebooks) is the Internet. For example, Google Books (http://books.google.com), Project Gutenberg (www.gutenberg.org), Apple's iTunes store, and some public libraries provide access to thousands of digital texts, including classic literature, contemporary fiction, and nonfiction. The wide selection of digital texts and their built in capabilities for accommodation and individualization can offer adolescents with LD more enticing reading options than might typically be found in classroom or school libraries. Digital texts can also be a valuable tool in helping adolescents with LD access the general education curriculum. For example, if a ninth grade English class is reading *Romeo and Juliet* by Shakespeare, students with LD could use a digital copy of the text so that they can easily look up unknown words or phrases and have parts read aloud to them. Similar benefits would apply to content area textbooks used in science and social studies classes.

Providing adolescents with LD opportunities to learn with digital texts supports not only their academic achievement but also their postsecondary goals. Facility with digital texts and technologies is a skill that experts believe is especially important as students near graduation and begin to look for employment or pursue post secondary education (Biancarosa &

Snow, 2006; U.S. Department of Commerce, 2011). According to the U.S. Department of Commerce, 62% of working Americans use the Internet as a primary tool in their jobs. Moreover, digital literacy is important as an increasing number of daily activities in higher education, health care, and banking are commonly conducted online (U.S. Department of Commerce, 2011).

Putting It All Together

Helping adolescents with LD improve their reading skills is a critical yet complicated task. One important element in planning responsive reading instruction for adolescents with LD is text selection. What might proper text selection look like in practice?

- *Step 1. Determine students' approximate reading level.* Some schools administer schoolwide reading assessments to determine students' reading levels, in which case teachers can request the data for their students. If the school does not administer such an assessment, teachers can administer an assessment like an IRI in their classroom. It is important that students' reading levels are monitored throughout the school year so that they accurately reflect changes in students' reading progress across the year.
- *Step 2. Administer a reading interest inventory to determine students' interests.*
- *Step 3. Locate materials that appear to match individual student's reading levels and interests.* Some book publishers provide the approximate reading level of a book on the front or back cover, or the levels can be looked up online. If the reading level for a book is unclear or unknown, readability estimates can be calculated. If teachers are having difficulty locating books or technology-based texts that are written on an appropriate level and that match students' interests, collaborating with others may be helpful. Teachers can consult school media specialists or curriculum coordinators to find materials within the school. If the school does not have enough appropriate materials, teachers can (a) collaborate with administrators to try to allocate funds to purchase books, (b) work with the local public library to borrow books, or (c) write a minigrant to purchase books. Teachers can also select ebooks that are available on the Internet. In addition to evaluating books based on their reading level and whether they match students' interests, it is also important to ensure that any depictions of diverse groups are accurate and respectful. Finally, as much as possible, books should include a technology component. This could include having a CD or digital copy of the book or web-based links and resources.
- *Step 4. Verify that books are a good fit for students.* While a student is reading a book, conduct a running record to verify that the book is not at the student's frustration level.

It is important to note that proper text selection is only one element of a quality, comprehensive reading program for adolescents with LD. To address all of the necessary elements adequately is beyond the scope of this article. See Table 2 for a list of organizations and research centers that maintain websites that provide resources related to adolescent literacy, particularly reading instruction for adolescents with disabilities and struggling readers. In addition to providing information related to text selection, these organizations also address other aspects of secondary reading instruction (e.g., reading assessments, content area literacy, comprehension instruction). The websites found in Table 2 include research reports, lesson plans, teaching strategies, professional development opportunities, and discussion forums that may be helpful initial resources for educators.

Texts that match a student's reading ability and interests will help motivate them to read and remain engaged during reading instruction. These texts should be (a) written on the student's instructional level, (b) appealing to adolescents' interests, and (c) representative of diverse perspectives, genres, and formats. High-interest/low-readability texts can serve as effective and efficient resources for teachers who are struggling to find reading material that meets older students' needs. With the right texts at their disposal, educators will be one step closer to helping adolescents with LD become more engaged in reading.

References

Allington, R. L. (2001). *What really matters for struggling readers: Designing research-based programs.* New York, NY: Longman.

Alvermann, D. E. (2002). Effective literacy instruction for adolescents. *Journal of Literacy Research, 34,* 189–208. doi: 10.1207/s15548430jlr3402_4

Barton, P. (2000). *What jobs require: Literacy, education and training, 1940–2006.* Princeton, NJ: ETS.

Bean, T. W., Readence, J. E., & Baldwin, R. S. (2008). *Content area literacy: An integrated approach.* Dubuque, IA: Kendall/Hunt.

Biancarosa, C., & Snow, C. E. (2006). *Reading next—A vision for action and research in middle and high school literacy: A report to Carnegie Corporation of New York* (2nd ed.). Washington, DC: Alliance for Excellent Education.

Boone, R., & Higgins, K. (2003). Reading, writing, and publishing digital text. *Remedial and Special Education, 24,* 132–140.

Clay, M. (1991). *Becoming literate: The construction of inner control.* Auckland, NZ: Heinemann.

Daniel, S. S., Walsh, A. K., Goldston, D. B., Arnold, E. M., Reboussin, B. A., & Wood, F. B. (2006). Suicidality, school dropout, and reading problems among adolescents. *Journal of Learning Disabilities, 39,* 507–514. doi: 10.1177/00222194060390060301

Table 2   Web Sites Related to Adolescent Literacy.

Organization	Web Site	Materials About Adolescent Literacy or Adolescent Struggling Readers
All About Adolescent Literacy (AdLit.org)	www.adlit.org	Free classroom materials
		Description of research-based reading strategies
		Professional development modules
		Research reports
Alliance for Excellent Education	www.all4ed.org/adolescent_literacy	Research and policy reports
		Case studies of school districts
Center on Instruction	www.centeroninstruction.org	Professional development modules
		Webinars
		Conference information
Florida Center for Reading Research (FCRR)	www.fcrr.org	Professional development resources
		Research and policy reports
		Webinars
		Assessment materials and tools
ReadWriteThink	www.readwritethink.org	Lesson plans
		Student materials and printouts
		Professional development materials
		Classroom strategy guides
		Professional library recommendations
		Webinars
Vaughn Gross Center for Reading and Language Arts (VGC)	www.meadowscenter.org/vgc	Professional development materials
		Online professional development opportunities
		Lesson plans and classroom activities

Deshler, D. D., Ellis, E. S., & Lenz, B. K. (1996). *Teaching adolescents with learning disabilities.* Denver, CO: Love.

Edyburn, D. L., & Edyburn, K. D. (2012). Tools for creating accessible, tiered, and multilingual web-based curricula. *Intervention in School and Clinic, 47,* 199–205. doi: 10.1177/1053451211424603

Faggella-Luby, M., Schumaker, J. B., & Deshler, D. D. (2007). Embedded learning strategy instruction: Story structure pedagogy in heterogeneous secondary literature classes. *Learning Disability Quarterly, 30*(2), 131–147. doi: 10.2307/30035547

Faggella-Luby, M. N., Ware, S. M., & Capozzoli, A. (2009). Adolescent literacy—Reviewing adolescent literacy reports: Key components and critical questions. *Journal of Literacy Research, 41,* 453–475.

Fry, E. (1975). Fry's readability graph: Clarifications, validity, and extension to level 17. *Journal of Reading, 21,* 242–252.

Gajria, M., Jitendra, A. K., Stood, S., & Sacks, G. (2007). Improving comprehension of expository text in students with LD: A research synthesis. *Journal of Learning Disabilities, 40,* 210–225. doi: 10.1177/00222194070400030301

Guthrie, J. T., & Alao, S. (1997). Designing contexts to increase motivations for reading. *Educational Psychologist, 32,* 95–105. doi: 10.1207/s15326985ep3202_4

Guthrie, J. T., & Davis, M. H. (2003). Motivating struggling readers in middle school through an engagement model of classroom practice. *Reading and Writing Quarterly, 19,* 59–85.

Ivey, G., & Broaddus, K. (2001). "Just plain reading": A survey of what makes students want to read in middle school classrooms. *Reading Research Quarterly, 36,* 350–377.

Kamil, M. L., Borman, G. D., Dole, J., Kral, C. C., Salinger, T., & Torgesen, J. (2008). *Improving adolescent literacy: Effective classroom and intervention practices: A practice guide.* Washington, DC: National Center for Education Evaluation and Regional Assistance.

Kincaid, J. P., Fishburne, R. P., Rogers, R. L., & Chissom, B. S. (1975). *Derivation of new readability formulas (automated readability index, fog count, and Flesch reading ease formula) for Navy enlisted personnel* (Navy Training Command Research Branch Report, 8–75). Millington, TN: Naval Technical Training, U.S. Naval Air Station.

Kutner, M., Greenberg, E., Jin, Y., Boyle, B., Hsu, Y., & Dunleavy, E. (2007). *Literacy in everyday life: Results from the 2003 National Assessment of Adult Literacy* (NCES 2007-480). Washington, DC: U.S. Department of Education, National Center for Education Statistics.

Lenters, K. (2006). Resistance, struggle, and the adolescent reader. *Journal of Adolescent and Adult Literacy, 50*(2), 136–146.

Malmgren, K. W., & Trezek, B. (2009). Literacy instruction for secondary students with disabilities. *Focus on Exceptional Children, 41*(6), 1–12.

Marshall, J. C., & Campbell, Y. C. (2006). Toward independence: Working toward fluency. In J. S. Schumm (Ed.), *Reading: Assessment and instruction for all readers* (pp. 163–189). New York, NY: Guilford.

National Center for Education Statistics. (2003). *The condition of education 2003.* Washington, DC: Author.

National Joint Committee on Learning Disabilities. (2008). *Adolescent literacy and older students with learning disabilities.* Retrieved from www.ldonline.org/about/partners/njcld

O'Connor, R., Bell, K., Harty, K., Larkin, L., Sackor, S., & Zigmond, N. (2002). Teaching reading to poor readers in the intermediate grades: A comparison of text difficulty. *Journal of Educational Psychology, 94,* 474–485.

Pisha, B., & Stahl, S. (2005). The promise of new learning environments for students with disabilities. *Intervention in School and Clinic, 41,* 67–75. doi: 10.1177/10534512050410020601

Pitcher, S. M., Martinez, G., Dicembre, E. A., Fewster, D., & McCormick, M. K. (2010). The literacy needs of adolescents in their own words. *Journal of Adolescent and Adult Literacy, 53*(8), 636–645.

Raygor, A. L. (1977). The Raygor Readability Estimate: A quick and easy way to determine difficulty. In P. D. Pearson (Ed.), *Reading: Theory, research and practice* (pp. 259–263). Clemson, SC: National Reading Conference.

Reutzel, D. R., & Cooter, R. B. (2012). *Teaching children to read: The teacher makes the difference* (6th ed.). Upper Saddle River, NJ: Pearson/Merrill Hall.

Rog, L. J., & Burton, W. (2001). Matching texts and readers: leveling early reading materials for assessment and instruction. *Reading Teacher, 55*(4), 348–357.

Rose, D. H., & Meyer, A. (2002). *Teaching every student in the digital age: Universal design for learning.* Alexandria, VA: ASCD.

Scammacca, N., Roberts, G., Vaughn, S., Edmonds, M., Wexler, J., & Torgesen, J. K. (2007). *Interventions for adolescent struggling readers: A meta-analysis with implications for practice.* Portsmouth, NH: RMC Research Corp., Center on Instruction.

Stanovich, K. (1986). Matthew effects in reading: Some consequences of individual differences in the acquisition of literacy. *Reading Research Quarterly, 21,* 360–407.

Tyner, B. (2009). *Small-group reading instruction: A differentiated teaching model for beginning and struggling readers* (2nd ed.). Newark, DE: International Reading Association.

U.S. Department of Commerce. (2011). *Fact sheet: Digital literacy.* Retrieved from www.commerce.gov/news/fact-sheets/2011/05/13/fact-sheet-digital-literacy

U.S. Department of Education. (2011). *The nation's report card* [Data file]. Retrieved from http://nationsreportcard.gov/reading_2011/nat_g8.asp?tab_id=tab2&subtab_id=Tab_7#chart

Worthy, J., Moorman, M., & Turner, M. (1999). What Johnny likes to read is hard to find in school. *Reading Research Quarterly, 34,* 12–27.

Critical Thinking

1. Who else might benefit from using the high interest/low readability books and strategies suggested in this article?

2. So why is it important to be concerned about the reading ability of this specific group of adolescents? Why not use these books with other students?

3. Using one of your personal interests, prepare a list of five high interest/low readability (use 6th grade as reading level) books of any genre. Review them and report your findings in class.

Create Central

www.mhhe.com/createcentral

Internet References

All about Adolescent Literacy
www.adlit.org/

MELINDA LEKO is an assistant professor at the Department of Rehabilitation Psychology and Special Education at UW-Madison.

CHARLOTTE MUNDY currently teaches undergraduate classes focusing on literacy acquisition and development.

HYUN JU KANG and **SUJATA DATAR** are doctoral students in the Department of Rehabilitation Psychology and Special Education at UW-Madison.

Article   Prepared by: Rebecca B. Evers, *Winthrop University*

Using Family Message Journals to Improve Student Writing and Strengthen the School-Home Partnership

LYNDA M. VALERIE AND SHEILA FOSS-SWANSON

Learning Outcomes

After reading this article, you will be able to:

- Plan actions to establish a School-Home Partnership for your classroom.

Dear Mom,

We have to send mune for a yoyo . . . and tomorrow is the picture day and we learned a life cycle of a pumpkins.

Love,

Troy

Troy wrote this message in his family message journal (FMJ). FMJs are notebooks in which students write about some aspect of their school day: a new lesson, an anecdote, an upcoming event. The students bring these journals home each day and a family member writes back.

As educators, our interest in using FMJs to improve student writing emerged from four areas of concern.

- Where do we fit writing instruction and practice into the curriculum?
- How do we motivate students to write?
- How can we engage all students in multiple writing opportunities so that they develop as writers?
- How can we foster home-school partnerships?

Answering these and other questions as they arose became part of the rationale for implementing FMJs in our classrooms. In true educator style, we first began by speaking with colleagues and reviewing the literature.

The Case for Writing

Classroom teachers gather ideas, strategies, and lessons that appeal to and are adapted for all students to foster literacy learning. Several ideas that assist with reading instruction and writing have emerged in the field, including using computers to include new literacies. For teachers, fostering a love of writing in students is often challenging. For students, navigating the thought from head to fingers is sometimes a Herculean task. Teachers often ask such questions as the following:

- Do we have to bother with writing?
- Is learning to write still necessary for today's students?
- Learning to write takes so much time and practice; where can teachers find the time?

Learning to write is crucial to literacy development. Teaching writing, even spending time on writing in elementary classes, often comes after teaching reading and math—and sometimes after art and music or as a substitute for recess. The reasons for limited time dedicated to writing are many; however, the benefits that early learners derive from writing are compelling. First, writing communicates in myriad ways: a thank-you note, a birthday card, a family story, a consumer complaint, or a persuasive request. Writing is a practical, essential life skill. Beyond practicalities, writing is a basic part of learning. Murray (2009) and Elbow (2004) both view writing as a thinking process that goes beyond merely recording thoughts. Many sources, such as National Writing Project & Nagin (2003), the National Council of Teachers of English (NCTE; 2004), and Routman (2005) reiterate the view that the act of writing generates ideas, helps develop higher order thinking skills, and can result in higher test scores.

Writing is not an isolated competence; educational literature also documents the interdependence of reading and writing

(Knipper & Duggan, 2006; Rasinski & Padak, 2009; Tompkins, 2009). Students need to write, not only to develop as writers and thinkers but also to develop as readers. Writing must therefore take a necessary front-and-center place in the school curriculum. How can teachers best use time spent on writing, and how can they appeal to even the most reluctant writers? As part of the literature review for this article, we found an article by Wollman-Bonilla (2001), which eventually led us to FMJs.

The Case for Family Literacy

Two components of family literacy articles pertained to particularly to writing as a core part of the classroom: to increase interactive activities between parents and children and to foster age appropriate education to prepare students for success in school and life experiences (Amstutz, 2000). From the time that a child is born until he or she is 18 years old, the child spends only 11% of the time in formal education. Teachers must therefore tap into the 89% of time that students are outside the traditional classroom, because when family and school are connected, students succeed.

Family literacy encourages a partnership that is based on commonalties of home and school. It encompasses the reading, writing, listening, speaking, and thinking that take place within the family. Discourse begins at home, where students utter their first words to communicate with and to be a part of their families. Students' exposure to books and other forms of written communication are based on the interests of their families. When students reach school, they are already "somebody." Rowsell and Pahl (2007) contend that children's interests can be traced back to the home, where the process of "meaning making" begins with discourse within the family. This discourse becomes "sedimented" in the child's identity and finds its way into texts that the child creates. Literacy is infused with meaning that families create (Rowsell & Pahl, 2007).

FMJs are an effective way to connect home and school through written communication and can be the link to increase writing time/motivation. Instructionally, FMJs are a wonderful starting point in teaching writing to children. When they are included into an established daily routine, they provide a built-in authentic purpose for writing, increase writing time, and facilitate communication between school and home.

What Can a Family Message Journal Teach Children?

Using FMJs to communicate with family members provides students a daily writing opportunity for a real audience. Children learn the value of writing for a variety of purposes including taking stock of new information, remembering responsibilities and requests, generating and developing ideas, connecting new information with the known, expressing personal feelings or wishes, recalling experiences, and sharing messages. The messages can be a reflection about a subject or concept that relates to curriculum or can inform parents about school-related events and activities (Wollman-Bonilla, 2000). The family member writes a daily reply to the student.

Writing to a family member of his or her choosing gives the student the luxury of knowing the relationship, humor, beliefs, and stance of his or her reader. When the teacher asks students to tell the family member about a specific lesson or event that occurred during the school day, the student can use sociocultural schema to share what he or she believes will interest the reader. Because the student has participated in oral conversations with the chosen family member, she or he can decide what crucial information to include in the message about the writer's school day. The writer benefits from immediate feedback about the message when the family member reads and discusses the journal entry. Further discourse takes place when the family member writes a reply. The family member is continuing the role of teacher by modeling how to write a journal reply. Young writers communicate more effectively when given opportunities to write for authentic purposes.

Successful FMJs require understanding of and aptitude for audience awareness. "Writing is simultaneously an individual struggle and a social undertaking" (Holliway, 2004, p. 1). Audience awareness consists of selecting and ordering language to develop texts that are recognizable to readers. It involves understanding the experiences, expectations, and beliefs of the addressed audience. Research has defined *audience awareness* as shared perspective, as trying to place oneself in the shoes of the audience, and as the ability to consider an absent reality (Carvalho & Brandao, 2002; Holliway, 2004; Langer & Flihan, 2000; Wollman Bonilla, 2001). According to Olsen (1994) and Witte (1992), as cited by Holliway, "Establishing reciprocity among the reader, writer, and text is the hallmark of experienced writing" (p. 335). This reciprocity requires much support from the combined social interactive areas of oral discourse, wide reading, and authentic writing for real-world purposes. In this way, writing in an FMJ also contributes to building oral discourse abilities, another essential life skill.

Implementation

We introduced FMJs in a first-grade urban classroom with a diverse student population. Subsequently, educators have initiated FMJs in several other settings, spanning prekindergarten through middle school.

Once FMJs are established as a way to help develop writing for students at all levels, the teacher can implement the practice in the classroom. The process can be used with all students and to increase communication with parents of students with disabilities. On the first day of school, the teacher began by establishing the idea of the home-school connection through Read Aloud. The book *The Gardener* by Sarah Stewart (1997) worked well because it tells a story in which the character shares her day-to-day activities through letter writing. Part of the class discussion focused on how the main character would have felt if she had not stayed connected with her family through message writing.

Next, the teacher introduced journal writing using a writer's workshop format. The teacher wrote a sample journal entry to a family member and used this activity to generate a discussion about writing to an audience. The class then created a family word bank, including words such as *mom, dad, grandma, grandpa, brother, sister, cousin,* as well as types of pets, stuffed animals, and imaginary friends.

After the teacher instructed students to write about something that they had done in school that day, the students wrote their first message. Depending on the developmental level of the student, they either drew a picture or wrote a sentence. The students who drew a picture labeled it with a beginning letter, a word, or a sentence using sound spelling.

On the inside cover of the FMJ, each student glued a preprinted letter and signed her or his name. The letter explained to family members how to write daily replies back to students. At morning meeting time on the following day, the teacher asked one or two students to share their messages and their family replies.

The class often engaged in role play of the interaction that took place at home between the student and the family member with the teacher playing the home responder. For example, a student wrote, "I went to art." The teacher said, "What did you do in art?" The student and teacher then engaged in discourse about vital information that the student might add to the message. The student decided to add that he painted a seascape and described the colors and materials that he used to create his artwork. This role play took place periodically throughout the year and was a good way to include all students in the process. After a time, Lucy, a child with special needs, became especially adept at playing the mother. When a student wrote "I went to gym," the class would echo Lucy by chanting, "What did you *do* in gym?" Writing in the FMJ became a daily routine and part of the classroom culture. On the rare occasion that we had to skip writing in the FMJs, the students would comment, "But we didn't write in our journals!"

Because audience awareness plays a big part in FMJ writing, part of the teacher's role when implementing FMJs in the classroom is to teach audience awareness through direct instruction and to facilitate the students' writing to their families. When writers consider the perspective of their readers, they tend to add more detail and interest to their written work. The writer has to consider information that is missing from oral discourse and provide it for the reader. Writers take readers' expectations into account and benefit from reader feedback. Writers who are aware of their audience may be more critical readers as well. In the process of writing their FMJs, students are learning to write and writing to learn. According to The National Commission on Writing in America's Schools and Colleges (2003), "If students are to make knowledge their own, they must struggle with the details, wrestle with the facts, and rework raw information and dimly understood concepts into language they can communicate to someone else" (p. 9).

In the original research that inspired our FMJ practice (Wollman-Bonilla, 2000), the teacher wrote a message on the board and the students copied it in their journals. It was many weeks before the teacher asked students to develop their own messages. To modify this practice, the teacher began to just write essential information on the board, such as "Field trip, Karabin Farm, Friday, October 12th. No uniforms required. Chaperones needed." For some students, that information was almost the entirety of their message. Others built on the bare facts as their writing abilities grew.

Dear Mom,

Can you come to my field trip to pick apples? 1 am not scared.

Love,

Mackenzie

No other notices went home informing parents about field trips, chaperones, picture day, book fairs, school concerts, and other activities. Students—and family members too—knew that the individual message journals were the source for important information. This technique worked well, and students felt responsible for communicating to family members about school events. Below is an example of an informative student message.

Dear Dad,

Please come to meet my teacher. Please come at 6:30 tomorrow.

Love,

Aditya

In true writers' workshop fashion, mini-lessons focused on FMJ issues as needed. Even though there is probably no end to the number of possible mini-lessons that teachers can use to help refine FMJ messages, the core examples continually revisited throughout the year included

- Consider your reader. What do you want him or her to know about your school day? What would appeal to him or her?
- Add details to your message. Your reader wants to know what materials and colors you used in art and what you painted.
- Write a persuasive message to get what you want.
- Include important information in communications about school events, including the date, time, place, what to wear, and what to bring.
- Explain your thinking when describing new learning.
- Create a picture with words to help yourself recall an experience that you want to remember, such as a field trip to an apple orchard.
- Learn the parts of a letter, including the date, greeting, message, closing, and signature.

The teacher taught audience awareness mini-lessons to encourage writers to consider their readers. Writers learned to include important information in a message so that a family member who was not at school could understand the student's message.

When Nathan read his bare-bones message to the class the next morning,

Dear daddy,

I had Art.

Love,

Nathan

he heard the chant from his classmates, "But, what did you *do* in art?" Nathan went back to his seat and added to his message "I mad a seascape."

Using Family Journals to Improve Writing and Strengthen the School-Home Partnership by L. M. Valerie and S. Foss-Swanson

77

Writers learned how to write persuasively and receive a positive response. In the following example, a student wrote home to ask for money for the school book fair:

Dear Mom and Dad

Please can I have MonEy for the Holiday Shop? We will shop on thursday. Please can I have a new toy for the toy drive too? I want to give a new toy to a kid who dont have one.

Love,

Juan

Persuasive writing empowers students and encourages discourse between students and members of their family.

A teacher might ask students to take out their FMJs after a math lesson and write to someone at home to explain the concept of greater than and less than.

Dear Mom,

we learnd about comparing numbrs. 10 is grater than 4.

Asking a student to analyze and synthesize a new concept by explaining it in a written message to a family member is rigorous, authentic, and purposeful.

By using their FMJs, students learned to reread, edit, and revise messages before taking them home to share with family members. When a message was not clear, the teacher asked the writer to clarify and provide additional information that he or she had omitted from the message. The writer also benefited from immediate feedback from the reader and learned what to include the next time. Over the school year, the students progressed through the developmental stages of writing, as evidenced in their FMJs. Students who began the year by drawing to communicate about their day eventually began to rely on print to relay their messages and then used the format of letter writing. One hallmark of progress was when postscripts began to appear—first on the family member's messages and then, without explicit mention, on students' messages.

Dear MoM,

I had a great day at the movies today. It was vary fun. I am riting very good now. Have a great day mom.

P.S. I love how you are proud of me!

Possible Problems and Solutions

One issue to consider when using FMJs is whether a child in the classroom has a family member who can write back in the conventional way. Allington and Cunningham (2006) describe four categories of family involvement: involved in school and supportive of child, uninvolved in school and supportive of child, involved in school but not supportive of child, and uninvolved in school and not supportive of child. Educators can adapt the use of FMJs so that students from all these categories can develop their writing.

Involved in School and Supportive of Child

The children who may benefit most from FMJs are those from this type of family. Their parents foster the school-home partnership. These children learn and grow in school and during the 89% of time spent outside school. These families write faithfully each evening in FMJs; and their children learn and develop a rich vocabulary, while their journals relate a plethora of information about their school days, often in priceless words and pictures.

Uninvolved in School but Supportive of Child

As teachers, this group of parents surprised us the most because without FMJs there was almost no school contact. We were unsure if these students were receiving any support at home and doubted that most of these parents would write back to their children. We were surprised and pleased that they did. We were excited and encouraged to read the journal exchanges between these students and their parents. We learned about family relationships, dynamics, the level of support at home, and how family members felt about what their children were learning in school. One parent became more involved by corresponding with the teacher occasionally.

The teacher can also address concerns about non-English-speaking families or families with limited English proficiency by using FMJs. Some family responders did not speak, read, or write in English. These families wrote their replies in their native language even though the student had written to them in English. The family member typically read his or her note to the student, and the student translated it orally the next day in class when sharing.

For example, one teacher had a student from Bosnia whose mother wrote her responses in her native language. When the student came to school, a parent of a classmate who brought his child to school each morning would read the message and translate it for her. Even if a child forgets the translation, the important discourse about school has still taken place between the family member and the child. The child is still writing daily in English for authentic purposes, and the family member and child are still talking about school at home. Some parents who do not read or write have simply signed their names each evening after the child has read and/or translated the message. The ultimate goal of the FMJs is to encourage students and their families to have conversations about school.

For students using assistive technology (AT) to communicate, parents and teachers need to evaluate the most effective method of response and communication for the FMJ. Educators should consider involving the district AT specialist to help with communication. Also, if parents are not comfortable with the technology, anyone can respond to the FMJ. Some parents may feel restricted by AT or even by the limited time to respond. In such situations, other family members (for example, siblings, aunts, uncles, cousins, or grandparents) can take turns responding.

Involved in School but Not Supportive of Child

Sometimes parents may contribute to school activities or lead parent organizations but not appear to support their own child. Rather than responding to content the parent may be overly critical of writing mechanics and focus on spelling or neatness. Having a one-on-one discussion with this type of parent has usually remedied this issue; the teacher should point out that the primary purposes of the FMJ are to share information and write for authentic purposes. For example, one parent began to circle every word that her first grader spelled incorrectly and made her write it over. The child became completely unmotivated to write anything at all. The teacher sat down with the parent and explained that invented spelling was developmentally appropriate for her child and persuaded the parent to circle only one word per day in the journal and to use it for a home spelling lesson. Open communication between the teacher and parent is critical, especially for this type of parent.

Uninvolved in School and Not Supportive of Child

This type of parent has been extremely rare when teachers have used FMJs. In those instances, the educator can help arrange for an alternative responder. A member of the extended family, an older student, or a school staff member (not the teacher), such as a school secretary, librarian, or community volunteer, can serve as an alternative responder. When a child does not have a family member who will write to him or her at all, choose a student from another classroom, usually one at a higher grade level, to visit the classroom each morning for 5 minutes and write a reply. Sometimes, the child is initially disinclined to have someone who is not a member of his or her family write in the FMJ. However, once the surrogate responder begins to write, comment, and ask questions about the child's FMJ, the student usually begins to respond and enjoy the experience with the alternative responder.

Differentiation

All students follow the same developmental stages of writing; they just do it at different rates, ages, and grade levels. Because FMJs allow each student to communicate at his or her developmental level, education becomes differentiated by design. Throughout our 5 years of incorporating FMJs into literacy instruction, we have successfully adapted the concept for students identified with special needs, including students with autism, students who use a wheelchair, nonverbal students, and students with limited range of motion. In addition, several upper elementary and middle school teachers have incorporated FMJs as an intervention for their students with writing difficulties. Although teachers can use their own ideas, the following are some options for differentiation:

- Picture menus that use such software as Boardmaker help students choose symbol-based representations of activities done during the day.

- Several varieties of alternative keyboards can be programmed to include frequently used phrases, letter templates, or pictures instead of letters and words.
- Software such as Kurzweil allows students and family members to listen to written words on a computer.
- Educators can pair a student who is at an advanced stage of writing development with one who is less advanced and have them write together, or one student can dictate while the other one writes.
- A tech-savvy student might keep an FMJ on a computer, using various fonts, picture inserts, and drawing programs to which family members can respond at home.
- Advanced students might post to an online web log to create a classroom FMJ that informs and updates parents about classroom and school events and invites parents to offer comments and responses.
- Higher order thinkers might develop a peer journal in which they write as themselves to a pet or imaginary friend and another student writes back in the voice of the pet or imaginary friend.

How Can Educators Use FMJs for Assessment?

Once teachers implement FMJs in their classroom they can easily begin to use them for assessment. We have found that if students are demonstrating audience awareness in their written messages, this factor can be used to document a student's growth. One simple way to illustrate growth is to compare the message from the first day of school with subsequent messages. For example, Isabella's first-day entry consisted of a drawing of herself, which she labeled *Jimm*. The student was using this message as her way of communicating that she had gym class that day. The discourse between this student and her mother when Isabella presented her journal entry to her mother was probably something like the following:

Mom: Did you meet a girl named Jimm today?

Isabella: No mom, we went to gym today!

Mom: Oh, I see. Well, the word gym is spelled differently. You spell it g-y-m. Maybe if you had drawn yourself kicking a ball and wrote the word ball, I would have understood it better.

Isabella: Okay, next time I'll do that!

Only 2 months later, in October, that same student wrote the following:

Dear MoM,

I wot to rit to 100 but onle riding at scol I wot to mack a necliss in the hundreds club

PS I wet to Jim we ridid the bics and rann it wus fun we had a grat day I had fun at Jim

love

Isabella

This message translates as

> Dear Mom,
>
> I want to write to one hundred, but only writing at school. I want to make a necklace in the hundreds club.
>
> P.S. I went to gym. We rode bikes and ran. It was fun. We had a great day. I had fun at gym.
>
> Love,
>
> Isabella

Isabella wrote her message in letter format, with the date, greeting, message, closing, and signature. Her writing had developed enough that she was attempting to write sentences, and she even included a postscript that imitated her mother's previous use of that element. Isabella used a mix of invented spelling and conventional spelling. She included background information that her audience would need to understand about writing to 100 and being allowed to make a necklace when she was able to accomplish that task. She wrote more about her experience in gym class, mentioning the activities in gym. Overall, she clearly demonstrated growth in her writing. This type of comparative evaluation is useful in portfolio assessments and in showcasing to students and families the level of growth that has occurred.

Teacher Inquiry

We also found that FMJs answered some of our original concerns about time and motivation, as well as building home-school partnerships. For further assessment, we also used comparison data that demonstrated growth in student writing, and we implemented a teacher inquiry project adapted from Wollman-Bonilla (2001) on FMJs and audience awareness.

The FMJs provided a means to gather and analyze student work that demonstrated audience awareness by counting rhetorical moves. Wollman-Bonilla (2001) identified a *rhetorical move* as a text feature that has been recognized as verification of audience awareness. We used four specific rhetorical moves to evaluate FMJs.

Naming Moves

A naming move positions the audience and writer by addressing readers and cuing them to their expected stance. A writer who names or addresses the audience member directly is using a naming move. For example, when a student writes "Dear Mom," the word *mom* is a naming move; and when a student writes "I can't wait for you to see it," the word *you* also is a naming move.

Context Moves

A context move provides background information that the writer believes that the audience needs. Isabella used a context move when she wrote "I wot to rit to 100 but onle riding at scoi I wot to mack a necliss in the hundreds club." She provided background information so that her mother would understand that she had to write numbers to 100, but she could only write them in school rather than at home. As a reward for demonstrating this skill, she would be able to make a "hundreds club necklace."

Strategy Moves

A strategy move keeps the reader's interest and appeals their emotions, concerns, or sense of humor. Juan used a strategy move by appealing to his parents' emotions when he explained why he wanted a new toy for the toy drive: "I want to give a new toy to a kid who dont have one."

Response Moves

When students use a response move, they can state, explain, or accommodate the reader's potential concerns or objections. For example, "I know it's probably not a good idea, but can I sleep over at Dexter's house?" is a response move because the student anticipates the response of the parent and addresses it in his message before the parent can respond.

Results

Our inquiry indicated that children in first grade had the sociocognitive capacity to demonstrate audience awareness. Overall, our results were similar to those of the Wollman-Bonilla (2001) study. Students demonstrated audience awareness when writing to family members, and they used rhetorical moves that educators could count and assess. The study supports the idea that writing authentic, purposeful messages to family members causes students to consider their audience and to appeal to the individual beliefs and expectations of their readers. We originally collected data on only two rhetorical moves: naming moves and context moves. We were surprised to discover that first-grade students also used strategy moves and response moves abundantly in their FMJs. The students' writing became more sophisticated over the course of the school year. We believe that the close connection between the writer and the reader, as well as the immediate feedback, both oral and written, enhanced the students' writing progress.

Recommendations

Existing research focuses on audience awareness; therefore, future research could focus on how audience awareness in writing relates to reading progress. Another recommendation for further study is to examine whether the newfound skill of demonstrating audience awareness transfers to other types of students' written work. Perhaps further research might focus on quantifying how families who participate in communicating through FMJs are more involved than other parents in the school lives of their children or whether they believe that they are more connected and informed.

Benefits

FMJ serves the teacher, the school, the family, and the student. These intertwined benefits build upon one another.

Teachers

One advantage of FMJ writing is that after establishing FMJs, teachers require little planning time and no grading time, yet students increase the time that they spend on writing.

One second-grade teacher reported that her principal, after reviewing grade-level monthly writing prompts, noted the increase in student writing stamina and asked what had brought about the change. The teacher told her principal about FMJ. That teacher had students write in their journals during the last 20 minutes of each school day, while she circulated and helped students prepare for dismissal. Another special education teacher stated that nothing had ever worked like the FMJ to motivate students to write and to increase their output. The teacher found the FMJ to be an activity in which her students could and did fully participate. One fifth-grade urban teacher noted that the FMJ helped with classroom management:

> We had Art today and you might as well ground me for what I did in Art today. One made the most awful choice of my life. I pushed someone into the table and he banged his head. I lost control of my actions and I made a bad choice. We apologized to each other and promised not to fight ever again.

This student had already written about problems and solutions before there was a need for a parent and teacher discussion.

School

The FMJs help create a community of writers. Any activity that motivates students to write more and improve their writing achievement benefits the school in obvious ways. Several classrooms, grade levels, or the whole school might use FMJs. When older students have served as the reader and corresponding writer, students formed relationships beyond their grade level. The ongoing communication with families resulted in more families that felt that they were connected with the school and believed that they were informed about their child's education.

Educators noted more casual visits from parents and short informal conversations. Parents came to parent conferences prepared to discuss their child's progress in a meaningful manner. Parents seemed to follow closely what and how their children were writing in the journals. One parent began to circle one word a day that her child had misspelled and helped the child learn to spell it correctly. Another parent noticed that the penmanship of her child had started to decline. That parent wrote a message to the child stating that she would not read the messages unless the child chose to write neatly. Other parents wrote reminders for good behavior during the school day. Still others wrote to their children reminding them to bring home all their homework. Overall, the increase in communication went beyond the classroom but focused on school and life.

Families

Families can finally obtain an answer to the age-old question: "What did you learn in school today?" FMJs, by their nature, set up a natural structure that encourages families to discuss the connections between home and school. When these connections strengthen, everyone benefits, especially the students.

Students

The outcome for this group was significant. As teachers, we incorporated FMJs into the classroom because this tool helped us answer our original questions: Where do we fit writing instruction and practice into the curriculum? How do we motivate and engage all students in multiple writing opportunities so that they develop as writers? We found that asking students to write daily to retell happenings, relay information, and compose requests to an essential and authentic audience was powerful. In that process, the students developed as writers and as communicators, and become more adept at connecting to school, home, and the community beyond—the ultimate goal of writing.

References

Allington, R., & Cunningham, P. (2006). *Schools that work.* Boston, MA: Pearson.

Amstutz, D. D. (2000). Family literacy: Implications for public school practice. *Education and Urban Society, 32,* 207–220.

Carvalho, J., & Brandao, J. (2002). Developing audience awareness in writing. *Journal of Research in Reading, 25,* 271–282.

Elbow, P. (2004). Write first: Putting writing before reading is an effective approach to teaching and learning. *Educational Leadership, 62*(2), 10.

Holliway, D. R. (2004). Through the eyes of my reader: Strategy for improving audience perspective in children's descriptive writing. *Journal of Research in Childhood Education, 18,* 334–349.

Knipper, K., & Duggan, T. (2006). Writing to learn across the curriculum: Tools for comprehension in content area classes. *The Reading Teacher, 59,* 462–470.

Langer, J., & Flihan, S. (2000). *Writing and reading relationship: Constructivist tasks.* Retrieved from cela.albany.edu/publication/article/writeread.htm

Murray, D. (2009). *The essential Don Murray: Lessons from America's greatest writing teacher.* Portsmouth, NH: Boynton/Cook Print.

The National Commission on Writing in American Schools and Colleges. (2003). *The neglected "r": The need for a writing revolution.* New York, NY: College Board.

National Council of Teachers of English (NCTE). (2004). *NCTE beliefs about the teaching of writing.* Retrieved from www.ncte.org/positions/statements/writingbeliefs

The National Writing Project, & Nagin, C. (2003). *Because writing matters: Improving student writing in our schools.* Berkeley, CA: Jossey-Bass.

Olsen, D. (1994). *The world on paper.* Cambridge, MA: Cambridge University Press.

Rasinski, T, & Padak, N. (2009). Write soon! *The Reading Teacher, 62,* 618–620.

Routman, R. (2005). *Writing essentials.* Portsmouth, NH: Heinemann.

Rowsell, J., & Pahl, K. (2007). Sedimented identities in texts: Instances of practice. *Reading Research Quarterly, 42,* 388–403.

Stewart, S. (1997). *The gardener.* New York, NY: Holtzbrinck.

Tompkins, G. (2009). *Language arts: Patterns of practice.* Upper Saddle River, NJ: Pearson.

Witte, S. (1992). Context, text, intertext: Toward a constructionist semiotic of writing. *Written Communication, 9,* 237–308.

Using Family Journals to Improve Writing and Strengthen the School-Home Partnership by L. M. Valerie and S. Foss-Swanson

81

Wollman-Bonilla, J. E. (2000). *Family message journals: Teaching writing through family involvement.* Urbana, IL: National Council of Teachers of English.

Wollman-Bonilla, J. E. (2001). Can first graders demonstrate audience awareness? *Reading Research Quarterly, 36,* 184–201.

Critical Thinking

1. What are some of the important reasons for a teacher to use FMJs to establish a relationship with family members other than working on student/family literacy?

2. Even if you do not teach in an early childhood classroom the FMJ could be a useful method of communication. Make a list of ways you could incorporate FMJ into your content area or grade level.

3. As with any other classroom activity, there can be unexpected positives and negatives from the teacher's point of view. Find a friend or class peer to discuss this article and think about unintended consequences. Explain how you might plan for such events.

Create Central

www.mhhe.com/createcentral

Internet References

All about Adolescent Literacy
www.adlit.org/

Read, Write, Think
www.readwritethink.org/

LYNDA M. VALERIE teaches in the Department of Reading and Language Arts at Central Connecticut State University SHEILA FOSS-SWANSON teaches at the Gaffney Elementary School in New Britain, CT.

Article   Prepared by: Rebecca B. Evers, *Winthrop University*

Go Figure

Math and the Common Core

MARILYN BURNS

Learning Outcomes

After reading this article, you will be able to:

- Discuss the mental process a child might take to think about math problems.

A t a recent family dinner, my 11-year-old grandson, J. D., asked me how long ago I wrote *The I Hate Mathematics! Book*. I brought out a copy and asked him to check the copyright date, which was 1975.

"How long ago was that?" I asked. All of us around the table started to figure. After a few moments, we all agreed it was 37 years from 1975 to 2012.

"How did you figure out the answer?" I asked. (The math teacher part of me couldn't resist.)

J. D.'s 15-year-old sister, Hope, explained, "I knew it was 25 years to 2000, so I added 12 more and got 37." My husband Jeffrey did it the same way, but elaborated, "To add 25 plus 12, I added 10 and then 2." Everyone was nodding, except for J. D.

"That's not what I did," he said. His mother Deb encouraged him to explain.

J. D. said, "From 1975 to 2000 is 20 plus 5, and from 2000 to 2012 is 10 plus 2. So 20 plus 10 is 30, and 5 plus 2 is 7. It's 37."

It was quiet around the table. Then Hope said, "I don't get it." Jeffrey added, "That seems like a complicated way to figure."

"Tell me again," Deb said, trying to understand.

I was glad that Deb asked J. D. to explain again because I wasn't immediately clear about how he was thinking. I'd solved the problem the way Hope and Jeffrey did, and I had difficulty pulling myself away from the strategy we'd used to engage with the strategy J. D. had used, even as I could see that the way the rest of us solved it made little sense to him. I was reminded that one of the challenges of teaching is to listen to how students reason, rather than listening for responses we expect to hear.

Although I didn't initially understand J. D.'s reasoning, after thinking for a bit, I did—and I realized it was mathematically sound. Like the rest of us, J. D. used the year 2000 as a benchmark. He knew that it was 25 years from 1975 to 2000, and 12 more years from 2000 to 2012. To add 25 and 12, he decomposed each into its place value parts, added the tens (20 + 10) first, then added the ones (5 + 2), and then combined 30 and 7.

Math Talk and Common Core

At the time of this table talk, I was beginning to write this article about the Common Core State Standards and mathematics. I wanted to point out what's familiar in these standards and to give teachers clear access to what's different about them. I wanted to emphasize what has made me passionate about the Common Core standards—which is their two-part structure: Standards for Mathematical Practice and Standards for Mathematical Content, both equally important.

Let me start with a short description of these parts. The Standards for Mathematical Practice (referred to throughout this article as the practice standards) include the same eight standards for all grades (see "The Common Core State Standards for Mathematical Practice,"). These practice standards describe the "expertise that mathematics educators at all levels should seek to develop in their students"—that is, the ways we want students to engage with the mathematics they're learning.[1]

In contrast, the Standards for Mathematical Content include many more standards, which are different for each grade. These content standards "define what students should understand and be able to do." They are organized into domains, each of which includes clusters of related standards so as to present mathematics as a subject of closely related, connected ideas. Teaching to the Common Core standards calls for making both the practice standards and the content standards integral to classroom instruction.

So how do the Common Core standards relate to J. D. and the problem of figuring out how long ago 1975 was? This is a traditional word problem, like those that have long been part of elementary school math. In the Common Core content standards, references to whole-number word problems appear at various grade levels. In grade 4, for example, under the Operations and Algebraic Thinking domain, one cluster of standards is "use the four operations with whole numbers to solve problems." In the Number and Operations in Base Ten domain, one cluster heading is "use place value understanding and properties of operations to perform multi-digit arithmetic." Although the Common Core language may differ from the language in various states' existing math standards, the word problem we solved at dinner illustrates a typical content expectation in all of them.

Examining my family's conversation as we solved this problem can help explain the spirit and intent of the Common Core practice standards. Figuring out how long ago the book was written called for making sense of a problem that required quantitative reasoning (Practice Standards 1 and 2). We presented our arguments for how we modeled the problem with mathematics (Standards 3 and 4). We were concerned with the precision of our answers (Standard 6). Some of us questioned how J. D. reasoned (Standard 3), and Jeffrey and J. D. explained how they broke numbers apart into their place value components (Standard 7).

Embracing the Common Core standards doesn't mean that it's essential to attend to every practice standard in all math lessons. All the Standards for Mathematical Practice are important, but different ones are appropriate at different times. For example, solving the problem in this anecdote didn't provide the opportunity to express regularity in repeated reasoning (Standard 8). Also, Practice Standard 5 calls for strategically using appropriate tools that students would have access to in the classroom, such as paper and pencil, concrete models, or calculators. None of these math tools were available at the dinner table, so we engaged in mental computation. Actually, computing in our heads exemplified the expertise called for in the practice standards.

Needed: Numerical Reasoning Skills

Assessing students' facility with numerical reasoning is essential to implementing the math standards. Although the Common Core standards are all about helping students make sense of math and become mathematical thinkers, arithmetic is still the cornerstone of the Standards for Mathematical Content through 5th grade. But even when teaching the basics of arithmetic—perhaps *especially* when teaching the basics of arithmetic—the Standards for Mathematical Practice should be at the forefront of math instruction. This means, for example, that students should be able not only to figure out the answer to a problem like 15×12, but also to demonstrate an understanding of multiplication as defined by the practice standards.

Solving problems mentally too often receives limited attention in classrooms compared with paper-and-pencil computation. Although developing written computation skills is important, mental computation helps develop facility with many of the practice standards—for example, reasoning quantitatively, constructing a viable argument, and looking for and making use of structure. Mental computation is also explicitly called for in the content standards. And it's an essential life skill — for example, when dividing checks at restaurants, deciding when to leave to arrive on time for appointments, adjusting recipes, or estimating how much you'd save if you bought

something on sale. Figuring mentally is often sufficient — and more efficient than reaching for a tool.

The Math Reasoning Inventory (MRI), an online formative assessment tool I created with a team of colleagues with funding from the Bill and Melinda Gates Foundation, focuses on numerical reasoning (see "What Is the Math Reasoning Inventory?"). Our charge was to help teachers assess how their students would respond to the kind of questions the Common Core standards expect entering middle school students to answer. The core of the assessment is one-on-one interviews in which students explain how they solved problems. The website (http://mathreasoninginventory.com) hosts video clips showing students' mathematical reasoning in action.

Watching these videos is helpful because observing students mentally solve math problems and explain their reasoning helps bring meaning to the practice standards. We're all familiar with what to expect when students solve 15×12 using paper and pencil. But what should educators expect to see when they ask students to figure out the answer to 15×12 mentally? What would be evidence of understanding and mathematical expertise as defined by the Common Core standards?

Following are descriptions of how four students, three 5th graders and one 6th grader, responded when asked to mentally figure 15×12. For each student, the assessor stated the problem aloud and showed it written on a card. After each student responded, the assessor asked, "How did you figure out the answer?" Each of these students arrived at the correct answer of 180, but in a different way. (See clips of these short interviews by going to https://mathreasoninginventory.com/Home/VideoLibrary and searching by the student's name, and then by the specific math problem.)

Monica's Reasoning

Just as J. D. decomposed 12 into its place-value parts to add it more easily to 25, Monica decomposed 12 into $10 + 2$ and multiplied each part by 15. She explained, "I did 15 times 10, and it was 150. Then I did 15 times 2, which is 30, and it was ... 180." Monica used the distributive property. Her method can be represented symbolically as $15 \times 12 = (15 \times 10) + (15 \times 2) = 150 + 30 = 180$.

Alberto's Reasoning

Alberto also used the distributive property but in a way that initially surprised me. He started with something he knew— 12×12. He explained, "I did 12 times 12, [which is] 144, then I did 3 times 12 and I got 36, so I added 144 plus 36." If you watch this interview online, you'll see my surprise as Alberto explained his method. Alberto decomposed the first factor, 15, not into its place value parts, but instead into 12 plus 3. His method can be represented symbolically as $15 \times 12 = (12 \times 12) + (3 \times 12) = 144 + 36 = 180$.

Malcolm's Reasoning

Malcolm used the distributive property, but broke apart the 15 instead of the 12 so he could first multiply 10 times 12 and then 5 times 12. He explained, "I broke apart the 15 and then 10 plus 5, and then I did 10 times 12, which equals 120, and then I did 12 times 5, which equals 60, and then I added it all together and got 180." Malcolm's method can be represented symbolically as $15 \times 12 = (10 \times 12) + (5 \times 12) = 120 + 60 = 180$.

Cecilia's Reasoning

Cecilia used a very different method to figure out the answer. As she talked, she used her finger to "write" on the desktop to show how she was manipulating the numbers, as if using paper and pencil. Cecilia explained, "First, I'm breaking it into steps, and I'm doing 5 times 2. Then I leave the zero here and then I bring the 1 up here. Then 2 times 1 is 2, plus 1 is 3, so that's 30. And then 1 times 5 is . . . I mean, put a zero. Then 5 times 1 is 5, and then 1 times 1 is 1. So then the answer is 180."

Although Cecilia didn't have paper and pencil available, she simulated using them. Her method for this one problem doesn't necessarily indicate a lack of ability to reason numerically, but it would be a concern if she relied on algorithms as her only strategy for computing mentally.

It may seem surprising that students use different methods to solve the same arithmetic problem. Consider, however, that students usually write different topic sentences for the same writing assignment or that students in discussions often restate what someone else said in their own words, using alternate constructions to explain essentially the same idea. Why would we expect all students in math class to reason in the same way?

Notice how each of these learners exhibited the Common Core's practice standards. Each child persevered to solve a problem that called for quantitative reasoning (Standards 1 and 2). They each gave a viable argument (Standard 3); attended to precision (Standard 6); and used structure, breaking numbers apart to apply the distributive property (Standard 7—and a key understanding for algebra).

Natasha's Mileage Problem

It's also revealing to hear how another student, Natasha, reasoned through her solution to a different problem. The problem reads, "Molly ran 1.5 miles each day for 20 days. How many miles did she run altogether?"

In the clip, Natasha sits for a few moments looking at the problem written on a card. She hesitantly begins to explain: "I'm thinking that, I know that, in 2 days she ran 3 miles, because 1.5 times 2 would be 3 miles . . . 3 point zero. And 2 times 10 would be . . . ." Natasha stops, continues to think, scratches behind her ear, and then points again to the card, rereading the problem to herself. After being prompted to talk, she says, "OK, I know 2 days was 3 . . . 3 miles . . . and there's 20 days. So 2 times 10 is 20, so . . . ." Natasha pauses again to think, still looking at the problem on the card. After a moment, she says hesitantly, "30 miles?" She gets more confident as she constructs an argument that leads to the correct answer: "I got 30 miles because I did 15 . . . 2 days is 3 miles, and 2 times 20 days . . . 2 times blank is 20, and I got 10, and 10 times 3 is 30 miles."[2]

I've shown this video clip to many teachers, and the reaction is always the same. Everyone is tense. Watching Natasha struggle is difficult, almost excruciating. Although the clip is less than two minutes long, it seems interminable to watch Natasha as she focuses on the problem. In this clip, we see evidence of almost all the Standards for Mathematical Practice (except for 5 and 8). Natasha makes sense of problems and perseveres, impressively, in solving them. She reasons abstractly and quantitatively and constructs a viable argument—although because this was a one-on-one interview, there's no opportunity for her to critique others' reasoning. She models with mathematics (using proportional reasoning); attends to precision (she corrects her own language several times); and looks for and makes use of structure.

What We Learn From Listening

Analyzing Natasha's interview—as well as the other videotaped examples on the Math Reasoning Inventory site—shows the value of listening to students explain their reasoning. There is no way we would have learned so much about Natasha's use of the practice standards if she'd solved the problem independently with paper and pencil. The inventory is designed to assess students and then instantly provide a detailed report of the reasoning strategies and understandings that they do and don't demonstrate, which enables teachers to focus on strengthening any deficient reasoning strategies and underlying understandings about mathematics.

When teachers listen to students' math reasoning like this and realize that many students they're listening to can't demonstrate a particular strategy or understandings, instruction should change. Developing reasoning strategies and understandings should become part of the classroom culture, and at the forefront.

What Is the Math Reasoning Inventory?

The Math Reasoning Inventory (MRI) is an online tool that helps teachers assess their students' numerical proficiency. MRI focuses on the numerical skills and understandings required by the Common Core State Standards for Mathematics for students entering middle school. There are three assessments in MRI—Whole Numbers, Decimals, and Fractions. Questions are based on content from the Common Core standards up to 6th grade. Each assessment includes an interview and a short written computation section. During the interview, which is the core of MRI, the teacher asks students to explain how they figured out answers.

The MRI website (https://mathreasoning inventory.com) provides, free of charge, complete instructions and support for administering these assessments. The site also enables teachers to generate individual and class reports that analyze their students' math reasoning. It provides specific information about the reasoning strategies and understandings required for numerical proficiency and includes a library of more than 80 videos that show students solving problems during interviews.

It's important not to think about "fixing" students who don't demonstrate particular skills or understanding, because partial understanding and confusion are part of the learning process — students learn in their own ways, at their own paces. But an assessment tool like the Math Reasoning Inventory can identify areas of weaknesses in the class and should guide us to teach in ways that reinforce students who are experiencing math success while giving more support to those who need it.

We should not judge students' numerical proficiency solely on their ability to compute with paper and pencil. We've all known students who can borrow, carry, and invert and multiply yet are unaware when their answers are unreasonable. These students typically lack numerical intuition and don't see the sense in mathematics. The challenge of the Common Core standards is to help all students develop enough mathematical expertise to be prepared for college or the workplace—and successful futures.

References

National Governors Association Center for Best Practices & Council of Chief State School Officers. (2010). *Common Core Standards for Mathematics*. Washington. DC: Authors. Retrieved from www.corestandards.org/Math.

Natasha clearly meant "1.5" when she said "15." Students' language is sometimes imprecise even when their mathematical thinking is correct.

Note

1. The students shown are from a racially diverse school with a high percentage of low-income students and English language learners. Embracing the tenets of the Common Core initiative is a priority at the school; teachers have worked to help students develop the academic vocabulary they need to communicate mathematical reasoning.

Critical Thinking

1. Use a Venn diagram to compare your state's previous mathematics standards with the Common Core Mathematic standards. Be prepared to share your results.

2. Go to The Teaching Channel to watch Lynn Simpson teach reasoning about division @ https://www.teachingchannel.org/videos/common-core-teaching-division How does her teaching correspond to what the teachers in the article are doing?

3. There are critics of the Common Core. You may have read those critics in education journals. After reading this article and watching Ms. Simpson teach, how would to respond to those who think CCSS are taking schools in the wrong direction?

Create Central

www.mhhe.com/createcentral

Internet References

National Library of Virtual Manipulatives
http://nlvm.usu.edu/

MARILYN BURNS (mburns 1941 @gmail.com) is the founder of Math Solution in Sausalito, California, which provides professional development and resources; www.mathsolutions.com

Article   Prepared by: Rebecca B. Evers, *Winthrop University*

Too Much Too Soon? Common Core Math Standards in the Early Years

Laura Fricke Main

Learning Outcomes

After reading this article, you will be able to:

- Debate the issues presented to early childhood teachers in the new Common Core Math Standards.

The Common Core Math Standards have been written swiftly with a lofty implementation goal. The aim of the common core standards initiative is to have "fewer, clearer, higher standards" (Phillips and Wong 2010), yet the final document in its entirety is approximately 500 pages (Mathis 2010). While the standards have promise, there is much work to be done as a nation before we are ready to implement them, especially with our youngest students.

The Revision Process

A draft of the common core standards for mathematics was released on March 10, 2010 with a public comment period ending on April 2, 2010. At that point, the National Council for Teachers of Mathematics (NCTM) released a statement in support of the basic goals and aims of the initiative as well as having specific concerns (NCTM 2010). NCTM pointed out "a few serious placement issues" about the learning progressions being overambitious and beyond the bounds of what is knows from research (NCTM 2010). The position paper details examples of concerns including place value expectations in Kindergarten that would likely sacrifice understanding in a rush for rote responses as well as concerns about the term "the standard algorithm" when really it references the United States standard algorithm, which is one of many algorithms of which none is superior (NCTM 2010). Upon examination of the *Common Core State Standards for Mathematics* (CCSSO and NCA Center 2010), it does not appear as if these changes have been considered; however, the NCTM did endorse the final *Common Core State Standards for Mathematics* (Gewertz 2010) which was released in June, 2010.

The Common Core Standards

In the "Introduction to the Common Core State Standards", the Council of Chief State School Officers (CCSSO) and the National Governors Association Center for Best Practices (NGA Center) claim that the final version of the standards are the result of feedback from (a) the general public; (b) teachers; (c) parents; (d) business leaders; (e) states; and (f) content area experts, and that the standards themselves are informed by the standards of other high performing nations (CCSSO and NCA Center 2010). The Thomas B. Fordham Institute found that the academic standards in the common core are superior to the standards in 33 individual states (Carmichael et al. 2010). It seems that the word "informed" does not imply research-based because, if the initiative continues at the same pace and is implemented nation-wide, it places the United States at risk of performing a high stakes national experiment on our students. This is especially of concern to our youngest students, who seem to have the most to lose if these standards are implemented as written.

Investment in Standards

In 2010, in a joint position paper issued on the Common Core Standards, The National Association for the Education of Young Children (NAEYC) and the National Association of Early Childhood Specialists in State Departments of Education (NAECS-SDE) makes a claim for the urgency of:

- Comprehensive curricula and assessments
- Professional development for teachers and administrators
- Resources

Even if the Common Core standards were superior, the standards alone are not sufficient for appropriate implementation. Early learning standards require effective curriculum, classroom practices, and teaching strategies that connect the interests and abilities of children and promote their development and learning (NAEYC 2002). Professional development is essential for early childhood teachers and administrators to gain the knowledge, skills and dispositions needed to implement early learning standards (NAEYC 2002). This is true of any new initiative, yet the rush to implement the Common Core as written seems to not account for this need. Darling-Hammond (2010) warns that it is important to invest not only in well-designed assessments, but also in teacher expertise (including professional development, instructional assistance, hiring and retention) and curriculum resources. It does not appear, at least at this time, that there is time for this important work to occur.

The Promise of Standards

Munson (2011), who is president and executive director of the nonprofit research organization Common Core, (a separate organization from the Common Core Standards), advocates for a renewed focus on content knowledge as opposed to overemphasis on skills alone. This position seems to take the stance of advocating for the Standards for Mathematical Practice over the Standards for Mathematical Content in the current Common Core Standards. The practice standards, as overarching principles, are powerful, yet when coupled with the details of the Content Standards in the current Common Core, may seem less important to practitioners. There is a line buried in the introduction to the Standards for Mathematical Practice which warns, "Designers of curricula, assessments, and professional development should all attend to the need to connect the mathematical practices to the mathematical content in mathematics instruction" (www.corestandards.org). While the Mathematical Practices emphasize understanding, it will take leadership at the state and local levels to emphasize these over the discrete standards which, on balance, lean more towards skill development.

Munson (2011) points out that the Common Core Standards are not curriculum in and of themselves and will mean little if implemented ineffectively. Reys and Lappan (2007) argue that in order to implement coherent, rigorous curriculum for all students, there is a need for leadership, cooperation and collaboration. Curriculum is needed for implementation and is another reason to delay implementation so that there is time to research, select and align local curricula appropriately.

NAEYC and NAECS-SDE (2010) agree that standards that are challenging, achievable, and appropriate to children's development are important for the success of every child. The question is not, "Should we have standards?" but instead, "Are the Common Core Standards, as written, appropriate?" It seems that there is more work to do and more discussions that need to occur before implementing the Common Core on a national scale.

Criticism of the Common Core

The development of the Common Core Standards was quick (approximately 1 year) with little input from school-based practitioners, yet in most standards efforts, there is both extensive practitioner involvement and public hearings conducted over the course of several years (Mathis 2010).

Mathis (2010) condemns the core standards with his claims that standards alone do not determine how well each state performs because those with high standards do no better (or worse) than those which have been identified as having low standards. Mathis (2010) also points out that very little evidence supports that having national academic standards will improve the quality of American public education and the push towards having these standards may pull the attention from other needed reforms in schools.

International Comparisons

Milgram (2010) condemns the Common Core Standards noting that there are "many serious flaws". He claims that he was not able to certify that the Common Core Mathematics Standards are benchmarked at the same level as standards of other high achieving countries (Milgram 2010).

The Trends in International Mathematics and Science Study (TIMSS) demonstrate that on eighth grade math and science tests, eight of the 10 top scoring countries had national standards, but so did nine of the 10 lowest scoring countries in math (Kohn 2010). McCluskey (2010) points out that on the most recent TIMSS to include high school seniors, done in 1995, the United States finished poorly in the combined math and science literacy scale, fourth from the last. The three nations it outperformed all had national standards, but 3 out of the 5 top performing countries did not have national standards, including the top performer (McCluskey 2010). Another study found no correlation between the rigor of a particular state's standards and its National Association for Educational Progress (NAEP) scores (Whitehurst 2009).

The introduction to the Common Core State Standards claims that all research has been considered (www.corestandards.org/assets/ccssi-introduction.pdf), yet an example of a particular standard for young children that appears to lack a research base is the kindergarten place value standard:

Work with Numbers 11–19 to gain Foundations for Place Value.

K.NBT.1. Compose and decompose numbers from 11 to 19 into ten ones and some further ones, e.g., by using objects or drawings, and record each composition or decomposition by a drawing or equation (such as 18 = 10 + 8); understand that these numbers are composed of ten ones and one, two, three, four, five, six, seven, eight, or nine ones.

This particular standard is repeated in first grade as well which makes it unclear why it is a kindergarten standard at all. The first grade place value standard is:

Understand Place Value.
1.NBT.2. Understand that the two digits of a two-digit number represents amounts of tens and ones. Understand the following as special cases:

a. 10 can be thought of as a bundle of ten ones- called a "ten."
b. The numbers from 11 to 19 are composed of ten and one, two, three, four, five, six, seven, eight or nine ones.
c. The numbers 10, 20, 30, 40, 50, 60, 70, 80, 90 refer to one, two, three, four, five, six, seven, eight or nine tens (and 0 ones).

It seems that these standards expect children to progress at an unprecedented rate through the primary years that seems to require our youngest students to make a leap that research out of Western Australia suggests that they are not ready to make developmentally. The research found that children enter what is called the partitioning phase between the ages 6 and 9 and by the end of this phase, usually between ages 9 and 11, children can partition at least two and three digit numbers into parts (Western Australian Minister for Education 2006). While certainly some children in kindergarten and first grade can achieve these standards, is this truly achievable for all students even with the best curriculum and the best instruction? While a range of development is acknowledged by the writers of the Common Core in the introduction to the Common Core State Standards for Mathematics, the standards themselves are meant to "provide a consistent, clear understanding of what students are expected to learn" (www.corestandards.org). It seems as if there is more work to be done before making this claim. The introduction to the Common Core State Standards acknowledges that there is "more to be learned about the most essential knowledge for student success" (www.corestandards.org), yet it appears we are forging forward without this full understanding.

Standards and Assessment

In all likelihood, the core standards will be accompanied by a national standardized test (Kohn 2010). Ravitch (2010), referring her 180° turn on her position on No Child Left Behind (NCLB), states that the nations with successful school systems do not narrowly focus success in their schools on two skill-based subjects as measured by standardized test scores. Ravitch (2010) states that a good accountability system should include professional judgment and other measures of student achievement as opposed to simply test scores. She takes this one step further, warning that schools who expect only the basic skills from their students will not produce graduates who are college or workplace ready (Ravitch 2010). Her concern is that, by overemphasizing test scores to the exclusion of other goals, one may undermine both a love of learning and the desire to acquire knowledge, which are necessary for intrinsic motivation (Ravitch 2010). Mathis (2010) points out that the standards have not been field tested and that it is unclear whether the tests that will be used to measure the outcomes of the standards will have validity to justify the consequences that will likely arise.

Standards and Young Children

In a position statement, the National Association for the Education of Young Children (NAEYC) recognized the ethical responsibility to use standards; however it is unrealistic to expect that standards be fully implemented without the benefit of policies and funding that supports a system of high-quality developmentally appropriate experiences for all children (NAEYC 2009). In a joint position statement by NAEYC and the National Association of Early Childhood Specialists in the State Departments of Education (NAECS-SDE), the process of developing early learning standards should rely on expertise, stakeholder involvement and regular evaluation and review; the ways in which standards are developed and reviewed contribute to their credibility and effectiveness (NAEYC 2002).

In the joint position statement on the Common Core, NAEYC and NAECS-SDE (2010) remind that standards are not new to early childhood education, but that the characteristics of early childhood must be considered and that a developmental continuum of standards, curriculum and assessments would better support the transitions of young children from the early years into later schooling.

In reading a joint position statement of NAEYC and NCTM, which was adopted in 2002 and updated in 2010, it appears that there is indeed much work to be done prior to the implementation of the Common Core. The position statement argues that to support high quality mathematics education, institutions, program developers, and policy makers should:

a. create more effective early childhood teacher preparation and continuing professional development;
b. use collaborative processes to develop alignment of appropriate high-quality standards, curriculum and assessment;
c. design structures and policies that support ongoing teacher learning, teamwork and planning; and
d. provide resources to overcome barriers to young children's proficiencies at mathematics at the classroom, community, institutional and system-wide levels (NAEYC and NCTM 2010).

The position statement supports that high-quality, challenging and accessible mathematics is a fundamental foundation to future mathematics learning (NAEYC 2009). According to Bredekamp (2004), the challenges of such a task, especially for young children, are to ensure that:

- innovation is not stifled;
- children are not put into inappropriate categories;
- individual or cultural differences are not ignored;
- the end result is not a narrow, superficial teaching that fails to give children a solid foundation.

More Time is Needed

Mathis (2010) recommends that:

a. the initiative continue, but that it take the form of a low stakes advisory and assistance tool for the states as a way of improving curriculum and professional development;
b. Common Core standards be subjected to extensive validation, trials and revisions before they are implemented thus allowing for careful examination and experimentation by school-based practitioners; and
c. Policymakers not implement high stakes accountability when the assessments used to measure such accountability are inadequate.

These recommendations are sound and, if considered, would allow states and in turn local districts to have time to improve curriculum and professional development opportunities for teachers in mathematics while the Common Core standards themselves are subjected to scientifically-based research. Assessments would be able to be properly developed that are aligned with the standards and would also be subjected to the same time of scientific scrutiny as the standards themselves prior to being used for high stakes purposes.

Recommendations

Given the swiftness of the initiative, it would be wise to use caution when moving forward with the common core standards as written. Cooperation, collaboration and professional development is needed before we experiment with our children. In considering the Common Core Standards as a working draft, educators would then have the opportunity to develop curriculum, assessments and professional development that would allow for the initiative to progress, albeit at a slower pace. Our youngest learners deserve the most scrutiny as they seem to have the most to lose should this initiative fail. The pace is too swift and the details of the expectations for our youngest students are not being carefully linked with the research. I would urge early childhood educators to read the standards carefully and engage in a national conversation prior to implementation of the Common Core Mathematics Standards.

References

Bredekamp, S. (2004). Standards for preschool and kindergarten mathematics education. In D. H. Clements, J. Sarama, & A. M. DiBiase (Eds.), *Engaging young children in mathematics: standards for early childhood mathematics education* (pp. 77–82). Mahwah, NJ: Lawrence Erlbaum.

Carmichael, S. B., Martino, G., Porter-Magee, K., Wilson, W. S., Fairchild, D., Haydel, E., Senechal, D., & Winkler, A. M. (2010). *The state of the slate standards and the common core-2010*. Washington: Thomas B. Fordham Institute. Retrieved from www.edexcellence.net/index.cfm/news_the-state-of-state-standards-and-the-common-core-in-2010.

Council of Chief State School Officers & National Governors Association Center for Best Practices. (2010). *Common core state standards for mathematics*. Common Core State Standards Initiative. Retrieved from www.corestandards.org/assets/CCSSI_Math%20Standards.pdf.

Council of Chief State School Officers & National Governors Association Center for Best Practices. (2010). *Introduction to the common core state standards*. Common Core State Standards Initiative. Retrieved from www.corestandards.org/assets/ccssi-introduction.pdf.

Council of Chief State School Officers & National Governors Association Center for Best Practices. (2010). *Introduction. Standards for mathematical practice*. Common Core State Standards Initiative. Retreived from www.corestandards.org/the-standards/mathematics/introduction/standards-for-mathematical-practice.

Darling-Hammond, L. (2010). *The flat world and education: How America's commitment to equity will determine our future*. New York, NY: Teachers College Press.

Gewertz, C. (2010, June 9). Allies shift focus toward promoting standards adoption. *Education Week, 29*(33), 1, 18–19.

Kohn, A. (2010, January 14). *Debunking the case for national standards: One size fits all mandates and their dangers*. Retrieved from www.alfiekohn.org/teaching/edweek/national.htm.

Mathis, W. J. (2010). *The "common core" standards initiative: An effective reform tool?* Boulder and Tempe: Education and the Public Interest Center & Education Policy Research Unit. Retrieved from www.epicpolicy.org/publication/common-core-standards.

McCluskey, N. (2010, February 17). *Behind the curtain: Assessing the case for national curriculum standards*. Washington: CATO Foundation, policy analysis 66. Retrieved from www.cato.org/pub_display.php?pub_id=11217.

Milgram, R. J. (2010). *Review of final draft core standards*. Testimony to the California Academic Content Standards Commission. Retrieved from www.concernedabouteducation.posterous.com/review-of-common-core-math-standards.

Munson, L. (2011). What students really need to learn: Top-performing nations set their instructional sights on far more than basic reading and math skills. *Educational Leadership, 68*(6), 10–14.

National Association for the Education of Young Children. (2009). *Developmentally appropriate practice in early childhood programs serving children from birth through age 8*. Washington: National Association for the Education of Young Children. Retrieved from www.naeyc.org/files/naeyc/file/positions/PSDAP.pdf.

National Association for the Education of Young Children & National Association of Early Childhood Specialists in State Departments of Education. (2002). *Early learning standards: Creating the conditions for success*. Washington: National Association for the Education of Young Children. Retrieved from www.naeyc.org/files/naeyc/file/positions/position_statement.pdf.

National Association for the Education of Young Children & National Association of Early Childhood Specialists in State Departments of Education. (2010). *Joint statement of the National Association for the Education of Young Children and the National Association of the Early Childhood Specialists in State Departments of Education on the common core standards initiative related to kindergarten through third grade*. Washington: National Association for the Education of Young Children. Retrieved from www.naeyc.org/files/naeyc/file/policy/NAEYC-NAECS-SDE-Core-Standards-Statement.pdf.

National Association for the Education of Young Children & National Council of Teachers of Mathematics. (2010). *Early childhood mathematics: Promoting good beginnings*. Washington: National Association for the Education of Young Children. Retrieved from www.naeyc.org/files/naeyc/file/positions/psmath.pdf.

National Council of Teachers of Mathematics. (2010). *NCTM public comments on the common core standards for mathematics*. Retrieved from www.nctm.org/about/content.aspx?id=25186.

Phillips, V., & Wong, C. (2010). Tying together the common core of standards, instruction and assessment. *Phi Delta Kappan, 91*(5), 37–42.

Ravitch, D. (2010). *The death and life of the great American school system*. New York, NY: Basic Books.

Reys, B., & Lappan, G. (2007). Consensus or confusion? The intended math curriculum in state-level standards. *Phi Delta Kappan, 88*(9), 676–680.

Western Australian Minister for Education. (2006). *First steps in mathematics volume 1: Understand whole and decimal numbers, understand fractional numbers*. Beverly, MA: STEPS Professional Development.

Whitehurst, G, (2009, October 14). *Don't forget curriculum.* Providence: Brown Center Letters on Education, #3. Retrieved February 11, 2010, from www.brookings.edu/papers/2009/1014_ curriculum_whitehurst.aspx.

Critical Thinking

1. Have you seen the Common Core Math Standards? If not, go to www.corestandards.org/the-standards/mathematics to find the standards for the grade you teach. What is your first reaction?

2. Based on the grade you will be or are teaching, do you agree with Main's criticism of the standards? Provide specific rationales for your answer.

3. Review the articles in Unit 1 that discuss our international standing in mathematics. Do you believe that we need national standards rather than local standards? What might be the benefits of national standards? What might be the negative consequences of national standards?

4. Has your state adopted the Common Core? If possible, find a local administrator or teacher to discuss their professional opinion of the standards. Prepare a response to share in class discussion.

Create Central

www.mhhe.com/createcentral

Internet References

National Council of Teachers of Mathematics
    www.nctm.org

LAURA FRICKE MAIN teaches at Western Connecticut State University.

Main, Laura Fricke. From *Early Childhood Education Journal*, September 2011, pp. 73–77. Copyright © 2011 by Springer Science and Business Media. Reprinted by permission via Rightslink.

Unit 4

UNIT

Prepared by: Rebecca B. Evers, *Winthrop University*

Improve School Climate to Improve Student Performance

All of us are situated in social, political, and economic circumstances, which inform and develop our values. Our values are usually derived from principles of conduct that we learn in each of our histories of interaction with ourselves (as they form) and in interaction with others. This is to say that societal values develop in a cultural context. Teachers cannot hide all of their moral preferences. They can, however, learn to conduct just and open discussions of moral topics without succumbing to the temptation to indoctrinate students with their own views. In democratic societies, such as the United States, alternative sets of values and morals co-exist. What teachers perceive to be worthwhile and defensible behavior informs our reflections on what we as educators should teach. We are immediately conscious of some of the values that affect our behavior, but we may not be as aware of what informs our preferences. Values that we hold without being conscious of them are referred to as tacit values: these are values derived indirectly after reasoned reflection on our thoughts about teaching and learning. Much of our knowledge about teaching is tacit knowledge, which we need to bring into conscious cognition by analyzing the concepts that drive practice. We need to acknowledge how all of our values inform—and influence—our thoughts about teaching. Teachers grapple with the dilemma of their own values versus the values of their students.

Students need to develop a sense of genuine caring both for themselves and others. Teacher must model and teach students how to be a caring community of learners by building positive relationships with the students, their parents, and the community outside the school. The articles in this unit offer practices and suggestions to help teachers create caring communities of learners.

Age appropriate social skills are an important component of caring communities of learners. Sparks argues labeling between the sexes may cause boys and girls to mature and learn differently. Further, she asserts that through teacher modeling, in a classroom that is free of labels and gender expectations, a more integrated classroom can be developed where social skills and productive relationships are created.

In Zakin's article, *Hand to Hand,* there are four primary assertions: getting along with others in a multicultural society is essential; for the best results, teach tolerance to young children; this skill should be explicitly taught in preschool curriculum; and art is the perfect teaching tool. Once that has been said, the author explains why and how to teach tolerance within the early childhood classroom and provides step-by-step instructions for use in K-6 classrooms including student comments. Creative art teachers would be able to implement this technique in higher grades with little adjustments.

Tommie Lindsey is a teacher who cared enough about the students in his Oakland, CA high school to have high expectations for them and for him. Over the years, he worked with young African-American men and women to build trust and a relationship as he taught skills of forensics and later established a class in life skills. His work has been the topic of an award winning documentary film and he has been awarded grants to fund his work. His article with Mabie explains the four student supports he provides in the life skills class. Lehman echoes much of what Lindsey says and does, when he argues only assuring that teacher candidates are highly qualified in their subject area is not enough. Attention must be given to the importance of the candidates' drive to do what is necessary to engage students. Lehman believes it is the enthusiasm for one's students that produces lifelong learners.

Establishing positive relationships and making sure that we use the appropriate currency to motivate students does not mean we are "fluffy" or "soft" in our attention to the real work of schools. In the article, *She's Strict for a Good Reason,* researchers share the stories of 31 teachers whose students are high achievers in low-performing, high-poverty, and high-minority schools. How do they do it when others around them are failing? The researchers found these teachers had common behaviors in the classroom and held similar beliefs about their responsibilities as teachers.

Article   Prepared by: *Rebecca B. Evers, Winthrop University*

Scholars Say Pupils Gain Social Skills In Coed Classes

SARAH D. SPARKS

Learning Outcomes

After reading this article, you will be able to:

- Debate the pros and cons of coed classes

Preschool teacher Jacque Radke started the school year at Kenilworth Elementary in Phoenix with a pretty typical bunch of 3-, 4-, and 5-year-olds. Some of the girls had started to form cliques and "no boys allowed" lunch tables, while Ms. Radke and her instructional assistant worried that one quiet little girl was getting shunted to the sidelines by the boys.

Generally, boys and girls become more polarized through their first years in school. Now, researchers have started to explore how to span that sex divide and are finding that more-equitable coed classrooms can have social and academic benefits for boys and girls alike.

While children of both sexes play together as toddlers, by the end of kindergarten, they spend only 9 percent of their playtime with children of the other sex, according to research by Lise S. Eliot, an associate professor of neuroscience at the Chicago Medical School.

"Separation is a fact of human childhood and is equally common among young monkeys and apes," Ms. Eliot says in the 2009 Houghton Mifflin Harcourt book *Pink Brain, Blue Brain: How Small Differences Grow Into Troublesome Gaps and What We Can Do About It.* That early separation, she says, creates "two separate cultures that persist throughout childhood."

But researchers at the American Educational Research Association's annual conference, held in Vancouver, British Columbia, last month, stressed that while all children naturally develop gender identity, classroom demographics and teacher practices can make a big difference in how and whether students develop sex-based stereotypes and prejudices.

Not 'Hard-Wired'

In a meta-analysis of studies based on more than 7 million children in kindergarten through 11th grade, Janet S. Hyde, a psychology professor at the University of Wisconsin-Madison found small average gender differences in such areas as activity level (favoring boys) and ability to focus (favoring girls), but no significant differences in mathematics or reading comprehension and "no solid evidence that boys and girls actually learn differently."

"You never hear a good, modern neuroscientist say the brain is hard-wired," Ms. Hyde said. "In fact, it is characterized by great neural plasticity, so . . . any differences you see are at least as likely caused by differences in the experiences of males and females as to any kind of anatomical differences present from birth."

Even if boys and girls don't learn differently, classroom demographics can change how students learn, according to research by Erin E. Pahlke, an assistant research professor of social and family dynamics at Arizona State University in Tempe. Ms. Pahlke analyzed the achievement of more than 21,000 pupils in the federal Early Childhood Longitudinal Study-Kindergarten Cohort, and found that as the percentage of girls in a kindergarten or 1st grade classroom increased, the reading and math achievement of both boys and girls at the end of 1st grade rose, too.

Moreover, boys and girls in classes near sex parity had better self-control than those of either sex in a class in which they were the dominant majority, 80 percent or more.

Ms. Pahlke said she was still digging into the reasons why coed parity might be beneficial, but a few things jumped out at her. For one, teachers reported classes with more girls as better behaved, which could translate into better interpersonal skills and more time on task for learning, yet she cautioned that girls do not behave better when they are the overwhelming majority in the classroom.

Teacher Modeling

Teacher stereotypes about student abilities may also be tempered in a more balanced classroom, Ms. Pahlke said. Prior research has shown that teachers' own beliefs about gender stereotypes—such as that girls perform worse in math, or boys in reading—can bring down their students' performance.

"In a class where teachers see there are more boys in the classroom, and I would argue teachers are hyperaware of these issues, . . . maybe in a math class where they have more boys they say: 'Oh, boys are better in math. I can use more-advanced-math approaches in my classroom,'" Ms. Pahlke said, "and it could work the other way in reading."

Seemingly benign and insignificant practices, such as greeting students with "Good morning, boys and girls," or seating students boy-girl-boy-girl, can have big and unintended consequences, according to other, ongoing studies of social labeling and group identity.

Rebecca S. Bigler, an associate professor of psychology at the University of Texas at Austin, has studied how children develop a sense of group differences and biases, especially related to gender and race.

Both Ms. Radke, the Phoenix preschool teacher, and her instructional assistant Erica K Flynn, said they routinely referred to their preschool classes by gender.

"Growing up, I'd always seen, oh, boys are in this line and girls are in this line, and I'd not thought anything about it," Ms. Flynn said.

Yet even casually organizing students by gender or mentioning it in a way that labels causes boys and girls to develop the idea that gender is fundamentally oppositional, in ways the teacher has not mentioned or discussed, Ms. Bigler's and other research has shown.

"If you compare it to race, if you said to your 1st grade classrooms, 'Good morning, whites and Latinos; let's have the Latinos get your pencils,' what would happen is you would go to federal prison," Ms. Bigler said. "Labeling children routinely by race in your classroom is a violation of federal law, and, of course, you can do this routinely with gender."

While infants as young as 6 months can differentiate people by gender, they can also differentiate by any number of other characteristics, from ethnicity to hat wearing, she said. They look to an adult's behavior to decide which differences are important in a given context.

"Children can attend to any salient difference set out in their environment," Ms. Bigler said. "Labeling is especially powerful," she noted; using a noun description like calling someone a "hat wearer," rather than saying "he likes to wear hats often," makes the description seem more permanent and intrinsic in children's minds.

In one series of experiments discussed at the research conference, elementary school students were separated into two random groups and given either red or blue shirts to wear for the duration of the summer session. In some classrooms, the teachers were asked to hand out the shirts and never mention them again. In others, teachers were asked to use them casually to group students—asking students to form a red line and a blue line, using separate red and blue cubbies or asking, "Let's have the red students turn in their books now."

In some versions, the blue- and red-shirted pupils were put in separate classrooms.

At the end of the summer session, Ms. Bigler said, "what we find is when teachers use groups to label children in their classrooms, you get the formation of stereotyping and prejudice, and when teachers ignore the presence of those groups in their classrooms, you do not find stereotyping and prejudice."

That sort of adult modeling may help explain why children in their first few years of school are far more rigidly oriented along gender lines than toddlers or even the adults they will become.

During that period of schooling, children begin to play and interact overwhelmingly with others of their own sex and become less comfortable interacting with those of the other sex, according to Laura D. Hanish, the co-director of the Lives of Girls and Boys: Initiatives on Gender Development and Relationships project at Arizona State.

Ms. Hanish's research found that when boys and girls played mostly with same-sex classmates in preschool, they began to behave in more gender-stereotyped ways: Boys played farther from teachers, became more aggressive, and used more "rough and tumble" play over time; girls moved closer to teachers and included more gendered play.

"As girls play with other girls, they start to become more skilled in the interactional styles and patterns typical of girls and less skilled in the interactional styles and patterns associated with boys," Ms. Hanish said. "You start to see increasing segregation. Children develop a fairly limited set of interaction skills: less understanding, appreciation, respect of one another.

"All of that can translate into a host of problems across classrooms," she said. "It can translate to less effective interactions across academic tasks, harassment, bullying."

Building Relationships

The Sanford Harmony Program at Arizona State is working with schools to ease the polarization of boys and girls in early grades without preventing normal gender identification. In Phoenix, Ms. Radke and Ms. Flynn are part of an experimental curriculum intended to re-engage boys and girls in two critical transition grades, preschool and 5th grade.

The educators received professional development on gender biases and child development, including research on teacher labeling.

"It was an eye-opening thing realizing how many times I was inadvertently categorizing the children in biases based on whether they were boys or girls," Ms. Radke recalled. "There was personal self-awareness that came out."

Throughout this school year, Ms. Radke and Ms. Flynn have not directly discussed gender with their students, but each week, every child is paired with a new "class buddy" of the other sex. Every day, buddies do a different activity together, from art projects and music to active physical games outside.

The program also includes regular activities to teach the children social skills, such as listening, sharing, and cooperation.

In a preliminary study of 94 preschool and 199 5th grade low-income students in matched classrooms, Ms. Hanish found students who participated in the buddy matching and social curriculum were more socially competent, less aggressive, less exclusionary, and showed better social skills toward both boys and girls.

Teachers of students in the program also reported that those children were better behaved and better at following directions than those from nonparticipating classrooms.

The Phoenix educators said the program has made a big difference in their students' general behavior and their relationships with one another over the course of the year.

"Every Monday, they're excited to come in and see who their new buddy is," Ms. Radke said. "What we began to see was on their own, they would sit with their buddy for the sit-down, read-aloud activity. . . . Not every buddy partnership works well, but I resisted the temptation to change it, because there were a lot of odd couples that ended up working well."

The cliquishness at the beginning of the year has dissipated, Ms. Flynn said, and across the board, students are now more likely to play together, cooperate, and help each other. Even the youngest girl has become accepted by her bigger classmates and speaks more often.

"Before, there was a lot more arguing," Ms. Radke said. "Now, well hear them say 'good job' or 'it's OK'—really supportive words. It's like they're kinder to each other."

Moreover, she said, the small-scale bullying that was common earlier in the year, such as telling a child he was not a friend, or she couldn't sit with a particular group at lunch, has vanished.

"I truly believe that as the children engage in structured buddy activities, they are learning to know each other, and this connection is reflected by growth in their patience and tolerance as they interact together throughout the day," Ms. Radke said. "Not hearing that [bullying] language is a huge change in our class."

Critical Thinking

1. Research cited in this article found that there is "no solid evidence that boys and girls actually learn differently" and that "any differences . . . likely caused by difference in experiences. . . ." What evidence was provided to illustrate the accuracy of these statements? What questions remain for you?

2. Based on what you have read in this article, how would you vote if a referendum for single gender classrooms came to your school district? Would your vote change if you were a parent rather than a teacher? Provide at least two reasons for each of your answers.

Create Central

www.mhhe.com/createcentral

Internet References

What Kids Can Do
  http://www.whatkidscando.org/

SARAH D. SPARKS covers education research and tracks education happenings in Idaho, Maine, South Carolina, and Tennessee

Article   Prepared by: Rebecca B. Evers, *Winthrop University*

Hand to Hand
Teaching Tolerance and Social Justice One Child at a Time

ANDREA ZAKIN

Learning Outcomes

After reading this article, you will be able to:

- Design a plan for establishing positive relationships with and among your students.

- Design a plan for integrating social justice into your grade level curriculum or content area.

Many educators (Cohen, 2006, 2007; Jones, 2004; Stevens & Charles, 2005) believe that teaching tolerance is a pedagogical imperative, while others relegate children's moral development to the purview of parents. Still others (Barrier-Ferreira, 2008; Jones, 2004; Mustakova-Poussardt, 2004; Paley and the Teaching Tolerance Project, 1998) go beyond tolerance to promote instruction in social justice. Tolerance connotes patience, forbearance, and impartiality, as well as open-mindedness. In early childhood, possessing tolerance would refer to children's burgeoning awareness of themselves in relation to others, and the capability to accept appearance and behavior different from one's own. But is teaching tolerance, additionally considered the ability to care and have empathy for others, enough? Perhaps it is more appropriate to teach preschool children tolerance in conjunction with social justice, the principles and habits of mind that guide individuals to actively treat others with fairness, respect, and responsibility ("Social justice," n.d.). Social justice for preschool children would indicate an ability to treat others with fairness, even if that means putting the needs of others above one's own. It may be that teaching tolerance for very young children essentially sets the stage for a more developed understanding of tolerance and justice to grow as children move on to elementary school and beyond.

This article maintains that: 1) the capability to get along with others in a multicultural community is an essential life skill that must be explicitly taught in school (Stevens & Charles, 2005); 2) teaching tolerance and social justice is best initiated when children are young (Paley and the Teaching Tolerance Project,

1998); 3) tolerance and social justice should be included in preschool and school curricula; and 4) art is a perfect vehicle for teaching tolerance and social justice. Although it is difficult to know where tolerance ends and social justice begins, social justice incorporates action and not just talk. For preschoolers, this would mean actively demonstrating tolerance and acceptance of others during everyday activities.

I decided to work with a group of young children and their teachers in a preschool setting that would welcome interdisciplinary activities predicated on art making, with the goal of exploring diversity in terms of skin color. The purpose of the unit was to discover if young children could and would explore differences verbally and through art. Investigating skin color can be considered a first step in teaching tolerance and social justice. Preschool children learn to accept themselves and others, to treat other people with fairness and respect, and to translate that understanding into action by participating in continuing activities that help others in their classroom, school, and community. As children mature in upper elementary school, and into middle and high school, they also can explore the difficulties of accepting differences, learn why some people consider diversity to be threatening, and discover how acceptance of differences among people makes them feel. To be meaningful, teaching tolerance and social justice cannot just be a solitary or rare occurrence; the topic must be carefully sequenced and integrated into ongoing school curricula.

Why Teach Tolerance and Social Justice?

Today's schools are more diverse than ever before. Yet, the concerted emphasis on academic achievement (quantified by standardized assessment) precludes sufficient attention to children's social and interpersonal growth, including their ability to learn with and from others, particularly those different from themselves (Cohen, 2007; Edmondson, Fetro, Drolet, & Ritzel, 2007; Inlay, 2005; Merrow, 2004; Mustakova-Poussardt, 2004). Often, there is simply not enough time or teacher sophistication to teach children how to accept difference with regard to race, ethnicity, culture, religion, socioeconomic background, gender orientation, and ability.

Contrary to common belief, the research shows that young children are aware of differences such as skin color; they just do not pay much attention to it (Masko, 2005). If, however, they are free to comment on and learn about diversity from an early age, they are less likely to internalize unspoken negative messages about difference as they grow older, which can culminate in a learned hierarchy that is then enacted throughout their lives (Jones, 2004; Masko, 2005). Children, therefore, require help to acknowledge and make sense of diversity so that they can begin to develop empathy for others rather than judging them for being different from themselves (Paley et al., 1998). School is a key place for children to learn about diversity, and their ability to accept difference is dependent on teacher attitude (Hollingsworth, Didelot, & Smith, 2003).

Even when preschoolers feel free to remark on skin color, for instance, this easy frankness is unlikely to continue in the years to come. Yet articulating difference tends to diffuse it, rendering it interesting but unthreatening (Hollingsworth et al., 2003; Richards, Brown, & Forde, 2007). Thus, teaching tolerance should happen early and often. Unfortunately, discussion of controversial issues, such as diversity of skin color, is not a common occurrence even in the social studies classroom, an expected site of such exchanges (Nystrand, Gamoran, & Carbonaro, 1998).

For young children, tolerating and accepting diversity start with recognition of the self in relation to others, which leads to an appreciation of difference and similarity. Appreciation of difference reveals individual uniqueness, and enhances self-acceptance and self-esteem, while appreciation of similarity furthers identification with others, including those in the classroom community. Both difference and similarity stem from observation—the ability to discern and make sense of perceived details. This is another reason why art should be central to a teaching tolerance curriculum.

It is eminently possible to incorporate teaching tolerance and social justice with social studies, particularly in an integrated curriculum (see Table 1). Pelo (2008) claims that early childhood programs predicated on social justice prioritize anti-bias, culturally sensitive teaching and learning. Teachers call attention to the ways in which people are different and the ways in which people are the same, honoring individual and group identity. They intentionally introduce issues of fairness and unfairness, and coach children to think critically and to take action. Teachers learn about children's family and cultural identities and integrate those identities into the daily life of the classroom, at the same time as they acknowledge the ways in which their own cultural identities shape their teaching.

Preschools that promote social justice encourage young children to share, wait their turn, care for a friend who feels sad, help a child who is hurt, and refrain from grabbing, fighting, or using harmful words. Since the literature encourages meeting differences head-on, I decided to design a series of interconnected, interdisciplinary art activities. Then, I located a school that embraced teaching tolerance and social justice, had

attributes such as those Pelo describes above, and would welcome a collaboratively taught unit.

Teaching Tolerance and Social Justice through Art

As an art educator who also teaches general education teacher candidates, I contend that art is an indispensable tool in an integrated curriculum, a helpful adjunct for students with different learning styles, and an expedient way to teach tolerance and social justice. Art is a subject that allows children to concretely express their thoughts and feelings about themselves and the world around them (Freedman, 2000; Greene, 2007; Smith, 1993). In addition to allowing for the expression of emotion, art also involves cognitive and metacognitive functioning, thus motivating children to reflect on how they think and learn in a seamless integration of their thinking and feeling selves (Eisner, 2002; Gardner, 1993, 1999; Greene, 2007).

More specifically, multicultural art education can help children learn to appreciate and understand difference as well as the worldviews and belief systems of other cultures. Ballengee-Morris and Stuhr (2001) consider multicultural art education to be an integral part of school reform that teaches students to look at cultural traditions, including their own, as well as that of others, from critical and multiple perspectives. Young children need a means of expressing their feelings. Eisner (2002) maintains that art provides students with a language to articulate and take ownership of these ideas. Multicultural art activities, moreover, seem tailor-made for a preK-6 social studies curriculum.

The Project

While the project is equally appropriate for preschool and elementary school-age children, I elected to work with 4- and 5-year-old children because the age range bridges preschool and elementary school, and because teaching tolerance should start young. The lessons incorporate literacy (reading and oral communication) and social studies (awareness of self and others, and of differences in skin color the world over) with art (art making and response to art). The curriculum unit, based on close observation, brings skin color to center stage in children's awareness. It becomes a topic in ongoing class conversations, helping children to learn that while everyone is of a certain color, no color is better or worse than any other. The combination of concrete, focused, artistic exploration, in conjunction with open discussion, widens boundaries and awakens consciousness.

The Preschool

During initial meetings with the director and teachers, I became familiar with the school's educational philosophy, premises, classes, teachers, and children. The preschool, a parent-run cooperative located in the Bronx, New York, accepts children ages 2 to 5, who continue on to attend neighborhood

Table 1 Relationship of Teaching Tolerance and Social Justice/Multicultural Art Activities and PreK-6th-Grade Social Studies Curriculum

Grade	Social Studies Curriculum	Actualized through Multicultural / Teaching Tolerance Art Activities
Pre-kindergarten-1st grade	Kindergarten curriculum emphasizes the self in relation to others. Focus is on interdisciplinary activities that enhance children's awareness of their unique qualities as well as their similarities with others. Through written and oral narrative, young children learn about values, ideas, and traditions by relating to others within their classroom community. 1st-grade curriculum emphasizes the family in relation to other families (past and present) and their traditions, and explores children's identity and roles as members of their family and community.	Mixing skin tone, stamping hand prints, painting one's hand with multicultural paint, and creating a self-portrait collage using multicultural paper show young children that their skin tone is unique and that everyone has a skin color. Consequendy, they become aware of who they are in relation to the group. Reading children's picturebooks that present children of different colors and in various countries, and viewing the Native American poster, reinforces children's beginning understanding of the similarities and differences between themselves and others, including the traditions of their families and those of others.
2nd-3rd grade	2nd-grade curriculum emphasizes different kinds of communities, particularly the child's community as a model of other communities elsewhere. Focus includes children's contributions to their community. 3rd-grade curriculum emphasizes an examination of world communities, including the nature of, and similarities and differences among, different cultures and civilizations.	The activities mentioned above contribute to children's beginning understandings of their identity in terms of similarities and differences within their families and their communities, starting with their classroom community. Children take on more responsibility by completing the art activities by themselves or with the help of a partner. Children learn about the traditions of others by reading children's picturebooks that portray children from around the world and provide a scientific explanation for the existence of different skin colors, and by studying the artwork of world artists.
4th-6th grade	4th-grade curriculum emphasizes local history and government (e.g., children's families, school, and community), including an exploration of Native American and colonial American cultures. 5th-grade curriculum extends this investigation to a national level and includes countries in geographic proximity to the United States. 6th-grade curriculum emphasizes the interdependence of all peoples, with a particular focus on Eastern countries.	The activities mentioned above contribute to children's deepening understandings of themselves (as part of a larger community) in relation to others in their country and in other countries. Additional art activities (self-portrait object/face) explore representations of the self in relation to world artists.

kindergarten programs. Sixty-six children attended the preschool the year I completed my research. The families are diverse in terms of ethnicity, race, income, profession, and family style. There were 20 children in the 4s/5s classroom (nine boys and eleven girls). Nine children were Hispanic, one was African American, six were white, and four were biracial.

The nursery school describes its environment as one in which children learn to learn, and are encouraged to develop theit natural curiosity and creativity and pursue their own interests. The curriculum is child-centered and activity-based and uses multiple modalities. Free individual exploration is balanced by teacher-led group activities. Social, emotional, and ethical development is considered just as important as cognitive growth. While the nursery school incorporates diversity into its curriculum through the use of picturebooks, they had not explored difference through art and were eager to do so.

Curriculum and Implementation

In my teaching, I try to include some of the ideas and approaches delineated in the *Starting Small* (Paley etal., 1998) book and video, instructional materials created to help preK-12 grade teachers promote respect, equity, and justice in their classrooms. I recalled a color-mixing activity in *Starting Small* that an early childhood teacher used to build community in her classroom. The teacher mixed "multicultural paint" (i.e., paint in a variety of skin tones) to match the hand of each student. The activity teaches students that while everyone is of a certain color, no color is better or worse than any other. They also learn that each skin color has a specific name: caramel, ebony, cinnamon, and peach, rather than black, white, yellow, and red. A student may be a combination of beige and olive, but not white, since, as one young child stated in the video, no one is white "like socks." Name-calling based on skin color is virtually eradicated, because "caramel" or "cinnamon" does not work as taunts, and skin color, no longer symbolic, becomes a mere descriptor.

I decided to extend the multicultural color-mixing exercise in a variety of concrete ways. First, the children, with adult help, would mix their skin tone (session one); then, they would make handprints with their skin color paint (session two); next, they would paint a tracing of their hand with their particular skin tone (session three); and finally, they would participate in a culminating self-portrait activity, along with a group discussion during circle time (session four). The non-threatening activities—in which the hand would serve as a symbol of the self—would be augmented by reading related picturebooks and examples from collaboratively selected cultural and art history materials. The final activity in session four involved responding to an artwork, in this case, a Native American poster.

I worked primarily with the head teacher, with help from assistant teachers and a student teacher. The director participated whenever possible. The division of labor between the head teacher and me occurred naturally; we designated responsibilities beforehand, but felt free to change roles during instruction. While I arrived with an armful of children's picturebooks, the school also made suggestions—the final determination was made collaboratively. The teacher led circle time (which usually followed the main activity session) and read related picturebooks, and I was in charge of the main art activity, with the help of assistant and student teachers. Other related art activities occurred concurrently. Children circulated from station to station. We decided that all children would participate in the primary teaching tolerance activity (which I led), but in small groups. The head teacher subtly directed children to my table when other children had finished the activity.

The project took place over four class sessions, each approximately four hours in length and spanning circle time as well as other activities (such as snack time). Prior to and during instruction, the head teacher and I would touch base and fine-tune our respective responsibilities. Only in the final class did I read during circle time as a form of closure, and only because the teacher deemed the children ready to accept me in that role.

The project is not meant as a "recipe" for teachers to blindly follow, but does show how even a kernel of an idea can grow. The unit of study described in this article is appropriate for preschool through 1st grade and occupies the top segment of Table 2. Activities for 2nd- to 6th-grade students also are provided to demonstrate the sequence of a teaching tolerance/social justice preK-6 curriculum. For example, for older children (2nd-6th grade), it is possible to adapt, as I did, an excerpt from Barry Lopez's (1998) memoir *A Passage of Hands,* which contains a review of his life from the vantage point of his hands. (See Lopez reference in Table 2.) The Lopez essay shows students that self-reflection gives meaning to one's life, and that a metaphor, such as one's hands, can encapsulate that meaning. As Lopez (1998) comments in his essay, "I know [my hands] have a history, though I cannot remember where it starts" (p. 211).

Books formed an important part of our curricular unit by identifying topics and shaping questions for discussion. (See Appendix for list and Table 2 for grade level designation.) Prior to my visit, the head teacher read books related to skin tone diversity to the children and led discussions on the subject during the morning circle time. These activities continued during my four days of instruction. The conversations began with questions on sections of the text, and progressed to dialogue among the children. The head teacher, assistant teachers, and I felt free to join in to redirect the discussion and to ask additional questions.

The Introductory Skin Color-Mixing Activity: Session One

On the day of the first instructional session, the classroom was set up to accommodate a variety of activities, each tangentially related to teaching tolerance: playdough mixed in different skin tone colors on one table, multicultural dolls in the block area, multicultural magic markers on the drawing table, age-appropriate books on skin color and diversity in the reading center, and multicultural paint in the painting section, where I would be conducting the activity. Several areas always provided the opportunity for independent artistic exploration. During circle time, the head teacher read the picturebook *The Colors of Us* (Katz, 1999), which describes the wide range of brown skin tones featured in a young girl's community and the task of mixing paint to portray those colors. This provided an easy transition to the color-mixing project. According to the head teacher, the book conversations on tolerance were more extensive and focused than were usual circle time discussions, and elicited more in-depth responses from the children than customary. A sample follows. (Adult comments are noted in italics. Children's names have been changed.)

- The head teacher asked the children: *"What skin color are you?"* Children took turns pointing out the skin color of a child depicted in the book that was closest to their own and responded: "I'm this one." "This one is me."
- The teacher posed the question: *"Does it matter what skin color you are?"* The children answered, "No, it doesn't matter."
- *"What's different?"* "We have different skin colors." "Different sleeves." "Different hands. Some of them have nail polish."
- *"What's the same?"* "We're people."
- *"Do we have friends with different skin colors?"* "Yes." "Jesse's a different skin color. He's lighter than me."

The dialogue shows that the children were interested in discussing diversity and were able to relate difference in terms of skin color to difference in other areas, such as clothes. Approximately half of the children were able to identify their correct skin tone in the book *All the Colors We Are* (Kissinger, 1994).

Following circle time, the head teacher circulated around the room, helping as needed, while the assistant, student teachers, and I worked one-on-one with each child in the central

Table 2 Teaching Tolerance through Multicultural Art Education with Related PreK-6 Art Activities

Complete book titles are found in the Appendix.

Age Group	Art Activities	Readings	Cultural/Art History
Preschool-1st grade	1) Mixing skin color with multicultural paint/handprint stamping with mixed skin color on individual and/or group paper or board 2) Drawing contour of hand and painting skin tone within it, stating favorite activity performed with one's hands 3) Self-portrait face or full-length self-portrait collage, using multicultural paper and found objects	*Hands Are Not for Hitting; Hands Can; I Call My Hand Gentle; Yo! Yes?; The Colors of Us; The Skin You Live In; Skin Again*	*We Are All One* (1984): Native American poster of moccasins from the Smithsonian Institute's National Museum of the American Indian
2nd-3rd grade	Same as 1-3 above except instead of teacher assistance, pairs of children work together to help each other hold the paper for stampings outlining hand, etc. Additional activities: 4) Painting large self-portrait face with facial details and skin tone observed in mirror 5) Creating large-scale full-length self-portrait in favorite action with skin tone and clothing details using paint and collage	*Shades of Black; Whoever You Are; The Colors of Us; The Skin You Live In; Skin Again* Barry Lopez (1998): *A Passage of Hands* from *About This Life*	Chuck Close fingerprint paintings: *Georgia Fingerprint I*, 1984–85; Eduardo Kingman: *Abatido*, 1968; van Gogh: *Shoes*, 1888
4th-6th grade	Same as 1–5 above with students taking on increasing responsibility for art production. Additional activities: 6) Painting an object as a form of self-portrait (related to van Gogh's shoes or room) or self-portrait using shoes (related to Native American poster) 7) Self-portrait face using fingerprints and ink from stamp pad (related to Chuck Close fingerprint paintings) and/or 8) Self-portrait face using printrnaking roller to create thin layer of black paint on self-portrait drawn on styrofoam tray (free from supermarket meat counter), using paper towel to remove ink in dabs (related to Chuck Close fingerprint paintings)	*All the Colors We Are: The Story of How We Get Our Skin Color; The Black Book of Colors* Barry Lopez (1998); *A Passage of Hands* from *About This Life*	Chuck Close fingerprint paintings: *Fannyl Fingerpainting*, 1985, *Georgia Fingerprint I*, 1984–85, *Large Phil Fingerprint*, 1979; Eduardo Kingman: *Abatido*, 1968, *La Lavanico*, 1956; van Gogh; *Shoes*, 1888, *Room, Aries*, 1888, *Self-portrait With Bandaged Ear*, 1889, *Self-portrait With a Pipe*, 1889, *Self-portrait With Grey Felt Hat*, 1887–88, *Self portrait With Pipe and Straw Hat*, 1888; *We Are All One*: Native American poster

art area. Together, child and adult viewed the paint jars and experimented with colors to find the ones that most closely matched the child's skin tone. The assistant teacher or I introduced the activity by saying, "Today, we're going to mix your skin color." Next, we pointed to the paint bottles, which were lined up in order from lightest to darkest, and asked, "Which color do you think is most like your color skin?" When the child selected a particular bottle, the adult would say, "O.K., let's try that one first. . . ." The adult squirted a small amount of paint into a spoon and then applied the paint to the top of the child's hand with her finger. If the color "disappeared" into the skin, it was the right selection. If not, paint from other bottles was added until the color blended into the skin. We mixed the paint in small plastic baby food containers that we subsequently marked with the child's name and paint color. For instance, a child might be a combination of beige and peach or olive and cinnamon. All the children had something to say about their skin color:

- *"Is your skin color darker or lighter?"* "My skin is darker." "I'm not that color." "I'm darker, darker, darker." "It looks like a tree color." "My skin smells like chocolate."
- "I have my own skin color."
- (A conversation among three children.) "I have pink skin." "Nobody has pink skin. It's only pink when your cheeks gets red." "When you don't wear sunscreen, you turn red." "My shirt is pink." "Nails are different 'cause [I] have nail polish." "My *titi* (aunt) is pink."

The children talked while mixing their skin tones, and commented on the evolving color as it was mixed. They also were interested in noting how skin color changes, for instance, in response to the sun. Most of the children found their mixed skin color acceptable, but one child felt her blended color should be darker.

Stamping Hands with Skin Tone: Session Two

Next, we used a brush to paint the palm of each child's hand. The children proceeded to stamp their handprints onto black and white papers as they saw fit. With repainted hands, the children also left handprints on a large black board; the handprints radiated out from the center, similar to a Smithsonian Museum poster titled "We Are All One" (1984), in which moccasins from different Native American groups span outward from the middle of the page. Since the purpose of the project was to build community, I thought it important for an artifact commemorating the classroom community to remain in the school. The children enjoyed stamping their handprints; a sampling of children's comments follows.

- "Look! I made a snow angel with my hands!"
- (A conversation among several children): "We have a lot of different skin color in this class." "They are all skin color." "We have different eyes." "We have different color hair." "We have different hand colors."

Because the group project contained all the children's handprints on one page, it provided children with the opportunity to view the diversity of skin tones in the class.

Hand Silhouette and Skin Color: Session Three

In the next session, the teacher read aloud Mem Fox's (2001) *Whoever You Are*. The book explores the external differences of children the world over while emphasizing the inherent similarities. The young children were quick to point out differences (unusual types of clothes and differently colored skin, eyes, and hair) and similarities, the attributes all children possess in common:

- "We're all people."
- "We all have skin."
- "We all have bodies."
- "And skeletons."
- "And bones."
- "And heads."

- "We all eat."
- "We all cry."
- "We all laugh."

The book reading and discussion were followed by an art project and the same, center-related activities as before, with the addition of finger painting using different skin tones. While drawing with multicultural colored markers and painting with multicultural finger paint, children commented:

- "They're kind of different colors, like dark brown and light brown."
- "One is darker and one is lighter because they're people's different skin colors."
- "My skin is almost this one."
- "My skin is brownish lightish."
- "My skin is brownish darkish."
- "I wonder what kind is mine."
- "I color myself."

The conversations initiated during circle time continued during center time.

The art activity called for the children to draw a silhouette of their hand (with or without assistance, as they wished), and to paint inside the contour of the hand with the previously mixed skin color. They also read the book *I Call My Hand Gentle* (Haan, 2003), which displays the different activities that hands can perform. The children were asked what the hands in the book could do. They responded:

- "Eat strawberries."
- "Pick flowers."
- "It can hug."
- "Let's hug."
- "It can throw."
- "It can hold something."
- "Like an umbrella."

The discussion was fluid and far-reaching. The purpose of the Haan book is to build caring for others by taking responsibility for one's behavior, since hands cannot perform actions on their own—an idea with which the children concurred. The book discussion ended with the children acknowledging their neighbors by shaking hands with them.

The final task required the children to specify the favorite activity they do with their hands. The following remarks ensued, starting with the comment, "I like . . .

- ". . . painting with my hands."
- ". . . washing with my hands."
- ". . . to play with my toys."
- ". . . to hug."
- ". . . to clap with my hands."
- ". . . to hold my mother's hand."
- ". . . to draw."
- ". . . to tickle with my hands."

As one teacher commented, "We do all these things—*no matter what our skin color is.*" Although the children freely participated in the discussion, it was the teacher who made connections between feelings about diversity of skin color and the kinds of actions that hands can perform. All of the children contributed positive activities, such as hug, play, clap, and hold.

A teacher asked a group of children: *Do you think it matters what color your skin is?* Children's responses ranged from a chorus of "No's" to "Yes. It matters because it's a different skin color." The head teacher believed that the child who made the latter comment likely meant that everyone's skin color should be acknowledged as different and unique. The teacher mentioned that this particular child was a sophisticated thinker capable of making such distinctions. The child was among the few who desired the mixed skin color to be as dark as her own skin tone. All the children, however, proclaimed that it would not matter what color your skin was, because your friends and family would always love you.

Multicultural Self-Portrait Activity: Session Four (Part I)

In this activity, children selected a paper that was cut in an oval (to represent a face) from among a dozen possible skin-toned papers. They glued their "faces" onto a colored background paper of their choice, and proceeded to a table on which a variety of found objects (yarn, beads, small round papers suitable for eyes, etc.) were placed. They selected objects to represent their facial features, brought their collection back to their stations, and glued the objects into place. Mirrors were placed nearby for consultation. Then, they dictated a statement proclaiming what they most liked about their self-portrait project. Comments included:

- "Mine [my face] is oval."
- "I like my hair. My hair is getting longer."
- "Mine [my eyes] are blue."
- [Picking out differently colored background papers] "Purple and green are my favorite colors."
- "This is how I'm wearing my hair today."
- "I have lots of hair."
- "I need a star."

The children produced a wealth of commentary while engaged in the self-portrait activity. Many of the comments were detailed in nature. It is possible that the preceding discussions about skin tone diversity contributed to both the quantity and specificity of remarks. The children's remarks also may have been inspired by their assiduous studying of their faces in mirrors as they worked. It was evident that the children were invested in sharing what was unique and different about themselves.

Naming the Group Art Project: Session Four (Part II)

It soon came time to "name" the poster with all the children's handprints. A discussion ensued about what should be put in the empty middle space, something that would acknowledge the collaborative process of the project. The conversation also included responding to the "We Are All One" poster that depicts a variety of moccasins radiating outward from the center of the page.

- One child commented, "I like it because all our friends' hands are in it. It has all our friends in it."
- The teacher responded, *"Yes, in this classroom, we're all friends."*
- Child: "I think we should put a rainbow in it. A rainbow of us."
- Teacher: *"A rainbow of us. How about that?"*
- Children: "Yeah."
- Teacher: *"OK, we did it. It will read 'It has all our friends in it. A rainbow of us.'"*

The final discussion was interesting because a degree of abstraction was involved in identifying a name that captured the dual nature (individual/community) of the children's poster, as well as the ability to relate that picture to the Native American poster. The children were able to make connections between the two artworks. The head teacher led the naming of the children's poster while I guided the discussion about the Native American poster.

It would seem that the term "rainbow" refers to the range of skin color displayed on the poster rather than the placement of hands in a rainbow formation. The project served as closure for the unit on diversity and allowed the children to witness, on one page, the "rainbow" of skin tones represented by their class.

Teaching Tolerance: A Necessary Component of Classroom Discourse

The children's comments show that they felt free to express their thoughts and feelings about skin color—their own and that of others. The preschool children were accustomed to reading about diversity; they were familiar with several of the books I brought to the school as well as others on the topic. While the depth and breadth of exploration was a new experience, the preschool children actively participated in the extended literacy, social studies, and art curriculum. Although the children had created self-portraits previously, they had not mixed their skin tones or incorporated their skin colors into the self-portraits. In addition, they had not engaged in an extended unit of study on diversity, nor explored the topic through art.

Based on my experience with the project, I learned that the preschool children: 1) are interested in and enjoy exploring difference (and similarity); 2) are aware of differences in skin color but are not always cognizant of their own skin tone; 3) may (more often) initially choose a lighter skin color than their own, whereas some (less often) may possess the capacity to be precise about their skin tone selection; 4) enjoy relating new information about skin color complexity to their prior knowledge and experiences with it; 5) can explore skin color diversity through literacy-related art activities; 6) are able to focus on detailed, sequenced, extended art activities, such as color mixing, painting, and collage; and 7) have the capacity to explore and comprehend such philosophic issues as the interrelated nature of humanity (e.g., as illustrated by the circle of hands "Rainbow" project).

Discussions with the head teacher and school director revealed that they think that children, teachers, and staff

Appendix
Children's Books That Teach Tolerance and Acceptance of Diversity

Books About Hands

- *Hands Are Not for Hitting,* written by Martine Agassi, illustrated by Marieka Heinlen, 2002, Free Spirit Publishing, Minneapolis, MN.
  A board book for very young children that differentiates between the positive activities hands can perform (drawing, playing, eating) versus negative activities (such as hitting).

- *Hands Can,* written by Cheryl Willis Hudson, photographs by John-Francis Bourke, 2003, Candlewick Press, Cambridge, MA.
  A board book for very young children that specifies the activities that hands can do, such as wave, touch, and clap.

- *I Call My Hand Gentle,* written by Amanda Haan, illustrated by Marina Sagona, 2003, Viking Penguin Putnam Books, New York, NY.
  Highlights the positive activities (and some of the negative ones) that hands can perform, along with a message that emphasizes self-control (i.e., hands do what we tell them to do).

Books About Skin Color

- *All the Colors We Are: The Story of How We Get Our Skin Color,* written by Katie Kissinger, photographs by Wernher Krutein, 1994, Redleaf Press, St. Paul, MN.
  The book dispels myths about skin tone and provides a scientific explanation of why people have different skin color. In Spanish and English.

- *Shades of Black: A Celebration of Our Children,* written by Sandra L. Pinkney, photographs by Myles C. Pinkney, 2006, Scholastic, New York, NY.
  The book relates skin and hair color to colors in nature.

- *Whoever You Are,* written by Mem Fox, illustrated by Leslie Staub, 1997, First Voyager Books, Orlando, FL.
  The book shows how people all over the world may be different from one another but are all the same underneath.

- *All the Colors of the Earth,* written and illustrated by Sheila Hamanaka, 1994, Morrow Junior Books, New York, NY.
  The book relates skin color to colors in nature.

- *Yo! Yes?,* written and illustrated by Chris Raschka, 1993, Scholastic, New York, NY.
  The book is not specifically about difference, but shows a Hispanic and an African American boy interacting and playing together. (Caldecott Honor book.)

- *The Colors of Us,* written and illustrated by Karen Katz, 1999, Henry Holt & Co., New York, NY.
  The book shows a young girl's gradual awareness of the different skin colors of the people in her community.

- *The Skin You Live In,* written by Michael Tyler, illustrated by David Lee Csicsko, 2005, Chicago Children's Museum, Chicago, IL.
  The book celebrates the different colors and attributes of skin, both inside and outside.

- *Skin Again,* written by Bell Hooks, illustrated by Chris Raschka, 2004, Hyperion Books for Children, New York, NY.
  The book characterizes skin as merely a covering and emphasizes the unique qualities that lie underneath. The illustrations depict a range of skin tones.

Book About Color

(While there are many books in color and about color, the following book reveals a unique take on the idea of color.)

- *The Black Book of Colors,* written by Menena Cottin, illustrated by Rosanan Fatia, translated by Elisa Amado, 2008, Groundwood Books, Toronto, ON.
  The book, entirely in black, explores the qualities of color by asking readers to feel raised images with their fingertips and picture the color in their mind's eye. In English and Braille.

---

benefited from participation in the project. The head teacher stated that she learned that: 1) art is a valuable way to learn about diversity through hands-on exploration; 2) art, in conjunction with literacy and social studies, helps young children explore complex ideas; 3) young children enjoy sharing their ideas one-on-one with a teacher, including speaking into a tape recorder; 4) young children can respond to master artwork and relate their own work to it; 5) a concentrated focus on philosophic issues is possible within an extended art-based project; 6) ongoing participation in teaching tolerance and social justice activities is essential for young children; 7) color-mixing activities concretize the idea of diversity for young children through creating individual models that together constitute community; and 8) extended art-based projects permit in-depth, free exploration for young children of challenging, complex subjects, such as tolerance and social justice.

The teacher maintained that the teaching tolerance project reinforced a sense of community by raising multicultural awareness of both difference and similarity. She shared that in the following months, students often made remarks that could only have emanated from the project ("That's your color." "This is my color." "We're all different colors.") and displayed a new ease with the topic. She also believed that the project was "comforting" for the children with dark complexion, because it enhanced group acceptance of diversity by honoring children of all skin tones. Encouraging self-acceptance, a practice that should begin in preschool, is important when developing tolerance, as is the acceptance of others different from oneself.

The teacher noted, "Young children notice everything, but their observations are not accompanied by value judgments." This happens later, which is why teaching tolerance must start young and occur often. It also explains why teaching tolerance projects should be predicated on close observation, a skill central to art making. In art activities, noticing detail becomes interesting and educational, which dispels value judgments. The teacher and director assert that the project showed that preschool children can sustain participation in an extended unit of study, and that instruction in diversity should incorporate art, literacy, and social studies. They plan to incorporate art into future diversity projects and to expand the scope and frequency of teaching tolerance and social justice.

References

Ballengee-Morris, C, & Stuhr, P. L. (2001). Multicultural art and visual cultural education in a changing world. *Art Education, 54*(4), 6–13.

Barrier-Ferreira, J. (2008). Producing commodities or educating children? Nurturing the personal growth of students in the face of standardized testing. *Clearing House, 81*(3), 138–140.

Cohen, J. (2006). Social, emotional, ethical, and academic education: Creating a climate for learning, participation in democracy, and well-being. *Harvard Educational Review, 76*(2), 201–237.

Cohen, J. (2007). Evaluating and improving school climate. *Independent School, 67*(1), 18–26.

Edmondson, L., Fetro, J. V., Drolet, J. C., & Ritzel, D. O. (2007). Perceptions of physical and psychosocial aspects of a safe school. *American Journal of Health Studies, 22*(1), 1–9.

Eisner, E. W. (2002). *The arts and the creation of mind.* New Haven, CT: Yale University.

Fox, M. (2001). *Whoever you are.* Orlando, FL: First Voyager Books.

Freedman, K. (2000). Social perspectives on art education in the United States: Teaching visual culture in a democracy. *Studies in Art Education, 41*(4), 314–329.

Gardner, H. (1993). *Frames of mind: The theory of multiple intelligences* (10th ed.). New York, NY: Basic Books.

Gardner, H. (1999). *Intelligence reframed: Multiple intelligences for the twenty-first century.* New York, NY: Basic Books.

Greene, M. (2007). Art and imagination: Overcoming a desperate statis. In A. Ornstein, E. Pajak, & S. Ornstein (Eds.), *Contemporary issues in curriculum* (4th ed., pp. 32–38). Boston, MA: Allyn and Bacon.

Haan, A. (2003). *I call my hand gentle.* New York, NY: Viking Penguin Putnam Books.

Hollingsworth, L. A., Didelot, M. J., & Smith, J. O. (2003). REACH beyond tolerance: A framework for teaching children empathy and responsibility. *Journal of Humanistic Counseling, Education and Development, 42,* 139–151.

Inlay, L. (2005). Safe schools for the roller coaster years. *Educational Leadership, 62*(7), 41–43.

Jones, H. (2004). A research-based approach on teaching to diversity. *Journal of Instructional Psychology, 31*(1), 12–19.

Katz, K. (1999). *The colors of us.* New York, NY: Henry Holt & Co.

Kissinger, K. (1994). *All the colors we are.* St. Paul, MN: Redleaf.

Lopez, B. (1998). A passage of hands. *About this life: Journeys on the threshold of memory* (pp. 211–222). New York, NY: Random House.

Masko, A. L. (2005). "I think about it all the time": A 12-year-old girl's internal crisis with racism and the effects on her mental health. *The Urban Review, 37*(4), 329–350.

Merrow, J. (2004). The 3 kinds of school safety since 9/11. *Educational Digest, 70*(4), 4–15.

Mustakova-Poussardt, E. (2004). Education for critical moral consciousness. *Journal of Moral Education, 33*(3), 245–269.

Nystrand, M., Gamoran, A., & Carbonaro, W. (1998). *Towards an ecology of learning: The case of classroom discourse and its effects on writing in high school English and social studies.* Albany, NY: Center on English Learning Achievement.

Paley, V. G., & The Teaching Tolerance Project. (1998). Starting small: Teaching tolerance in preschool and the early grades. The Teaching Tolerance Project. Retrieved July 2, 2009, from www.tolerance.org/teach/resources/starting_small/jsp

Pelo, A. (2008). Embracing a vision of social justice in early childhood education. *Rethinking Schools Online, 23*(1). Retrieved December 5, 2009, from www.rethinkingschools.org/archive/23_01/embr231.shtml

Richards, H. V., Brown, A. F., & Forde, T. B. (2007). Addressing diversity in schools: Culturally responsive pedagogy. *Council for Exceptional Children, 39*(3), 64–68.

Smith, R. A. (1993). The question of multiculturalism. *Arts Education Policy Review, 94*(4), 2–19.

"Social justice." (n.d.) Retrieved December 20, 2009, from http://en.wikipedia.org/wiki/Social_Justice

Stevens, R., & Charles, J. (2005). Preparing teachers to teach tolerance. *Multicultural Perspectives, 7*(1), 17–25.

"We Are All One." (1984). (Poster). New York, NY: Smithsonian Institute, National Museum of the American Indian.

Critical Thinking

1. In the opening statement, Zakin acknowledges that there is some controversy about teaching tolerance and social justice. Which side of this debate are you on? Do you believe it is a pedagogical imperative or the purview of the parents? Why?

2. If parents in your school object to the teaching of tolerance, how might you involve them and help them understand the purpose of your work? Keep in mind that parents may be employed during the school day.

3. The author is an art educator, so naturally she used art as a teaching vehicle. Based on the content or grade you teach, construct a plan to teach a similar lesson/unit or to continue this teacher's work in a higher grade level.

4. If you are a prospective administrator, what would you do to support both parents and teachers in this work?

Create Central

www.mhhe.com/createcentral

Internet References

Teaching Tolerance
    www.tolerance.org
Teachers of Color
    www.teachersofcolor.com

ANDREA ZAKIN is an Assistant Professor at Lehman College.

Article

Prepared by: Rebecca B. Evers, *Winthrop University*

Life Skills Yield Stronger Academic Performance

A course for freshmen boys teaches them about the black experience and each other—and leads to improved self-concepts and academic performance.

TOMMIE LINDSEY JR. AND BENJAMIN MABIE

Learning Outcomes

After reading this article, you will be able to:

- Hypothesize why teaching life skills can improve achievement.

I have never encountered any children in a group who are not geniuses. There is no mystery how to teach them. The first thing you do is treat them like human beings and the second thing you do is love them.

—Asa Hilliard

That, unfortunately, appears to be an ever-unfulfilled expectation. Across the country, there is a collective failure to teach young black men. In 2009, the most recent aggregation of national reading and math scores, "white 8th graders scored an average of 26 points higher on the National Assessment of Educational Progress reading test than did black 8th graders, and an average of 31 points higher on the NAEP math test" (Koebler, 2011).

Socioeconomic marginalization only provides a partial explanation for the achievement gap. White students enmeshed in poverty do just as well in school as their African-American counterparts outside of poverty (Gabriel, 2010).

No community in America seems to be immune. In Union City, Calif., a Bay Area city riven with ethnic, religious, and racial peculiarities, black students comprise 10% of James Logan High School's population but a substantially smaller portion of its graduates. Even fewer go on to four-year colleges. This failure, coupled with high rates of delinquency and the social exclusion of black youths at Logan High, prompted speech and debate teacher Tommie Lindsey to create a "lifeskills" class exclusively for 9th grade African-American males.

Fifty-three students enrolled in the course in the 2007–08 school year. But a few months after its start, the program suffered a blow to its moral authority when a student in the class was gunned down while picking up his younger brother from middle school. Resultant racial tensions fractured the city and left many in the lifeskills class wondering why they should attend a school that failed to protect them. The class finished out the year, but then went on hiatus.

A few years later, many of the soon-to-be-graduating students from the first class encouraged Lindsey to offer the lifeskills program again.

In fall 2010, the lifeskills class was reborn with 40 students and five instructional aides—the latter drawn from a diverse group of students on Lindsey's speech and debate team. The aides were upperclassmen and received elective credits for the class, and the course was required for all 9th-grade African-American males, though opting-out was made possible some months before the school year began. The curriculum developed by this class has been implemented again for the 2011–12 school year, and planned for subsequent years.

To design the course, the teaching team borrowed liberally from the Motivational Framework for Culturally Responsive Teaching by Margery Ginsberg and Raymond Wlodkowski (2000) to fashion a model with four important supports: establishing inclusion, building security, enhancing meaning, and engendering competence.

#1. Establish Inclusion

Students bought into the inclusion concept almost from the beginning, but not without some convincing. It seemed the students had been conditioned to hold certain beliefs regarding skin color. Several of the young men's remarks would have made slavemaster Willie Lynch proud. But after studying passages from Lynch's speech, "The Making of the Slave," students understood the gross inhumanity of dividing them-selves by the tone of their skin. Then, taking a more positive approach, the class studied two poems—"America," by Claude McKay and "I, too, Sing America," by Langston Hughes, each addressing the significance of cultural identity. The discussion that followed reinforced the importance of that lesson.

As the year progressed, the curriculum content remained highly inclusive. While reading *The Autobiography of Malcolm X,* the teaching team constructed two activities—"Malcolm and Me" and "My Nightmare"—that asked students to compare and contrast the life of Malcolm and their lives. Such activities emphasized the importance of being able to share with each other, openly, honestly, and respectfully. During a discussion about soci-ety's pressure to be hypermasculine, for example, one student said he had tried on a dress and a bra when he was younger. While an observer might have expected the students to laugh at this admis-sion, that didn't happen. Empathy already had been established.

Having open conversations with each other also helped build positive relationships. A few months into the year, a musician visited the class to help students with an audiovisual produc-tion. Students organized themselves, separating into writers, actors, musicians, and various other roles associated with com-pleting the task. They gauged each other's strengths and weak-nesses and made sure everyone was included. Here, as always, bonding was the goal.

Student-to-student relationships were only half the puzzle. What was equally important were the relationships that the teacher and his senior aides built with each student. To build those strong teacher-student relationships, the teacher and aides shared personal stories whenever the entire class was sharing, and they always took part in the same activities as the students, which may have appeared embarrassing to students and senior aides alike. While the class was lucky enough to receive sing-ing assistance from the renowned choir director Sandra Iglehart, perfect pitch was far from the point. For example, while teach-ing the class "Lift Every Voice and Sing" and "Unchained Mel-odies," the teachers and aides were either part of the harmony of voices or asked to sing alone. Such acts worked wonders to strengthen the teacher-student relationships. The group effec-tively broke down the "I am the (superior) teacher; you are the (inferior) student" dichotomy so often found in classrooms. Our actions showed that we cared about them, that we loved them.

#2. Build Security

A student learns best in an environment where he feels com-fortable. A student will only get out of the class what he feels is worth putting into the class.

Despite their African-American cultural connection, this group was far from cohesive. Students who knew each other from middle school would inevitably group together, which was probably natural given the foreign environment in which they found themselves at high school. Even more interest-ing, however, was the denominator they used to draw a line between groups: skin color. Lighter students congregated with lighter students and darker students with darker students—even when they didn't have any prior acquaintance. The one African National student who spoke with an accent was almost univer-sally excluded.

Forming these groups was clearly a defense mechanism. None of the students had ever before been in a class composed entirely of African-American males; at most, they had only a few other black students in other classes. In a class entirely composed of that single group, they homed in on other physical traits, which resulted in a segregated class that mimicked the Jim Crow South where darker-skinned blacks were viewed as more primal and less white.

This was not acceptable. The students inherently had a poor understanding of their past, where whites encouraged segrega-tion among African-Americans to prevent a strong, cohesive front. The curriculum began by breaking down the distinction between skin color.

The year started by identifying the students' common enemy by reading the infamous Willie Lynch speech from 1712 that detailed the process of breaking slaves mainly by keeping them in a constant struggle with one another. Lynch urged the slave-master to divide the old from the young, the light skinned from the dark skinned, the short from the tall—the same divisions that the class was grappling with in the first weeks of school. Lynch concluded that this system of slavery would support itself for hundreds of years to come, as long as those in power could "leave the body, but take the mind." This showed students that divisions among them were a coordinated attack by society to separate them and to control them.

The idea of being controlled was unappealing to students as they recognized that slavery was not and is not merely the physical control of the body, but also the enslavement of the mind. One of the oft-repeated mantras throughout the year became "keep the body, take the mind." "Those words hurt," admitted one student, Jaelen, and yet the recognition "of my ancestors' suffering and struggle motivated me to change . . . my teachers noticed the improvement."

By the end of the year, everyone was freely associating with everyone else. The class was a safe environment in which every student equally participated, where there was no hierarchy and no exclusion.

Students often arrived to this first-period class as much as a half-hour early. For them, the classroom was a safe haven. Lindsey and his senior aides talked with them before class on any num-ber of subjects, approached them about their problems, and even offered morning tutoring. Some of the senior aides tutored stu-dents after class and even intervened with other teachers to support class members. The teaching team's interest in the students was reciprocated in the classroom through enhanced student interest in what was to be learned. Students understood that the class was structured to assure they did well; they weren't forced to do so. Students were always provided the security to make that choice.

#3. Enhance Meaning and Relevance

American writer Sydney J. Harris once noted that "the whole purpose of an education is to turn mirrors into windows." His argument was simple: Education is about the loss of objectivity—the ability to subtract ourselves from our own subjective experience or our own socioeconomic disposition, and analyze things from a transcendental position.

This idea has become all too popular in contemporary American education. The curriculum we pass on to students is far from relevant and certainly not meaningful—especially to black males. It seems as if our education could use a few more mirrors reflecting our personal character in the content we teach. As many students agree, one of the principal causes of the undereducation of students of color is the imposition of a curriculum that is utterly alien to their own experience. Amaris, a freshmen in the class, said, "The current curriculum either ignores our history or depicts the negative parts of our past," something he says can be detrimental to "students of color getting involved in learning." Students who are unable to identify or care about the work in front of them will become alienated from the process of learning altogether.

As a lifeskills elective, this course avoids the tangle of state-mandated standards and has the freedom to craft curriculum that promotes historical and cultural literacy related to the black American experience. Here is a brief sampling of our rigorous curriculum, which helps students make personal meaning of several California high school standards delivered in other classes:

- Basic rights and liberties, as well as the importance of navigating the criminal justice system;
- Thoughtful analysis of African-American poetry from Langston Hughes, Paul Laurence Dunbar, and Claude McKay;
- Historical and literary dissection of "Lift Every Voice and Sing," which is often called the black national anthem, accompanied by the students' performance of the hymn;
- Reading *The Autobiography of Malcolm X*;
- Historical lessons on "medical apartheid"—the exploitation and significance of Henrietta Lacks, the Tuskegee syphilis experiments, and other contemporary cases;
- Reading and discussing the writings of Willie Lynch; and
- Understanding the current state of black education in our district and nationwide.

This curriculum is both meaningful and relevant because it provides a context for all schooling to be important. First, students explore issues central to their identity. Second, students learn about the realities of the world around them, which provides meaning to the work that might otherwise alienate them.

At the end of nearly every lesson, the class returned to Willie Lynch's framework "leave the body, but take the mind." Students learned that earning an education is resisting racism. One of our students, Elijah, taught us that "there is an anti-intellectual stereotype for people of color and through education we break free of it." Their grades, not only in our class, but in all classes, improved as a result.

While most classrooms are far more pluralistic than ours, we believe that the framework we've used can be passed along to other educators. Last spring, the class began a unit on William Ernest

Henley's profound poem, "Invictus." While the poem is written by a white male, the central concepts of the class were driven home again. The students analyzed the poem, and then asked: "How does this relate to our own lives, or, how does this relate to African-American history?" The young men's aptitude for developing quick connections shined through, as their own experiences mirrored those of a man with whom they had little in common.

It is the act of holding up a mirror alongside the curriculum that guarantees success for all students. Once African-American males can see themselves in their schoolwork, nothing can impede their success.

#4. Establish Expectations

Lifeskills students said they were seldom expected to succeed. They told stories of how teachers neglected them in class, which influenced the future they expected for themselves. Teachers expected them to attend summer school, not college. During the first semester, most students laughed at the prospect of attaining reasonably high marks in high school; a few said they'd be able to make it to class on time.

Low expectations almost inevitably led individuals to resign themselves to mediocre performance. Thus, one of the primary goals of the course was creating external and internal expectations that would drive the young men toward college.

The teaching team began by asking students what they wanted from one another and from themselves. Students collaborated with the teaching team to establish classroom rules. By general consensus, they agreed they would not disrespect one another, would not wear hats in class, and would be in their seats on time. Because students helped set the class code, the teachers' external expectations were harmonized with the expectations students had for themselves.

However, students went beyond merely setting expectations to regulate discipline or behavior. They also pledged to each other that they would graduate together as a class. In this communal obligation, one could literally see the student's views of the future shifting toward a brighter end.

Students rose to those expectations. They didn't wear hats; they showed up on time. At the end of the first semester, the average GPA was 1.6; by the end of the second semester, it was 3.0. In January, 11 students were on the honor roll; by spring, that number jumped to 20, and the remainder of the class received "On a Roll" awards that signaled that students would likely be on the honor roll the next semester.

Our students are beginning to understand that, "The real gap is between African-American male's typical performance and the criterion levels of excellence, which are well within their reach. That is the gap that is unacceptable, given what we know about what good teaching can do, and given what we know about the genius of our children" (Perry, Steele, & Hilliard, 2004).

Conclusion

By embracing the Motivational Framework for Culturally Responsive Teaching (Ginsberg & Wlodkowski, 2000), our class has established an equitable, inclusive, and academic space for young black males to transcend the limitations of our pedagogic apartheid. The numbers speak for themselves: Reading scores for 9th-grade black males grew the most of any demographic in our school. But more important are the intangibles—a student's new sense of confidence that allows him to share his experience, thoughts, or feelings, a newfound love for reading, an ability to overcome intraracial hate or, even more destructive, self-hate.

The beauty of our lifeskills class is its simplicity. The district provided minimal funding, and aside from the senior aides, it functioned like a normal course. Any classroom could reproduce these results. Don't neglect any student's needs. Craft and link lessons to the identities of your students. Establish a sense of security and expect great things. In other words, treat them like human beings—and love them.

References

Gabriel, T. (2010, November 9). Proficiency of black students is found to be far lower than expected. *The New York Times,* www.nytimes.com/2010/11/09/education/09gap.html

Ginsberg, M.B. & Wlodkowski, R.J. (2000). *Creating highly motivating classrooms for all students: A schoolwide approach to powerful teaching with diverse learners.* San Francisco, CA: Jossey-Bass.

Koebler, J. (2011, July 15). Close achievement gap by discussing race, expert says. *United States News & World Report.*

Perry, T., Steele, C., & Hilliard, A. (2004). *Young, black, and gifted.* Boston, MA: Beacon Press.

Critical Thinking

1. At the beginning of this unit, there is a list of internet websites. Go to the website about the Motivational Framework for Culturally Responsive Teaching (MFCRT). Use that URL to visit the information. Once you have done that, compare the original intents with what happened in Lindsey's classroom.

2. What makes a program like this one work when others have not? Provide examples to support your answer.

3. What could you do in your classroom or school to include the supports from Culturally Responsive Teaching? Explain three to five specific actions or activities you would offer to students, faculty, and staff.

Create Central

www.mhhe.com/createcentral

Internet References

Youth and Education Law Project

www.law.stanford.edu/program/clinics/youtheducation/

TOMMIE LINDSEY, JR. is a Forensics coach, at James Logan High School. He graduated valedictorian from the University of San Francisco in Communication Arts and Social Science. Benjamin Mabie is a student at University of California, Santa Cruz. Instructional aides Miles Bridges, Scott Nicholson, and Shiran Sukumar also contributed to this article.

Lindsey, Jr., Tommie and Mabie, Benjamin. From *Phi Delta Kappan*, February 2012, pp. 33–36. Reprinted with permission of Phi Delta Kappa International, www.pdkintl.org All rights reserved. www.kappanmagazine.org

Article

Prepared by: Rebecca B. Evers, *Winthrop University*

Lesson of the Heart
An Extra-Credit Assignment

LINDA LEHMAN

Learning Outcomes

After reading this article, you will be able to:

- Describe what a highly effective teacher does to help students achieve.

In today's world of proficiency tests and state report cards, teachers feel increasing pressure to become more and more involved in the paperwork of teaching—test scores, benchmarks, grade-level indicators, record keeping. Important? Yes, very important.

But, what about the people work? Teaching occurs when teachers go beyond paperwork and invest hope in students. Children sense this investment and rise to be worthy of a teacher's belief in them. The most meaningful education occurs when a teacher nurtures a child's spirit as much as his mind and works toward educating the whole child. Instilling this commitment in future educators is a noble and essential challenge. But, how do we educate teachers to truly invest in children, to instill in them lofty goals and the faith that their creativity and imagination can lead to innovation?

Teacher candidates must learn that teaching is so much more than content and using strategies to teach it.

After 36 years in education, I now teach college students in early childhood art education courses and supervise student teachers. This rewarding experience allows me to use expertise I gained from years of valuable classroom experiences and from the talented colleagues I admired and emulated. Most teacher candidates come to college with a love of their content so learning new content comes naturally. But, this is the easy part of becoming a teacher. I also have found efficient methods to teach effective strategies and mechanics of successful lesson planning that incorporate state and national standards. Through valuable field experiences, teacher candidates witness best practices and put into action pedagogical skills they learned in college.

But, teacher candidates must also learn that teaching is so much more than content and using strategies to teach it. First, students must want to learn. How do we excite children to observe, envision, and innovate? How do we instill confidence that allows each student to take risks necessary for creative problem solving and true innovation? How do we appeal to a student's imagination and his tendency to totally lose himself in a journey or adventure? Most of all, how do we transmit to all students that we believe in them and have a sustained hope for them and what they can accomplish?

Critical, essential skills

I've been fortunate recently to work with several teacher candidates from our university who have demonstrated skills that should be considered critical and essential. Investing hope in students manifests itself in ways as unique as the candidates themselves. But, each teacher candidate has a particular strength that merits discussion and examination. Each of these are qualities that all teachers need to continuously invest in, hone, and polish.

I've seen many teacher candidates who have lit up a school. Upon entering a school where they're student teaching, invariably I'm approached by someone—a principal, the school secretary, or the cooperating teacher—who professes an appreciation of the candidate. Throughout the building, he or she is recognized as "a positive person" because they enjoy their students—all of them, not just the fun ones or the talented ones. They speak with students and colleagues with a genuine interest, enthusiasm, and commitment to make each conversation a full engagement of their minds and attention. Even when students demonstrate difficult or inappropriate behaviors, these student teachers convey concern and an expectation for the best possible solution. Their positive views, smiles, and enthusiastic acceptance of all students are genuine and contagious. A simple quality you might say is possibly naive or even pollyannaish? Not so. Ask students which teachers genuinely care about them, and you'll find that those are the classes with strong attendance, high student engagement, and, most importantly, hopeful students who are buoyed by their teacher's belief in their potential.

Not only have I taught teacher candidates, I've learned from them, too. Teacher candidate Julie taught me about a teacher's capacity for compassion. Barely in her 20s and from a very typical Midwest family, Julie showed a limitless capacity to care and an acute perception of those in need. She seemed to naturally and quickly sense in every class which students needed extra help, encouragement, or, in some cases, boundaries and guidance. In a quiet and kind voice, she consoled, encouraged, mended hearts, and tended wounds. She calmed the chaos in an autistic child's world and never gave up on the student who insisted that he was not worth caring for. Caring profoundly for others came naturally to Julie. Yet, she is the first person who would say that her life is the one that's been enriched and fulfilled even as we believe that her students have been the fortunate ones.

How many hours of planning and perfecting a lesson are required before teachers can savor the brief moment when that wide-eyed, open-mouthed gasp tells us we have our students' undivided attention? If you asked first-year art teacher Kelsey, she would cheerfully say that it doesn't matter. What matters is that it happens! And Kelsey is determined, if not driven, to motivate students to learn. Kelsey personifies the willingness to work hard and to care about the quality of that hard work. She knows that mundane or textbook ideas or even original ideas that are poorly executed don't excite students. Kelsey understands that students need—and deserve—lessons that engage, challenge, and push them into realms of understanding never before considered. Kelsey uses creative ideas such as building clay cakes to teach students art history. Firing a 2½-foot clay layer cake and then meticulously painting it in the style of Van Gogh or Seurat is only part of the visual display. Dozens of cupcakes spring forth, representing styles and periods from da Vinci to Warhol. Students become engaged and learning occurs in an atmosphere of creativity and high expectation that Kelsey has created in her first teaching position in West Muskingum High School in Ohio. Her students seem to energize her, and, before long, we wonder who motivates whom?

Nature vs. training

Many educators seem to believe that there are natural teachers, and there are trained teachers. And I must admit that personable, outgoing teacher candidates with engaging people skills do seem like naturals in the classroom. However, some of the intangibles that make up those natural teachers are not so intangible after all. They may not be all that natural either. They're dispositions of enthusiasm, of compassion, and of valuing hard work. They must have a work ethic that bears an unrelenting commitment to be conscientious about the quality of their work. In teacher preparation programs, these dispositions must be addressed with the same fervor that lifesaving skills are taught to doctors. Isn't that really what we are doing? Saving lives?

Teacher candidates need a passion for teaching and a drive to do whatever is necessary, even when it's uncomfortable, uncommon, or hard. Such efforts should not be considered extra, but essential. A purposeful, focused enthusiasm for one's students, a belief in their potential, along with heartfelt compassion and the perseverance to work until students succeed are not extras that make a good teacher great. They're the essential qualities necessary for students to thrive and teachers to survive in challenging, high-need districts. We can't expect the ordinary to do the extraordinary.

For many years, teaching was considered a safe, secure, and rewarding profession best suited for those who loved children and their summer vacations. Although I maintain that was never truly the case, today's educator must have a new tenacity, a new fierceness in the face of adversity, an unbridled enthusiasm, and a heart both soft and gizzard-tough. We need candidates who have a passion to teach, but, in preparing teachers, we must commit to inculcate enthusiasm, a strong and conscientious work ethic, and a depth of compassion. These aren't simply traits that we hope evolve over the years, but instead they're traits that are foundational and necessary in the preparation of every teacher. These are the core of what sustains a successful teacher as content evolves and pedagogical strategies follow yet another trend. Soft skills? Not at all. They are essential skills that must move from the dispositional small print to the headlines of teacher education.

Critical Thinking

1. What makes a teacher candidate become an excellent teacher? Lehman says it is a set of foundational traits or dispositions. What do you believe is the most important disposition a teacher must have? Be prepared to defend your answer with examples.

2. Including the teaching and assessing of dispositions in teacher preparation programs is a continuing debate among education professionals and the general public. Do you think a person can be taught to have the appropriate dispositions for teaching? How do you think this can be accomplished?

3. If you think teacher candidates can be taught to have certain dispositions for teaching, how would you assess those *dispositions?*

Create Central

www.mhhe.com/createcentral

Internet References

Motivational Framework for Culturally Responsive Teaching
   http://raymondwlodkowski.com/Materials/Fostering%20Motivation%20in%20Professional%20Development%20Programs.pdf

LINDA L. LEHMAN (l-lehman@onu.edu) is on the art education and early childhood education faculty at Ohio Northern University, Ada, Ohio.

Lehman, Linda. From *Phi Delta Kappan*, vol. 93, no. 8, May 2012, pp. 52–53. Reprinted with permission of Phi Delta Kappa International. All rights reserved. www.pdkintl.org

Article

Prepared by: Rebecca B. Evers, *Winthrop University.*

She's Strict for a Good Reason
Highly Effective Teachers in Low-Performing Urban Schools

Studying the work of highly effective teachers can help us better understand what really works to improve student learning and help us avoid practices that are complicated, trendy, and expensive.

For four years, we studied 31 highly effective teachers in nine low-performing urban schools in some of the most economically depressed neighborhoods in Los Angeles County, Calif. The first thing that struck us was how strict the teachers were. But it was a strictness that always was inseparable from a grander purpose, even in students' minds. For example, a 2nd grader admitted, "Ms. G kept me in the classroom to do my work. She is good-hearted to me." A high school math student wrote, "I think Mrs. E is such an effective teacher because of her discipline. People might think she is mean, but she is really not. She is strict. There is a difference. She believes every student can learn."

MARY POPLIN ET AL.

Learning Outcomes

After reading this article, you will be able to:

- Describe what a highly effective teacher does to help students achieve.

Are there highly effective teachers in low-performing urban schools?
If so, what instructional strategies do they use?
What are their personal characteristics?

The teachers we studied had the highest percentage of students moving up a level on the English/language arts or math subtests of the California Standards Test (CST) for two to three years. Toward the end of the school year, we asked their students why they thought their teacher taught them so much. One Latino 4th grader summed up much of what we discovered: "When I was in 1st grade and 2nd grade and 3rd grade, when I cried, my teachers coddled me. But when I got to Mrs. T's room, she said, 'Suck it up and get to work.' I think she's right. I need to work harder."

We began our study with three questions: Are there highly effective teachers in low-performing urban schools? If so, what instructional strategies do they use? And what are their personal characteristics?

There are highly effective teachers in these schools, and we chose 31 of them for our study. They included 24 women and seven men; 24 taught English/language arts, and seven taught math; 11 taught in elementary schools, nine in middle schools, and 11 in high schools. In the year they were observed, these teachers' CST data revealed that 51% of their students moved up a level, 34% maintained their levels, and only 15% dropped a level.

These results were very different from those of their peers teaching in the same schools. For example, in three high schools, we calculated every teacher's achievement and found disheartening data. Fifty percent of the English teachers and 60% of the math teachers had between 30% and 75% of their students dropping a level in a single year. Sixty-five percent of the English teachers and 68% of the math teachers had the same number or more students going down a level as going up.

Clearly, the highly effective teachers were different. What was happening in their classrooms? Who were these high performers?

The Classroom

Strictness. These teachers believed their strictness was necessary for effective teaching and learning and for safety and respect. Students also saw their teacher's strictness as serving larger purposes. Students explained that their teacher was strict "because she doesn't want us to get ripped off in life," "because she wants us to go to college," "because she wants us to be at the top of 2nd grade," "because she wants us to be winners and not losers," and "because he has faith in us to succeed."

Instructional intensity. The second most obvious characteristic was the intensity of academic work. There was rarely a time when instruction wasn't going on. Our first visit to the only elementary teacher identified for mathematics gains found Ms. N marching her 1st graders to the playground as they chanted, "3, 6, 9, 12, 15 . . . 30" As the year progressed, they learned to march by 2s through 9s; by May her "almost 2nd graders" could multiply. She told us that she appreciated the standards as guides —"to know what I'm responsible for teaching"—and that she always tried to "push the students just a little bit into 2nd grade."

The teachers transitioned from one activity to another quickly and easily. Many of them used timers, and students often were reminded of the time remaining for a particular activity. At one school, teachers met students in the hallway during the passing periods and talked with them. When the final bell rang, these teachers instructed students on exactly what should be on their desk when they sat down: "When you get inside the door, take your jackets off; get out your book, pencil, and notebooks; then put everything else in your backpack and under your desks." As students entered, conversations ended and students prepared for work.

Most teachers began with an overview of the day. In some cases, students were required to copy the daily agenda in their notebooks—"In case your parents ask you what you learned today, I want you to be able to tell them."

Movement. Perhaps the single most productive practice of most of these teachers was their frequent movement around the classroom to assist individual students. The time spent at students' desks provided feedback on the effectiveness of their instruction, kept students on track and focused, offered individual students extra instruction and encouragement, and even allowed for brief personal interactions between teachers and students. This simple, almost instinctive activity of walking around accomplished scores of purposes *naturally*—individualized and differentiated instruction, informal assessments, teacher reflection, teacher/student relationships, response to intervention (RTI), and classroom management.

By walking around, teachers came to know their students. For example, Mrs. M asked a middle school student whose head was on his desk what was wrong. He replied, "I don't feel so good." She headed toward him, proclaiming, "Remember what I always tell you, you'll feel much better when you get your work done. Here, let me help you." She stayed by his side until he had a good start on his work. We rarely knew which students were classified as special education or English language learners because teachers' personal assistance helped mask this.

> **The single most productive practice of most of these teachers was their frequent movement around the classroom to assist individual students.**

Traditional instruction. Traditional, explicit, teacher-directed instruction was by far the most dominant instructional practice. We were constantly reminded of Madeline Hunter's sequences—anticipatory set, input, modeling, checking for understanding, guided practice, monitoring, closure, independent practice, and review. Instruction was, for the most part, unabashedly and unapologetically from the state standards and official curriculum materials. Ms. N told us, "Open Court is very helpful and gives you good pacing." This surprised the team, as there had been a good deal of contention in Los Angeles over requiring this series.

Typically, following energetic content presentations and demonstrations, teachers entered into whole-class discussions. Students were called on randomly and had to use full sentences and high-level vocabulary. Teachers always *pushed* students (a term used by teachers and students). Ms. P said to one young girl, "That is absolutely correct! Now, can you say that like a 5th grader?" At one elementary school, teachers required students to reference the previous student's comment before offering their own; this encouraged students to pay attention to one another. Teachers followed instruction and discussion with independent practice. At this stage, they began moving around. One teacher said, "If I see two or three having trouble, I stop, go back, and teach it another way."

What we saw *least* was also instructive. There were very few constructivist projects in their classrooms. The ones we saw were short-lived, and they often appeared to be used more as practice or a reward for learning than as a route to it. Cooperative and collaborative learning activities were also limited except in two classes. Most cooperative activities were brief pair-shares. Some of our teachers were adamantly opposed to it. High school teacher Mr. Mc told us, "In school, I helped 500 students get a better grade, 495 of whom learned nothing from the experience." His counterpart, Mr. T, said, "It's not realistic." From the back of the room, the team often observed that even the best cooperative activities allowed for a good deal of irrelevant socializing.

When we asked teachers to describe their classrooms to a stranger, not one of the 31 used race, class, or ethnic terms.

Though the teachers were from a variety of ethnic groups, we saw very little evidence of overtly planned activities that directly addressed culture unless it was built into curriculum materials. Cloetta Veney (2008) studied two of our elementary schools' classrooms and concluded that they resembled those in the effective classroom literature of the 1980s more than today's cultural proficiency models. When we asked teachers to describe their classrooms to a stranger, not one of the 31 used race, class, or ethnic terms.

Pat Pawlak (2009) found that the students of these teachers said—60% more frequently than any other comment—that their teacher helped them because he or she *explained things over and over.* We consistently found that students expressed appreciation for explicit instruction with patience.

Exhorting virtues. Every few minutes, these teachers encouraged students to think about their future and to practice particular virtues. The top virtues were respecting self and others, working hard, being responsible, never giving up, doing excellent work, trying their best, being hopeful, thinking critically, being honest, and considering consequences. Respect was paramount, and even a small infraction drew quick rebuke and consequences.

Teachers always linked doing well in school to going to college and getting good jobs so that they could someday support their families and own houses and cars. Mrs. C told her students how missing one word on a spelling test lost her a job she desperately wanted and needed. Ms. P told of problems she had experienced in her life. One of her students told us, "She has passed through some trouble in her life and does not want that to happen to us. So, she is preparing us for troubles and telling us what is the best choice."

These teachers focused less on making the work immediately relevant than on making the link to their futures. Even 2nd graders knew this—"Ms. G is weird, strict, mean, and crazy. This classroom is smart and nerdy because she wants you to go to college."

Strong and respectful relationships. The teachers had a profound respect for students. There was a sense that teachers were genuinely optimistic for their students' futures. Teachers often provided students with a vision of their best selves. Middle school teacher Ms. P told us, "All students need to know that you respect them and care for them. Fortunately, that is very easy. I try to make sure every so often that I have said something personal to each of them." She bent down at a student's desk and said, "Alejandro, I can see you are very good at math. I look forward to seeing what you will do in your life." Now, Alejandro has heard from a respected adult outside his family that his math skills may play into his future.

Teachers often provided students with a vision of their best selves.

Respect for students is a more accurate description of what we saw than simply caring for the students. The teachers did not need the students to love them; they needed to see their students achieve. Ms. B said, "I'm hard on my students, but at the same time, they know it is out of love. I've had to fail some students. . . . When I see them in the hall, they still greet me. They tell me they wish they were back in my class—they say they know why they failed my class."

The High-Performing Teachers

Though they shared common strategies, the teachers were quite diverse—11 were black, nine white, seven Latino, three Middle Eastern Americans, and one Asian-American. Their ages ranged from 27 to 60, and years of experience from three to 33. Two-thirds of the teachers (23) were educated in nontraditional teacher education programs—teaching before they finished their credentials. Nearly half (14) were career changers. Almost one-third (9) were first-generation immigrants. While they were all highly effective, few fit the definitions of highly qualified in terms of National Board certifications and degrees.

The teachers were strong, no-nonsense, make-it-happen people who were optimistic for students' futures, responsible, hard working, emotionally stable, organized, and disciplined. They were also energetic, fit, trim, and appeared in good health. They were comfortable in their own skins and humorous. Ms. M told her high school students, "If you develop multiple personalities, you better assign one to do your homework."

What do they believe? Their most central beliefs include:

1. Every one of my students has much more potential than they use;
2. They have not been pushed to use it;
3. It is my responsibility to turn this situation around;
4. I am able; and
5. I want to do this for them.

Ms. M said simply, "They can do and be so much more."

Teachers didn't use the students' backgrounds as an excuse for not learning, and yet they were not naive about the challenges facing some students. They had confidence that what they did in the classroom would truly help students.

Teachers had a pragmatic attitude about testing. "It's required all your life," Mr. T told us. Mrs. C said of the district assessments, "I really like them, I like them a lot. I've been embarrassed by them a few times, but I am all for them." Ms. K said, "When students don't do well, I take it personally. I know I shouldn't, but I think that that bothers me." These teachers neither taught to the tests nor ignored them; tests were simply another resource.

Several additional incidents were instructive for those of us who work in teacher development, supervision, and evaluation.

First, not one of our teachers had any idea that they were more successful than their colleagues teaching similar students. The student achievement data that was available to them did not allow for such comparisons.

Second, in a couple of cases, the principals were resistant to a teacher who emerged from the data, urging us to observe a different teacher. However, none of the nominated teachers made the cut when we rechecked the data. To be honest, when we first entered their classrooms, we also were surprised because of our preconceptions about what effective instruction should and shouldn't look like.

An incident is instructive here: One day, Ms. N was visibly shaken after a visit from a district teacher development specialist. She told our team member that she must be a terrible teacher and didn't think that she should be in the study. The researcher told her that she certainly wasn't a bad teacher but, if she liked, the researcher could come back another day. This demonstrates the importance of knowing the achievement data before we target teachers for intervention. Many teachers in that school needed instructional interventions, but it is counter-productive to take a veteran teacher of 33 years who is highly effective year after year and to shake her confidence in order to make her use preferred strategies. Teachers who have demonstrated results should be granted considerable freedom in determining their classroom instruction.

The teachers respected their principals. The teachers were the authority in their classrooms, and their principals were their authorities. However, they did not seem to be particularly close to their principals because the teachers were more focused on the inside of their classrooms than on networking with administrators. One teacher summed up their relationships when she said, "We get along."

Conclusion

Our concerns about the limitations of traditional, explicit instruction may be unfounded. What we found were happy and engaged students obviously learning from committed, optimistic, disciplined teachers. These teachers were realistic; they did not set their goals too broadly (saving children) or too narrowly (passing the test). Their students were being taught that mathematics, reading, speaking, listening, writing, and the formation of character are necessary for life beyond their neighborhoods.

We need to be cautious about adopting complicated, trendy, and expensive practices. We need to re-evaluate our affection for cooperative/collaborative learning, extensive technology, project-based learning, and constructivism, as well as our disaffection with explicit direct instruction and strict discipline. These teachers were direct, strict, deeply committed, and respectful to students. Their students, in turn, respected them. Mr. L's math students said it best: "It takes a certain integrity to teach. Mr. L possesses that integrity." "One thing for sure, his attitude is always up. He never brings us down, but we all know he has faith in us to learn and succeed."

References

Pawlak, Pat. "Common Characteristics and Classroom Practices of Effective Teachers of High-Poverty and Diverse Students." Doctoral dissertation, Claremont Graduate University, 2009.

Veney, Cloetta. "The Multicultural Practices of Highly Effective Teachers of African American and Latino Students in Urban Schools." Doctoral dissertation, Claremont Graduate University, 2008.

Critical Thinking

1. Make a list of all the actions taken by highly effective teachers in the classroom section of the article. As a student, have you been in classrooms where teachers practiced those strategies? What do you remember most about that classroom or teacher?

2. Who are these highly effective teachers? Describe the characteristics of these teachers. Any surprises for you in those characteristics?

3. Are you surprised by their attitudes toward standardized testing? Why do you think it is not a serious concern for them?

4. The researchers said, "To be honest, when we first entered their classrooms, we also were surprised because of our perceptions about what effective instruction should and shouldn't look like." What did they see that they were not expecting? What was missing from the classroom that they thought would be there?

5. If you could talk to these teachers, what would you say? What questions would you ask?

Create Central

www.mhhe.com/createcentral

Internet References

Coalition of Essential Schools
    www.essentialschools.org

MARY POPLIN is a professor of education at Claremont Graduate University, Claremont, Calif. **JOHN RIVERA** is a professor and special projects assistant to the president, San Diego City College, San Diego, Calif., and the study's policy director. **DENA DURISH** is coordinator for alternative routes to licensure programs for Clark County School District, Las Vegas, Nev. **LINDA HOFF** is director of teacher education at Fresno Pacific University, Fresno, Calif. **SUSAN KAWELL** is an instructor at California State University, Los Angeles, Calif. **PAT PAWLAK** is a program administrator in instructional services at Pomona Unified School District, Pomona, Calif. **IVANNIA SOTO HINMAN** is an assistant professor of education at Whittier College, Whittier, Calif. **LAURA STRAUS** is an instructor at the University of Montana Western, Dillon, Mont. **CLOETTA VENEY** is an administrative director at Azusa Pacific University, Azusa.

From *Phi Delta Kappan*, by Mary Poplin et. al., vol. 92, no. 5, 2011, pp. 39–43. Reprinted with permission of Phi Delta Kappa International, www.pdkintl.org, 2009. All rights reserved.

Unit 5

UNIT

Prepared by: Rebecca B. Evers, *Winthrop University*

Teaching English Language Learners

The concepts of culture and diversity encompass all the customs, traditions, and institutions that people develop as they create and experience their history and identity as a community. In the United States, very different cultures coexist within the civic framework of a shared constitutional tradition that guarantees equality before the law. So, many people are united as one nation by our constitutional heritage. Some of us are proud to say that we are a nation of immigrants. Our country is becoming more multicultural with every passing decade. As educators, we have a unique opportunity to encourage and educate our diverse learners. The articles in this unit reflect upon all the concerns mentioned above. You can establish a classroom that is a place of caring and nurturing for your students, multicultural-friendly, equitable, and free from bigotry, where diverse students are not just tolerated but are wanted, welcomed, and accepted. Respect for all children and their capacity is the baseline for good teaching. Students must feel significant and cared for by all members of the classroom. Our diverse children should be exposed to an academically challenging curriculum that expects much from them and equips them for the real world.

The number of children (ages 5–17) who spoke a language other than English at home almost tripled (from 4.7 to 11.2 million) from 1980 to 2009. Among these children, the percentage who spoke English with difficulty decreased between 1980 and 2009. In 1980, 41 percent of these children spoke English with difficulty whereas in 2009 the number was 24 percent. This may be associated with increased school enrollment. Between 1980 and 2009, school enrollment of 5- to 17-year-old children who spoke a language other than English was up from 90 percent to 93 percent. In 2009, 16 percent of Hispanic and Asian children spoke a language other than English at home or spoke English with difficulty whereas only 6 percent of Pacific Islanders, 3 percent of American Indians/Alaska Natives, and 1 percent each of Whites, Blacks, and children of two or more races were not proficient English speakers. If we compare these students by age, the youngest had the most difficulty speaking English easily; while seven percent of children ages 5–9 and only four percent of adolescents ages 14–17 spoke English with difficulty (U.S. Department of Education, National Center for Education Statistics, 2012).

On average, Hispanic students never perform as well as other students, not even in kindergarten. In some states, the Hispanic school-age population has nearly doubled since 1987 and is approaching one-half of all students. Unfortunately these students are more likely to attend a hypersegregated school, where the population is 90–100 percent minority and they are less likely to read or do math at grade level or earn a college degree. In fact, they drop out of high school at higher rates than all other categories of the student population (Coleman and Goldenberg, 2010).

These data appear to indicate that teachers and schools are making an impact on second language acquisition of students who do not speak English at home. The articles in this unit focus on the concept that caring, culturally responsive instruction from teachers with positive attitudes who look for student's assets can and will help English language learners be successful learners in school.

To begin the unit, Lee suggests new ways to talk about students from other countries and cultural backgrounds. For example, we might consider that these students have experiences that make them culturally different but not culturally deficit. A shift in our thinking can make a powerful difference in how we approach and teach these students. Further, Lee offers examples from the schools in the International Network. The Network school in New York City has a graduation rate that is more than double the other schools in the city. There are lessons to be learned from those teachers.

Ferlazzo uses a Mexican folktale to illustrate his point that international students come to our schools with experiences, prior knowledge, strengths, and skills which teachers can use to increase reading levels and higher-order thinking. His own experience as a community organizer prior to teaching gave him a framework for organizing his classroom and teaching. His Organizing Cycle has five actions for the teacher and student to use. He describes this as a balancing act for teachers to help students develop life-long reading and thinking skills.

Finally, Konrad, Joseph, and Itoi offer guided notes and graphic organizers as a research-based strategy to support learning of international students in our public schools. They suggest that taking notes during lectures, class discussion, and reading texts is challenging for many students. Further, teaching all students to use guided notes can be helpful to both ELLs and those with learning and language disabilities. The use of symbols in the notes is helpful to all language learners. There are examples of guided notes across several grade levels and content areas.

References

Coleman, R. & Goldenberg, (2010). *What Does Research Say about Effective Practices for English Learners?, Kappa Delta Pi Record*, Winter 2010.

U.S. Department of Education, National Center for Education Statistics. (2012). *The Condition of Education 2011* (NCES 2011-045), Indicator 6.

Article   Prepared by: Rebecca B. Evers, *Winthrop University*

New Talk about ELL Students

Culturally responsive schooling can and does help immigrant English learners succeed in school while learning the language.

Stacey J. Lee

Learning Outcomes

After reading this article, you will be able to:

- Explain the importance of knowing the academic language skills of the students who are ELL in your classroom.

- Determine appropriate teaching methods to use in teaching content to students who are ELL.

Students from immigrant families, including foreignborn children and those born in the United States to immigrant parents, are a large and growing segment of the student population. In 2005, the U.S. had about 11 million school-aged children of immigrants, making them about one-fifth of the school-aged population (Rong & Preissle, 2008). Students from immigrant families are diverse in terms of ethnicity, race, religion, language background, English proficiency, immigration status, and social class. These differences in background make a profound difference in how they negotiate schooling.

Immigrant youth who enter the U.S. as adolescents, in particular, face significant challenges. Research suggests that immigrant English learners score lower on standardized tests, graduate from high school at lower rates and drop out at higher rates than their native English-speaking peers.

Students who arrive in the U.S. as adolescents often develop the social English necessary to chat with friends and consume popular culture quickly. But students need four to seven years to develop academic English (Hakuta, Butler, & Witt, 2000), which may make it challenging to have the academic English necessary to graduate from high school in four years. Late-entry ELLs face particular difficulties in states with high school exit exams because of these language issues.

Immigrant students' prior educational experiences play a central role in their educational achievement in the U.S. About 6% of newcomer immigrant students have experienced interrupted formal education in their home countries; in places like New York City, about 10% of all ELLs are students with interrupted formal education (Bartlett & Garcia, 2011; Advocates

for Children, 2010). These youth are typically two or more years behind their same-age peers in school, and many aren't literate in their native languages.

Immigrant English learners are typically tracked into ELL classes that focus almost exclusively on acquiring English, often to the exclusion of academic content (Callahan, 2005; Callahan, Wilkinson, Muller, & Frisco, 2009). Too often, educators assume English learners can't do academic work until they're fully proficient in English (Callahan, 2005). Instead of offering students access to academic subjects and the opportunity to develop critical and independent thinking, schools too often subject ELLs to vocabulary drills.

When they do exit ELL programs, they're often unprepared to handle the academic content in mainstream classes because they haven't been prepared to do so. When ELL placement limits access to academic subject matter, there are long-term negative effects on students' achievement and future educational opportunities.

Educators often view immigrant cultures and languages as barriers to academic success. Instead of building on students' backgrounds, the assimilationist perspective encourages educators to disregard native languages and cultures (Lee, 2005; Valenzuela, 1999), which alienates both the immigrant youth and their families from schools.

Lessons from The Internationals

The issue for educators is what schools can do to improve educational opportunities for these youth. What are the elements of a successful educational program for newcomer immigrant English learners? How can schools provide these students with an academically enriching, culturally responsive, and socially supportive education?

In the last few years, my colleagues and I have been studying high schools in the Internationals Network for Public Schools in New York City, which points to the possibilities and challenges of providing newcomer immigrant English learners with a high-quality education.

Schools in the Internationals Network have a reputation for successfully educating immigrant students from diverse backgrounds. One study of the three oldest International High Schools in New York City reveals that the final graduation rate for students who entered in 1998 was 88.7%, compared to a graduation rate of 49.6% for a similar population citywide during this period (Fine, Stoudt, & Futch, 2005). Students in these schools come from over 70 countries, speak over 60 languages, and 80% of the students are eligible for free or reduced-price lunch. Students arrive at the Internationals with diverse educational backgrounds, including many who have experienced interrupted formal educations. Students' English literacy ranges from early elementary to approaching grade level.

The 15 schools in the Internationals Network are designed to serve the unique academic, social, and emotional needs of recently arrived immigrant youth who are English learners. Teachers work in interdisciplinary teams, which foster teacher collaboration. Most teams include an ESL-certified teacher, and all teachers receive professional development on language acquisition. These schools build on students' cultural and linguistic identities through an interdisciplinary course of study that fosters learning English through content.

Cultural and Linguistic Identities

Scholars who embrace sociocultural perspectives have argued that the educational challenges experienced by students from culturally and linguistically different backgrounds, including immigrant ELLs, are the result of unrecognized and unappreciated cultural differences not cultural deficits (Gay, 2000; Ladson-Billings, 1995; Moll et al., 1992). These scholars have highlighted the importance of drawing on students' cultures, native languages, identities, and communities in promoting high academic engagement and achievement. Teachers in the Internationals regularly draw on student experiences and cultures to involve students in academic discussions. Teachers collaborate across disciplinary boundaries to create interdisciplinary curricula that often center on themes relevant to students' lives.

In one recent study at a network high school, we focused on teachers' efforts to create an interdisciplinary American studies curriculum that was relevant to students' identities, including units on immigration and globalization (Lee & Walsh, in press). During the unit on immigration, the English teacher posted the following questions on the walls: "How is identity related to inclusion and exclusion, belonging and not belonging? How are you, personally, becoming a part or not becoming a part of the United States? How are immigrants included and excluded from life in the United States?"

As the teacher's questions suggest, students were constantly asked to think about their own immigration experiences. In English and history classes, students were encouraged to reflect on their family's immigration experiences as a way of making sense of the history of immigration in the U.S. and current immigration policies (Lee & Walsh, in press). Research on the Internationals Network of Public Schools reveals that students are eager to share aspects of their cultural backgrounds with peers from other countries, and they regularly draw on experiences in their native countries to make sense of classroom

material (Fine, Stoudt, & Futch, 2005; Jaffe-Walter & Lee, 2011; Lee & Walsh, in press).

Learning English Through Content

Teaching academic English is central to the mission of schools in the Internationals Network. Because of the vast number of languages spoken by students, English is the language of instruction in all but two Network schools. The approach to language instruction at the Internationals reflects what some scholars call a "plurilingual" perspective, which centers on individual students' linguistic, cultural, and schooling experiences. A dynamic plurilingual perspective responds to the complex language practices of individual students, recognizes that language practices are occurring in an increasingly multilingual global society (Garcia, Sylvan, & Witt, 2011). Students are encouraged to use their native languages to build their English skills and classrooms are often filled with the sounds of languages from around the world.

Teachers work in teams to develop methodologies that help students simultaneously develop content knowledge and the academic English associated with a particular subject. The central strategies used by teachers include systematic scaffolding of content along with language. Scaffolding often includes giving students opportunities to make visual representations of their ideas or acting out a critical scene in a book before beginning writing. The immigration unit, for example, included a visual arts component in which students posed for self-portraits with three artifacts that were meaningful to them. The artifacts (e.g., family photos in their native countries and in their apartments in New York City, religious items, or music) were then used as prompts to get students to talk about and later write about their immigration experiences. Teachers accommodate the range of English proficiency levels in any given class by differentiating instruction. In English classes, for example, students read about the same theme (e.g., immigration, African-American experiences) through different books matched to their individual reading levels (Lee & Walsh, in press).

> **Too often, the work of educating English learners is seen as the sole responsibility of the ELL or bilingual staff in a school.**

Social Capital

In another study, my colleague and I found that teachers and other staff at the Internationals recognize the many obstacles facing students, and they work together to create nurturing school cultures that support academic success, including helping students make postsecondary plans (Jaffe-Walter & Lee, 2011).

At some Network schools, discussions about postsecondary options occur in weekly advisory periods; in others, students take career development classes in which students research different colleges and careers and complete college applications. Teachers and staff in both models emphasize going on to higher education and help students at every step of the college application and financial aid process. Network schools also provide internships, which expose students to a variety of career choices.

Challenges

Schools in the Internationals Network have created educational opportunities for newcomer ELLs that build on student strengths and respond to student needs. The schools also enable teachers to collaborate in responding to students' academic, social, and emotional needs. The reality of students' previous education and current lives means that not all students graduate from high school in four years, but Network schools work with students to give them extra time to fulfill requirements when necessary. However, high-stakes testing has presented additional obstacles for teachers and students in these schools.

In New York, all students, including newcomer ELLs, must pass five Regents exams to earn a high school diploma. Since this new mandate began, ELLs have consistently struggled to pass the exams, and dropout rates among this group have increased. In 2005, for example, only 33.2% of ELLs in New York City passed the English part of the Regents exam (Menken, 2008). Indeed, our research suggests that ELL students face substantial hurdles in passing these exams, and many must retake the exams again and again before earning passing scores (Lee & Walsh, in press).

Internationals Network teachers are trying to prepare students for these high-stakes tests while maintaining a commitment to curriculum that is culturally responsive. Significantly, the professional communities and the culture of collaboration allow teachers to negotiate challenges created by accountability policies while maintaining a commitment to providing an academically rich and cultural and linguistically relevant pedagogy (Jaffe-Walter, 2008).

What Does It Take?

What are the lessons from the Internationals Network of Public Schools? What does it take to provide newcomer immigrant English learners with a culturally responsive and academically challenging education? Too often, the work of educating English learners is seen as the sole responsibility of the ELL or bilingual staff in a school. This model leaves the ELL staff and their students marginalized and isolated in schools. Given the complexity of working with late-entry immigrant English learners, the lone teacher who is isolated in his or her classroom would be easily overwhelmed.

Too often, educators assume English learners can't do academic work until they're fully proficient in English

Research in Internationals Network schools and other schools known for successfully educating newcomer ELLs points to the importance of having schoolwide investment in working with immigrant English learners. At schools in the Internationals Network, instructional teams allow teachers to collaborate across disciplinary boundaries and across specializations to serve student needs. Significantly, ESL-certified teachers work as coequals with subject-area teachers to address language issues across subject areas.

Similarly, in their research at a bilingual high school for Dominican immigrant youth in New York City, Lesley Bartlett and Ofelia Garcia highlight the centrality of the school's "collective effort oriented toward the edification of an entire community" (2011, p. 232). Furthermore, staff members have positive attitudes towards students' cultural and linguistic differences and seek to build on the students' backgrounds. Once again, the instructional teams play a central role in helping teachers negotiate their work as team members share responsibility for working together to learn about students and to construct learning opportunities that reflect students' cultural and linguistic differences.

Can other schools recreate the Internationals' model? Most successful schools for newcomer ELLs are in large urban areas where many teachers have experience dealing with diversity. While most immigrant students do attend schools in urban centers, increasing numbers of immigrant ELLs are settling in small towns, suburbs, and rural communities in the Midwest and South with little experience dealing with cultural, racial, or linguistic diversity.

Schools in many of these smaller communities lack the resources and expertise to address the educational needs of immigrant ELLs. Furthermore, these districts and their teachers are generally isolated from institutions that could provide support. Research is needed on how to create successful models of education for immigrant ELLs in smaller districts. The research on Internationals suggests that smaller districts may want to start by offering professional development on cultural and linguistic diversity, which emphasizes collaboration and schoolwide commitment to serving immigrant ELLs.

References

Advocates for Children. (2010). *Students with interrupted formal education: A challenge for New York City public schools.* New York, NY: Author. www.advocatesforchildren.org/

Bartlett L. & Garcia, O. (2011). *Additive schooling in subtractive times: Bilingual education and Dominican immigrant youth in the Heights.* Nashville, TN: Vanderbilt University Press.

Callahan, R. (2005). Tracking and high school English learners: Limiting opportunity to learn. *American Educational Research Journal, 42* (2), 305–328.

Callahan, R., Wilkinson, L., Muller, C., & Frisco, M. (2009). ESL placement and schools: Effects on immigrant achievement. *Educational Policy, 23* (2), 355–384.

Fine, M., Stoudt, B., & Futch, V. (2005). *The Internationals Network for public schools: A quantitative and qualitative cohort analysis of graduation and dropout rates. Teaching and learning in a transcultural academic environment.* New York, NY: The Graduate Center, City University of New York.

Garcia, O., Sylvan, C., & Witt, D. (2011). Pedagogies and practices in multilingual classrooms: Singularities in pluralities. *Modern Language Journal, 95* (3), 385–400.

Gay, G. (2000). *Culturally responsive teaching: Theory, research, and practice.* New York, NY: Teachers College Press.

Hakuta, K., Butler, Y.G., & Witt, D. (2000). *How long does it take English learners to attain proficiency?* Stanford, CA: University of California Linguistic Minority Research Institute.

Jaffe-Walter, R. (2008). Negotiating mandates and memory: Inside a small schools network for immigrant youth. *Teachers College Record, 110* (9), 2040–2066.

Jaffe-Walter, R. & Lee, S. (2011). To trust in my root and to take that to go forward: Supporting college access for first-generation immigrant youth. *Anthropology & Education Quarterly, 42* (3), 281–296.

Ladson-Billings, G. (1995). Toward a culturally relevant pedagogy. *American Educational Research Journal, 32* (3), 465–491.

Lee, S. (2005). *Up against whiteness: Race, school, and immigrant youth.* New York, NY: Teachers College Press.

Lee, S. & Walsh, D. (In press). Resistance and accommodation: Social justice education for immigrant youth in an era of high-stakes testing. *Encyclopaedia: Journal of Phenomenology and Education.*

Menken, K. (2008). *English learners left behind: Standardized testing as language policy.* Clevedon, England: Multilingual Matters.

Moll, L., Amanti, C., Neff, D., & Gonzalez, N. (1992). Funds of knowledge for teaching: Using a qualitative approach to connect homes and classrooms. *Theory into Practice, 31,* 132–141.

Rong, X.L. & Preissle, J. (2008). *Educating immigrant students in the 21st century: What educators need to know.* Thousand Oaks, CA: Corwin.

Valenzuela, A. (1999). *Subtractive schooling: U.S.-Mexican youth and the politics of caring.* Albany, NY: State University of New York Press.

Critical Thinking

1. Lee suggests teachers see students who are English Language Learners as culturally different rather than as culturally deficient. How will this shift in attitude improve the outcomes for students?

2. What was your "aha" moment in this article and how will that affect your future teaching?

3. Do you see any pitfalls in implementing the philosophy and actions suggested in this article? What are they and why do you think these will occur?

Create Central

www.mhhe.com/createcentral

Internet References

What works for English Language Learners
http://ies.ed.gov/ncee/wwc/topic.aspx?sid=6

STACEY J. LEE (slee@education.wisc.edu) is a professor of educational policy studies at the University of Wisconsin-Madison, Madison, Wis.

Lee, Stacey J. From *Phi Delta Kappan*, vol. 9, no. 6, 2012, pp. 66–69. Reprinted with permission of Phi Delta Kappa International. All rights reserved. www.pdkintl.org

Article   Prepared by: Rebecca B. Evers, *Winthrop University*

Get Organized Around Assets

The steps community organizers use to help change people's lives can help teachers improve English language learners' reading.

LARRY FERLAZZO

Learning Outcomes

After reading this article, you will be able to:

- Apply appropriate support materials to lesson plans for students who are ELL.

- Outline appropriate ways to include multicultural activities into content area lessons.

Nobody thought Juan was very capable. People didn't take him seriously when he said he wanted some land to farm. Finally, he was given a small plot, but everyone laughed because they believed it was poor soil and Juan wouldn't be successful. Juan, though, was a hard worker, and he had the knowledge that his friends the Zanate birds shared with him. Following their advice, he planted what are known as the "three sisters": corn, beans, and squash. The birds—and the indigenous people of Mexico—know that these three plants complement one another during the growing season. The townspeople were shocked to see the success of Juan's harvest. From that day forward he was known as Juan Zanate.

In this Mexican folktale, as told in the picture book *The Harvest Birds* (Children's Book Press, 1995), people had a low opinion of Juan's ability. However, through his determination and his use of inner gifts—which most people didn't see he had—Juan succeeded beyond his neighbors' imaginations. Educators often perceive English language learners the way that Juan's neighbors viewed him—through a lens of deficits. But what if we viewed them with a focus on assets? The word assets derives from the French word *assez*, meaning "very much, a great deal." Most English language learners (ELLs) bring *a* great deal of life experience and skills to the classroom, and teachers can help them apply those skills to reading. If we use instructional strategies to maximize these students' strengths, we can help them make tremendous strides in reading and higher-order thinking.

Assets and Community Organizing

Before I became a high school English as a second language teacher 9 years ago, I spent 19 years as a community organizer, primarily in immigrant neighborhoods and with institutions focused on immigrants. Organizing is a process of helping people—many of whom might be reluctant to change—learn new skills and engage in the world in a way that improves their situation. Organizing means helping people use their assets—their experiences, traditions, and stories—to reimagine themselves and their dreams. It's about helping them tap into their intrinsic motivation and embark on a journey of action, discovery, and learning. I call the process that successful organizers use *the organizing cycle*. As a teacher, I've adapted this cycle to help English language learners become accomplished readers and learners.

The organizing cycle includes five actions: Build strong relationships with students; access prior knowledge through stories; help students learn by doing; identify and mentor students' leadership potential; and promote the habit of reflection.

1. Build relationships

When teachers develop relationships with students by learning about their lives, interests, and hopes, everyone benefits. Numerous studies have tied positive student-teacher relationships to increased student achievement (Johnson, Johnson, & Roseth, 2006). As Robert Marzano (2007) writes, "If the relationship between the teacher and the students is good, then everything else that occurs in the classroom seems to be enhanced" (p. 150). Such relationships are particularly important for helping English language learners develop a feeling of safety in the classroom and see possibilities for their own academic success (Suarez-Orozco, Pimentel, & Martin, 2009).

Teachers who actively pursue positive relationships also gain understanding of the kind of background knowledge students bring with them. We can then more effectively connect students' life experiences with classroom content, particularly in identifying texts that will engage them and strengthen their comprehension.

In helping ELLs choose what to read—or choosing for them—teachers must achieve the delicate balance of finding material that is engaging and challenging; that connects to students' background knowledge and attaches new understandings to that knowledge; and that anchors new learning to their interests, self-identity, and goals. Asking older students to read ABC-style books geared to English-speaking kindergartners might not be the most effective way to generate a love of reading. Fortunately, there are thousands of free "talking stories" available online, which offer audio support and animated illustrations to accompany texts of both fiction and nonfiction. Talking stories make high-interest and challenging texts accessible to ELLs. In addition, numerous education publishers have developed texts that meet these criteria, including graphic novels.

The way you introduce a reading may be as important as what text you choose. Before I assigned one class of predominantly Hmong immigrant students to read a text on American Indian tribes, I asked them to explain to me the structure of the 20 Hmong clans and each clan's culture, including its leadership style, loyalty expectations, and system of resolving conflicts.

Next, I asked students to look for connections between their knowledge of Hmong clans and the text on American Indians as they read. Once they began the reading, class engagement was off the charts. Students had difficulty restraining themselves from shouting out similarities they were finding.

I later asked students to reflect on whether they would have been as engaged with this text if they hadn't made connections to Hmong clans. The answer was a universal no. Students had seen vividly the difference it made to bring personal meaning to a text, and many of them applied the strategy of making connections during the rest of the year.

2. Access prior knowledge through stories

Renate and Geoffrey Caine (1994) describe the brain's two types of memory systems: taxon and locale. Taxon learning consists of lists, basic skills, and habits. Locale memory, on the other hand, involves creating stories out of a person's life experiences—weaving taxon memories into a sophisticated sense of meaning. For example, our taxon memories enable us to know how to open the door to our home with a key. Our locale memories connect that skill with related experiences and skills so that we know how to proceed if we lose our key.

Many schools today focus on taxon learning, which responds more to extrinsic motivation and is resistant to change once a fact or habit has been learned. Locale learning is more responsive to intrinsic motivation and is always evolving. The Caines believe that teaching skills in the context of students' stories—their experiences and memories and the way they've internally organized them—taps locale memory.

I used my Hmong and Latino immigrant students' locale memories to strengthen their reading skills during a unit on feudalism. The textbook's authors listed several key facts about feudalism: People spent most of their time working in the fields, they didn't own the land they farmed, and their homes had one or two rooms. The book flatly declared that feudalism had ended with the Renaissance. Instead of having students memorize these facts (taxon memory), I asked students to think about them, write about whether they'd experienced any of these conditions in their home culture, and ask their parents and grandparents the same question (locale memory). Every student commented that they were either experiencing some of those "feudal" conditions currently or had done so very recently, either before their families emigrated or while they lived in refugee camps. The class concluded that the textbook was mistaken in saying feudalism had ended.

Examining parallels between their lives and the lives of people in the Middle Ages strongly engaged students. Many clamored to read more challenging texts about the Middle Ages. This unit provided countless opportunities for my students to learn reading strategies, academic vocabulary, and grammar. They embraced those opportunities because the lessons took place within the framework of their own stories and those of their families.

3. Help students learn by doing

John Dewey (1916) popularized the phrase learning by doing, which means that students learn more from solving problems on their own than from just being told how to do so. Recently, this concept has been framed as creating learner-centered classrooms. Certain elements of a learner-centered classroom—such as inductive teaching methods, problem-based learning, or project-based learning—are ideal for strengthening English language learners' reading abilities.

Inductive teaching makes learners active agents in their pursuit of English language skills. Teaching inductively means providing students with several examples from which they detect a pattern and form a concept or rule. It embraces Jerome Bruner's (1996) definition of knowledge as the ability to "derive the unknown from the known" (p. 51). In deductive teaching, in contrast, a teacher provides a rule or hypothesis and students practice applying it.

One effective inductive strategy is the Picture Word Inductive Model (Calhoun, 1999). In this model, the teacher displays an enlarged photo showing various objects and people in the classroom, surrounded by white space. Students and teacher together label objects in the picture. Working in language notebooks or on a poster board, students create categories (such as *furniture*) and sort words from the picture (and others they find) into these categories. Eventually students use the words in fill-in-the-blank sentences, categorize and combine these sentences into paragraphs, and may ultimately work them into a longer piece of writing.

I tried this technique by taking a photo of students at work in my beginning English as a second language class, which is composed of Latino, Southeast Asian, and Arab immigrants who've been in the United States for periods ranging from one week to four months. After enlarging the photo, laminating it on a poster board, and hanging it on a wall, I asked students to join me up front. As students pointed out items in the photo for which they knew the word, we printed that word on the poster with an arrow pointing to the object. We also spelled each word aloud together and ended by pronouncing the whole word. The poster quickly filled with 25 English words.

Students individually copied these words onto a copy of the photo I had made for each learner. Each student then developed categories for the words (such as people or words with an e in them) and wrote several more words that fit those categories.

To extend this work into composition, students completed a sheet of 10 multiple-choice close-format sentences about the photo, such as The _____ sits at her _____ (teacher, desk, student, dog).

They grouped those 10 sentences into such categories as sentences describing actions, and each learner composed several new sentences for each category. The following day, these beginning English speakers learned about composing paragraphs and converted their sentences into paragraphs for a simple descriptive essay.

Text data sets are another teaching tool that helps language learners develop more sophisticated reading and writing ability. A text data set also uses categorization, but instead of completing cloze sentences, students work with a series of short expository sentences or paragraphs (see fig. 1). Learners generally categorize these short sentences, giving reasons that each

Figure 1 Sample Text Data Set

A teacher might assign beginning ELL students to group these sentences into categories (such as numbers, colors, size, age, weather, and temperature); compose their own similar sentences for each category; and use the sentences in a short, descriptive essay.

1. There are 22 students in class.
2. Choua is wearing a black shirt.
3. Mr. Ferlazzo is an old teacher.
4. Walter is tall.
5. Luther Burbank is a big school.
6. Johanna has a blue pencil.
7. There are 26 desks in the classroom.
8. Ms. Smith has short hair.
9. Chue has a young sister.
10. Today is a sunny day.
11. The boy is wearing white shoes.
12. Tomorrow will be a rainy day.
13. The rice is very hot.
14. Ms. Vue has a little baby.

sentence belongs in a specific category. Students then compose new sentences in the same format, which they then convert into paragraphs and an essay.

Teachers can use inductive strategies like these to help students learn about phonics concepts, common grammatical errors, and other key content.

4. Foster leadership potential

A good community organizer looks for signs that the leadership skills of people she or he is working with are emerging. A sense of self-efficacy and a willingness to take risks and learn from mistakes are indicators that individuals are ready to lead. Self-confidence and risk taking are also qualities that help second language learners become successful readers. Language acquisition scholar Stephen Krashen (2002) cites H. D. Brown's conclusion that "the person with high self-esteem is able to reach out beyond himself more freely, to be less inhibited, and because of his ego strength, to make the necessary mistakes involved in language learning."

Teachers can help ELLs develop self-confidence and willingness to take risks by cultivating a supportive classroom community. Besides fostering good student-teacher relationships, another way to support students' leadership qualities is to strengthen their belief in their own competence by teaching them strategies they can use to attack any learning challenge. For example, the teacher might

- Coach students in self-reflective activities and encourage students to use these activities to monitor whether they have been successful or unsuccessful at a learning task—and why.
- Teach and reinforce reading-comprehension strategies, such as monitor and repair. Using this strategy, students first determine whether they believe an unknown word or phrase is important to understanding the passage in which they've encountered that word. If it is, the student tries various methods—using a dictionary, seeking context clues, rereading the passage, and so on—to comprehend the word and check their understanding of the surrounding passage. Of course, choosing engaging readings and lessons is important here; students need to care about understanding a text before they seek to comprehend it.
- Help students refine their skill at detecting patterns. Pattern identification—from seeing that sentences contain nouns and verbs, to detecting patterns like the consistent presence of a protagonist and a climax in fiction—can have a major impact on enhancing understanding.

Teachers can help ELLs develop a sense of self-efficacy as readers by knowing each student's personal interests and offering students the opportunity to read challenging books connected to these motivating interests. The often damaging system of book "leveling" can leave students feeling restricted. If a book addresses a topic of interest to the student, we might be surprised at the effort he or she will exert to comprehend the content.

5. Promote reflection

The word *reflection* comes from the Latin reflexionem, meaning "a bending back." In reflection, people bend back to think about what they are doing and what they have done. We evaluate our thoughts and actions and come to conclusions about our strengths, weaknesses, and what we might do differently. For learners, the most important step is to take such conclusions and apply them to future thinking and action. Reflection can thus function as a means of formative assessment.

To help students reflect on their progress, teachers might involve them in activities like summarizing daily learning, self-assessing, and goal setting. We might help learners explore whether what they learned today was relevant to their lives outside the classroom—and how—or even evaluate the instructional strategies we or other teachers use.

Many teachers at my school have students, including ELLs, complete close assessments throughout the year to evaluate their reading comprehension and vocabulary development. We have students read out loud to us to evaluate fluency. Teachers share these assessment results with students, who reflect on them and use the results to identify their own reading goals and the strategies they'll use to accomplish them. The reflection component makes the process highly motivating. As one student told me, "There's something about my making a goal that pushes me harder to get to it."

The Balancing Act

A member of a community group once described to me the contrast between two organizers she'd worked with. She had learned a lot of information from one, she said, but she'd learned how to think from the other. As we work with language learners or other struggling readers, teachers must ask ourselves, When we teach, is our goal to impart information or to help students develop reading and thinking skills for a lifetime? It's not an either/or choice; an effective teacher keeps the two in balance. Holding the five steps of the organizing cycle in mind can help.

References

Bruner, J. (1996). *The culture of education.* Cambridge, MA: Harvard University Press.

Caine, R. N., & Caine, G. (1994). *Making connections: Teaching and the human brain.* Menlo Park, CA: Addison Wesley.

Calhoun, E. F. (1999). *Teaching beginning reading and writing with the Picture Word Inductive Model.* Alexandria, VA: ASCD.

Dewey, J. (1916). *Democracy and education.* New York: Macmillan.

Johnson, D., Johnson, R., & Roseth, C. (2006). Do peer relationships affect achievement? The Cooperative Link, 21(1). Retrieved from *www.co-operation.org/wp-content/uploads/2011/01/Volume-211.pdf*

Krashen, S. (2002). Second language acquisition and second language learning. Retrieved from author at *www.sdkrashen.com/SL%5FAcquisition%5Fand%5FLearning*

Marzano, R. J. (2007). *The art and science of teaching.* Alexandria, VA: ASCD.

Suarez-Orozco, C., Pimental, A., & Martin, M. (2009). The significance of relationships: Academic engagement and achievement among newcomer immigrant youth. *Teachers College Record*, 111(3), 712–749.

Critical Thinking

1. Ferlazzo speaks of viewing students who do not speak English through the lens of deficits and discusses his work as a community organizer. Why might you as teacher be wise to think of yourself as a community organizer?

2. Think about your own classroom or an experience you had in a classroom. What could you have done to initiate the five actions of the organizing cycle?

3. Can you think of other groups of students who would benefit from this assets view? Who are they? Why do you believe teachers need to shift their view of this additional group you selected?

Create Central

www.mhhe.com/createcentral

Internet References

The Center for Comprehensive School Reform and Improvement
The link for Resources for English Language Learners is
www.centerforcsri.org/index.php?option=com_content&task=view&id=678&Itemid=126
Doing What Works from the US Department of Education
http://dww.ed.gov/

LARRY FERLAZZO (mrlerlazzo@aol.com) teaches English and social studies at Luther Burbank High School in Sacramento, California, and blogs at http://larryferlazzo.edublogs.org. His latest book, *The ESL Teacher's Survival Guide,* coauthored with Katie Hull-Sypnieski, is forthcoming from Jossey Bass.

Ferlazzo, Larry. From *Educational Leadership*, vol. 69, no 6. March 2012, pp. 44–48. Copyright © 2012 by ASCD. Reprinted by permission. The Association for Supervision and Curriculum Development is a worldwide community of educators advocating sound policies and sharing best practices to achieve the success of each learner. To learn more, visit ASCD at www.ascd.org. Reprinted by permission via Copyright Clearance Center.

Article

Prepared by: Rebecca B. Evers, *Winthrop University*

Using Guided Notes to Enhance Instruction for All Students

Moira Konrad, Laurice M. Joseph, and Madoka Itoi

Learning Outcomes

After reading this article, you will be able to:

- Design guided notes for lectures and activities in your grade level or content area.
- Determine strategies to use in secondary content area classrooms to increase student achievement.

- Pay special attention to this main idea
- Engage in a written reflection
- Put down your pencil and listen to a story
- Try a challenge problem

Instructional time constraints and increased accountability require teachers to accomplish more in less time. All students are expected to make academic gains each year (i.e., adequate yearly progress); thus, teachers need to increase their instructional efficiency. One way to increase efficiency is to teach new skills and content directly through lecture (Heward, 2001). During teacher-directed lectures, students are expected to take notes to help them obtain important information.

However, for many students, taking notes from lectures or reading material can be challenging, especially for those who have learning disabilities (Hughes & Suritsky, 1994). These students often perceive traditional note-taking as labor-intensive and frustrating due to difficulties in deciphering relevant information during lectures (Barbetta & Skaruppa, 1995; Stringfellow & Miller, 2005). Additionally, listening to a lecture and taking notes at the same time poses a real challenge (Barbetta & Skaruppa, 1995). Therefore, students may choose not to take notes during lectures and play a more passive role during classroom instruction.

An alternative to traditional note-taking is a method called *guided notes*. Guided notes are "teacher-prepared handouts that 'guide' a student through a lecture with standard cues and prepared space in which to write the key facts, concepts, and/or relationships" (Heward, 1994, p. 304). Research has demonstrated that guided notes improve outcomes for students with a range of ages, skills, and abilities (Konrad, Joseph, &

Eveleigh, 2009). Specifically, guided notes increase active student responding (Austin, Lee, Thibeault, Carr, & Bailey, 2002; Blackwell & McLaughlin, 2005; Heward, 1994), improve the accuracy of students' notes (Sweeney et al., 1999), and improve students' quiz and test performance (Patterson, 2005). Additionally, research has revealed that students prefer to use guided notes over taking their own notes (Konrad et al., 2009) or using preprinted notes (Neef, McCord, & Ferreri, 2006). Not only do guided notes help students attend to lectures better, this form of note taking serves as a model for helping students learn how to take better notes on their own.

Developing Guided Notes

According to Heward (2001), guided notes are created by first developing an outline of the lecture using presentation software such as PowerPoint or overhead transparencies, focusing on the most important concepts that students need to learn. A handout consisting of blanks where important information (e.g., content that will be included on follow-up assessments) is omitted accompanies the teacher's lecture notes (see Figure 1 for a sample page from a set of guided notes). The students fill in the blanks with key concepts as they listen to the lecture. An adequate number of blanks is distributed throughout the handout to encourage active engagement, and each blank should contain enough space so students can record all essential information. In general, each blank on the guided notes should require students to record one to three words (Sweeney et al., 1999), but varying the length may help students attend to the lecture. Consider including in the guided notes one-word, two-word, or three-word responses (and occasionally four- or five-word responses for older students) in an unpredictable pattern to help keep students alert and on their toes.

For students who have difficulties with fine motor tasks, teachers can modify guided notes by (a) making the blanks shorter (i.e., requiring the students to write fewer words), (b) giving the students choices to circle, (c) allowing students to select and paste (e.g., with hook-and-loop fasteners or stickers) the correct responses, or (d) using assistive technology (e.g., computer software or adaptive assistive devices) to permit students to select correct responses.

Clouds

Directions: Follow along with your teacher and fill in your guided notes.

<u>What Are Clouds?</u>

★ A cloud is a collection of _____ of _____.

<u>What Are the Different Kinds of Clouds?</u>

★ There are many different types of _____:

Cirrus

Types of _____

Stratus

<u>How Do I Know What Type of Clouds Are in the Sky?</u>

- Cirrus clouds
  - Most common
  - Made of _____
  - Thin and _____ _____
  - Predict _____ weather

Draw a picture of a cirrus cloud.

- Cumulous clouds
  - Often called "_____" clouds
  - _____ and _____
  - Can develop into large _____ or _____ clouds

Draw a picture of a cumulous cloud.

Figure 1 Sample page from a set of guided notes with embedded graphic organizers

---

In addition to the blanks, which serve as cues to prompt students to write information provided during the lecture, teachers can use symbols to help students anticipate what to expect (Heward, 2001). For example, consider using a star symbol to indicate main ideas so students know which information is most important and will likely appear on upcoming tests. See Table 1 for several examples of symbols teachers can use to cue students. Start with just two or three symbols; use them consistently; and as students get more comfortable and proficient with guided notes, you can gradually add other cues.

A lecture does not need to be a dry, monotonous delivery of material, and teachers who use guided notes do not have to forgo their personal teaching styles. Teachers can keep lectures interesting by interspersing stories, examples, and personal experiences (Konrad et al., 2009). One way to do this might be to include cues in the guided notes (perhaps indicated by a

Table 1   Examples of Symbol Cues
Teachers Can Use within Guided Notes

Symbol	Cue
★	Pay special attention to this main idea
①	Here is some supplemental information that is interesting but will not be tested
👂	Put down your pencil and listen to a story or anecdote
✏	Engage in a written reflection
?	Try a challenge problem
📖	Read from your book and answer these questions
💬	Discuss a concept with a classmate
🏠	Complete these exercises for homework
✗	Here is a new tool for learning
⇄	Connect what we just learned to something you already knew
❑	Stop and self-monitor your behavior; have you been on-task?

specific symbol; see Table 1) that signal students to listen to a supplemental story. It is important that the anecdotes are relevant, purposeful, and strategically integrated into the lecture and that students know what they should take away from these stories.

Distinguishing essential from nonessential content during a lecture is challenging for many students (Stringfellow & Miller, 2005). This may especially be the case for students whose native language is not English. Guided notes may be a less cumbersome way of helping English language learners (ELL) take notes while simultaneously attending to the language as well as the relevant content conveyed during the lecture (Tam & Scott, 1996). Teachers may want to work with ELL specialists and/or translators to include, within the guided notes, translations of key words and phrases in the students' native language(s).

Combining Guided Notes with Other Effective Teaching Strategies

Guided notes should be combined with other evidence-based teaching strategies to increase their effectiveness. For example, as an alternative to the traditional method of involving students in class question–answer sessions (i.e., the teacher poses a question and calls on a student who has raised his or her hand), choral responding and response cards allow all students to respond in unison (Heward, 1994; Randolph, 2007). When teachers lecture using guided notes, they can stop at strategic points to review what has been covered by having all students respond to questions or prompts using choral responding or

response cards. The teacher simply asks a question, provides a brief thinking pause, and gives a signal (e.g., a snap or a verbal cue such as "class" or "show me") for all students to respond. On the signal, students either respond orally (choral response), by writing on small white boards (write-on response cards); or by selecting cards or items to hold up, such as preprinted response cards (Heward, 1994; Randolph, 2007).

Partially completed graphic organizers, such as story or geography maps, word webs, and Venn diagrams, may be embedded into guided notes to aid in labeling essential elements and gaining an understanding about relationships among concepts (Dye, 2000). See Figure 1 for an example of how a graphic organizer can be embedded into guided notes.

The teacher can also create worksheets that follow a *model-lead-test* teaching sequence and then have the students complete it along with the teacher. For example, when teaching an algorithm to solve equations, students can complete guided notes to learn the rule and then follow the teacher through the model-lead-test sequence with practice problems. The teacher should complete the first few problems (i.e., model) while the students fill in the correct answers on their guided notes (i.e., teacher-directed worksheets). The teacher should then complete the next set of problems with the help of students in the class (i.e., lead) as they are completing the problems on their guided notes. Finally, students should complete the last few problems independently (i.e., test), while the teacher monitors. The teacher can then provide the correct answers on the overhead for students to self-correct or can collect the notes and use the last set of problems as a way to assess that lesson's objective(s).

Similarly, when teaching a spelling rule (e.g., the first doubling rule), students can complete guided notes while the teacher states (and writes) the rule. The rule should be followed by examples (e.g., hop + ing = hopping) and nonexamples (e.g., jump + ing ≠ jumpping) for practice with discriminating between words that require doubling from those that do not. The teacher should walk students through the first example(s) to show them how and when to apply the rule (i.e., model), while the students follow along on their guided notes. The teacher can gradually fade assistance as students practice with additional examples (i.e., lead) until they are able to apply the rule independently (i.e., test). See Figure 2 for an example of the first page of a teacher-directed worksheet on the first doubling rule.

When students are expected to read material independently, teachers can provide them with guided notes to prompt them to attend to main ideas and important details, reflect on content, and check for understanding. For instance, when students are reading a chapter in a history textbook, they can record key concepts as well as stop and think about how events are related at certain signal points inserted throughout their guided notes. When guided notes are used in this manner, students can receive guidance on the salient features of text without direct teacher assistance. It is important to note that for students to benefit from using guided notes, reading assignments should be at their independent reading levels. Furthermore, once students have finished reading and filling in the guided notes independently, they should have access to the completed guided notes so they can self-correct their notes before using them to study (Lazarus, 1993).

Teacher-directed Worksheet on the First Doubling Rule
(I–I–I Rule)

- Today's rule is called the "First _____ Rule" or the _____ Rule.
- Here's the rule:
  - ○ In words with
    - _____ _____,
    - ending in _____ _____,
    - after _____ vowel,
    - double the final consonant before adding a vowel suffix.
  - ○ Why's this rule called the I–I–I rule? (Let's circle all the Is in the rule.)

Examples

- Watch Me:
  - ○ The word is **hop** and I want to add the suffix–ing
    - Is the word one syllable? _____
    - Does the word end in one consonant? _____
    - Does that consonant come after one vowel? _____
    - So, do we follow the I–I–I rule? _____
    - Double the final consonant before adding the vowel suffix:
      hop + ing = _____
- Let's Try One Together:
  - ○ The word is **sit** and I want to add the suffix –ing
    - Is the word one syllable? _____
    - Does the word end in one consonant? _____
    - Does that consonant come after one vowel? _____
    - So, do we follow the I–I–I rule? _____
    - Double the final consonant before adding the vowel suffix:
      sit + ing = _____
- Your Turn:
  - ○ The word is **run** and I want to add the suffix –ing
    - Is the word one syllable? _____
    - Does the word end in one consonant? _____
    - Does that consonant come after one vowel? _____
    - So, do we follow the I–I–I rule? _____
    - Double the final consonant before adding the vowel suffix:
      run + ing = _____

Non-Examples

- Watch Me:
  - ○ The word is **play** and I want to add the suffix –ing
    - Is the word one syllable? _____
    - Does the word end in one consonant? _____
    - Does that consonant come after one vowel?
    - So, do we follow the I–I–I rule? _____
    - Just add the vowel suffix: play + ing = _____

Figure 2   Sample page from a teacher-directed worksheet

Completing and Studying Guided Notes

Guided notes can serve as a tool to facilitate students' preparing for upcoming assessments, and one advantage of using guided notes is that students are more likely to leave class with a complete and accurate set of notes (Konrad et al., 2009) from which to study. However, some students may need close monitoring as they complete the guided notes, particularly when they are first learning how to use them. Monitoring student use of guided notes may be easily accomplished in an inclusive classroom where team-teaching occurs (Konrad et al., 2009). For instance, while one teacher is lecturing to the class, the other can assist by monitoring and providing feedback to all students on the accuracy of their guided notes. Furthermore, some students may need additional contingencies to use guided notes. For example, teachers can award bonus points for complete and accurate notes. If teachers collect guided notes on an unpredictable schedule, students know that they should be ready to turn them in at any time. This also makes monitoring student note-taking and delivering contingent reinforcement less cumbersome to manage on a day-to-day basis. Another way to motivate students to complete guided notes is to give in-class, open-note quizzes immediately following lectures. Teachers should design these quizzes so that students with complete guided notes will be able to do well.

Characters in *The Giver* by Lois Lowry (1993)

Directions: Follow along with your teacher and classmates as you learn about and discuss the characters in the novel. Once you have completed the guided notes, fold the page in half to quiz yourself. Be sure to quiz yourself from left to right **AND** from right to left. You can also pair up with a classmate and quiz each other. When you quiz each other, be sure to mix up the order in which you ask the questions.

Characteristics	Character
1. Who is the main character in the novel?	1. _____
2. Write three adjectives that describe the main character.	2. a. _____ b. _____ c. _____
3. Which character is pale-eye, bearded, and tired?	3. _____
4. What is Jonas' mother's profession?	4. _____
5. What is Jonas' father's profession?	5. _____
6. Write three adjectives that describe Asher.	6. a. _____ b. _____ c. _____
7. Write three adjectives that describe Lily.	7. a. _____ b. _____ c. _____
8. Write three adjectives that describe Fiona.	8. a. _____ b. _____ c. _____
9. Which character receives the assignment to become Caretaker of the Old?	9. _____
10. Which character has the most honored profession/assignment in the Community?	10. _____

Figure 3   Sample page from columnar guided notes

Even when students are absent, they should be held accountable for learning the content that was covered during their absence. Teachers can leave a blank copy of the guided notes along with a copy of the completed notes in a "While You Were Out" folder. Students can then learn to complete the guided notes from the missed lecture(s) upon their return. This way, students who are not at school can still have opportunities for active responding.

Once students have a set of accurate lecture notes, they should be taught and encouraged to use those notes to study for upcoming quizzes and exams. To promote active studying, instructors can format guided notes in columns with questions, prompts, or main ideas on the left side and answers or supporting details on the right side (see Figure 3) (Weishaar & Boyle, 1999). Students can then learn to fold the paper down the middle to quiz themselves. This format may also serve as a model for students learning to take their own notes.

Additionally, teachers can help students create study cards (Itoi, 2004; Wood, 2005) by printing their guided notes on both sides of a sheet so that one side allows students to take notes, whereas the other side consists of questions relevant to the information on the guided notes side of the card. Figures 4 and 5 illustrate how a set of guided note study cards should be formatted. Specifically, the completed guided notes become the backs of the study cards (i.e., answers); and the questions, which are printed on the back of the original set of guided notes, become the front sides. With this format, students can simply cut out the notes to create a set of flashcards. Teachers should lead structured review sessions to show students how to study with flash-cards and should emphasize repeated practice in which students read the question to themselves, say the answer, and check the answer by referring back to the information recorded on the guided notes.

Guided Notes: Parts of Speech	_____ is used to name a person, animal, place, thing, and abstract idea. Examples:
Name _____ Date _____ Directions: These guided notes will be the backs of your study cards. Complete them with the teacher and wait for instructions on how to cut them into cards and use them to study. 1 (back)	_____ _____ 2 (back)
_____ tells you the action or the state of being. Examples: _____ _____ 3 (back)	_____ tells you something extra about the person or objects. Examples: _____ _____ 4 (back)
_____ tells you something extra about the verb, an adjective, or another adverb by answering questions such as "how" "when" or "how much." Examples: _____ _____ 5 (back)	_____ is always used with a noun and tells you something extra about a noun. There are only three of them: _____ _____ 6 (back)

Figure 4 Sample back page from a set of guided notes study cards

When instructors combine guided notes with in-class review time, learning outcomes are enhanced (Lazarus, 1993). A review session using a set of guided notes study cards easily can take place in a peer-tutoring context, in which students teach one another under the direction of a teacher (e.g., Veerkamp, Kamps, & Cooper, 2007). Teachers should simply divide students into pairs and provide each student with a peer-tutoring folder (Heward, 2006), which contains the guided notes study cards in a "Go" pocket. Students take turns reading the questions and answering them by saying aloud the words in the blanks from the guided notes. Once students master a card, it can be moved into a different pocket in the folder (e.g., mastered).

Promoting Higher Order Thinking

In addition to assisting students with studying for exams, guided notes can also be used to promote higher order thinking. For example, teachers can encourage students to reflect on the lecture by including within the guided notes stopping points for students to pause and think critically, ask questions, connect with personal experience, relate to prior knowledge, and generate new ideas.

Reciprocal teaching may also be implemented during a class lecture similar to the way in which this method is implemented in a reading group (Palinscar & Brown, 1984; van Garderen,

2004). After the teacher has created and modeled a lecture using guided notes, students in the class can take turns creating guided notes and leading the class through a minilecture using their prepared guided notes. Students who lead the class need to be well prepared so that they can respond to questions and clarify responses made by their classmates. The instructor may ask two students to cocreate and colead a lecture using guided notes. Students will need structure and guidance throughout this process, and teachers will need to use their best judgment in determining if this form of reciprocal teaching is appropriate for their classroom given the diverse characteristics and needs of their students.

Conclusion

With so much material to cover in so little time, guided notes can be helpful for teachers in holding themselves accountable for reaching daily objectives. Teachers may want to create a packet of guided notes that corresponds to an instructional unit and decide (ahead of time) which pages will be covered on which days. This can help the teacher strategically plan ahead and stay on task during lectures rather than straying off topic. Teachers should design assessments (e.g., quizzes, exams) that are direct measures of mastery of material covered within the guided notes. They should use the data from

What part of speech is used to name a person, animal, place, thing, or abstract idea? Give two examples. 2 (front)	**Study Cards: Parts of Speech** Directions: Ask yourself or a peer the questions or prompts, try to answer the questions, and check the back of the card to see if you are correct. Put them into two piles (corrects and incorrects). Be sure to do more studying with the incorrects! 1 (front)
What part of speech is used to tell you something extra about a person or objects? Give two examples. 4 (front)	What part of speech tells you the action or the state of being? Give two examples. 3 (front)
What part of speech is used with a noun and tells you something extra about the noun? (There are only three of these.) Name all three. 6 (front)	What part of speech tells you something extra about a verb, an adjective, or another _____ by answering questions such as how, when, or how much? Give two examples. 5 (front)

Figure 5   Sample front page from a set of guided notes study cards

these assessments to evaluate the effectiveness of their lessons and make appropriate instructional adjustments as needed.

The suggestions offered here are not exhaustive of all possible ways guided notes can be implemented. This versatile tool not only facilitates students' attention to lecture, ease in studying for exams, and improved test performance, it helps teachers organize and pace their delivery of lecture content.

References

Austin, J. L., Lee, M. G., Thibeault, M. D., Carr, J. E., & Bailey, J. S. (2002). Effects of guided notes on university students' responding and recall of information. *Journal of Behavioral Education, 11,* 243–254.

Barbetta, F. M., & Skaruppa, C. L. (1995). Looking for a way to improve your behavior analysis lectures? Try guided notes. *The Behavior Analyst, 18,* 155–160.

Blackwell, A. J., & McLaughlin, T. F. (2005). Using guided notes, choral responding, and response cards to increase student performance. *International Journal of Special Education, 20,* 1–5.

Dye, G. A. (2000). Graphic organizers to the rescue! Helping students link—and remember—information. *TEACHING Exceptional Children, 32*(3), 72–76.

Heward, W. L. (1994). Three "low-tech" strategies for increasing the frequency of active student response during group instruction.

In R. Gardner, D. M. Sainato, J. O. Cooper, T. E. Heron, W. L. Heward, J. Eshleman, & T. A. Grossi (Eds.), *Behavior analysis in education: Focus on measurably superior instruction* (pp. 283–320). Monterey, CA: Brooks/Cole.

Heward, W. L. (2001). *Guided notes: Improving the effectiveness of your lectures.* Columbus: Ohio State University Partnership Grant for Improving the Quality of Education for Students With Disabilities.

Heward, W. L. (2006). *Exceptional children: An introduction to special education.* Upper Saddle River, NJ: Prentice Hall.

Hughes, C. A., & Suritsky, S. K. (1994). Note-taking skills of university students with and without learning disabilities. *Journal of Learning Disabilities, 27,* 20–24.

Itoi, M. (2004). *Effects of guided notes study cards on the accuracy of lecture notes and next-day quiz scores of students in a 7th grade social studies classroom.* Unpublished master's thesis, Ohio State University, Columbus.

Konrad, M., Joseph, L. M., & Eveleigh, E. (2009). A meta-analytic review of guided notes. *Education & Treatment of Children, 32,* 421–444.

Lazarus, B. D. (1993). Guided notes: Effects with secondary and post secondary students with mild disabilities. *Education and Treatment of Children, 16,* 272–289.

Lowry, L. (1993). *The giver.* New York, NY: Dell Laurel-Leaf.

Neef, N. A., McCord, B. E., & Ferreri, S. J. (2006). Effects of guided notes versus completed notes during lectures on college students' quiz performance. *Journal of Applied Behavior Analysis, 39,* 123–130.

Palinscar, A. S., & Brown, A. L. (1984). Reciprocal teaching of comprehension fostering and comprehension monitoring activities. *Cognition and Instruction, 1,* 117–175.

Patterson, K. B. (2005). Increasing positive outcomes for African American males in special education with the use of guided notes. *Journal of Negro Education, 74,* 311–320.

Randolph, J. J. (2007). Meta-analysis of the effects of response cards on student achievement, participation, and intervals of off-task behavior. *Journal of Positive Behavior Interventions, 9,* 113–128.

Stringfellow, J. L., & Miller, S. P. (2005). Enhancing student performance in secondary classrooms while providing access to the general education curriculum using lecture format. *TEACHING Exceptional Children Plus, 1*(6), 2–16.

Sweeney, W. J., Ehrhardt, A. M., Gardner, R., Jones, L., Greenfield, R., & Fribley, S. (1999). Using guided notes with academically at-risk high school students during a remedial summer social studies class. *Psychology in the Schools, 36,* 305–318.

Tam, B. K. Y., & Scott, M. L. (1996). Three group instructional strategies for students with limited English proficiency in vocational education. *Journal of Vocational Special Needs Education, 19*(1), 31–36.

van Garderen, D. (2004). Reciprocal teaching as a comprehension strategy for understanding mathematical word problems. *Reading & Writing Quarterly, 20,* 225–229.

Veerkamp, M. B., Kamps, D. M., & Cooper, L. (2007). The effects of classwide peer tutoring on the reading achievement of urban middle school students. *Education and Treatment of Children, 30,* 21–51.

Weishaar, M. K., & Boyle, J. R. (1999). Note-taking strategies for students with disabilities. *Clearing House, 72,* 392–395.

Wood, C. L. (2005). *Effects of random study checks and guided notes study cards on middle school special education students' notetaking accuracy and science vocabulary quiz scores.* Retrieved from OhioLINK Electronic Thesis and Dissertations Center.

Critical Thinking

1. Guided notes can be helpful to students with learning disabilities; so why would it be included in a unit on English Language Learners? Why would Guided Notes be useful for them?

2. While guided notes are generally used for taking notes during a lecture in class, how else might teachers use this strategy to provide equitable access to the curriculum and support student learning?

3. Find a lesson plan or activity that you have taught or find one from another source. Now prepare guided notes to support a student who has difficulty writing or using Standard English in a classroom setting.

4. Some teachers consider providing notes of any kind to students as coddling or enabling helplessness. However, after reading this article you have determined that you will use this strategy. What would you say to relieve the concerns these teachers have about enabling?

Create Central

www.mhhe.com/createcentral

Internet References

Larry Ferlazzo's educational blog
http://larryferlazzo.edublogs.org/
Study Guides and Strategies
A link to more information about Guided Notes is at
www.studygs.net/guidednotes.htm

MOIRA KONRAD, PhD, is an assistant professor of special education at Ohio State University. Her current interests include self-determination and literacy development for youth with disabilities. **LAURICE M. JOSEPH, PhD,** is an associate professor of school psychology at Ohio State University. Her current interests include academic interventions, students with disabilities, and applied behavior analysis. **MADOKA ITOI, PhD,** is a senior clinician at Spectrum Center. Her current interests include analyzing intervention efficiency and effectiveness for students with disabilities in the educational context.

Declaration of Conflicting Interest—The author(s) declared no conflicts of interest with respect to the authorship and/or publication of this article.

Funding—The author(s) received no financial support for the research and/or authorship of this article.

Unit 6

Technology Supports Learning

UNIT

Prepared by: Rebecca B. Evers, *Winthrop University*

Technology Supports Learning

Technology has been a change agent in education. After experiencing early motion pictures in 1913, Thomas Edison declared that books would become obsolete in schools because we would be able to learn everything from movies. Most recently we have heard similar claims about digital books from advocates of Kindle, Nook, iPad, and other e-readers and sellers of audio books. What is really happening in our schools? Are textbooks disappearing? Is everyone connected? Are our students sitting all day laboring over a keyboard and staring at a screen? In this unit we will explore both the potential of the digital technology and the challenges of using this technology for teaching and learning.

There are significant trends noted by Bitter and Pierson (2002) that are important to this discussion. The first is the shift in demographics within our student population. We are seeing an increased numbers of students who do not live in traditional family structures, who have special needs at both the high and low ends of achievement, who are English Language Learners, or who live in poverty. For many of these students, the ability to access sophisticated technology may not exist in their homes or neighborhoods. Hence, schools are the only place where they can be exposed to and learn about the usage of technology. These students, many of whom will need technology to access the curriculum, will pose a considerable challenge to public schools. An additional challenge, according to Bitter and Pierson, will be the acceleration of technological change that correspondingly increases the pace of change in our knowledge base. Keeping up in one's field of expertise or areas of interest has become a full-time job of its own.

In most schools, regardless of where the school is regionally or economically, most teachers who use computers do so because computers make their jobs easier and help them complete tasks more efficiently. The computer can do things the teacher cannot or is unwilling to do. We use them to keep digital grade books that will correctly calculate final grades in a flash; search for information to use in lectures; create photos and clip art to illustrate our PowerPoints; obtain lesson plans to meet state standards; and communicate with peers down the hall, the principal, and even with parents. But too often the teacher's computer may be the only computer in a classroom. There may be a computer lab down the hall or a few computers in the media center, but very few schools have laptops or handhelds for all students. So almost 100 years ago, Thomas Edison may have been a bit hasty to declare books a thing of the past. In the Education 98/99, we published an article, *The Silicon Classroom* by Kaplan and Rogers (1996) which declared that schools were rushing to spend billions on computers without a clue on what

to do with them. In this issue, we are publishing an article that outlines the challenges that schools face today in implementing computer usage in the classroom. Why haven't we seen greater strides made to bring every school into the digital age? We hope the articles presented in this unit will challenge you to consider how you should and will use technology to provide access to information within your content area curriculum to all students.

The first article is meant to provide a glimpse of what is possible and what challenges still remain. Despite the increased use of technology across the nation's schools, too many school districts still ban cell phones from their buildings. However, some teachers are finding interesting ways to use phones during instruction; giving life to the old saying, "if you can't beat them, then join them." For example: Calculators may be available in math and even in science classes, but what about their use in social studies and language arts classes where students may want to average grades or percentages in class elections. Digital cameras can be used to document notes on the board from class discussions, posters they need to remember, or even a slide from a multimedia presentation; then there are field trips and role plays/skits in class. Internet access may be needed when none is available in the classroom and/or home. Dictionaries allow students with disabilities, who are ELL, or even gifted, to look up a definition of a new word (Melville, 2005). As Kolb follows Sarah into her 7th grade class, she notes that students are using their cell phones to complete an opinion poll before class begins and as class continues the students repeatedly use their phone to participate in class, gather new information, and complete assessments. Such activities cause Kolb to refer to the cell phone as the Swiss Army knife of digital tools. Further, using the cell phone in class allows the teacher to teach important lessons about using cell phones in life. Finally, she outlines interesting ways to use cell phones for instruction.

Crossman begins by reminding us that too many teachers and schools are using 19th century methods to teach 21st century students. He asserts that a rebellion is happening in schools as young students are unable to relate to the teaching methods and materials presented in most classrooms. This is a non-violent rebellion, but it is nonetheless very disturbing and destructive. In conclusion, Crossman offers solutions to the problems he has described.

If we are in the middle of a rebellion or revolution, even a non-violent one, we will need weapons to take into battle. Tucker's article on collaborative technology provides an interesting array of weapons or rather technology tools that are easily accessible to teachers and their students. Most of us know about Google Docs, but how does that software support student learning?

She explains how she uses the free software, *Collaborize Classroom,* to teach communication skills and facilitate group discussion. The tools mentioned here will be useful to teachers who are considering using the relatively new teaching method of *Flipping* discussed in the last two articles of this unit.

Álvarez describes her journey from being a teacher who looked for reasons and rationales for why students were failing in her classes to a teacher who looked for solutions. Her primary solution was to *flip* her classroom. After she explains why and how she *flipped,* she notes the student successes and explains why parents approved of the flip and used the resources made available to them as well as their children. This article is a good place to start if you are not sure what flipping a classroom means. The Cohen and Brugar article will take you to the next step as they explain why they wanted to flip their classes. Further, they note that three themes emerged as they review student surveys and assessment data. Students demonstrated increased levels of confidence, collaboration, and comprehension. You will find their list of five things to remember when developing video instruction.

Hopefully the articles in this unit will stimulate your imagination to consider using more technology in your classroom or using what you have more creatively.

References

Bitter, G. & M. Pierson. 2002. *Using Technology in the Classroom.* Boston, MA: Allyn and Bacon.

Melville, E (2005). Cell Phones: Nuisance or Necessity. *Teaching Today.* Retrieved on 15 May 2012 from http://privateschool. about.com/gi/o.htm?zi=1/XJ&zTi=1&sdn=privateschool&cdn= education&tm=26&gps=234_220_1066_560&f=20&tt=13&bt =1&bts=1&zu=http%3A//www.glencoe.com/sec/teachingtoday/ educationupclose.phtml/52

Article   Prepared by: Rebecca B. Evers, *Winthrop University*

Adventures with Cell Phones

Teachers are finding creative ways to turn the basic cell phone from a digital distraction into a versatile learning tool.

LIZ KOLB

Learning Outcomes

After reading this article, you will be able to:

- Consider the ways that technology has changes schooling.

- Determine how cell phone technology might be used for educational purposes in your teaching situation.

When 7th grader Sarah walked into her history classroom a few minutes before class began, she immediately took out her cell phone and began text messaging. She wasn't texting her friends, though. Instead, she was participating in the class brainstorming poll that her teacher had projected on the whiteboard. The teacher was using Poll Everywhere (www.polleverywhere.com) to ask students to give their opinion about the most important cause of the United States Civil War (slavery, states' rights vs. federal rights, the election of Lincoln, social issues, or financial issues). Sarah sent in her response, and then watched the percentages in the bar graph on the whiteboard change as more students texted in their votes.

When class began, Sarah's teacher asked the students to send another text message, this time explaining their reason for the selection they made. Sarah sent her answer, but as she watched other students' responses pop up on the whiteboard, she began to think about other viewpoints. Because the answers were anonymous, students felt comfortable giving their honest opinions.

After the teacher led the students in briefly reviewing the range of comments they had sent to the brainstorming board, she put the students into groups and asked them to create an 8–10 minute podcast debating the merits of two different viewpoints on the major cause of the war. To research their two viewpoints, the groups used their mobile phones to search different sources on the mobile Internet. Once they gathered their data and developed their podcast, they called in to the teacher's Google Voice number and recorded their podcast in her private account. The podcasts immediately became downloadable

MP3 files. Later, the teacher would listen to them on her phone, evaluate them, and text message her feedback to the students.

As students left class, the teacher told them to use their phones to take a picture of the bar code she had posted by the doorway. When they did so, Lincoln's Gettysburg Address and a short video from Ken Burns's documentary *The Civil War* appeared on their phones, along with their homework assignment—read the text, watch the video, and then send a 140-character text-message summary of the Gettysburg Address to the class brainstorming board. The next day in class, the students would compare and evaluate the various summaries.

Why Cell Phones Are Important in Learning

When I was a high school technology coordinator and secondary social studies teacher, I wrote strong policies to keep student cell phones out of my school because of the distraction and cheating they could cause. Today, I hear many other educators express the same concerns. They worry that allowing cell phones in schools will lead to more problems with cheating, distraction, sexting, or general laziness in learning.

Although I believe we should not ignore these concerns, I've changed my perspective in the last five years. After using cell phones in my own teaching at the University of Michigan, I've become a strong advocate for allowing teachers and schools to use them as a learning tool. Here are a few reasons why.

Class time is precious. Cell phones can help teachers increase the amount of class time spent on teaching and learning. First, because most students already know how to use a cell phone (often better than their teachers do), there is no need to consume class time teaching students to use new instructional hardware and software. In addition, integrating cell phones into learning means that many technology-based activities can occur outside the classroom, freeing up class time to focus on learning content. Students do not even need to bring their cell phones into the classroom to use them for learning—they can collect images, videos, and audio recordings on their cell phones for homework and send them to the teacher or a class website.

Cell phones can save money. The great majority of students own a cell phone—98% of 9th-12th graders, 83% of 6th-8th graders, and 43% of 2nd-5th graders (Project Tomorrow, 2010). When schools tap into this resource, they get the benefits of technology without spending money on additional expensive hardware and software. If students do not own a cell phone, many cell phone activities can also be done over a landline (with a toll-free number) or via the Internet.

Students love them. It's indisputable—students are incredibly fond of their cell phones. They never leave home without them. Integrating their favorite device into learning can get students more engaged with classroom content.

Cell phones facilitate learning anytime, anywhere, from any source, at any pace. Twenty-first century students don't want learning to be confined to a classroom or even a library. They want to be able to learn anytime (even at 2:00 A.M.); anywhere (even at the mall); from any source (for example, researching lunar eclipses by connecting with the NASA website, Wikipedia, a space observatory in South Africa, and their own interest group on Facebook); and at their own pace. A cell phone lends itself to this type of learning. With it, students can connect to the Internet while they wait in line, document current events while those events are happening, or text message with others in their learning group about a project on the go.

Students need preparation for 21st century jobs. The abilities to text message, take mobile photos and videos, and connect to the Internet by cell phone will almost certainly be required for many future jobs. Although students know how to do many of these activities, they do not usually understand how these skills could be helpful in their future professions. If schools model how to use cell phones to organize, network, schedule, and gather data, students may see their phone as a tool for future professional growth rather than just a toy.

Students need to learn mobile etiquette and safety. Fifty-two percent of 10-17-year-olds who use cell phones say they send text messages while watching a movie in the theater; 28% send messages at the dinner table (Dias, 2007). Additionally, students often do not understand the repercussions of sending potentially embarrassing text messages (which are often not private and can be retrieved by cell phone companies); using inappropriate chat language; or publishing mobile media on the Internet without permission. Cell phone instructional activities give educators the opportunity to talk with their students about mobile etiquette.

Mobile phones can empower students who are visually or hearing impaired. For example, by coupling the phone with websites like Dial2Do (www.Dial2Do.com), students who are visually impaired can send speech-to-text e-mails, blog posts, tweets, reminders, posts on a Google calendar, and so on. In addition, these students can listen to podcasts, web pages, e-mails, or Google calendar posts. With Dial2Do, students who are hearing impaired can take advantage of text-messaging features to participate in activities that normally require oral communication—they can use sites like Google Voice (www.google.com/voice) to view text transcripts of voice-mail messages.

Learning Activities with Cell Phones

Teachers are leading students in exciting learning activities with cell phones. All the following activities can be done with a basic cell phone that has a camera and text-messaging capabilities (no need for a smartphone).

Activity 1: Podcasting, Oral Recordings, or Oral Quizzes

Probably the easiest activity to do with a cell phone is to create instant podcasts and oral recordings. Many resources on the Internet allow students to post their phone calls online as audio files or podcasts. Teachers can also create a Google Voice account (www.google.com/voice) that provides a free local phone number—associated with the teacher's phone or a voice mailbox—on which students can leave recorded homework assignments or test answers.

For example, a Spanish instructor uses her Google Voice account to give oral quizzes. Through Google Voice, she sends a text message to her 23 Spanish two students telling them when their oral quiz is ready. The students call in to the teacher's Google Voice number, listen to a greeting she has created giving them their quiz instructions, and then speak their answers. When each student hangs up, his or her quiz becomes an MP3 file in the teacher's private Google space. The Spanish teacher then receives an e-mail or text message that she has a new voice-mail message. She can call in to Google Voice or log in online to hear the quizzes. In addition, the teacher can send a text message to each student directly from Google Voice with the student's individual evaluation.

Because Google Voice archives voice-mail and text-message communication, there is a running record of all activities and progress. If the teacher chooses, she could make the oral quizzes into podcasts by uploading them to a podcasting service, such as iTunes, and requiring students to subscribe to the podcast.

Activity 2: Mobile Geotagging

Mobile geotagging is the ability to post media (photos, video, audio, or text) from a mobile phone to a specific point on a map. Although geotagging usually requires a global positioning system (GPS) or Bluetooth, some websites couple with basic cell phones to allow geotagging. For example, Flagr (www.flagr.com) allows users to create public, semiprivate, or private maps. Anyone who has a Flagr account and is a member of a particular map's group can send a photo or text message to a specific point on that map.

Teachers in many subject areas can use geotagging to enhance learning. For example, students in a middle school biology class who are studying different biological species can take pictures of species in their local community and then send each picture and a description of the habitat where they found the species to the class Flagr map. Back in the classroom, the teacher opens the Flagr map, and the students begin to identify the species and discuss why they were found in each particular habitat.

Another site that captures locations through mobile phones, GeoGraffiti (www.geograffiti.com), creates voice-marks—audio postings to specific map locations. For example, a history teacher assigns his students to create an audio tour about local history. The students go to various historical monuments and buildings in the community and then phone in historical summaries of the significance of these sites to GeoGraffiti, which places the oral recordings in the appropriate geographic locations on the map. This activity enables students to research local history, practice public speaking, and learn geography in one assignment.

Activity 3: Digital Storybooks

Although there are many ways to create digital storybooks (such as Photostory, iMovie, Jumpcut, and VoiceThread), many of these resources depend on computer or Internet access. This means that students cannot create the digital stories anytime, anywhere. Yodio (www.yodio.com) enables students to create and participate in individual or collaborative digital storybooks using a mobile phone.

For example, a class of 1st graders on a trip to the zoo creates a collaborative digital storybook with Yodio concerning what they learned about the animals on the trip. Each parent chaperone has a group of four or five students, who take turns calling in to the Yodio phone number (on the parent chaperone's phone) and recording their observations about an animal, perhaps even capturing the animal's sound. Students also take a picture of their chosen animal with the cell phone. Back at school, the students log in to Yodio and create a digital storybook combining their recorded narrations and photos.

Activity 4: Student Organization

Students often have mixed results when they use hard-copy assignment notebooks to organize their school assignments. Cell phones can help with organization if students take advantage of services like Jott (www.jott.com) or Dial2Do (www.dial2do.com). These voice-to-text services enable users to call in reminders to themselves, send e-mails or text messages to groups of people, create posts, create a schedule on a Google calendar, listen to their Google calendar, listen to their e-mail, and even listen to podcasts and webpages on the go. For example, a high school student who does not have Internet access at home could call in to Dial2Do to check on homework assignments and set up homework reminders.

Activity 5: Photo Projects

Imagine a homework assignment in which 4th grade mathematics students take pictures of different polygons they see in their everyday lives and instantly send them (along with a short text message describing the type of polygon) to a private space online. The next day in class, the teacher opens the private space and uses it to illustrate polygons and their connection to students' lives, leading to a lesson on how to measure these polygons.

This activity can be done using the photo-sharing sites Flickr (www.flickr.com) and Photobucket (www.photobucket.com). Both sites have a private mobile address that can be used

Using Cell Phones Appropriately

Before you begin using mobile phones for instruction, teach students how to use their devices appropriately, legally, and safely. Here are some sample activities:

- Show and discuss the brief video *Digital Dossier* (www.youtube.com/watch?v=79IYZVYIVLA)—which describes all the digital records that accumulate about a typical person from conception to death—to make students aware that all mobile messages, media uses, and calls are part of their permanent record.
- Discuss how to stay safe in the mobile world, using websites like ConnectSafely (www.connectsafely.org), which includes social network safety tips for teens and parents.
- For middle and high school students, show the MTV special on sexting (www.mtv.com/news/articles/1631123/20100203/asher_roth.jhtml) and encourage them to take the sexting quiz online (www.athinline.org).
- Give students a survey assessing what they know about mobile phone use (their own phones as well as the public nature of their text messages, GPS location, and phone records). Discuss the results. For elementary students, you can use the WoogieWorld website. At www.woogiworld.com/educators, students can sign up to play games that teach them cybersafety, cyberethics, cybersecurity, and cyberhealth.
- With middle and high school students, discuss examples of students and professionals who have lost jobs or been in court as a result of text messaging, sexting, or media sharing via cell phone. For example, see www.oprah.com/packages/no-phone-zone.html (texting while driving) and www.mtv.com/news/articles/1608002/20090327/story.jhtml or www.cnn.com/2009/CRIME/04/07/sexting.busts (sexting).
- Develop consequences for inappropriate actions conducted on cell phones—focusing on the act itself, rather than the tool used to conduct the act. For example, school rules are commonly already in place to prohibit cheating, failing to pay attention in class, or saying or doing something inappropriate during class.
- Keep parents informed of any cell phone activities the class conducts through permission forms, parent information nights, and even by inviting parents to participate (via their mobile phones) in the activities.

on any mobile phone; all the teacher needs to do is set up the mobile account and give students the address.

Activity 6: Classroom Response Systems

Classroom Response Systems (sometimes called *clickers*) are an exciting and engaging way for students to take instant polls and quizzes or even to record attendance, but these systems can be costly for schools. Resources like Poll Everywhere (www.polleverywhere.com), Wiffiti (www.wiffiti.com), and TextTheMob (www.textthemob.com) enable teachers to turn basic cell phones into classroom performance clickers at no charge. Students can send poll responses and ideas achieved through brainstorming directly to an interactive webpage—either in the classroom to see instant results or outside the classroom to send in responses that the class can view and discuss the next day.

For example, when students walk into their math class, the teacher projects onto an interactive whiteboard the question, How do you define a right angle? The students use their cell phones to text in their definitions, which instantly appear on the whiteboard and serve as the introduction to the lesson.

Activity 7: Information Gathering

Teachers can design instructional activities that help students learn how to use their cell phones as an anytime, anywhere research and information-gathering device. For example, while on a field trip to historical Williamsburg, Virginia, a teacher tells his class to send any questions that occur to them to the free information site ChaCha (www.chacha.com). One student wonders why a certain building was constructed in such an odd way. No tour guides are around to help, so he calls 1-800-chacha, asks his question, and gets a text-message answer back in minutes.

The Future Is Here

Many teachers are discovering that a basic cell phone can be the Swiss army knife of digital learning tools. Even if they did not grow up in the digital generation themselves, they have come to accept the mobile phone as a ubiquitous presence in the everyday lives of both elementary and secondary students. I share these educators' belief that it's time to stop banning mobile phones and start integrating them into learning.

A basic cell phone can be the Swiss army knife of digital learning tools.

References

Dias, S. (2007, July 2). Mobile cell phone usage soars in summer. *The Washington Post.* Retrieved from www.voices.washingtonpost.com/posttech/2007/teen_cell_phone_usage_soars_in.html

Project Tomorrow. (2010). *Creating our future: Students speak up about their vision for 21st century learning.* Retrieved from www.tomorrow.org/speakup/pdfs/SUNational Findings2009.pdf

Critical Thinking

1. Why do you think administrators are so opposed to allowing cell phones in schools?

2. Does the school where you teach or the college you are attending have a policy on cell phones? Did you agree with that policy before you read this article? What do you think now?

3. Design an activity to use a cell phone for learning or assessment in your content area. Prepare to share the plan in a class discussion.

Create Central

www.mhhe.com/createcentral

Internet References

Center for Applied Special Technology
http://cast.org/
www.cast.org/teachingeverystudent/

LIZ KOLB is a lecturer in learning technologies, School of Education, University of Michigan. She is the author of *Toys to Tools: Connecting Student Cell Phones to Education* (International Society for Technology in Education, 2008); elikeren@umich.edu.

Article   Prepared by: Rebecca B. Evers, *Winthrop University*

From the Three *R*s to the Four *C*s
Radically Redesigning K-12 Education

The battle against nonliteracy has focused on teaching everyone to read and write text. But new technologies that facilitate more holistic learning styles, engaging all of the learner's senses, may open the locked stores of global knowledge for all. Instead of reading, 'riting, and 'rithmetic, we'll move to critical thinking, creative thinking, "compspeak," and calculators.

WILLIAM CROSSMAN

Learning Outcomes

After reading this article, you will be able to:

- Explain how technology supports the four *C*s in your content area or grade level.

From the moment that Jessica Everyperson was born, her brain, central nervous system, and all of her senses shifted into high gear to access and to try to understand the incredible new informational environment that surrounded her. She had to make sense of new sights, sounds, tastes, smells, tactile experiences, and even new body positions.

Jessica approached her new world with all of her senses operating together at peak performance as she tried to make sense of it all. Her new reality was dynamic, constantly changing from millisecond to millisecond, and she immediately and instinctively began to interact with the new information that poured through her senses.

Jessica's cognitive ability to access new information interactively, and to use all of her senses at once to optimize her perception of that ever-changing information, is all about her hardwiring. Jessica, like all "everypersons" everywhere, was innately, biogenetically hardwired to access information in this way.

For Jessica's first four or five years, her all-sensory, interactive cognitive skills blossomed with amazing rapidity. Every moment provided her with new integrated-sensory learning experiences that helped to consolidate her "unity of consciousness," as the ancient Greek philosophers called it. Because each learning experience was all-sensory, Jessica's perception of reality was truly holistic. This meant that the ways she processed, interpreted, and understood her perceptions were also holistic. Jessica was therefore developing the ability to both perceive and understand the many sides of a situation—the cognitive skills that form the basis of critical thinking and lead to a broad and compassionate worldview.

During those preschool years, she also became proficient in using the variety of information technologies (ITs) that continued to be introduced into her environment: radio, TV, movies, computers, video games, cell phones, iPods, etc. Early on, she stopped watching TV, which engaged only her eyes and ears, and switched to video games, which engaged her eyes, ears, and touch/tactility. Before she could even read a word, Jessica had become a multimodal multitasker, talking on her cell phone while listening to her iPod and playing a video game.

At this point in her young life, Jessica was feeling very good about her ability to swim in the vast sea of information using the assortment of emerging ITs. Not surprisingly, she was also feeling very good about herself.

Then, Jessica started school!

The Brightness Dims: Hello K-12, Hello Three *R*s (Reading, 'Riting, 'Rithmetic)

On Jessica's first day in kindergarten, her teacher was really nice, but the message that the school system communicated to Jessica and her schoolmates was harsh. Although none of the teachers or administrators ever stated it in such blatant terms, the message, as expressed via Jessica's school's mandated course curriculum and defined student learning outcomes (SLOs), was this: Reading/writing is the only acceptable way to access information. This is the way we do it in "modern" society. Text literacy is the foundation of all coherent and logical thinking, of all real learning and knowledge, and even of morality and personal responsibility. It is, in fact, the cornerstone of civilization itself.

And the message continued: Since you don't know how to read or write yet, Jessica, you really don't know anything of value, you have no useful cognitive skills, and you have no real ways to process the experiences and/or the data that enter your brain through your senses. So, Jessica, from now on, through all of your years of schooling—through your entire K-12 education—you and we, your teachers, must focus all of our attention on your acquiring those reading and writing skills.

The United States Department of Education holds every school system in the United States accountable for instilling reading skills, as well as math skills, in every one of its students, and it requires students to take a battery of standardized tests every year to see if both their reading scores and math scores are going up.

If the test scores trend upward, the schools are rewarded. If they stay level or decline, the schools are punished with funding cuts and threatened with forced closure. Schools literally pin their long-term survival on just two variables: First, do the tests show that students can read and write, and second, do the tests show that students can do math?

From that moment on, Jessica's learning experience took a radical downward turn. Instead of accessing a dynamic, ever-changing reality, she was going to have to focus almost entirely on a static reality that just sat there on the page or computer screen: text. Instead of accessing information using all of her integrated senses simultaneously, she was going to have to use only her eyes. And instead of experiencing information interactively—as a two-way street that she could change by using her interactive technologies—she was going to have to experience information as a one-way street: by absorbing the text in front of her without being able to change it.

Welcome, Jessica, to the three Rs, the essence of K-12 education. Of course, Jessica and her schoolmates, particularly in middle and high school, will take other courses: history, chemistry, political science, and so on. However, these other courses count for almost nothing when students go on to college, where they have to take these subjects all over again (history 101, chemistry 101, political science 101), or when they enter the vocational, business, and professional world, where they have to receive specialized training for their new jobs. College admissions directors and workplace employers really expect only one narrow set of SLOs from students who graduate with a high school diploma: that the students should have acquired a basic level of text literacy.

Jessica, like almost all of her kindergarten schoolmates, struggled to adjust to this major cognitive shift. Actually, for the first year or so, Jessica was excited and motivated to learn to read and write by the special allure of written language itself. The alphabet, and putting the letters together to make words, was like a secret code that grown-ups used to store and retrieve information. The prospect of learning to read and write made Jessica feel that she was taking a step into the grown-up world.

However, this initial novelty and excitement of decoding text soon wore off, and most of the children in Jessica's first, second, and third-grade classes, including Jessica herself, had a hard time keeping up. By the fourth grade, numbers of students were falling further and further behind the stated text-literacy SLOs for their grade level. Their self-confidence was getting severely damaged, and they were feeling more and more alienated from school and education itself. Not surprisingly, Jessica was no longer feeling very good about herself.

Young People's Rebellion against The Three *R*s and Text Literacy

What's going on here with Jessica and young people in general? Our children are actually very intelligent. From the earliest age, their brains are like sponges soaking up and interpreting experiences and information that floods their senses. Almost all young children love to learn about everything, including about the learning process itself. They're continually asking "why?" in an effort to understand the world around them. It's a survival mechanism that we humans have evolved over millennia, much like the newborn deer kids that can stand and run minutes after they're born.

Young people's failure to excel, or to even reach proficiency, in reading and writing in K-12 is reflected in the school literacy rates that continue to fall or, at best, remain stagnant decade after decade. Look no further than the National Assessment of Educational Progress, an annual test that most experts consider a fairly accurate gauge of reading scores throughout the United States. The scores for 12th-graders declined from 292 in 1992 to 188 in 2009, while the scores of students in other grades only negligibly improved during that same time period—this despite gargantuan amounts of time, resources, and hundreds of billions of dollars that school systems burned through in an attempt to bring them up.

Yet another reflection of young people's dissatisfaction with reading is the tragic rising dropout rates of middle-school and high-school students, particularly African American and Latino students. The question that parents and educators need to ask themselves is: Do children become less intelligent as they pass through the K-12 years?

The answer is No! Studies consistently show that, although young people's text-literacy rates are falling, their IQs (intelligence quotients) are rising at an average of three points every 10 years. Researchers have been noting this trend for decades and call it the "Flynn Effect," after James Flynn, a New Zealand political science professor who first documented it.

What's going on here is that young people today are rebelling against reading, writing, and written language itself. They are actively rejecting text as their IT of choice for accessing information. They feel that it's no longer necessary to become text literate—that it is no longer relevant to or for their lives.

Instead, young people are choosing to access information using the full range of emerging ITs available to them, the ITs that utilize the fullness of their all-sensory, interactive cognitive powers. Because their K-12 education is all about learning to gather information via text, young people are rejecting the three *R*s-based educational system, as well. Why, Jessica is asking, do I need to spend years learning to read Shakespeare's *Hamlet* when I can download it and listen to it, or listen to it via audio book CD, or watch a movie or DVD of it, or interact with it via an educational video game of the play?

We may be tempted to point out to Jessica and her fellow text rejecters that, when they're text messaging, they are in fact writing and reading. But it's not really the writing and reading of any actual written language—and Jessica knows it. Texting uses a system of symbols that more closely resembles a pictographic or hieroglyphic written language than an alphabetic one. "♥2u" may be understandable as three symbols combined into a pictogram, but it's not written English.

In my opinion, "♥2u" exemplifies not a flourishing commitment to text literacy among young people, but rather the rejection of actual text literacy and a further step in the devolution of text/written language as a useful IT in electronically developed societies.

Replacing Text in Schools—and Everywhere Else

What is text/written language, anyway? It's an ancient technology for storing and retrieving information. We store information by writing it, and we retrieve it by reading it. Between 6,000 and 10,000 years ago, many of our ancestors' hunter-gatherer societies settled on the land and began what's known as the "agricultural revolution." That new land settlement led to private property and increased production and trade of goods, which generated a huge new influx of information. Unable to keep all this information in their memories, our ancestors created systems of written records that evolved over millennia into today's written languages.

But this ancient IT is already becoming obsolete. Text has run its historic course and is now rapidly getting replaced in every area of our lives by the ever-increasing array of emerging ITs driven by voice, video, and body movement/gesture/touch rather than the written word. In my view, this is a positive step forward in the evolution of human technology, and it carries great potential for a total positive redesign of K-12 education. Four "engines" are driving this shift away from text:

First, evolutionarily and genetically, we humans are innately hardwired to access information and communicate by speaking, listening, and using all of our other senses. At age one, Jessica just started speaking, while other one-year-olds who were unable to speak and/or hear just began signing. It came naturally to them, unlike reading and writing, which no one just starts doing naturally and which require schooling.

Second, technologically, we humans are driven to develop technologies that allow us to access information and communicate using all of our cognitive hardwiring and all of our senses. Also, we tend to replace older technologies with newer technologies that do the same job more quickly, efficiently, and universally. Taken together, this "engine" helps to explain why, since the late 1800s, we have been on an urgent mission to develop nontext-driven ITs—from Thomas Edison's wax-cylinder phonograph to Nintendo's Wii—whose purpose is to replace text-driven ITs.

Third, as noted above, young people in the electronically developed countries are, by the millions, rejecting old text-driven ITs in favor of all-sensory, nontext ITs. This helps to explain why Jessica and her friends can't wait until school is over so they can close their school books, hurry home, fire up their videogame consoles, talk on their cell phones, and text each other using their creative symbols and abbreviations.

Fourth, based on my study and research, I've concluded that the great majority of the world's people, from the youth to the elderly and everyone in between, are either nonliterate—unable to read or write at all—or functionally nonliterate. By "functionally nonliterate," I mean that a person can perhaps recognize the letters of their alphabet, can perhaps write and read their name and a few other words, but cannot really use the written word to store, retrieve, and communicate information in their daily lives.

Since the world's storehouse of information is almost entirely in the form of written language, these billions of people have been left out of the information loop and the so-called "computer revolution." If we gave a laptop computer to everyone in the world and said, "Here, fly into the world of information, access the Internet and the Worldwide Web," they would reply, "I'm sorry, but I can't use this thing because I can't read text off the screen and I can't write words on the keyboard."

Because access to the information of our society and our world is necessary for survival, it is therefore a human right. So the billions of people who are being denied access to information because they can't read or write are being denied their human rights. They are now demanding to be included in the "global conversation" without having to learn to read and write.

Three great potential opportunities for K-12 education in the coming decades arise out of this shift away from text.

- Using nontext-driven ITs will finally enable the billions of nonliterate and functionally nonliterate people around the world to claim and exercise their right to enter, access, add to, and learn from the world's storehouse of information via the Internet and World Wide Web.
- Voice-recognition technology's instantaneous language-translation function will allow everyone to speak to everyone else using their own native languages, and so language barriers will melt away. Consider the rate of improvement in voice-recognition technology over the last decade. As David Pogue points out in a 2010 *Scientific American* article, "In the beginning, you had to train these programs by reading a 45-minute script into your microphone so that the program could learn your voice. As the technology improved over the years, that training session fell to 20 minutes, to 10, to five—and now you don't have to train the software at all. You just start dictating, and you get (by my testing) 99.9% accuracy. That's still one word wrong every couple of pages, but it's impressive."
- People whose disabilities prevent them from reading, writing, and/or signing will be able to select specific functions of their all-sensory ITs that enable them to access all information.

The Brightness Returns: Goodbye, Three *R*s; Hello, Four IT Cs

Every minute that Jessica and her friends spend getting information and communicating using video games, iPods, cell phones, and other nontext ITs, they're developing new cognitive skills.

Their new listening, speaking, visual, tactile, memory, interactive, multitasking, multimodal skills allow them to access information and communicate faster and more efficiently than ever before. I believe that Jessica and her friends are developing the very skills that will be required for successful K-12 learning as we move into the coming age of postliterate K-12 education.

Something good is also happening to Jessica's brain and consciousness as she uses her all-sensory, interactive ITs. Jessica is retraining her brain, central nervous system, and senses. She is reconfiguring her consciousness so that it more closely resembles its original, unified, integrated, pre-three Rs state. Jessica's worldview is broadening because she's perceiving and understanding the world more holistically. And she's feeling good about herself again.

Jessica's story—and there are millions of Jessicas struggling to succeed in our three Rs-based classrooms today—points the way to a new strategy for K-12 education in the twenty-first century. Basing K-12 education on the three Rs is a strategy for failure. We have the emerging ITs on which we can build a new K-12 strategy, one that has the potential to eliminate young people's academic nonsuccess and sense of failure and replace it with academic success and self-confidence.

Instead of the three Rs, we need to move on to the Four Cs: critical thinking, creative thinking, comp-speak (the skills needed to access information using all-sensory talking computers), and calculators (for basic applied math).

As text/written language falls more and more out of use as society's IT of choice for accessing information, so will the text-based three Rs. It's a trend that's already starting to happen. Videos as teaching-learning tools are surpassing textbooks in innumerable K-12 classrooms. Instructional interactive videos (we won't be calling them video "games" anymore) are already entering our classrooms as the next big IIT—instructional information technology—because students want to be interactive with information.

As the three Rs exit the K-12 scene, they'll leave a huge gap to be filled. What better way to fill that gap than by helping young people to become better critical and creative thinkers—the most crucial cognitive skills they'll need to help them build a more sustainable, peaceful, equitable, and just world? In order to store and retrieve the information they'll need to develop and practice these thinking skills, they'll also need to systematically acquire the all-sensory, interactive skills to access that information: the comp-speak skills.

These compspeak skills are the very same skills that Jessica and her classmates have been developing unsystematically by using their all-sensory ITs, but systematic training in listening, speaking, visuality, memory, and the other compspeak skills should be a central component of their post-three Rs education. It's ironic, and definitely shortsighted, that, in a difficult economic and budget-cutting climate, classes that support these compspeak skills are the first to be cut: music (listening, visual, body movement, memory), art (visual, body movement), physical education and dance (body movement, memory), speech (speaking, listening, memory), and theater arts (all of the above).

Over the next decades, we will continue to replace text-driven ITs with all-sensory-driven ITs and, by 2050, we will have recreated an oral culture in our electronically developed countries and K-12 classrooms. Our great-great-grandchildren won't know how to read or write—and it won't matter. They'll be as competent accessing information using their nontext ITs as we highly text-literates are today using the written word.

Critical Thinking

1. Reflect on the concerns Crossman outlines in this article. Do you agree that how we teach may be causing the very problems we are trying to remediate? Explain your answer.

2. Why do you think that teachers are not using more 21st-century teaching methods and materials, such as technology?

3. There are teachers who are using project-based learning (PBL) as a way to meet the needs of Jessica and her peers. Go to Edutopia's page on PBL www.edutopia.org/project-based-learning to find a video or page that you might use in your content area or grade level teaching. Be prepared to share in class discussion to explain your reason for the project you selected.

Create Central

www.mhhe.com/createcentral

Internet References

The Teaching Channel
    www.teachingchannel.org/
Open Thinking Wiki
    couros.wikispaces.com/TechAndMediaLiteracyVids

WILLIAM CROSSMAN is a philosopher, futurist, professor, human-rights activist, speaker, consultant, and composer/pianist. He is founder/director of the CompSpeak 2050 Institute for the Study of Talking Computers and Oral Cultures (www.compspeak2050.org). E-mail: willcross@aol.com.

Some of the ideas discussed in this article are discussed in greater depth in the author's book *VIVO [Voice-In/Voice-Out]: The Coming Age of Talking Computers* (Regent Press, 2004). This article is adapted from an earlier version in *Creating the School You Want: Learning @ Tomorrow's Edge* (Rowman & Littlefield, 2010), edited by Arthur Shostak and used with his permission.

Article   Prepared by: Rebecca B. Evers, *Winthrop University*

Common Core Standards: Transforming Teaching with Collaborative Technology

CATLIN TUCKER

Learning Outcomes

After reading this article, you will be able to:

- Describe how core standards can be adapted to all students with disabilities.

- Discuss what you consider necessary to improve teaching of students with disabilities.

The concept of group work—collaborative efforts by students—intrigued me from the earliest days of my teaching career.

I understood the myriad benefits of grouping students together to tackle challenges, explore topics, and work jointly to create a finished product. Unfortunately, the reality, in most cases, was very different from what I had hoped to achieve. There was no equity in student contributions during group tasks. One student usually dominated the work while the others chatted about random, unrelated topics. There was never enough time, and the finished product was almost always disappointing. It was not until I was able to embrace a blended learning model that combined online engagement with work in the classroom that I was successful in having students complete collaborative tasks.

Collaboration is an essential skill to success beyond high school. The Common Core Standards require students to "use technology, including the Internet, to produce and publish writing and to interact and collaborate with others." In addition to collaborating online, students must "prepare for and participate effectively in a range of [real-time] conversations and collaborations with diverse partners, building on others' ideas and expressing their own clearly and persuasively."

The process of working with others to produce or create something requires strong communication skills, a willingness to be open minded, and the understanding that the group's potential far exceeds any one individual's contributions. So how do we support students in cultivating the skills that are necessary for successful collaboration?

Luckily, educators today have access to a wide array of free technology geared toward fostering collaboration online. The relative ease of using these tools to group students, encourage communication, and drive creative problem solving make it possible to blend instructional mediums to engage students both inside and outside the classroom. Teachers are no longer limited to in-class group work to help students develop these competencies.

Collaboration requires that students be actively involved in the learning process. This is a new role for many students, who are used to sitting quietly in class passively consuming information. As a result, students need to learn how to actively engage with their peers to tackle academic challenges and become confident producers of information if they are going to be competitive beyond secondary school.

As schools deal with massive budget cuts across the nation, many teachers do not have the necessary professional development to support them in transitioning to the Common Core Standards. Increasingly, librarians and media specialists are becoming leaders on school campuses to support teachers in exploring technology and effectively integrating it into their curriculum.

I want to highlight some of the tools available to educators that can help them support their students in developing their communication and collaboration skills. Many of these tools offer educators the opportunity to share their best practices and lessons with each other. It is becoming easier for educators who may live and work on opposite sides of the globe to collaborate and learn from one another. With the guidance of a librarian and media specialists, teachers can explore how technology can be used to replace and improve what they already do instead of adding to their workload. They can also learn how to access a growing wealth of teacher-generated resources available on the Internet.

Collaborize Classroom: Online Discussions

I use Collaborize Classroom, a free online discussion platform, to teach communication skills and facilitate group discussions, debates, writing assignments, and group work. Most learning management systems have threaded discussions or a discussion board; however, I selected Collaborize Classroom because it focuses entirely on dynamic discussions. There is a variety of question types to structure discussions, teachers can embed media, and there is a results page where the outcomes of a conversation can be published in a colorful chart.

Teachers in upper elementary through postsecondary are using this discussion site to create online learning communities to complement their in-class work. The Common Core Standards state that students as early as kindergarten, "with guidance and support from adults, explore a variety of digital tools to produce and publish writing, including in collaboration with peers." This writing standard, which stresses the use of online tools to publish and collaborate, make it necessary for teachers to explore safe spaces where they can begin to cultivate these skills.

Results Page

Taking discussions online makes it possible for teachers to overcome many of the barriers that impede in-class conversations. Instead of a few students dominating the discussion, there is equity in the contributions. Students have the time and space to consider a question, articulate a response, and read the responses posted by their peers. This asynchronous flexibility makes it possible for every student to have a voice, which is necessary if they are "to understand other perspectives and cultures." This realization that other students in a class have different points of view or are influenced by their cultural backgrounds and past experiences is a necessary component of being college and career ready.

Online discussions are also an effective tool to teach students how to communicate in a respectful, supportive, and substantive way. These communication skills must be taught with intention. Too often teachers assume that students, as "digital natives," know how to navigate this space. They spend hours updating Facebook pages and firing off text messages, but they rarely see the impact their words have on others. They do not see the expression on the faces of the people receiving their messages. It is critical that they learn how to communicate orally and in writing, in person and online, to be successful in our rapidly evolving global economy.

I realized quickly that I needed to create a safe space online in the same way that I created a safe space in my classroom. I began by giving students a "Dos and Don'ts List for Online Communication" to ensure that students knew exactly what was appropriate in their online interactions. I engaged them in fun icebreaker activities to foster relationship building. Then we slowly built on that foundation, and I provided strategies for "Saying Something Substantial." I wanted to make sure students knew how to contribute to the conversation in a substantive way to ensure that the quality of conversations remained high.

This early work supporting students paid off as they quickly learned how to engage in academic conversations in a respectful and substantive manner. They also learned how to drive dynamic discussions without my involvement. These skills were the groundwork for the successful collaboration that blossomed out of their ability to clearly express themselves, engage respectfully with their classmates, and understand that the other thirty students in our class were incredibly valuable resources.

More than anything I did with my students, online discussions were essential in cultivating communication skills and raising awareness about our collective intelligence, which is so critical to successful collaboration.

I was surprised when the communication skills they developed online translated so seamlessly to the classroom. Students entered my class talking about discussions from the previous night. They began using each other's names in class and referring to specific ideas shared in the online space. As a result, our in-class discussions and group work were transformed. Students were more confident in their abilities and more eager to participate.

Teacher librarians can model the use of online discussions by inviting teachers to participate in an online book club using a technology like Collaborize Classroom. Engaging with other staff members using a specific technology provides teachers with an opportunity to explore the technology in a comfortable and enjoyable context.

Introducing a technology and allowing teachers to "play" with it helps them overcome many of the fears that can create a barrier to use. If teachers see the value of their online conversations, they are more likely to use the technology with their own students. It is also helpful to provide teachers with resources to support their efforts integrating technology. For teacher librarians interested in exploring this idea, there are resources available to them and the teachers on their campus regardless of the online discussion platform they use. There is a Collaborize Classroom Book Club sheet that provides an overview and a Book Club Facilitator's Guide with best practices, tips, and examples.

The Collaborize Classroom Topic Library makes it possible for teachers using the discussion site to archive and share their discussion topics with a global audience of educators. Currently, the Topic Library—a free extension of Collaborize Classroom—has over three thousand teacher-designed topics for a variety of subject areas and grade levels.

Google Docs

Google offers an array of free tools aimed at making collaboration simple. Google Docs is a suite of applications that include documents, forms, spreadsheets, drawings, and presentations. These can be shared with a single student, a group of students, or an entire class to allow easy synchronous or asynchronous work on a shared document.

Google Docs offers a vehicle to teach students how to communicate and collaborate while simultaneously helping them develop strong content knowledge. For example, English teachers who want to teach students how to read actively to comprehend complex texts can use a Google document to engage students in group annotations and discussions.

Teachers can copy and paste texts into the left column of a document and allow students to annotate and discuss the text in the right column. This makes it possible for students to use tools like "Define" or "Research" within the document to "determine or clarify the meaning of unknown and multiple-meaning words and phrases by using context clues, analyzing meaningful word parts, and consulting general and specialized reference materials."

In addition to identifying vocabulary that is unfamiliar, students are encouraged to "read closely to determine what the text says explicitly and to make logical inferences from it." This can be a challenging task, so it is helpful if students are encouraged to discuss the text and ask questions using the "Comments" feature or the real-time chat feature within a document. This creates a support network of peers who can offer insights and answer questions. Instead of traditional pen and paper homework, which leaves many students floundering when they encounter a question they do not understand, this is more engaging and fosters relationship building. As students lean on one another for support, ask questions, share ideas, and learn from each other, they begin to recognize peers as valuable resources in the class.

History and social science teachers who want to empower students can use Google Docs to group students and allow them to research a topic, become experts, and present that information to the class. This approach to flipping a lecture by allowing students to research and present the content addresses multiple Common Core Standards in a single activity.

First, students must research their topic using a shared Google Doc and utilize the "Research" tool. In doing so, students address writing anchor standards by conducting "short as well as more sustained research projects" and "gather relevant information from multiple print and digital sources."

Using the research tool inside of the Google document makes it possible for students to explore digital resources as a group to evaluate those online resources, identify key pieces of information, and discuss the importance of the facts they've found in relation to their topic. This teaches students to look at information with a critical eye, then consider how to present that information in a way that will interest other students.

Google Docs also makes it possible for students to create dynamic multimedia presentations to share their ideas with the class. It is important that students become media literate and learn how to communicate using images and video in addition to text.

Students today are inundated with media, but many do not think critically about the impact or purpose of media. Providing students with opportunities to create presentations requires that they "integrate and evaluate information presented in diverse media and formats, including visually, quantitatively, and orally." They have to think about details like citation or how an image might add to or detract from the content in their presentation. There are times when a picture can say more than words, but there are moments when a picture will distract or confuse an audience. These nuances of working with media are important to discuss with students to ensure that they are able to "present information, findings, and supporting evidence such that listeners can follow the line of reasoning and the organization, development, and style are appropriate to task, purpose, and audience."

The Common Core Standards for math emphasize several points that I think are important to discuss in this conversation about collaboration. When I was in high school, my math class consisted of reviewing a chapter in the math book then solving a collection of problems. Needless to say, the whole experience was not inspiring. I did not see the relevance of the formulas I was learning to life beyond the classroom

As I read through the Common Core math standards, I was excited to see a focus on real-world problem solving, higher-order thinking, and writing. Mathematically proficient students "construct viable arguments and critique the reasoning of others." They must be able to "Justify their conclusions, communicate them to others, and respond to the arguments of others." This requires that students be able to articulate their process and think critically about the way their peers have approached a mathematical problem A Google document can be used to present students with real-world scenarios that require problem solving and creative thinking. For example, [take] two different types of hair gel. . . . These two products essentially do the same thing, but this challenges students to look closely at the information about each gel. How many ounces does the bottle contain? How much is recommended for use? What types of ingredients are used? How much do they cost? Then they have to articulate a position about which hair gel they think is the "best deal" and support that position with evidence and a clear explanation.

I selected hair gel because it is a product many of my high school students are clearly using a lot of, so I knew it was relevant. It's a simple assignment that deals with a real-life scenario—bargain shopping—but also involves several variables and does not have a clear "right" answer. The task engages students in conversation and debate requiring that they clearly state their reasoning and evaluate the reasoning of their peers.

I could have used any number of items to create this document. Teachers who want to engage their students in designing problems for their peers to solve can empower students to create the product comparisons then share them with the class.

Teachers can also use technology to transform traditional exercises . . . . Adding online engagement makes the process more collaborative and interesting. Any teacher presenting students with a challenge can engage them in groups using Google Docs to brainstorm what they know about the problem, what they want to know, what they learned, and how they can apply their knowledge. The beauty is that their interactions and ideas are captured online and remain there for future reference and reflection.

Teacher librarians who want to share Google Docs with teachers on their campus should encourage teachers to begin by signing up for Gmail, which automatically provides them access to the full suite of Google apps. The template gallery available through Google Docs is a great resource for teachers using Google to create templates to collaborate and share their best practices.

Librarians model the use of Google tools by sharing documents with teachers who have a Gmail address so they can explore the potential for collaboration available via Google Docs. Modeling at every age level is effective for teaching. The more teachers have experience using a tool, the more likely they are to incorporate that into their teaching practice.

Most teachers are so overworked and overwhelmed by the current state of education that it is daunting to imagine shifting to a new set of national standards. Add to that the task of learning to integrate technology into their curriculum, and it becomes a staggering undertaking. If teachers understood that they could effectively teach a wide range of standards simultaneously with a single online assignment, this shift might not feel so overwhelming. The trick is to show teachers how to leverage the online space and their students' connectivity to actively engage students in collaborative tasks both inside and outside the classroom to prepare them for success beyond high school.

Critical Thinking

1. Tucker quotes a Common Core Standard that states students as young as kindergarten should use digital tools during writing activities in collaboration with peers. What is your opinion of beginning collaborative technology use at this age? Justify your answer.

2. Based on the information in the article, your own knowledge of collaborative technology and social media, and your chosen content area, develop two classroom activities that will involve students in collaborative technology for learning.

Create Central

www.mhhe.com/createcentral

Internet References

Quest Garden
 www.questgarden.com
Go2web20
 www.go2web20.net

CATLIN TUCKER is a Google Certified Teacher and CUE Lead Learner who has taught English language arts in Sonoma County since 2001. She authored Blended Learning for Grades 4–12: Leveraging the Power of Technology to Create Student-Centered Classrooms. She writes an education technology blog at www.catlintucker.com and is active on Twitter@CTuckerEnglish.

Article

Prepared by: Rebecca B. Evers, *Winthrop University*

Flipping the Classroom: Homework in Class, Lessons at Home

BRENDA ÁLVAREZ
From the National Education Association

Learning Outcomes

After reading this article, you will be able to:

- Find resources for free or low-cost technology to support collaborative learning in a flipped classroom.

Leo Tolstoy once said, "Everyone thinks of changing the world, but no one thinks of changing himself." That is until you meet Rob Townsend, a physical science teacher at Clintondale High School in Clinton Township, MI, and his school principal, Greg Green.

Green once asked Townsend why so many of his students fail his class the first semester. Townsend's initial response went something along the lines of "them not doing their homework, if they were in class at all."

Built in 1959, in a solidly working class community, Clintondale High School had prided itself on its academic performance and its strong relationship with the community. A half century later, the reality had changed. The 800-strong student body now comes from a diverse socioeconomic background, with 73% qualifying for free or reduced lunch; the population mix went from 35% minority to 65%; and for the past nine years the school has run at a budget deficit.

The climate and financial changes coupled with an increase in student need and decrease of school staff has contributed to the struggles of Clintondale. The result: In 2009, more than 50% of freshman students failed English, and school leaders had 736 discipline cases for 165 students.

So when asked why students were failing, it was easy for Townsend to point the finger at students. But the question was so powerful that it moved Townsend to action.

"I sat down determined to write a report on why these failures were happening," said Townsend, a 12-year Clintondale veteran and a member of the local Clintondale Education Association. "I wanted to be able to throw it on Principal Green's desk and say 'Ha! Look at this! Now where does the fault lie?'"

But after some honest reflection, Townsend recognized that a laundry list of problems would be useless. Instead, he set out to find solutions.

His report turned into an investigation, uncovering the reasons behind student absences and missing homework assignments. Townsend's research found that students lived too far to walk to school, had unreliable transportation, or depended on city buses that often run late.

A large percentage of Clintondale students live in Detroit. Students who live in Detroit typically wake up at five o'clock in the morning to make the 12-mile journey to the school. If a bus is late, the students' entire day is muddled.

When it came to missing homework assignments, Townsend found that it was because students didn't understand the material.

"After spending the majority of the class time explaining concepts and lessons while students took notes, or even doing a class-wide activity with the students, I was still unable to see if they understood and comprehended the concepts before they left with their homework assignments," said Townsend.

Townsend realized that it was silly to give homework to students who couldn't do it at home. He thought: "One way to create more class time and not lose education time was to have them take notes at home and do the work in class."

This concept fit with Green's desire to move the school toward using more technology. He encouraged Townsend to incorporate more internet-based programs that allowed students to take notes and access resources online, allowing students to receive extra support at home.

Green researched companies that could support reverse instruction, and came across Techsmith, which provides screen capture and recording software. Through the help of a grant from Techsmith, "flipping the classroom" was launched.

"This now gave us a chance to expand our school [instruction] without stressing staff out," said Green, referring to how the technology could be applied once and used by various educators. "It's maximizing our ability to teach."

Flipping the classroom allows an educator to record a lesson plan on video in the same fashion it would be presented to students. The structure of the video is an overview of the lesson, the content, and ends with a summary. Educators can insert their voice, video clips, photographs and images, as well as work out problems in their own writing within the video, which is less than 10 minutes long.

Students can access the lessons on any computer or smart phone. School leaders also opened the doors to the library and computer lab before school, during lunch, and after school for students without access to a computer.

"We made it convenient for students," said Townsend. "They no longer had to find a quiet area where they could sit and concentrate. All they needed to do was find 10 minutes to watch a video and take notes," he added.

By taking notes at home, an additional 30 minutes of class time was added to learning time. This extra time allowed Townsend to directly work with students on projects, lab assignments, or activities, ensuring along the way that students understood the material. He was also able to identify students who needed extra help or were too shy to raise a hand requesting help.

Other benefits of flipping the classroom include:

- Notes are now available at home for students who were absent;
- Students are less frustrated and disruptive in class because there is someone on hand to help one-on-one;
- A much larger percentage of assignments are completed and to a much higher quality;
- When an educator is absent from class, a video can be made for that day and a substitute teacher has a clearer idea of what was covered and how to help students.

Parental Approval

This new instructional model also sparked an interest among parents. They now had a direct link to their child's school instruction, and it gave parents the opportunity to be actively engaged in their child's education.

"Parents liked the idea of going online and watching the videos for themselves," said Townsend. "If their child was struggling with the assignment, the parent could watch the video and learn alongside their child," offering support along the way.

A year later, educators saw dramatic changes in students' core subject areas. According to Green, by reversing the instructional model, the failure rate in critical subjects had dramatically decreased. In English Language Arts, the percentage of students failing fell from 52% to 19%; in math, a drop from 44% to 13%; in science, it declined from 41% to 19%; and in social studies, fewer than 10% of students failed, compared with nearly a third the previous year.

"This is what makes sense for our school and we want the best for our students," said Green. "The flip approach holds the golden key for students because educators can control and eliminate learning obstacles, and it allows teachers to give their best presentations and share resources," said Green.

Reversing the instruction has received widespread support from the education community, including the Clintondale

Education Association (CEA), whose leaders were supportive of the new instructional model.

The association helped reduce the concerns from educators of being replaced by technology. From the onset, Ken Austin, president of CEA made sure this new model was a volunteer-based program, with the flexibility of opting in and out, or using it as a major part or a small portion of an educator's class time. In addition, the association worked with administrators to ensure educators were fairly compensated for extra working hours. "We want the students and school to succeed," said Austin. "The goal of changing the instruction is to get out of this 5% business," referring to the U.S. Department of Education's label of the nation's lowest-performing schools.

Educators and school leaders at Clintondale, along with the local association, are transforming one of the nation's lower-performing schools by taking a hard look at themselves and their professional practice, and collaboratively changing the strategies to an approach that is modern, relevant, and student centered.

Critical Thinking

1. Your principal believes that you are a progressive teacher who is "tech-savy". Therefore, he has asked you to prepare a presentation for the Parent-Teacher-Student Association at your school to explain Flipping the Classroom. He is concerned that parents and possibly teachers will have questions about the practical side of flipping. Possible questions are about students who do not have computers at home or who have many extra-curricular sports or music activities. Prepare short presentation that explains flipping and addresses these concerns.

2. You did such a good job in your presentation that the PTSA wants to give you money to purchase technology to use for flipping your class. After researching the possibilities you have found three items you want or need to flip your class. Explain why you need all three of these items by developing lessons that would be enhanced by flipping and especially by using these specific technologies.

Create Central

www.mhhe.com/createcentral

Internet References

No limits 2 learning: Celebrating human potential through assistive technology
    www.nolimitstolearning.blogspot.com

BRENDA ÁLVAREZ writes for the National Education Association. Condensed with permission, from the National Education Association's website, September 30, 2011. To read the full version of the article, visit www.neapriorityschools.org.

Álvarez, Brenda. From *Education Digest*, April 2012, pp. 18–21. Copyright © 2012 by National Education Association. Reprinted by permission.

Article   Prepared by: Rebecca B. Evers, *Winthrop University*

I Want That . . .

Flipping the Classroom

SHEILA COHEN AND KRISTY BRUGAR

Learning Outcomes

After reading this article, you will be able to:

• Design an instructional unit where technology is the primary delivery system for the content.

As she listened to her colleague's description of the rich discussion that had taken place in his English classroom, Mrs. Cohen moaned, "I want that!" When she asked him how such deep conversations are possible in a middle grades classroom, he replied that the students read the chapter the night before, marked in the margins of their books things they thought were important or didn't understand, and then came to class prepared for the discussion.

Mrs. Cohen (co-author of this article) decided to give it a try. She assigned her students the next section of their math book for homework and suggested they take margin notes. She hoped the assignment would help drive the discussion about the new topic she was introducing.

However, her experiment was not as successful as she'd hoped. First, the mathematics text does not have the same narrative qualities as a book such as *The Adventures of Tom Sawyer,* which her colleague's students were reading. Second, the students had difficulty with the technical terms associated with new concepts.

When Mrs. Cohen tried to engage them in a deep conversation, the students had very little to say. She needed a new tactic. She decided to "flip" her classroom and create engaging visuals for her students to review and react to.

Flipping Instruction

A flipped classroom is one in which students view a video that replaces live instruction at home and do "homework" in class. Thus, class time is available for students to work with one another and in small groups or individually with the teacher.

Jon Bergmann and his colleagues in "The Flipped Class: What It Is and What It Is Not" *(www.thedailyriff.com/articles/the-flipped-class-conversation-689.php)* identify several advantages to flipped classrooms:

1. Students are responsible for their own learning.
2. Videos are archived so students can revisit and review material as necessary.
3. Students and teachers have increased personal interaction.
4. Teachers provide personalized instruction.

Over a two-month period, Mrs. Cohen created 30 video lectures: 15 for Math 6/Honors and 15 for Pre-Algebra. Each video focused on a single concept and was between 10 and 15 minutes long.

In advance of filming the videos, she prepared whiteboards with key ideas, thus providing visual engagement to complement the audio engagement of the video. Mrs. Cohen felt strongly that she should talk to her students in the videos, so during filming, she addressed them through eye contact and direct questioning.

At the conclusion of each video, Mrs. Cohen gave the students the prompt to record two things they learned about the topic of the video and one question they had about the material—a strategy she referred to as a 2–1.

The students brought their video lecture notes and the 2–1 to class. The 2–1 served as a starting point for the class session. Mrs. Cohen began the class by asking students to share things they had learned from the video. As students shared, she recorded key aspects from the video lecture on the whiteboard. She encouraged students to add this information to their notes. After students identified the key aspects of the concept, she asked them to share their questions, which they discussed as a class.

Then, Mrs. Cohen gave students collaborative *homework* to complete in class. Students were assigned to small groups to work through the work. During this time, Mrs. Cohen was able to meet with students one-on-one. After approximately 20 minutes, the whole class reviewed the assignment.

Test of Success

During the two-month "flip," Mrs. Cohen collected various data, including student test scores, homework, researcher observations, and data from two student surveys (mid-point and final) and one parent survey (mid-point). Based on these data, she identified three themes: confidence, collaboration, and comprehension.

Confidence.

The "flipped classroom" helped students develop confidence in their role as math students. In a mid-point survey, a student remarked, "Now I know more about what we're talking about so I can talk without feeling stupid."

Students developed confidence because this type of instruction empowers them to "take charge" of their learning. They are able to stop, start, and rewind the video, and watch it as many times as they need to, thus controlling when and how often they get the information.

They are able to think through the concepts and formulate questions organically and bring well-thought-out and well-articulated questions to class to help clarify their understanding.

The independent experiences associated with the video lectures allow students to process the material on their own and be involved in class discussion. Each student progresses at his or her own pace, leading to confidence in their understanding of the concepts. One student shared, "Since the video lectures, I am more comfortable with participation in class discussion because I feel that I know what I am talking about."

Collaboration.

Mrs. Cohen's students collaborated to understand the material. The students were the driving force of whole-class discussions. They used the notes they took from the videos to discuss, clarify information, inquire about material that was unclear, and synthesize information for themselves and others.

As students transitioned from whole group to small groups so they could collaborate on homework, they moved from comparing answers (What did you get for number 5?) to discussing how they got their answers (How did you get that? What did I do wrong?).

In reflecting on the experience, one student said, "I get to help out my class mates and refresh my memory." This student realized that by explaining and helping others, he was solidifying his understanding of the mathematical concepts.

Comprehension.

Prior to the flip, if students were confused about the material covered in class, they would have to set up a meeting with Mrs. Cohen outside the allotted class time—during study hall or before or after school. If they could not find a time to meet that day, the student would fall further behind. Thus, the student was confused about the concept from yesterday, but now his comprehension of new material was also in jeopardy.

The "flipped classroom" approach afforded Mrs. Cohen the opportunity to work one-on-one with students. If a student was

still struggling with material, she was able to pull that student out of the group and give individual instruction for 5 or 10 minutes.

A significant percentage of students moved their class averages from the B range to the A range between the second trimester grades and the third trimester grades. At the end of the third trimester, a review showed only one student fell into the grade percentage below. Overall, students shifted into the next grade level or maintained their average.

Mrs. Cohen continues to provide information during class, but now students are learning to listen better and then formulate their own notes rather than waiting for her to tell them what's important. She is using a variety of instructional strategies to meet the needs of her students and increase their involvement in their own learning.

---

5 Things to Remember When Video Lecturing

If you are interested in creating your own video lectures, here are a few things to remember.

1. **Keep it short.** Remember that your students will stop and start the video, so their time commitment will be longer than the video itself.
2. **Talk to your students.** Remember that *your* students are viewing and listening to the video. Talk to them in the way you would in class.
3. **Give students a purpose for viewing the video.** Remember this should not be a passive experience; it should be an active learning opportunity. Just as in class, ask questions, pose problems, and give them time to grapple with the material.
4. **Prepare students for class.** Remember that the video should prepare students for the class session. At the end of the video, ask students to write down two things they have learned about the topic and frame one question. The comments and questions they bring to class generate great discussion.
5. **Get feedback.** Remember to ask your colleagues, parents, and most important, your students about the video lecture experiences. Ask students for regular verbal feedback in class. Consider conducting several surveys of both parents and students.

Critical Thinking

1. Ms. Cohen's data indicated that her students developed confidence, collaboration, and comprehension as they participated in the flipped classes. What else might she have hoped her students would learn to do or what other knowledge might they have gained during this two-month trial?

2. Ms. Cohen used video lectures to flip her class. List five other teaching methods or activities a teacher might use to flip. Which would be your preference? Explain why.

Create Central

www.mhhe.com/createcentral

Internet References

Classroom Window survey:
http://bit.ly/NFK2kL

Example of "one take" video lesson:
www.youtube.com/watch?v=2W7cliCmXxc

Flipped Classroom Training Program:
http://go.ncsu.edu/fctp

The FIZZ Project:
www.fi.ncsu.edu/project/fizz/

SHEILA COHEN is a sixth grade math teacher at Cranbrook Kingswood Middle School for Boys in Bloomfield Hills, Michigan. E-mail: scohen@cranbrook.edu

KRISTY BRUGAR is an assistant professor of social studies education at Wayne State University, Detroit, Michigan. E-mail: av6556@wayne.edu

Unit 7

UNIT

Prepared by: Rebecca B. Evers, *Winthrop University*

Collaboration

Hopefully we have reached the point where we understand the need to work collectivity and collaboratively to solve the problems facing our public school system, but that may not make it easy to actualize, as old habits are the most difficult habits to break. If we look back over the history of education, in almost every photograph of every classroom we will see a group of students with one teacher. That is the image of school burned into our collective memories. That was what I saw for the first 20 years of my teaching career in every school where I taught. How hard might it be to change that mindset?

That mindset alone can be a roadblock to effective and productive collaboration. Other possible roadblocks are teacher perceptions, time to engage with other teachers, lack of focus, and taking the time to develop collaboration skills. First, false perceptions can destroy collaboration before it even begins. Teachers often prefer to work alone and they perceive collaboration and co-teaching as invasive. The reason can be as simple as they like to have a classroom of their "own" students. Other reasons might include mistrust of others or a concern that if they make even one, small mistake, they will be found lacking and others will publicly point out their faults. Some teachers see any critical feedback as personal criticism or an assault on their academic freedom. Secondly, finding time for collaboration is difficult. Conflicting teaching and planning schedules, as well as other duties such as bus duty, record keeping responsibilities, and grading can take up all of a teacher's non-teaching time. It may be impossible to meet before or after school as personal lives may take precedent. Thirdly, focus during collaboration meetings can be lost to personal conversations or to situations that appeared suddenly. Dealing with distractions can consume meeting time so quickly. And finally, we must understand the need for training and time to develop the skills needed for this intimate relationship. Collaboration, like a marriage, takes time to emerge into a lasting relationship.

The primary early childhood (EC) professional organizations consider a family-centered practice to be the best and most effective practice. One may assume that collaboration is critical in establishing a family-center practice. Therefore, teacher preparation programs should include opportunities for pre-service EC educators to learn how to partner and collaborate with families. Conclusions drawn by Sewell's article indicate that preparation programs often do not emphasize the importance of teacher-family partnerships enough for pre-service teachers to be able to effectively include families in their teaching practice. Suggestions for change are offered.

We may think that working with others should happen when we feel it is beneficial to us, helpful to our students, or when we feel it is necessary. However, DuFour insists that we must collaborate even when we do not want to work with others. His premise is that professionals in fields outside education are not allowed to do whatever they please or want in the workplace, and that professionals in other endeavors are required and compelled to work interdependently to achieve common goals. According to the data he presents, the students of those teachers who do collaborate have higher achievement levels. His ideas about collaboration and professional learning communities may have merit, but read the article to make up your own mind.

One way for teachers to collaborate is to co-teach classes. Most often co-teaching is seen as something teachers do to meet the needs of students with disabilities in the general education classroom. Certainly that may be how most of us think of it and is the primary focus of Conderman's article. However as you read, think about other reasons for co-teaching and places where co-teaching would benefit both the teachers and the K-12 students. Co-teaching is generally thought to be when two teachers share the primary responsibility for teaching the same group of students at the same time. Teachers plan, teach, and assess the students together. But this may not be a perfect union, teachers may not agree on what to teach, how to teach it, who will teach what, or how to assess student learning. Who is going to do all of the grading, copying, and setting up? Co-teaching can fail before the teachers even enter the classroom. Conderman addresses the possible conflicts and how people approach conflict. He has proactive strategies as well as "do's and don'ts." The advice in this practical article will support your co-teaching efforts as a novice or veteran teacher.

As a nation, citizens of the U.S. spend millions each year on self-help books of one kind or the other; on relationships, child-rearing, getting what we want, and being better in our professional endeavors. Surely we need help understanding the person with whom we are trying to collaborate or co-teach. Is there a book for that? Perhaps not a book, but Miller's article has an interesting thesis that we have "curriculum style." Could knowledge of our own style help us be better teachers or articulate our needs to a potential teaching partner or team members? She admits that labeling and describing ideologies offers little more than a glimpse at a possible explanation for behavior. The four styles she describes are certainly possible sources of support or conflict as we move into collaborative relationships. Like speed dating, this survey may not lead to a lasting relationship, but it might—and that is what fuels our belief that we will find the right person by understanding our own and their behaviors.

This unit began with an article about working with parents and ends with two articles that illustrate two circumstances where parents and families can support the work of schools. Students with challenging behaviors are among the most difficult to teach. If these students have IEPs, we must establish Behavioral Intervention Plans (BIPs) for them. BIPs work best if they are carried out in all settings found in the student's day, including home, especially home, as the students spend a majority of their time at home. Park, Alber-Morgan, and Fleming have provided steps and examples of how to solicit family help and support. This article is an excellent source of information for any teacher who wants family support when working with a child who has a behavior concern.

The final article illustrates how school needs can blend into community needs in a collaborative relationship that supports children and senior citizens. In South Carolina, a community has established a Grandparent program where senior citizens are matched with students who need extra help or extra attention. This turns out to be a win-win situation: a perfect collaboration.

Article Prepared by: Rebecca B. Evers, *Winthrop University*

Are We Adequately Preparing Teachers to Partner with Families?

TAMARA SEWELL

Learning Outcomes

After reading this article, you will be able to:

- Describe a family-centered classroom.
- State reasons why involving parents in your classroom is important to student learning.

Introduction

Young children are the center of their family and as such their families are a wellspring of knowledge when it comes to their child's development and learning. Early childhood teachers have regular opportunities to interact with families and gather knowledge to influence their teaching practices. However, challenges arise when a teacher has not been prepared to partner effectively with families and to best serve children within the context of the family.

According to the Council for Exceptional Children's Division for Early Childhood (DEC), "practitioners in early education and intervention must be prepared to work with families whose cultural, ethnic, linguistic, and social backgrounds differ from their own" (Stayton et al. 2003, p. 11). "Class lectures, simulations, and supervised home visits with families, as well as interviews and informal conversations" (Hyson 2003, p. 140) are integral to the pre-service teachers' learning process.

The DEC's preparation program standards for early childhood professionals were developed in conjunction with the National Association for the Education of Young Children (NAEYC) and the National Board for Professional Teaching Standards (NBPTS). The DEC's program standards emphasize that the professional become involved as equal partners with families early on and that a reciprocal relationship should be maintained throughout the partnership. Additionally, because families vary in terms of priorities, resources, concerns, cultural background, views of education, and how they support their children's development and learning, training should involve families that are diverse in nature (Stayton et al. 2003). Providing comprehensive training to professionals has the potential to increase the implementation and effectiveness of family-centered practices.

Research concerning teacher preparation in the field of early childhood is limited, particularly in the area of family-centered practices. Several surveys have focused on this increasingly important topic, but results are, at best, inconsistent. However, there are two distinct issues that are repeated throughout the literature: teacher perceptions of families and the focus on family partnership in teacher preparation programs.

What Are Teachers' Perceptions of Family-Centered Practice?

Teachers and administrators struggle to partner with families due to the lack of preparation. In 2006, MetLife surveyed 1,001 public school teachers and found that "teachers consider engaging and working with parents as their greatest challenge and the area they were least prepared to manage during their first year" (Harvard Family Research Project 2006, p. 1). More specifically 31% of the teachers reported that the greatest challenge was in encouraging involvement and communicating with the family (Markow et al. 2006). The dearth of training opportunities has resulted in teachers feeling ill-prepared to work with families, which creates a multitude of challenges for the teacher, child, and family.

In-service training opportunities and topics impact practitioner perceptions and practices. Bruder et al. (2009) completed electronic surveys and phone interviews with 51 Part C coordinators and 49 coordinators of 619 programs regarding the implementation of professional development that is both systematic and sustainable. Thirty-nine of the Part C states and 35 of the 619 respondents reported offering in-service training systems that were systematic and sustainable. The training content for both Part C and 619 was based on administrative or consultant recommendations. Only 11 of the 51 Part C coordinators reported training content regarding partnering with families and none of the 619 respondents reported inclusion of family content.

Rothenberg and McDermot of the Sage College School of Education expanded on the MetLife survey by creating focus groups to gain a qualitative understanding of the nature of family-centeredness and its implementation. Teachers who were involved in the groups reported that they actually avoided working with families and found such work to be unappealing. Parents involved in the focus groups reported that they only felt comfortable working with those teachers that treated children and families with respect and high regard (Harvard Family Research Project 2006). Based on these views, it is easy to see that an unproductive cycle of teachers and families avoiding interaction is easily formed and maintained.

How Are We Preparing Teachers to Work with Families?

The Center to Inform Personnel Preparation, Policy and Practice in Early Intervention and Early Childhood Special Education (n.d.) conducted a survey of 5,659 institutions offering degree programs for all services under IDEA. Of the 1,131 respondents, 86.43% reported that they offer at least one course related to families, specifically with a focus on families with children ages three to five. Another survey, by The National Prekindergarten Center in 2004, reported a more conservative percentage of only 61% who reported that they offered at least one course dedicated to preparing professionals to work with families (Maxwell et al. 2006).

In order to establish the amount of family-centered content taught in early childhood teacher preparation programs, Rupiper and Marvin (2004) surveyed 82 institutions across the United States. Results demonstrated that family-centered content was infused across course curriculum. Twenty-eight institutions indicated that family-centered content was taught in an independent undergraduate course. Course credit hours ranged from two to eight with most respondents indicating three credit hours. Primary content of the family-centered coursework included knowledge of families, IFSP skills, respecting diversity, communication skills, and knowledge of teamwork.

Chang et al. (2005) reported on a national survey of early childhood teacher preparation programs completed in 1999 by the National Center for Early Development and Learning. One of the purposes of the study was to quantify the amount and type of coursework and practicum experiences related to families, collaboration, and home visiting required by early childhood preparation programs (Chang et al. 2005). The sample included 438 associate and bachelor level programs in 47 states that prepare individuals to work with children ranging in age from birth to four years. Participants were asked to complete a survey that included questions about required coursework and practical experiences related to families. Just under 60% of both associates and bachelor's degree programs offered at least one families course. Data also showed that students often had practical experiences with families, including home visits, without having had any in-class preparation prior to or in conjunction with the experience.

The Centre for Community Child Health in Australia (2003) convened focus groups based on common issues found in the literature on the subject of early childhood teacher preparation. One of the major issues identified by the focus groups was that students were unprepared for work with young and developing families. In particular, members of the focus group believed that although family-centered philosophies, beliefs, and practices are incorporated into course content, opportunities for students to apply and demonstrate comprehension are limited (Centre for Community Child Health 2003).

In an effort to establish how family-centered practice was taught to future teachers, Sewell (2007) conducted a critical study surveying 21 undergraduate early intervention/early childhood special education teacher preparation programs. Participants were asked to specify how family-centered practices were taught as well as how students were afforded the opportunity to articulate and apply those practices. Approximately 38% of the respondents indicated that family-centered practice was taught in an independent course. Ninety percent of the respondents indicated that more than 50% of family-centered focus was infused across course content. Eighty-one percent of respondents indicated that family-centered methods courses were linked to field experiences, however, direct contact with families during these experiences was often limited due to the nature of the placements. Echoing The Centre for Community Child Health in Australia's (2003) and Chang et al. (2005) results, participants indicated that students were taught family-centered practices and had moderate opportunities to articulate them but very little opportunity to actually apply the practices with families.

To gain a comprehensive understanding of early childhood teacher preparation program's strengths and weaknesses, Bruder and Dunst (2005) surveyed programs to determine where training emphasis was placed in regards to the following factors: family-centered practice, cross-disciplinary models, service coordination, development of IFSPs, and natural environments. Eight disciplines serving children under IDEA were examined, and a total of 449 programs completed a 30-item survey. Results indicated family-centered intervention was the only practice that constituted primary emphasis across all eight disciplines; however, none of the disciplines felt as though they were adequately prepared to work with families. The researchers recommend embedding family-centered practices into teacher preparation programs in order to prepare students to work effectively with children and families (Bruder and Dunst 2005).

Are We Influencing Preservice Teachers' Perceptions?

Teacher's perceptions of families impact their interactions with families. Murray and Mandell (2004) evaluated two pre-service programs designed to prepare graduates to provide family-centered services using the Family-Centered Pre-service Model (FCPM). The FCPM program was based on the teacher preparation professional standards developed by both NAEYC and DEC. The researchers interviewed 22 students to examine attitudes and beliefs, as well as aptitude, about issues relating to diversity. Students were also asked to report on family-centered practices that they had the opportunity to apply (Murray and Mandell 2004).

Prior to the program, approximately 70% of the participants had little experience with families and a limited understanding of family-centered practices. The FCPM program was effective in changing the students' attitudes and beliefs about working with diverse families and increasing the students understanding of families in general. In addition, didactic teaching in conjunction with experiential practice resulted in increased participant confidence to effectively utilize and apply practices (Murray and Mandell 2004).

Additional research exploring pre-service teachers' perceptions and experiences of preparedness training was conducted by Blasi (2002). Twenty-six students enrolled in a course titled "Principles of Interprofessional Collaboration," completed pre- and post-test questionnaires. At the time of the pre-test, 38% of the students felt prepared to work with children and families. Upon completion of the course, 58% of the students felt prepared. This increase is due to the fact that students "realized the importance of valuing and respecting parents as their children's first and most important teachers, and . . . saw their role in working with families as more of a 'shared power' within a 'family-first' perspective" (Blasi 2002, p. 115). The limited positive results of the course further illuminate the need to expand and increase the emphasis on family-centered learning opportunities beyond a single course.

Giallourakis et al. (2005) developed a measure to explore the specific beliefs, skills, and practices of graduate students in the field of early childhood education. The survey results indicated that a moderate level of family involvement is included in programs, but has little impact on how students perceive their education. As would be expected, frequency of contact was correlated with beliefs and practices on family-centered approaches. The two themes that evolved from the survey responses were increased empathy and awareness as well as the application of new skills in relation to family-centered practice. One student shared that the experience greatly impacted his/her perspective and work in helping him/her realize "that even the least participatory parent still holds immense knowledge regarding their child and family, and the needs and resources of the family" (Giallourakis et al. 2005, p. 4).

Students' expressive writing also gives insight into their perceptions of family-centered practice. Pang and Wert (2010) conducted a study of 87 undergraduate students enrolled in an introduction to early intervention course that introduced students to family-centered philosophy and practices. The students completed pre and post essays about their beliefs vis-à-vis the involvement of families in early intervention service delivery and how they would involve families in their practice as early interventionists. The researchers found that at both the pre and post points of the study, students recognized the importance of family involvement; however, in their post essays students placed more emphasis on actual practices, involvement of the family as a whole unit, the roles that families and professionals play, the importance of involving pre-service teachers with families early, and the challenges related to implementing family-centered practices (Pang and Wert 2010). Pre-service students involved in the study recognized family support as a critical component of early intervention services and noted that

family partnerships facilitated carryover of functional skills into multiple settings. This carryover reduced the pressure on the teacher to provide the primary support, increased both family and teacher understanding of the child's development and progress, and improved functionality of team goals.

Bingham and Abernathy (2007) used concept mapping to illuminate 49 pre-service students' changing attitudes and perceptions throughout a 16 week course on the topic of partnering with families. The students completed a pre- and post-course concept map depicting their perceptions about serving individuals with disabilities and their families. Differences between pre- and post-course perceptions included the expansion of the idea of communication from "getting the job done" to "advocating for children and families" and "a more reciprocal interaction with families" with students "relinquishing the role of power broker and embracing the role of advocate" (Bingham and Abernathy 2007, p. 52). Students saw the teacher's role as more collaborative not only with families, but also the community at large. However, not all results were as encouraging. In the pre-course maps, 73% of the students positioned the teacher as the expert. The post-course maps showed only a 8% change in this perception of roles. "Regardless of the numerous activities in which they participated and the family stories they heard, they did not move away from seeing the focus of the class on the special education system and its requirements" (Bingham and Abernathy 2007, p. 55). Bingham and Abernathy hypothesize that perhaps the strong focus on the administrative aspect of working with children with special needs (the Individuals with Disabilities Education Act requirements, documentation, education plans, etc.) overwhelm the students and therefore overshadow the importance of reciprocal family partnerships.

Results from the focus groups based on the MetLife survey spurred Rothenberg and McDermot to begin implementing new strategies in coursework. Practicum students were required to hold routine conferences with parents from a strengths-based perspective. These conferences were meant to focus on positive news about children, while also allowing parents to voice the views, goals, and dreams that they have for their children. Requiring family visits provided the students with insight into the child's world within the context of the family. Seasoned supervising teachers felt that the students' work with the families would create problems, but the families were quite receptive to the extra involvement and the students reported enjoying the contact with families and found that working with families resulted in positive outcomes for the children (Harvard Family Research Project 2006).

Conclusion

Partnering with families is best and effective practice and can only enhance children's development and learning. Nevertheless, many teachers find the idea of partnering with families a daunting and unmanageable task due to lack of preparation and training. All too often preparation does not emphasize the importance of partnering with families enough to enable pre-service teachers to practically apply the knowledge.

Increased and focused student contact with families throughout their teacher training is clearly necessary. Involvement of families in the development of coursework and in-service trainings as well as the delivery of course content and fieldwork opportunities is a key to improving student comprehension of the importance of family partnership. This concept ensures that course content is realistic and offers real-life examples. Families can act as co-instructors or guest speakers and share their experiences and lives through practical field experiences.

The research demonstrates that even one course can impact pre-service teachers' perceptions regarding partnerships with families. But, one course is not sufficient to adequately prepare teachers to work reciprocally with families. Theoretically, infusing family-centeredness throughout early childhood course work is the best option. However, programs must consider that "content taught, including both emphasis and pedagogical style, varies according to each individual instructor's knowledge and experience" (Sewell 2007, p. 61). Infusion of content across coursework is ideal as long as the emphasis of content is regulated and aligned with course objectives and practical experience so that regardless of instructor, students receive consistent information. In addition, ongoing in-service training is imperative in order to not only educate practicing teachers, but to support them in their daily practice with families.

It is vital for both early childhood teacher preparation programs and in-service trainers to ensure pre-service students and practicing teachers are adequately prepared to partner with families in order to best serve the needs of the child and family.

References

Bingham, A., & Abernathy, T. V. (2007). Promoting family-centered teaching: Can one course make a difference? *Issues in Teacher Education, 16*(1), 37–60.

Blasi, M. W. (2002). An asset model: Preparing pre-service teachers to work with children and families "of promise". *Journal of Research in Childhood Education, 17*(1), 106–121.

Bruder, M. B., & Dunst, C. J. (2005). Personnel preparation in recommended early intervention practices: Degree of emphasis across disciplines. *Topics in Early Childhood Special Education, 25*(1), 25–33.

Bruder, M. B., Morgro-Wilson, C., Stayton, V. D., & Dietrich, S. L. (2009). The national status of in-service professional development systems for early intervention and early childhood special education practitioners. *Infants and Young Children, 22*(1), 13–20.

Centre for Community Child Health. (2003). *Final report on research to inform the development of a capacity building program.* Canberra, ACT: Australian Council for Children and Parenting, Commonwealth Department of Family and Community Services.

Chang, F., Early, D. M., & Winton, P. J. (2005). Early childhood teacher preparation in special education at 2- and 4-year institutions of higher education. *Journal of Early Intervention, 27*(2), 110–124.

Giallourakis, A., Pretti-Frontczak, K., & Cook, B. (2005). *Understanding family involvement in the preparation of graduate students: Measuring family-centered beliefs, skills,*

systems, and practices. Cambridge, MA: Harvard Family Research Project.

Harvard Family Research Project. (2006). Is teacher preparation key to improving teacher practices with families? What are the alternatives? *FINE Network.* Retrieved from www.gse.harvard.edu/hfrp/projects/fine/memberinsights.html.

Hyson, M. (Ed.). (2003). *Preparing early childhood professionals: NAEYC's standards for programs.* Washington, DC: National Association for the Education of Young Children.

Markow, D., Moessner, C., & Horowitz, H. (Eds.). (2006). *The MetLife survey of the American teacher: Expectations and Experiences.* New York: Metropolitan Life Insurance Company.

Maxwell, K. L., Lim, C.-I., & Early, D. M. (2006). *Early childhood teacher preparation programs in the United States: National report.* Chapel Hill, NC: The University of North Carolina, FPG Child Development Institute.

Murray, M. M., & Mandell, C. J. (2004). Evaluation of a family-centered early childhood special education pre-service model by program graduates. *Topics in Early Childhood Special Education, 24*(4), 238–249.

Pang, Y., & Wert, B. (2010). Preservice teachers' attitudes towards family-centered practices in early intervention: An implication for teacher education. *Educational Research, 1*(8), 253–262.

Rupiper, M., & Marvin, C. (2004). Preparing teachers for family-centered services: A survey of pre-service curriculum content. *Teacher Education and Special Education, 27*(4), 384–395.

Sewell, T. (2007). Family-centered practice in early intervention and early childhood special education personnel preparation. (Doctoral dissertation). Retrieved from Proquest. (Publication number AAT 3273938).

Stayton, V. D., Miller, P. S., & Dinnebeil, L. A. (Eds.). (2003). *DEC Personnel preparation in early childhood special education: Implementing the DEC recommended practices.* Longmont, CO: Sopris West.

The Center to Inform Personnel Preparation, Policy and Practice in Early Intervention and Early Childhood Special Education. (n.d.). *Part C data report.* Retrieved from www.uconnucedd.org/publications/files/PPDataPartCweb.pdf.

Critical Thinking

1. Describe what your actions to create a Family-Centered classroom would include. Share your reasons.

2. Give three reasons why involving parents in your classroom is important to your teaching and student learning. Cite information from articles in this unit.

3. Why do you think that the results of the course completed in the research by Bingham and Abernathy in 2007 were not more encouraging?

4. As an administrator, you have determined that teachers need to involve parents more in the decision making and learning experiences of their children. Based on this article and others in this edition, what kind of professional development might you plan for your teachers and families?

Create Central

www.mhhe.com/createcentral

Internet References

The National Coalition for Parent Involvement in Education (NCPIE)

www.ncpie.org

TAMARA SEWELL teaches at the Bankstreet College of Education and she is the Supervised Fieldwork Advisor.

Article ⎯⎯⎯⎯⎯⎯⎯⎯⎯ Prepared by: Rebecca B. Evers, *Winthrop University*

Work Together
But Only If You Want To

We cannot waste another quarter century inviting or encouraging educators to collaborate.

R ICK D U F OUR

Learning Outcomes

After reading this article, you will be able to:

- Use alternative methods to meet with families.

- Understand why collaboration is important to student learning.

Teachers work in isolation from one another. They view their classrooms as their personal domains, have little access to the ideas or strategies of their colleagues, and prefer to be left alone rather than engage with their colleagues or principals. Their professional practice is shrouded in a veil of privacy and personal autonomy and is not a subject for collective discussion or analysis. Their schools offer no infrastructure to support collaboration or continuous improvement, and, in fact, the very structure of their schools serves as a powerful force for preserving the status quo. This situation will not change by merely encouraging teachers to collaborate, but will instead require embedding professional collaboration in the routine practice of the school.

Sound familiar? These were the conclusions of John Goodlad's study of schooling published in *Phi Delta Kappan* in 1983. Unfortunately, these findings have been reiterated in countless studies from that date to the present. The reason for the persistence of this professional isolation—not merely of teachers, but of educators in general—is relatively simple. The structure and culture of the organizations in which they work haven't supported, required, or even expected them to collaborate.

Attempts to promote collaboration among educators inevitably collide with this tradition of isolation. Defenders of this tradition argue that professional autonomy gives each educator the freedom to opt in or out of any collaborative process. *Requiring* educators to work together violates their right as professionals to work in isolation and can result only in "contrived congeniality" rather than a true collaborative culture (Hargreaves 1991). Some critics of systematic collaboration even offer a conspiracy theory, arguing that any effort to embed collaborative processes into the school day represents an administrative ploy to compel teachers to do the bidding of others and demonstrates a lack of commitment to empowering teachers. Thus proponents of volunteerism greet any attempt to ensure that educators work together with the addendum, "but only if they want to."

I've searched for the dictionary that defines "professional" as one who is free to do as he or she chooses. I can't find it. I see references to occupations in which people must engage in specialized training in order to enter the field and are expected to stay current in the practices of the field. I see references to expertise and to an expectation that members will adhere to certain standards and an ethical code of conduct. I simply cannot find any dictionary that defines a professional as someone who can do whatever he or she pleases.

Professional Doesn't Mean Autonomous

Time spent in collaboration with colleagues is considered essential to success in most professions. When professional airline pilots prepare to take off, they coordinate their work with air traffic control. If the tower informs a pilot that he or she is to move to runway 24L and be fourth in line for takeoff, the pilot does not, as a professional, have the autonomy to declare, "I prefer runway 25 and I refuse to wait." He or she is not merely expected, but is actually *required* to work interdependently with others to achieve the common goal of a safe takeoff.

The law firm that represented our school district when I was superintendent required all of its attorneys to meet on a weekly basis to review the issues and strategies of various cases assigned to individual members. Each attorney presented the facts of the case and his or her thoughts on how to proceed. The others offered advice, suggested relevant precedents, and shared their experience and insights. Attending the meetings was not optional. One might say this law firm *coerced* its members to attend. The firm, however, believed that all of its clients should have the benefit of the collective expertise of the entire firm, not merely the single attorney to whom the case had been assigned.

When our school district underwent a major construction project, the professionals engaged in the project always worked as a team. Each week, architects, engineers, and the construction manager convened in a collaborative meeting to make certain they were pursuing a common objective according to their established plan. They monitored progress toward clearly defined benchmarks and observed agreed-on protocols for identifying and solving problems. The meetings were not optional, and it might be said that members were *compelled* to be there.

When I went for a comprehensive physical examination, a doctor who reviewed one of the tests initially recommended that I undergo an immediate angioplasty. The hospital protocol, however, *demanded* that his recommendation be reviewed by two specialists. Those specialists examined the data from the test, but they also sought additional information. Based on that information, the team concluded that the procedure was not necessary as long as I engaged in alternative treatments.

In each of these instances, the professional is expected to collaborate with others. In fact, collaborating effectively with others is a condition for membership in their profession. Certainly, they will spend a great deal of their time working individually and autonomously. The pilot will work in isolation during some portions of a flight. A lawyer in the courtroom must be able to respond to the immediate situation. The engineers, architects, and construction managers return to their individual realms to work at their respective tasks in the joint effort to complete their project. And the cardiologist will make decisions based on his or her individual judgment when in the operating room. In every case, however, these professionals are required to work with others on a regular basis, and a structure is created to ensure that they do so.

When schools are organized to support the collaborative culture of a professional learning community, classroom teachers continue to have tremendous latitude. Throughout most of their workday and work week they labor in their individual classrooms as they attempt to meet the needs of each student. But the school will also embed processes into the routine practice of its professionals to ensure that they co-labor in a coordinated and systematic effort to support the students they serve. Like the professionals described above, they work interdependently in the pursuit of common purposes and goals. They share their expertise with one another and make that expertise available to all of the students served by the team. They establish clear benchmarks and agreed on measures to monitor progress. They gather and jointly examine information regarding student learning to make more informed decisions and to enhance their practice. They will not have the opportunity to opt out, because the entire structure of the school will be designed to ensure that they collaborate with their colleagues.

The Weight of the Evidence

Professionals make decisions based on the evidence of the most promising strategy for meeting the needs of those they serve. In a profession, evidence trumps appeals to mindless precedent ("This is how I have always done it") or personal preference ("This is how I like to do it"). So, let's apply the standard of the "weight of the evidence" to the question, "Do schools best serve their students when educators work collaboratively or when each educator can elect to work in isolation?"

Professional Organizations

Almost all of the professional organizations in education, including the National Education Association and the American Federation of Teachers, have specifically endorsed the premise that educators should work collaboratively. In addition, advocacy organizations, such as the National Commission on Teaching and America's Future (NCTAF), also call on educators to work as members of a professional learning community. NCTAF's president wrote:

> Quality teaching is not an individual accomplishment, it is the result of a collaborative culture that empowers teachers to team up to improve student learning beyond what any of them can achieve alone. . . . The idea that a single teacher, working alone, can know and do everything to meet the diverse learning needs of 30 students every day throughout the school year has rarely worked, and it certainly won't meet the needs of learners in years to come. (Carroll 2009: 13)

Principals have been advised by their professional organizations that one of their key responsibilities and a core strategy for improving student achievement is building the capacity of staff to work as members of a collaborative professional learning community. When advocating collaboration, neither principal nor teacher professional associations have added the caveat, "but only if each person wants to."

Research

There is abundant research linking higher levels of student achievement to educators who work in the collaborative culture of a professional learning community. A recent study of schools and districts that doubled student achievement concluded, "it should be no surprise that one result of the multiplicity of activities was a collaborative, professional school culture . . . what is commonly called a 'professional learning community' today" (Odden and Archibald 2009: 78). A study of the best school systems in the world found that schools in those systems focused on providing the "high-quality, collaborative, job-focused professional development" characteristic of "professional learning communities" in which teachers work together to help each other improve classroom practice (Barber and Mourshed 2009: 30). The most comprehensive study of factors affecting schooling ever conducted concluded that the most powerful strategy for helping students learn at higher levels was ensuring that teachers work collaboratively in teams to establish the essential learnings all students must acquire, to gather evidence of student learning through an ongoing assessment process, and to use the evidence of student learning to discuss, evaluate, plan, and improve their instruction (Hattie 2009).

A useful exercise for a school or district that claims its purpose and priority is to help students learn at high levels is to gather all the evidence faculty can find that supports the idea that students learn better if educators work in isolation. At the same time, gather all the evidence that students learn at higher levels when educators work as members of collaborative teams. The website www.allthingsplc.info provides specific quotes from organizations and researchers who have concluded that a collaborative school culture raises student achievement. I'm unable to include research indicating students learn at higher levels when educators work in isolation, because I'm unaware of any.

If the group determines that the preponderance of evidence indicates the school will be more successful if its members work together rather than in isolation, then structures should be created to support collaboration, and all members of the staff should be required to participate. An individual's desire to work in isolation does not trump a professional's obligation to apply what is considered the most effective practice in his or her field.

The fact that schools create the infrastructure to ensure educators work as members of collaborative teams does not preclude those educators from forming additional, voluntary collaborative communities. Many educators use technology to form virtual communities based on common interests. However, these voluntary communities should not substitute for school structures and cultures in which working together interdependently is the norm.

Only on What We Want

A corollary to the volunteerism argument is that if educators work in collaborative teams, each team must have the autonomy to determine the focus of its work. The issue is presented as a question of power—who will have the authority to decide what we will collaborate about. In a mature profession united in a joint effort to best meet the needs of those it serves, the more relevant questions are: Can we agree that the purpose of our collaboration is to improve our professional practice and the learning of our students? Do we recognize that we must resolve certain critical questions if we are to accomplish that purpose? Can we demonstrate the discipline to focus on the right work?

Focusing on the Right Work

Collaboration is a means to an end. Collaboration alone will not improve a school, and in a toxic school culture, providing educators with time to collaborate is likely to reinforce the negative aspects of the culture and deteriorate into complaint sessions. Team meetings that focus on the deficiencies of students, better strategies for punishing students who wear hats, or determining who will pick up the field trip forms will not improve student achievement; however, in many schools topics like these dominate the discussion. Providing educators

with structures and time to support collaboration will not improve schools unless that time is focused on the right work.

What is the right work? As members of collaborative teams, educators in a PLC work collectively to develop a guaranteed and viable curriculum to ensure that students have access to the same essential knowledge and skills regardless of the teacher to whom they are assigned. The team gathers ongoing information regarding the learning of their students through a comprehensive, balanced assessment process that includes common formative assessments developed by the team. The team then jointly analyzes the evidence of student learning from the assessments and uses the information to improve the professional practice of individual members and collective effectiveness of the team. As members look at actual evidence of student proficiency in the knowledge and skills the team has deemed essential, on an assessment the team has agreed is valid, they are able to learn from one another and continually enhance their ability to meet the needs of their students.

Finally, in a professional learning community, the school creates a *systematic* process that ensures that students who are struggling receive additional time and support for learning. Rather than continuing with the education lottery, where what happens when a student experiences difficulty will depend almost solely on the individual teacher to whom that student is assigned, the school will create a multi-tiered, coordinated, and collective response to support that student.

Schools committed to higher levels of learning for both students and adults will not be content with the fact that a structure is in place to ensure that educators meet on a regular basis. They will recognize that the question, "What will we collaborate about," is so vital that it cannot be left to the discretion of each team. Educators in these schools will collectively identify the right work and then create processes to support teams as they focus their efforts on those matters that improve student learning.

Powerful Concepts Can Be Applied Badly

The concept of a collaborative culture of a professional learning community is powerful, but like all powerful concepts, it can be applied badly. Schools can create artificial, rather than meaningful and relevant, teams. Educators can make excuses for low student achievement rather than develop strategies to improve student learning. Teams can concentrate on matters unrelated to student learning. Getting along can be a greater priority than getting results. Administrators can micro-manage the process in ways that do not build collective capacity, or they can attempt to hold teams accountable for collaborating while failing to provide the time, support, parameters, resources, and clarity that are crucial to the success of teams.

Creating a PLC is fraught with difficulty, but that doesn't mean educators should reject the concept or allow individuals to opt out. If they are to be members of a *profession*, educators must work together in good faith to develop their collective capacity to implement this powerful concept effectively.

More than a quarter century has passed since Goodlad warned that overcoming the tradition of teacher isolation will require more than an invitation. We must do more than exhort people to work together. In order to establish schools in which interdependence and collaboration are the new norm, we must create the structures and cultures that *embed* collaboration in the routine practice of our schools, ensure that the collaborative efforts focus on the right work, and support educators as they build their capacity to work together rather than alone.

References

Barber, Michael, and Mona Mourshed. "Shaping the Future: How Good Education Systems Can Become Great in the Decade Ahead. Report on the International Education Roundtable." Singapore: McKinsey & Co., July 7, 2009. www.mckinsey .com/locations/southeastasia/knowledge/Education _Roundtable.pdf.

Carroll, Tom. "The Next Generation of Learning Teams." *Phi Delta Kappan* 91, no. 2 (October 2009): 8–13.

Hargreaves, Andrew. "Contrived Congeniality: The Micropolitics of Teacher Collaboration." In *The Politics of Life in Schools: Power, Conflict, and Cooperation,* ed. Joseph Blase: 46–72. Thousand Oaks, Calif.: Sage, 1991.

Hattie, John. *Visible Learning: A Synthesis of Over 800 Meta-Analyses Relating to Achievement.* New York: Routledge, 2009.

Odden, Allen R., and Sarah Archibald. *Doubling Student Performance . . . And Finding the Resources to Do It.* San Francisco: Corwin Press, 2009.

Critical Thinking

1. DuFour thinks that teachers can no longer work independently of others, but must engage in collaborative work with families and other educational professionals. Outline the major points of his case and note your opinion on the veracity of each.

2. Collaboration has long been thought of as a voluntary activity. DuFour says that concept is no longer permitted. What can administrators do to establish collaborative professional learning communities? What specific actions would support collaboration?

3. DuFour states that the question "what will we collaborate about" is too vital to be left to each team. So he has asked you to make a list of topics, problems, and activities that you think PLC teams should make primary responsibilities of their work. What are your top 3–5 items?

4. Do you think DuFour is really asking teachers to *collaborate* in the true sense of that concept, or is he simply saying that teachers must learn to "play together" to get the job done? Is there a difference between being able to work well in a team situation and being collaborative?

Create Central

www.mhhe.com/createcentral

Internet References

The IRIS Center (see Collaboration)
http://iris.peabody.vanderbilt.edu/resources.html

RICK DUFOUR is an education author and consultant on the implementation of the professional learning community concept in districts and schools. © 2011, Rick DuFour.

Article   Prepared by: Rebecca B. Evers, *Winthrop University*

Methods for Addressing Conflict in Cotaught Classrooms

GREG CONDERMAN[1]

Learning Outcomes

After reading this article, you will be able to:

- Use appropriate methods to defuse a conflict in a collaborative relationship, such as co-teaching.

- Construct a plan for involving families in a student's Behavior Intervention Plan.

Based only on their schedule and availability, Marci and Craig's high school assistant principal assigned them to coteach two sections of biology. Their personalities and teaching styles could not be more different. Marci is outgoing, fun, and spontaneous, whereas Craig is quiet, predictable, cautious, and serious. At the middle school, Esther and Margaret coteach sixth-grade language arts. Esther believes that students at this level need to explore to create meaning in the curriculum, whereas Margaret is a firm believer in explicit instruction and scripted lessons. Finally, Inge and Zack coteach second grade. Neither really understands his or her coteaching role, and Inge feels Zack is invading her space. These three teams, representing various subjects and grade levels, illustrate issues between coteachers that potentially could cause conflict. Without professionally addressing the issues, these teachers (all names are pseudonyms)—and the students they serve—may not experience the true benefits and intended outcomes of effective coteaching.

Coteaching represents one approach for supporting students with disabilities in the general education classroom. Friend and Cook (2010) defined coteaching as a "service delivery option for providing special education or related services to students with disabilities or other special needs while they remain in the general education classroom" (p. 109). They also emphasized that coteaching involves two or more professionals who jointly deliver instruction to a diverse group of students within a shared classroom space. Coteaching also assumes that teachers display mutual respect for each other, assume roles with parity, collectively develop specific mutual goals, assume accountability for outcomes, share resources, and communicate in ways their partner understands (Conderman, Bresnahan, & Pedersen,

2009). Therefore, effective coteaching depends, in part, on each teacher's interpersonal skills, willingness and ability to work collaboratively, and skills in successfully handling conflict.

These skills are critical because coteaching is a highly interactive endeavor that brings together two individuals with different professional backgrounds, beliefs, expertise, strengths, and needs. Although blending contrasting profiles can result in professional satisfaction and growth for coteachers and increased student academic performance (Villa, Thousand, & Nevin, 2008), coteachers are also likely to face more opportunities for potential conflict than when teaching on their own. When professionals from different disciplines with different frames of reference make decisions about student needs, they are likely to disagree about desired outcomes (Behfar, Peterson, Mannix, & Trochin, 2008). Clearly, when two or more people are together for any length of time, they will experience some conflict (Bolton, 1979).

Addressing conflict may actually produce positive outcomes. For example, appropriately addressing conflict may clarify each partner's issues, increase each person's involvement in the process and outcomes, promote professional and personal growth, strengthen interpersonal relationships, rebuild organizational systems, foster problem solving, promote flexible thinking and creativity, prevent stagnation, and encourage fun (Bolton, 1979; Dettmer, Thurston, Knackendoffel, & Dyck, 2009; Villa et al., 2008). Furthermore, addressing conflict allows partners to become aware of issues in the relationship, causes future decisions to be made more carefully, and clears the air of unexpressed resentments (Falikowski, 2007).

Despite these advantages of addressing conflict, several reasons explain why teachers may be ill equipped to address conflict. First, many special education teacher preparation programs inadequately prepare teachers for addressing conflict. Special education teachers indicate that much of their day is spent navigating adult-to-adult interactions, for which they feel ill prepared. Few authentic early clinical or student teaching opportunities are available for preservice candidates to gain such experiences before their first teaching position (Conderman, Morin, & Stephens, 2005). Similarly, many enter coteaching with minimal training in this area (Conderman, Bresnahan, et al., 2009). Consequently, coteachers may not know what to expect or how to begin their coteaching situation, which may lead to resistance, stress, and uncertainty. Traditionally, school professionals have been uncomfortable addressing conflict (Friend & Cook, 2010), thereby providing few good models for beginning, or even experienced, teachers. Collectively, these factors may contribute to coteaching partners feeling ill prepared to address and negotiate critical issues. Because of the unique structure of coteaching and its potential for conflict, this article focuses on conflict within the context of coteaching by providing background on conflict, indicating possible reasons and sources for coteaching conflict, and describing ways to professionally address such conflict.

The Nature and Sources of Conflict

Defining Conflict

One general definition is that conflict occurs when individuals experience unresolved differences in terms of needs, values, goals, and/or personalities (Dettmer et al., 2009). At times, coteachers may have opposing (a) needs in terms of their contributions to the classroom, classroom organization, and/or student expectations; (b) values regarding critical student academic and social outcomes, the role of family members, and/or student responsibilities; (c) goals for themselves, each other, and/or their class; and (d) personalities such as their sense of humor, frames of reference, ways they deal with conflict, and the amount of energy and enthusiasm they portray during instruction. Villa et al. (2008) used the term *controversy* to describe situations in which coteachers have incompatible ideas (e.g., using two totally different approaches to introduce a math concept) and must reach an agreement. Friend and Cook (2010) defined conflict as a type of struggle in which individuals perceive that others are interfering with their ability to attain goals. These authors also noted that conflict can occur (a) between individuals with the same goals (e.g., both coteachers agree that coplanning is important but disagree on their approach) and (b) because of power or perceived power (e.g., the more experienced teacher assumes he or she has more decision-making authority). Moore (1996) listed five different types of conflicts:

1. value-based conflicts (caused by different goals, ways of life, or ideology),
2. structural conflicts (caused by negative patterns of behavior or interaction or by unequal power, control, or resources),
3. relationship conflicts (caused by poor communication or miscommunication),
4. data-based conflicts (caused by lack of information, misinformation, different views on what is relevant, or different interpretations of data), and
5. interest-based conflicts (caused by different procedural, psychological, or substantive interests).

These various definitions and examples provide a framework for understanding some of the unique circumstances surrounding coteaching conflict.

Sources of Coteaching Conflict

Because coteaching involves working very closely with another professional through coplanning, coinstructing, and coassessing (Muraski & Boyer, 2008), opportunities for conflict are inevitable during any or all of these coteaching components. Figure 1 lists potential sources of conflict associated with coplanning, coinstructing, and coassessing. Coteaching teams can use Figure 1 as a checklist to assess potential sources of conflict by noting areas of concern and later planning ways to address identified concerns.

As noted in Figure 1, some teachers, perhaps those who have taught the same grade level or subject for multiple years, may not share the same need for coplanning as their novice coteacher, one who is new to the content area, or a partner whose planning style is very deliberate and detailed. Admittedly, teachers approach their lessons in various ways, so finding a suitable planning time and process may take time and effort. Similarly, differences in coinstructing may emerge as teachers reveal their preferences for certain coteaching models, strategies, materials, acceptable classroom noise levels, need for structure, and instructional role of each coteacher. Finally, coteachers may differ on their beliefs and practices regarding assessment. For example, some teachers believe grades motivate students, and they value frequent student monitoring and data collection as a way to indicate student growth and inform instruction. In contrast, others view grades as tools that reduce student creativity, or they rely on end-of-semester projects or tests as major indicators of student learning. Therefore, during coplanning, coinstructing, and coassessing, coteachers should expect differences of opinion and the need for dialogue to understand their partner.

In addition to potential sources of conflict related to coplanning, coinstructing, and coassessing, other circumstances may affect the coteaching partnership and cause conflict. Personality issues may result in conflict or, at the very least, make coteaching less desirable and less enjoyable than teaching solo. Teachers who were good colleagues may not always make the best coteachers, especially if personality differences affect teaching expectations or cause one coteacher to feel unequal or disrespected, or if one coteacher uses a personality trait or strength to gain student or parent support or popularity and isolate the coteaching partner. A coteacher with a dominant or outgoing personality should not be allowed to manipulate a quiet individual, as this may lead to feelings of resentment. Unclear or different expectations of coteaching, a sense of invading one's territory, and lack of content knowledge can cause conflict. Outside sources, such as jealousies from other coworkers, misunderstandings from colleagues that coteaching is easy, pressure to raise student test scores from the cotaught class, and unclear systems of teaching evaluations are additional sources of conflict unique to some cotaught classrooms. Finally, issues related to unprofessionalism (e.g., one coteacher

Figure 1   Checklist of potential sources of coteaching conflict

	Coplanning
	The team has not received training on coplanning
	The team does not have a common planning time
	One coteacher did not attend scheduled coplanning meeting(s)
	One or both coteachers were unprepared for coplanning meeting(s)
	Coteachers have different approaches to planning (e.g., detailed and sequential v. holistic or written v. verbal)
	Coteachers disagree on instructional sequence
	Coteachers disagree on coplanning format or form
	One or both coteachers are hesitant using a new planning approach
	One coteacher has little opportunity to contribute meaningfully to coplanning
	Coteachers assume same coplanning role (e.g., only special educator suggests accommodations) even when both could have contributed
	Other (list)
	Coinstructing
	One or both coteachers were unprepared for coinstructing
	Coteachers have different views/philosophies on teaching, learning, role of teacher, role of students, classroom management, etc.
	One coteacher always assumes lead role
	One coteacher always assumes support role
	One coteacher lacks content knowledge to deliver, support, or modify instruction
	Students view one coteacher as assistant, rather than teacher
	One coteacher feels more like assistant, rather than teacher
	One coteacher did not follow established plan
	One coteacher was not flexible with lesson when a change was needed
	Coteachers do not use parity in instruction, language, signals, and/or materials
	Other (list)
	Coassessing
	Coteachers only use types of assessments used in previous semesters
	Coteachers have different philosophies regarding grading
	Coteachers have different views on the role of assessment
	One coteacher changed the assessment without notifying the partner
	Teams rely on subjective feelings rather than objective data for making instructional decisions and student evaluations
	Only one teacher has access to student grades
	Only one teacher communicates with parents regarding student progress
	Coteachers did not reflect on lesson
	Coteachers blame each other for poor lesson delivery or inadequate student growth
	Coteachers always assume same role in assessment (e.g., only special educator makes assessment accommodations or modifications)
	Other (list)

who does not maintain confidentialities, independently changes student grades or scores, or says negative comments about the partner to others) are quite serious, undermine the coteaching relationship, and often require administrator intervention. All of these issues illustrate potential sources of conflict unique to coteaching.

Coteaching conflict may be especially evident with poorly matched teachers (such as Marci and Craig from our opening scenario), those who view teaching and learning in significantly different ways (such as Esther and Margaret), and those who are uncertain about their coteaching roles (such as Inge and Zack). These teams are especially likely to experience discord (Dettmer et al., 2009). When not addressed, such discord is likely to negatively interfere with the relationship between coteachers, the classroom climate, teaching skills, and student learning.

Proactive Strategies

Several proactive strategies, implemented by coteachers, can minimize the likelihood of conflict damaging the relationship. Although their implementation does not guarantee that conflict will not occur, the following strategies, based on research from business management, organizational behavior, and social and behavioral psychology (Song, Dyer, & Thieme, 2006), offer structure and support to teams and increase the likelihood that coteaching endeavors will run more smoothly.

Several resources also offer proactive support for coteaching teams (see Table 1). Coteachers are encouraged to consult such sources and complete the discussion activities or assessments with their coteacher before they enter their coteaching relationship. Completing informal assessments individually and then discussing results as a coteaching team clarifies each person's approach to addressing conflict and offers insight for partners to comfortably approach each other when conflict arises. Six specific proactive strategies follow.

1. *Discuss instructional-related issues before you begin.* Before coteaching, spend considerable time thoroughly discussing any and all issues that may impact the teaching relationship. Being honest with your partner about your teaching style; educational philosophies; views on classroom management; and thoughts on grading; as well as your teaching strengths, challenges, and goals, helps create a foundation with which to build a trusting and safe coteaching relationship. Your coteacher cannot read your mind. Being vulnerable may be scary, but sharing ideas early avoids later surprises. Taking notes while your coteacher shares shows interest and provides a record of your discussion. Realize that ongoing discussion of these topics is critical to understanding your partner's perspectives.

2. *Ask your coteacher how he or she wants to address conflict.* Based on life experiences, gender, culture, frame of reference, and perceptions of how conflict resolution was modeled, individuals display predispositions when faced with conflict. An individual's conflict style is a behavioral orientation of how to approach and handle conflict (Falikowski, 2007). Therefore, seek to understand your coteacher's views and methods of handling conflict and how he or she wishes to be treated when you have constructive criticism to share. Specifically, ask how your coteacher wishes you to address issues, and then make a commitment to respect those wishes. Some teachers desire direct feedback (e.g., "Just tell me"), whereas others prefer a softer approach (e.g., "Gradually prepare

Table 1   Resources for Coteachers

Resource	Brief description
Allesandra (2007)	Free 18-question online inventory (Platinum Rule.com) that provides information about one's interpersonal style, including preferences for handing conflict
Conderman, Bresnahan, et al. (2009)	Book that includes discussion questions and forms to guide coteachers, especially during the beginning coteaching stage
Dettmer et al. (2009)	Book that includes communication and conflict checklists and practice activities, tips for communicating effectively, and discussion questions for coteaching teams
Dieker (2006)	Coplanning book that includes a side-by-side view of each teacher's lesson contribution, with space to document interventions and student progress toward goals
Friend and Cook (2010)	Book that provides a 12-question conflict management-style survey with scoring directions which indicates a person's preference to control, compromise, build consensus, accommodate, or avoid conflict
Karten (2010)	Coplanning book with weekly/quarterly lesson plan formats, assessment, monitoring, record-keeping forms, and inclusive strategies
Miscisin (2007)	Short, free, online assessment (Truecolors.com) that provides information about one's approach to work
Murawski and Dieker (2004)	Article that offers numerous coteaching resources and questions/forms to use to prepare to coteach, clarify coteaching expectations, and promote instructional parity
Trent and Cox (2006)	Comprehensive, inexpensive, online inventory that analyzes how individuals solve problems, process information, manage change, and face risk, which includes a comprehensive report of one's profile
Villa et al. (2008)	Book that offers discussion questions and forms to guide coteachers, self-assessments, answers to frequently asked questions, and tips for promoting cooperation in cotaught classrooms

me for your concern"). Be sure to ask your coteacher what would upset him or her in the cotaught classroom, so you can avoid embarrassment or conflict. In short, clearly stated policies and procedures that have the understanding and support of both parties create orderly processes that mitigate unnecessary conflict (Bolton, 1979). Similarly, recognizing different individuals' communication or conflict resolution styles leads to understanding and can also maximize the group's problem-solving effectiveness (Broome, DeTurk, Kristjansdottir, Kanata, & Ganesan, 2002).

3. *Put plans in writing.* Coteachers who just discuss upcoming lessons are probably more likely to forget some of the details, materials, or assigned tasks, which can cause conflict. A written lesson plan that outlines each coteacher's roles and responsibilities helps document parity. Writing lesson plans also helps teachers reflect more accurately after the lesson. Similarly, teams can return to their written plan to verify their original intent. Coteachers can use published lesson plan books or develop their own lesson plan format detailing the responsibilities of each coteacher during specified lesson segments.

4. *Address issues early.* Do not allow a concern to fester. Most likely, the issue will not go away, and in fact, given additional time, it may bother you even more. Covert conflicts need to be made overt and resolved, or they will fester and destroy the potential for a positive coteaching relationship (Villa et al., 2008). Decide if the issue is worth addressing, and if so, share your concern privately with your coteacher using a preferred method of addressing conflict. Because body language and voice intonation play an important role in communicating, issues are best discussed through face-to-face discussions rather than shared through e-mail or other written exchanges (Conderman, Johnston-Rodriguez, & Hartman, 2009). Similarly, phone exchanges should be short and to the point (Turnbull & Turnbull, 2001).

5. *Use effective communication skills.* Because coteaching is a relationship, and relationships are built on communication, take time to study effective communication skills. Most important, listen to your coteacher to find out what is important to him or her. Ask questions. Also, when you are feeling upset, calm yourself down before addressing your coteacher, so you do not respond in anger. Some effective communication skills (Conderman, Bresnahan, et al., 2009; Conderman, Johnston-Rodreguez, et al., 2009) include the following:

   a. Open-ended questions that seek information, such as, "How do you feel about doing a jigsaw activity tomorrow for social studies?"

   b. "I" messages that share how you feel about an event, such as, "I am concerned that students felt rushed to get through the jigsaw activity today."

   c. Paraphrasing or summarizing, which provides a short or longer summary of the topic of discussion as a way to check for communication accuracy and understanding, such as, "So, before we go, let's make sure we are on the same page regarding our lesson introduction tomorrow. We agreed to both introduce the lesson tomorrow with our role play. Then you will verbally describe the steps of the new math skill while I model, on the smart board. Did I miss anything?"

   d. Response to affect, which shows empathy by using a feeling word to indicate how you think someone else feels, such as, "I would be frustrated, too, if Myrna yelled at me."

   e. The sandwich technique, in which a concern is shared between two neutral statements, such as, "Willemetta, there is something I need to share with you. Remember, we agreed to come to one another if something was upsetting us. Well, I heard from another teacher that you said I have poor control of the class. This hurts me and violates our promise of confidentiality. I value our professional relationship, so I wonder how we can ensure this will not happen again." Even though using these kinds of effective communication skills may feel artificial, when used sincerely, they clarify issues and intents, thus acting as a proactive conflict intervention.

6. *Do not expect perfection.* Each of you will make mistakes, especially in the beginning of the cotaught relationship. Expect some bumps in the road. Allow yourself and your partner some grace and breathing room. Forgiveness goes a long way. Humble yourself when you make an error and be willing to forgive your partner.

Conflict Approaches

Proactive strategies will reduce potential for conflict, but most likely they will not eliminate the conflict entirely. Therefore, coteachers need to be aware of ways of approaching conflict when proactive strategies are insufficient in addressing the issue. Generally, the education and business literature indicates five main approaches to handling conflict (Copley, 2008). These include avoiding, accommodating, compromising, collaborating, and dominating. Table 2 reviews these five approaches or styles along with considerations and a coteaching example. Although a teacher's use of any of these approaches is dependent upon the situation and her or his partner, teachers should be skilled in all five strategies (Johnson, 2008). Gross and Guerrero (2000) discovered that colleagues generally view a collaborative style, with its emphasis on being polite, prosocial, and adaptive, as most appropriate and effective. In contrast, colleagues perceived the accommodating and compromising styles as neutral and the dominating and avoiding styles as less appropriate. Individuals tend to choose a conflict approach based on the importance of the issue and the consequences to the relationship (Johnson, 2008).

Table 2 Common Ways of Addressing Conflict with Definitions and Examples

Approach	Considerations	Coteaching example
Avoiding	Reflect on the consequences of avoidance and decide whether you can live with the result Use avoiding when the issue is trivial, stakes are not high, confrontation will hurt a working relationship, or others can more effectively resolve the conflict (Falikowski, 2007)	Erika frequently joked with students during the first few minutes of class, which upset Woody, who perceived this behavior as unnecessary and a complete waste of time. After reflecting on Erika's behavior, Woody realized that joking with students actually produced a positive classroom environment and that the payoff was worth a few minutes of silliness.
Accommodating	If the same teacher always accommodates, an uneven power situation may emerge Accommodate when maintaining the relationship outweighs other considerations, the issue is not critical, time is limited, or interpersonal harmony and stability are valued more than the issue (Falikowski, 2007)	Even though Paula wanted to start class with a video clip, she agreed with Laura's idea of starting class with a role-play; similarly, even though Laura wanted to use an anticipation guide, she agreed to use guided notes, which was Paula's suggestion.
Compromising	Although commonly used, compromise is often a lose–lose situation as neither teacher gets what she or he really wants Compromise when individuals are equal in power and have strong interests in different solutions (Afzalur et al., 1992) or when important issues have no clear or simple solutions (Falikowski, 2007)	Because she wanted to assess students' ability to apply their newly learned essay-writing strategy, Julie wanted to develop an essay test, but Greg wanted to use a multiple choice test to save time on grading because grades were due Friday. The team agreed to a test containing multiple choice items and one short answer question in which students could apply part of their writing strategy.
Collaborating	This can be a win–win situation, especially if both teachers openly express their needs and are willing to be creative (Copley, 2008) Collaborate when maintaining the relationship is important, time is not a concern, or when it is important to merge differing perspectives (Falikowski, 2007)	Jeff wanted to use a class period to teach students how to use their homework planner, but Sarah thought this was not an effective use of instructional time. The team decided to develop an instructional video clip on using planners, place the clip on their website, and have students study the clip as a homework assignment.
Forcing	Seldom effective in coteaching but may be needed if multiple reminders have been unsuccessful, or if student achievement or behavior is deteriorating Use forcing cautiously and only when personal differences are difficult to change, fostering supportive relationships is not critical, the partner may take advantage of noncompetitive behavior, a decision must be made, or unpopular decisions need to be implemented (Falikowski, 2007)	Toni stopped attending agreed upon coplanning meetings with Lynette, even when Lynette agreed to meet at other times and use other coplanning formats that Toni suggested. Finally, Lynette e-mailed Toni (and copied the administrator) and indicated that the lesson plan would be submitted on time to the administrator with or without Toni's contribution.

The Five Conflict Approaches

An *avoiding* style indicates low concern for self and others (Copley, 2008). Individuals who avoid conflict may be afraid to discuss the issue with their partner, lack effective conflict resolution skills, or think that discussing the issue may make matters worse. However, the situation is unlikely to change unless or until coteachers communicate. Therefore, teachers should first decide if the issue really bothers them. If it does not, then avoiding may be an appropriate choice. This style is often appropriate when individuals are dealing with perceived tactical or minor issues (Afzalur, Garrett, & Buntzman, 1992).

An *accommodating* style involves low concern for self and high concern for others (Copley, 2008). Coteachers who accommodate attempt to diminish differences and emphasize commonalities to satisfy their partner's needs (Copley, 2008). This approach is also appropriate when the issue is not critical and/or when a partner feels he or she may be wrong. However, if one teacher habitually accommodates the other, resentment may occur (Bolton, 1979).

Coteachers may *compromise,* or meet in the middle, when their initial ideas or views are quite different, or when both parties are equally powerful. Compromising is associated with an intermediate level of concern for both self and others (Copley, 2008). This give-and-take style means that neither partner really has his or her needs met as each side gives up something to end the conflict or solve the problem.

Collaborating requires that coteachers rethink the situation with a different frame of reference and implement a third option they had not previously considered. This style is characterized by a high regard for self and others (Copley, 2008). Collaborating is associated with problem solving and generating multiple solutions and is appropriate for dealing with issues related to policies and long-range planning (Afzalur et al., 1992).

Finally, *dominating* involves imposing a solution on someone else and thus is associated with a win-lose perspective and a high concern for self and low concern for others. This approach may be used when a quick decision is required or when an unpopular course of action must be implemented (Afzalur et al., 1992).

An additional option if coteachers are at an impasse is to seek counsel from an administrator, experienced teacher, or mentor. Sometimes an impartial colleague can consider issues more objectively and guide mutual brainstorming efforts. If this option is chosen, both coteachers need to agree on whom to consult, when to collectively meet with that person, and that they will agree to solutions generated.

Dos and Don'ts

Regardless of which conflict approach is used, coteachers may find the general *dos* and *don'ts* guidelines in Table 3 helpful as they discuss issues. Often, in the heat of an argument or disagreement, emotions run high, people feel threatened and defensive, and they may say or do something that they will regret later.

These are exactly the occasions when teachers need to stop and think about whether their verbal and nonverbal behavior is fueling the conflict, or if their approach or reaction to their partner can support a healthy discussion of the issue. Coteachers can acknowledge interest in the partner's views through nodding, maintaining eye contact, leaning toward the person, and asking nonthreatening questions. Several additional suggestions in Table 3 emphasize the importance of listening carefully to your partner because in conflict resolution the first goal is to deal constructively with emotions (Bolton, 1979). One specific tip for understanding your partner is that you should speak for yourself only after you have first restated the ideas and feelings of your partner accurately and to your partner's satisfaction (Bolton, 1979). This step helps teachers clarify and process both feelings and accuracy of information before generating a plan. Making a plan validates the partner's concern, and taking notes allows partners to check for understanding. Respecting your partner's feelings and indicating a willingness to make changes helps repair conflict. Remembering that the coteacher probably did not intentionally mean to cause conflict reduces defensiveness and tempers the discussion.

Conclusion

Conflict is an inevitable part of life, and teachers are likely to experience more conflict with the rise of collaborative

Table 3   Dos and Don'ts for Handling Coteaching Conflict

Do	Don't
Reflect on why the issue bothers you before you talk to your coteacher (Friend & Cook, 2010)	Act impulsively or when angry
Pick the right time and place to talk to your coteacher (Conderman, Johnston-Rodriguez, et al., 2009)	Share confidentialities with others, gossip, or speak unprofessionally about your partner
Use effective communication skills to share your concern (Conderman, Johnston-Rodriguez, et al., 2009b)	Blame your coteacher, offer advice, or lecture (Dettmer et al., 2009)
Focus on the issue (Bolton, 1979)	Focus on personalities, the past, or other nonrelated issues
Choose the most appropriate conflict approach for the situation and the style and needs of your partner (Conderman, Johnston-Rodriguez, et al., 2009)	Avoid all conflict or use the same approach for every situation
Listen and use a calm voice when someone shares a concern with you and acknowledge what has been said (Dettmer et al., 2009)	Get defensive when someone shares their concerns with you; say "Calm down"; tell the person how they should behave or feel (Dettmer et al., 2009)
Ask, "How can we resolve this?" (Dettmer et al., 2009)	Exit the situation without closure
Be willing to make a list of results that you consider acceptable solutions (Dettmer et al., 2009)	Be unwilling to compromise
When feelings are strong, deal with the emotional aspects of conflict first (Bolton, 1979)	Ignore the feelings of your partner and rush to a solution
Select solutions that will best meet both teacher's needs (Bolton, 1979)	Quickly and forcefully note the personal advantages of your suggestions
Agree on a written plan with outcomes and dates for accountability (Friend & Cook, 2010)	Rely on your memory for details of the plan
Evaluate the plan (Friend & Cook, 2010)	Be satisfied with sharing your feelings and discussing options
Thank your partner for coming to you with his or her concern	Take issues personally (Dettmer et al., 2009)

school-based practices such as coteaching. Addressing conflict is critical for the success of coteaching teams, so both teachers are empowered and feel a sense of parity. Coteachers need to be aware of conflict when it exists, diagnose its nature, and employ an appropriate problem-solving method that achieves the goals of both parties while maintaining the professional relationship (Dettmer et al., 2009). This may be difficult for some coteachers based on their frame of reference, past experiences with conflict, the school culture, or feelings of inferiority or intimidation. To support this process, coteachers are advised to be proactive by assessing how they typically address conflict; discussing ground rules for dealing with difficult issues, so that an agreed-upon system is in place; practicing effective communication skills; and acknowledging that neither partner is perfect. When conflict arises, teachers can also reflect upon which of the five approaches of dealing with conflict is most appropriate to use, given the importance of the issue and the effect that choice may have on the coteaching relationship. Coteachers who address conflict professionally by carefully listening to their partner and considering alternative solutions are more likely to experience the personal and professional rewards associated with coteaching, which include expanding their professional repertoire of knowledge and skills, creating respectful classrooms where each teacher's strengths are honored, and fostering a safe and productive learning atmosphere where all students learn.

References

Afzalur, R. M., Garrett, J. E., & Buntzman, G. F. (1992). Ethics of managing interpersonal conflict in organizations. *Journal of Business Ethics, 11*(5), 423–432.

Alessandra, T. (2007). *The platinum rule.* Retrieved May 19, 2010, from www.platinumrule.com/free-assessment.asp.

Behfar, K., Peterson, R. S., Mannix, E. A., & Trochin, W. M. K. (2008). The critical role of conflict resolution in teams: A closer look at the links between conflict type, conflict management strategies and team outcomes. *Journal of Applied Psychology, 93,* 170–188.

Bolton, R. (1979). *People skills: How to assert yourself listen to others, and resolve conflicts.* New York, NY: Simon & Schuster.

Broome, B. J., DeTurk, S., Kristjansdottir, E. S., Kanata, T., & Ganesan, P. (2002). Giving voice to diversity: An interactive approach to conflict management and decision-making in culturally diverse work environments. *Journal of Business and Management, 8*(3), 239–264.

Conderman, G., Bresnahan, V., & Pedersen, T. (2009). *Purposeful co-teaching: Real cases and effective strategies.* Thousand Oaks, CA: Corwin.

Conderman, G., Johnston-Rodriguez, S., & Hartman, P. (2009). Communicating and collaborating in co-taught classrooms. *TEACHING Exceptional Children Plus, 5*(5), Article 3. Retrieved June 6, 2010, from http://escholarship.bc.edu/education/tecplus/vol5/iss5/art3.

Conderman, G., Morin, J., & Stephens, J. T. (2005). Special education student teaching practices. *Preventing School Failure, 49*(3), 5–10.

Copley, L. (2008). *Conflict management styles: A predictor of likability and perceived effectiveness among subordinates.* Unpublished master's thesis, Indiana University, Indianapolis.

Dettmer, P., Thurston, L., Knackendoffel, A., & Dyck, N. (2009). *Collaboration, consultation, and teamwork for students with special needs* (6th ed.). Columbus, OH: Pearson.

Dieker, L. (2006). *The co-teaching lesson plan book: Academic year version.* Whitefish Bay, WI: Knowledge by Design.

Falikowski, A. (2007). *Mastering human relations* (4th ed.). Toronto: Pearson Education Canada.

Friend, M., & Cook, L. (2010). *Interactions: Collaborative skills for school professionals* (6th ed.). Boston, MA: Pearson.

Gross, M. A., & Guerrero, L. K. (2000). Managing conflict appropriately and effectively: An application of the competence model to Rahim's organizational conflict styles. *International Journal of Conflict Management, 11*(3), 200–226.

Johnson, D. W. (2008). *Reaching out. Interpersonal effectiveness and self-actualization* (10th ed.). Boston, MA: Allyn & Bacon.

Karten, T. (2010). *Inclusion lesson plan book for the 21st century.* Port Chester, NY: Dude Publishing.

Miscisin, M. (2007). *The true colors test.* Retrieved May 20, 2010, from www.true_colors_test.com.

Moore, C. (1996). *The mediation process: Practical strategies for resolving conflict.* San Francisco, CA: Jossey-Bass.

Murawski, W., & Boyer, L. (2008, November). *What is really happening in cotaught classes? One state knows!* Paper presented at the Teacher Education Division of the Council for Exceptional Children Conference, Dallas, TX.

Murawski, W., & Dieker, L. (2004). Tips and strategies for co-teaching at the secondary level. *TEACHING Exceptional Children, 36*(5), 52–58.

Song, M., Dyer, B., & Thieme, R. J. (2006). Conflict management and innovation performance: An integrated contingency perspective. *Journal of the Academy of Marketing Science, 34*(3), 341–356.

Trent, J., & Cox, R. (2006). *Leading from your strengths.* Scottsdale, AZ: Ministry Insights Intl.

Turnbull, A., & Turnbull, R. (2001). *Families, professionals, and exceptionality: Collaborating for empowerment* (4th ed.). Upper Saddle River, NJ: Pearson.

Villa, R. A., Thousand, J. A., & Nevin, A. I. (2008). *A guide to co-teaching: Practical tips for facilitating student learning.* Thousand Oaks, CA: Corwin.

Critical Thinking

1. Think about all of the times that you have collaborated with a peer or even with a person who was a supervisor. Now pick one experience that was especially memorable. What was best about that collaboration? What was unpleasant about that collaboration?

2. Have you ever tried to co-teach? Share your story about that event.

3. Even the best of collaborators with similar goals and ideals occasionally have conflict, particularly when the stakes are high, such as in a teaching situation. Why does this happen?

4. Table 2 lists common ways that collaborators address conflict. Which of these have you used to get out of a sticky situation? Why did you choose to use that method?

Create Central

www.mhhe.com/createcentral

Internet References

Education Oasis Working with Parents: Advice from teachers
www.educationoasis.com/resources/Articles/working_with_parents.htm

GREG CONDERMAN, EdD, is an associate professor of special education at Northern Illinois University. His research interests include coteaching and instructional methods for students with mild disabilities.

Declaration of Conflicting Interest—The author(s) declared no conflicts of interest with respect to the authorship and/or publication of this article.

Funding—The author(s) received no financial support for the research and/or authorship of this article.

Article   Prepared by: Rebecca B. Evers, *Winthrop University*

What's Your Style?

When teachers understand their own "curriculum style," they can make conscious decisions about incorporating other styles into their practice.

DONNA L. MILLER

Learning Outcomes

After reading this article, you will be able to:

- Understand how your personal style can affect your collaborative interactions.

Most of us approach life with a certain style. A comfort zone, philosophical stance, or belief system influences or motivates many of our actions and decisions. These behaviors are so entrenched by habit and convention that we often don't give them much thought, but to deconstruct this behavior might shed considerable light into corners where bias or even unawareness lurks. After all, how can we know that our way, our idea, or our belief is the best if we don't learn about anything else?

These tendencies to act may influence us at a subliminal level, so unless we bring them to light, we may never be able to give name to our actions. Employers, curious about leadership and personality styles and wishing to build effective teams, survey potential employees to maximize efficacy. They use measurement instruments like the Myers-Briggs Type Indicator to identify manifestations of perception and judgment, making cognitive behavior more understandable and useful. When it comes to curriculum development, similar sorting terms exist, and taking a survey can identify one's approach to teaching others. Such instruments don't purport to label or to evaluate but to provide feedback; they illustrate how behavior, which seems random, is actually motivated by preferences.

Four Curriculum Styles

Four common schools of thought in the curriculum arena are the linear, holistic, laissez-faire, and critical theorist approaches.

Linear Thinkers

Generally, to be linear means to favor structure, order, and maximum control of a particular environment. The linearist wants education to be as efficient as possible, both fiscally and

empirically. In essence, this model mimics scientific management in the way that Frederick Taylor used science to manage business. Franklin Bobbitt transported Taylor's ideas into schools, where they were further refined by Ralph Tyler (1949). Tyler outlined a curriculum plan that included selecting objectives, identifying useful learning experiences to further those objectives, organizing learning activities into a sequence or hierarchy, and evaluating the behavioral change. Diversity is not the ultimate goal in this model; this is a system that values procedure, routine, and the best way to do the job. Under the influence of such a design, standards control human effort, and predetermined outcomes require mastery, encouraging the worker or student to perform like a well-oiled machine. To establish such targets, one simply asks questions like "What constitutes the equivalent of a diploma?" or "What does a prototypical finished product look like?" Programs then provide the training to produce that outcome or meet that standard.

We don't need to look far to see these influences in schools. Scope and sequence charts, bell schedules, grade-level designs, and Bloom's Taxonomy all reflect linear characteristics. Furthermore, the prevalence of how-to books, social tendencies to rate performance against ideals, and our competitive spirit prove that linearism has permeated multiple aspects of life beyond school. Many of us find comfort in specifying content, articulating goals, following routines, and controlling variables. The more we value these elements, the more linear we are on the continuum.

Holists believe that as long as an object of study captures students' interest, moving on to another subject makes no sense.

Holists

While holists can also work within a schedule that devotes time to instruction, such practice cuts against their ideology. Holists believe that as long as an object of study captures students' interest, moving on to another subject makes no sense. Interest drives the learning experience, with consideration for whether an experience will open or close a student's world. Under such an organic design, curriculum emerges from negotiations among the student, teacher, and environment. Pragmatic in a Deweyan sense, the teacher arranges the environment to stimulate students to respond. By making suggestions, asking questions, and prompting student concern, teachers entice students to join an educational experience. Implied objectives become explicit through negotiation, and content emerges from students' curiosity. Such a design demands teacher awareness and knowledge in a wide variety of content to meet diverse interests. A teacher must also pay attention to each student and how that person encounters or interacts with the lesson. From such observations, teachers monitor lesson appeal or attraction and then devise ways to invite learning, making the experience palatable, meaningful, empowering, and significant. Holists don't divorce emotion from intellect; therefore, those espousing this philosophy honor a greater variety of learner preferences. In this model, power is more or less shared, boundaries are often crossed, and integrated learning experiences involve a quest for meaning. The holist pays attention to the emotional and creative components and to the aesthetics of learning, hoping to create citizens who are "productively idiosyncratic," a term coined by Elliot Eisner (1990). Such a focus assumes that enjoyable and enlightening experiences lead to learning. Fun is not their goal. Instead, they want educational experiences that are expansive and substantive. The holist wants students who become masters of their environment and citizens who are equipped to live in a democratic society. This belief explains their desire to share power; they wish to provide practice in engaging in genuine conversations to negotiate rules, to influence policy, and to effect change.

Laissez-Faire Advocates

The laissez-faire philosophy takes this freedom to act to another level. Hoping to maximize individual freedom without precipitating chaos, laissez-faire principles espouse no official curriculum. Freedom is at the heart of such schools, since the laissez-faire program wants to protect students from being violated by evaluation, coercion, and power paradigms that impede learning or work against individual readiness. This philosophy endorses other fundamental premises: All people possess natural traits, like curiosity, that predispose learning; the most enduring and profound learning occurs when initiated and pursued by the learners; all people are creative if allowed to develop unique talents; and freedom is essential to developing personal responsibility. Children are encouraged to explore their interests and passions, learn through play, and develop expertise in areas that suit them. Capitalizing on the enjoyment of seeing and searching, these philosophers align their thinking with Piaget, who suggested that we don't learn something until we recognize that we need to know it. With this approach, children freely explore ideas they wonder about. Learning stations provide students with options while allowing students to decide what they should do or why they should do it. The

key word here is *access*. Students have access to books, tools, and other resources that enable them to pursue their interests. In this "participatory democracy" (Gray and Chanoff 1984), students initiate all their own activities and create their own environments.

Critical Theorists

Finally, the critical theorists focus on the pursuit of social justice. Rather than deny the presence of power relationships, the critical theorist believes in talking about the elephants in the room. The teacher's job is to guide students to see social injustices, to make the chains visible, and to uncover subliminal messages. Once students are aware of these external, constraining forces, knowledge might help them combat the hegemony. Any curriculum, then, would invoke critical consciousness, advocate for social and educational transformation, and promote the demonstration of respect, understanding, appreciation, and inclusion. With an equitable and rigorous curriculum design, teachers help students enter the world independently, preparing them for leadership. Lessons maximize student and teacher interaction, center on authentic caring, and provide cultural and historical relevance. In this conspiratorial investigation, the teacher poses problems, and students encounter multiple points of view to enlarge their understanding of the world. Because the ultimate aim is social action outside the classroom, the curriculum encourages habits of mind and behavior norms that will enable students to both survive in the world and be agents of transformation. Because critical theorists believe current schools reproduce the status quo—preserving race, gender, class, and social stratifications—they wish to offer an alternative vision through a pedagogy of hope (Freire 1994) that instills the will, desire, knowledge, and skills needed to disrupt official meta-narratives and increase social justice.

Implications

Labeling and describing curriculum ideologies does little more than provide a glimpse at a possible explanation for behavior, since people and philosophies are much too complex to be summed up clearly in a few words, and generalizations generally omit someone. Besides, none of us are so tidy, so pure, or so easily identified that a label defines every part of us. Most of us possess a little of each of these habits of mind, but we generally espouse preferences that subconsciously or explicitly govern our actions.

But we should all know that there are many ways of seeing. Each has an element of truth, but none may be the whole truth. If we limit ourselves to one way of seeing and one truth, we not only limit our own intellectual development, but we limit our students' access to learning experiences. A competent thinker strives for a multifaceted vision since wisdom depends on adapting and examining multiple perspectives, even if one claims a purist stance. As we encounter new truths and research different ways of knowing, we must remember that those truths are always incomplete. Besides admitting that we can never know all there is to know, we must accept that all incoming data is refracted and discolored by the prism of our own personal understanding and experiences. These facets reflect a limited viewpoint. Although an alternative opinion may not be wrong, but simply different, such anomalies often lie so far out of our frame of reference that we reject them as faulty notions. Survey instruments help us validate our own behavior and facilitate our understanding and appreciation of differences in others.

Self-examination may also produce intellectual satisfaction because it makes one aware of personal curriculum style preferences and illuminates values and beliefs about teaching. Participants can reflect on their findings to consider possible explanations for their actions. Noticing how we form decisions and giving name to how we design curriculum may prompt some change in our teaching practices. Our discoveries may lead to a more productive focus and may take some of the mystery out of teaching.

References

Eisner, Elliot. "Who Decides What Schools Teach?" *Phi Delta Kappan* 71, no. 7 (1990): 523–526.

Freire, Paulo. *Pedagogy of Hope.* New York: Continuum Publishing, 1994.

Gray, Peter, and David Chanoff. "When Play Is Learning: A School Designed for Self-Directed Education." *Phi Delta Kappan* 65, no. 9 (1984): 608–611.

Tyler, Ralph W. *Basic Principles of Curriculum and Instruction.* Chicago: University of Chicago Press, 1949.

Critical Thinking

1. Based on what you learned in this article and what you know to be true of your own personality, what would be your top three needs from the people you might collaborate with during your career?

2. Do you think that knowledge of a "style" has any place in the collaboration discussion? If yes, explain why this knowledge would be beneficial in understanding how you might work in a professional learning community that is collaborative. If no, what would be more beneficial in understanding how you might work in a professional learning community that is collaborative?

3. Be a matchmaker. Which styles do think would work well together? Which would have conflicts and might not work collaboratively? This is just speculation, but you should be able to provide a rationale for your choices.

Create Central

www.mhhe.com/createcentral

Internet References

Allthingsplc.info
www.allthingsplc.info/

DONNA L. MILLER is an instructor in education at Aaniiih Nakoda College on the Fort Belknap Indian Reservation, Harlem, Mont.

Article   Prepared by: Rebecca B. Evers, *Winthrop University*

Collaborating with Parents to Implement Behavioral Interventions for Children with Challenging Behaviors

Ju Hee Park, Sheila R. Alber-Morgan, and Courtney Fleming

Learning Outcomes

After reading this article, you will be able to:

- Discuss the importance of parent involvement in the planning phase of behavioral intervention.
- Construct a plan for involving families in a student's Behavior Intervention Plan.

Over the past several decades, behavioral interventions have produced positive and significant outcomes for children with a wide range of challenging behaviors. However, the majority of these interventions have been primarily implemented by practitioners, often leaving parents as bystanders. Because parents probably have the most information regarding the extent and history of their child's difficulties and the most knowledge of their child's home environment, it is essential for parents to be actively involved in planning and implementing behavioral interventions in order to maximize their effectiveness (Ingersoll & Dvortcsak, 2006; Lucyshyn, Horner, Dunlap, Albin, & Ben, 2002).

In addition, when parents implement interventions consistently, positive outcomes are more likely to be maintained over time and generalized to new settings, situations, and behaviors (Kuhn, Lerman, & Vorndran, 2003). Therefore, it is critical for practitioners to encourage parents to take an active role in interventions that will improve their child's challenging behaviors. As a practitioner, understanding the family's strengths and needs is the first step in building rapport with parents. This step is followed by helping parents understand the behavioral approach, working with parents when planning and conducting an intervention, and motivating parents to continue using the intervention consistently. This article provides practitioners with a sequential process and suggestions for teaching parents to help plan and deliver effective interventions to their child.

Understanding Parents and the Family

To collaborate with parents, it is necessary to understand the family. Parents who have a child with disabilities may need to share their struggles with an understanding listener. When practitioners listen to parents and show genuine concern, parents and practitioners can begin to build a trusting relationship. Parents may then be more inclined to be actively involved in their child's learning. In addition, when practitioners listen carefully to parents, they can obtain a great deal of important information that will help with improving the child's challenging behaviors (Fox, Benito, & Dunlap, 2002). In particular, while listening to parents, practitioners can identify possible ways that parents can contribute to their child's success. In other words, parents' strengths and capabilities can be used to effectively address challenging behaviors (Lucyshyn et al., 2002). For example, a parent who can be patient will be more likely to implement interventions that take a substantial amount of time (e.g., using extinction to decrease a challenging behavior). Similarly, identifying a parent's challenges will help practitioners design interventions that will not exacerbate the problem. If a parent has too many demands on his or her time, the practitioner can plan alternative arrangements, such as having a sibling or grandparents help work with the child with disabilities.

Such efforts during the planning of an intervention will likely increase parent support of subsequent interventions. Moes and Frea (2000) found that when family activities, expectations, values, and interaction patterns were considered in the development of support plans for children with behavior disorders, challenging behaviors decreased and compliance increased. That is, focusing on family routines can help create an intervention that is more feasible and meaningful for the child and family (Lucyshyn, Blumberg, & Kayser, 2000).

Moreover, because the child's challenging behavior operates in the context of the family, it is important for practitioners to develop and sequence goals based on family input. In addition to identifying their needs and priorities, parents can provide important insight about how the child's challenging behaviors affect and are affected by the family. The following example illustrates how practitioners can begin to build rapport with the family.

Understanding Parents and Family

"Nathan Davis" is a 6-year-old boy who attends an inclusive first-grade classroom for most of the school day and also receives special education services in a resource room. He often engages in property destruction and aggression toward others. Nathan's mom works part time in the mornings, his dad works 10-hour days, and his grandmother lives with the family and assists with child care. Nathan also has two siblings, a 4-year-old brother and 7-year-old sister.

Ms. Foster, a behavior support specialist, has been contacted by the family for assistance because Nathan's behavior at home has become increasingly more destructive and aggressive. During an initial telephone conversation, Ms. Foster introduced herself to Nathan's mother and provided background information about the agency and her experience working with children with challenging behaviors. They set a meeting time when the whole family would be at home. To encourage productive dialogue, Ms. Foster asked the mother to gather some general information prior to the first meeting (e.g., Nathan's challenges, interests, strengths, and needs; family routines, activities, and concerns).

After a few minutes of rapport-building, Ms. Foster began the first meeting by talking to the Davis family about her background working with families such as theirs. Using open-ended questions, Ms. Foster engaged the family in a dialogue to obtain information about family routines, schedules, and activities (e.g., "It sounds like you have a pretty busy schedule. How do you coordinate your transportation?" "How is that working out for everyone?"). Ms. Foster continues this conversation with Nathan's mom and dad in order to get an idea of daily routines (e.g., "What activities does your family enjoy doing together?" "What is the typical bedtime routine for the children?"). By gathering such information, Ms. Foster can better identify aspects of their family life that are important to the Davis family.

The grandmother then takes the children to a different room and provides a play activity to allow Ms. Foster to discuss in further detail the challenges they are facing with Nathan. "You mentioned earlier that the children often play in the family room while you are making dinner. It sounds like Nathan enjoys this time with his brother and sister, but often becomes upset, like the other night when he had to wait his turn for the race car."

Mrs. Davis responds, "Cars are Nathan's favorite. We ask him to please share with his brother because he really likes them too. Even though we explain this, he still can't seem to wait, and ends up grabbing their toys instead, or pushing his brother away. I know he doesn't mean to hurt his brother." Ms. Foster nods as Mrs. Davis talks about the challenges of balancing the duties of being a working parent. Ms. Foster listens closely and asks Mr. Davis how this affects dinnertime. He adds

that he usually arrives home minutes before dinner starts and sometimes feels apprehensive about what he will find when walking in the door.

"Sometimes I walk in and the kids are running to greet me. Those nights are the best. But many nights as I approach the front door, I hear bickering between the kids, and I don't have the energy to handle the situation. It would be so nice to come home and see my wife smiling, and the kids playing together."

Ms. Foster sympathizes, "After a long day at work, this is probably not how you want to spend your evenings, is it?"

They share a smile and Mrs. Davis confirms, "No. I would really like some help with making this a positive and relaxing time for my family. I want to sit down to dinner and enjoy the company of my family, not tell Nathan that his brother is crying because his car is now broken."

Helping Parents Understand the Behavioral Approach

The next step to facilitating parental involvement in behavioral interventions is providing parents with information. In particular, practitioners should discuss the advantages and importance of behavioral interventions. Behavioral approaches (e.g., functional behavior assessment, positive behavior support) have been empirically validated for decreasing problem behavior in children (Heward, 2009). However, most parents have little knowledge about behavioral interventions. Thus, in an effort to establish a collaborative relationship, practitioners should discuss with parents the reasons the behavioral approach is appropriate for their child. This effort may motivate parents to serve as active partners in the implementation of interventions. Furthermore, it is necessary for practitioners to explain challenging behaviors from the behavioral perspective. This helps parents understand what specific environmental factors might be causing and maintaining their child's challenging behaviors. This is critical because, despite their good intentions, parents may be inadvertently reinforcing their child's challenging behaviors (e.g., paying attention to the child when he or she behaves inappropriately). By learning to examine the child's challenging behaviors from a behavioral perspective, parents gain important insights about how to change those behaviors (e.g., attending to appropriate behavior, ignoring inappropriate behavior).

By learning to examine the child's challenging behaviors from a behavioral perspective, parents gain important insights about how to change those behaviors.

Practitioners must also teach parents key behavioral concepts (e.g., the three-term contingency: antecedent, behavior, consequence) to help them understand the procedures they will be using (e.g., positive reinforcement). Practitioners should use clear and simple explanations for how these principles work.

For example, a child sees candy in the grocery store (antecedent), asks for the candy (behavior), and the parent says "no" (consequence). After the parent says "no" (antecedent), the child begins to whine (behavior) until the parent finally gives him the candy (consequence). If the child's future whining behavior increases, then positive reinforcement has occurred.

In order to effectively change their child's behavior, parents must also understand how behavioral principles operate on their own behavior. The child begins to whine (antecedent), the parent gives the child candy (behavior), and the child stops whining (consequence). As a consequence for providing candy, the parent is able to escape the child's whining. If the parent continues to give in to the child's whining in the future, negative reinforcement has occurred for the parent.

Furthermore, if the parent gives into the child's whining only sometimes, the child's whining behavior will probably be even stronger. Behavior that is reinforced on an intermittent schedule (i.e., not reinforced every time) occurs at higher rates and higher intensity than behaviors reinforced every time they occur. Helping parents understand how these principles work will provide them with valuable insights that will enable them to apply effective behavior change procedures for their children.

Helping Parents Understand the Behavioral Approach

Ms. Foster brought with her some general literature that she has compiled on behavioral interventions that she thinks will be useful and easily understood by the Davis family. These articles were selected based on the current needs of this family, such as increasing positive social interactions and communication with peers and decreasing problem behavior maintained by social attention. She has highlighted information the family would find most helpful (e.g., the purpose, procedures, and outcomes) and summarized each on a separate sheet of paper. She provided the summaries of the articles so that the Davis family can review the purpose and outcomes of each and then decide if they would like to read further about any specific intervention. Ms. Foster brought the full text of each article in the event that the family would like to read more. In discussing these types of interventions, she explains how research has made great advances in providing practitioners tools that have been shown to be effective with children displaying challenges such as Nathan's. Ms. Foster also discusses that the occurrence of certain events often precedes challenging behavior.

Mom interjects, "I notice that when his sister is very involved and busy playing with her dolls, Nathan grabs her dolls and pushes her. Sometimes he throws them at her too."

Dad adds "And oh, how that makes her mad!" Ms. Foster asks about Nathan's sister and how she responds to Nathan's behavior.

Both parents chime in, "She screams at him, 'Leave me alone! Those are mine! You are mean!' Then she tries to get her dolls back, sometimes chasing him around the house."

Mr. Davis comments that he was not raised to tolerate such behavior and that he steps in between the children when this

occurs and verbally scolds Nathan, requiring that he apologize to his sister.

"I don't believe Nathan understands that what he is doing is hurting his sister's feelings. So I do my best to explain this to Nathan and tell him why it is not the right thing to do. But this doesn't seem to make a difference because he still does this every time they play. She tries not to get upset, but this is hard for her too."

The conversation continues and Ms. Foster gathers information about the antecedents and consequences that the parents report. As the conversation unfolds, Ms. Foster decides that it would help to introduce to Mom and Dad the concept of attention maintained behavior. In their efforts to decrease Nathan's destructive behavior, they are actually reinforcing and maintaining it with a powerful reinforcer—attention.

"This can be very hard because we want to explain to our children what is and isn't acceptable. Especially in that moment that the problem occurs. From what you are saying, these reprimands are meant to stop the behavior from happening again and are not supposed to be an enjoyable event. But what can be difficult to keep in mind is that Nathan wants attention. He might want and need that guidance of how to verbally interact with his sister, such as 'Tell her you are sorry, Nathan.' Providing this verbal reprimand and mediation itself is a type of attention. And although this attention is not meant to be enjoyable for Nathan, it is attention of some type. This might help to understand a comment you made earlier, Mr. Davis, when you said you try to explain, but it doesn't seem to make a difference because he still acts out again later. Your reactions to Nathan's behavior are natural because you are providing guidance for your son that you believe will help him. I am sure you are doing what you feel is best, so what I would like to do is help show you how you can provide that guidance for him in a way that should help lead to the changes you want for Nathan."

Collaborating with Parents to Design Behavioral Interventions

Once parents learn basic concepts of the behavioral approach, practitioners need to have parents involved in planning behavioral interventions. This may begin with having parents observe the child's behaviors. Even though parents may spend time interacting with their child at home, they may not be aware of events that trigger their child's challenging behaviors. Through careful observation, parents come to find out when and under what circumstances the child engages in problematic behaviors at home and in community settings. If a child destroys property, the parent should observe their child's behavior to identify what happened before (i.e., antecedent) and after (i.e., consequence) the behavior. Such observation may provide direction for how to change the undesirable behavior.

Practitioners should then ask parents for additional information about the child's history, including preferences, strengths, learning or intervention programs, and communication skills. This allows practitioners to obtain useful information as well as to collaboratively design an effective intervention. Most parents have acquired extensive knowledge about their child over a relatively long period of time (Lucyshyn et al., 2002; O'Shea, O'Shea, Algozzine, & Hammitte, 2001). This information is essential in that it can be utilized to maximize the effectiveness of an intervention and to avoid unnecessary trials and errors in the process of designing a plan. For example, parents can help identify reinforcers (e.g., video games, stickers, praise, etc.) and punishers (e.g., loss of privileges) so that interventions can be designed more effectively.

After obtaining information from parents, practitioners should also discuss the goals and procedures of the intervention, which must be acceptable for parents. An example of an appropriate goal would be teaching the child to use communication skills (e.g., asking politely) when he wants something in order to replace inappropriate behavior (e.g., engaging in aggressive behavior). It is critical to involve parents in developing individual goals (Ingersoll & Dvortcsak, 2006) and in deciding the form and content of behavioral support (Mirenda, MacGregor, & Kelly-Keough, 2002).

Collaborating with Parents to Design Behavioral Interventions

In an effort to work with the parents in planning an intervention for Nathan, Ms. Foster used a training video that demonstrated brief clips of children engaging in problem behavior. The video clip showed a play interaction between two children. Prior to the start of the play time, an adult showed the children the toys they had available to play with, and reminded them of how to play nicely with each other (e.g., taking turns choosing an activity, keeping hands and feet to themselves, and sharing with each other). The children began playing, and as one child waited his turn, the mother in the video comments, "Wow! That was super—waiting your turn!" and pats him on the back. When the child attempts to grab the toy, the mother guides his hands back to his toy with a brief reminder, "You can change toys in a minute." After viewing the video, Ms. Foster and Nathan's parents discussed the observable events occurring before and after the problem behavior. Providing this example and discussion helped Nathan's parents look more objectively at their own child's problem behavior and its antecedents and consequences.

Ms. Foster also asked about Nathan's favorite toys and activities, as well as any involvement in school activities or previous services received. Mom reports that he has not had too many problems at school and that he has an aide who assists him. Ms. Foster uses the information she collects from these questions to compile a brief profile of the services received thus far and Nathan's strengths and needs.

After compiling family input, Ms. Foster conducts a functional behavior analysis (FBA) in the home environment in order to design a draft of the intervention. Ms. Foster suggests potential goals (increasing appropriate requests for items) and asks the parents what behaviors they would like to see Nathan increase. They agree that making appropriate requests should be a goal. They also would like Nathan to accept being told "no" without responding inappropriately.

Training Parents to Be Intervention Agents

The most active form of parent involvement in behavioral interventions may be serving as an intervention agent. Practitioners can successfully teach parents to implement specific procedures of a planned intervention. To train parents effectively, several components should be included in the parent training procedures including (a) teaching parents to identify and record their child's behavior, (b) teaching parents how to respond to problem behaviors, (c) modeling intervention procedures, (d) providing guided practice as well as frequent and specific feedback, and (e) encouraging parents to teach behavior strategies to other family members.

How to Define and Record Children's Behavior

To be effective behavior change agents, parents need to be taught to identify and record their child's behaviors. Parents and practitioners can generate a fist of their child's challenging behaviors and then prioritize them in order of importance. After selecting a problem behavior, the practitioner should ask the parents to describe what usually happens before (antecedent) the behavior occurs and what happens after (consequence). If the child breaks his toys by throwing them or banging them on the floor, the parent might observe this usually happens after the child experiences frustration while playing with the toy (e.g., unable to manipulate or operate the toy properly). The consequence for this behavior is usually attention in the form of a reprimand from the parent. When parents are able to examine how the antecedents and consequences function to maintain the problem behavior, they will have a greater understanding of how to address the problem.

In order to accurately record the frequency of the target behavior, the parents need to have a clear definition of the behavior stated in observable terms. The definition should be based on observations of the child. For example, the parents and practitioners may decide their objective is to decrease destructive behavior. They define destructive behavior as hitting, banging, throwing any object that is not intended for that purpose. For example, throwing a ball or hitting a drum with a drumstick is not destructive behavior, but throwing a telephone or hitting the coffee table with a drumstick is destructive behavior. After the parents have a clear definition of the target behavior, they can observe and record it.

Teaching Parents to Be Intervention Agents: Part 1

After observing and discussing Nathan's specific challenging behavior, the parents agree that his destruction of toys and household items is really making things difficult for the entire family. Ms. Foster shows Nathan's parents a few examples of data sheets they can use to record instances of problem behavior (see Figure 1). Mom and Dad agree on one of the data collection sheets because it seems easiest to use. Then Ms. Foster provides them with a binder containing many blank copies.

Figure 1 Example of a Data Collection Sheet

Date	Time	Destructive Behavior	Total
2/9/09	4:00–6:00	/////////	
	6:00–8:00	/////////	19
2/10/09	4:00–6:00	//////////	
	6:00–8:00	//////	16
2/11/09	4:00–6:00	//////////	
	6:00–8:00	//////////	20
2/12/09	4:00–6:00	//////	
	6:00–8:00	/////////////	19
2/13/09	4:00–6:00	//////////	
	6:00–8:00	///////////	21
2/16/09	4:00–6:00	//////////	
	6:00–8:00	////////////	22
2/17/09	4:00–6:00	/////////	
	6:00–8:00	//////////	19
2/18/09	4:00–6:00	//////	
	6:00–8:00	//////////	16
2/19/09	4:00–6:00	////	
	6:00–8:00	//////////	14
2/20/09	4:00–6:00	/////	
	6:00–8:00	//////////	15
2/23/09	4:00–6:00	////	
	6:00–8:00	//////	10
2/24/09	4:00–6:00	////	
	6:00–8:00	/////	9
2/25/09	4:00–6:00	/////	
	6:00–8:00	/////	10
2/26/09	4:00–6:00	///	
	6:00–8:00	/////	8
2/27/09	4:00–6:00	///	7
	6:00–8:00	////	

Ms. Foster uses modeling and guided practice to teach the Davises how to observe and record behavior. She shows them a video of a child engaging in destructive behavior and models how to tally each incidence explaining as she models. "He's stacking his blocks and right now he's playing appropriately. Look, he accidently knocked over his structure. He just threw one of the blocks at the wall. That's one, so I'm going to put a tally mark right here." After the parents observe for a few minutes, they practice observing and recording the child's videotaped behavior. When the parents are comfortable and accurate with the recording sheets, Ms. Foster asks them to use the recording sheets for Nathan's destructive behaviors. She explains that this information will be used in conjunction with

her own observations and that it will provide her with a more accurate overview of Nathan's behavior when she is unable to observe him directly.

How to Respond to Problem Behavior

Provide parents several alternatives to change the antecedents and consequences that maintain the behavior problem. For instance, providing the child with less frustrating activities or additional assistance may decrease the child's frustration and subsequent destructive behavior. In addition, the parent can change the consequences by withdrawing attention when the child breaks his toys. Furthermore, parents should praise the child whenever he plays with the toys in an appropriate manner. As an intervention agent, parents have to learn how to change the antecedents and consequences of the problem behavior and observe how the child responds.

Modeling. Even though parents may understand basic behavioral concepts and strategies, they still need to know how to apply these strategies to their own unique situations. Observation prepares parents to adjust a given strategy for use at home (Shea & Bauer, 1985). Parents can observe in settings where practitioners conduct behavior interventions. They can also watch videotaped materials in which other parents perform behavioral interventions with their children. Observing models may help parents better understand the procedures for implementing a strategy.

Guided Practice. After observation, the parents should have an adequate amount of time to practice what they learned in order to become more proficient with implementing the intervention. Parents should practice the skills verbally as well as physically under the guidance of practitioners (Shea & Bauer, 1985). Practitioners can also engage parents in role playing. Ongoing guidance should continue as practitioners observe parents working directly with their child.

Frequent and Specific Feedback. To promote successful implementation of behavioral interventions with their children, parents must be provided with frequent opportunities for immediate, specific feedback (Koegel, Koegel, & Schreibman, 1991). The more specific and immediate the feedback is, the more effective it will be. If it is impossible to provide immediate feedback, practitioners can arrange for parents to videotape sessions, and then provide feedback at a later time.

Encourage Parents to Teach Other Family Members

To maximize the effects of the intervention on the child's behavior, it would be helpful for as many significant others as possible to consistently provide the same intervention. Teaching family members (e.g., siblings, grandparents) how to prompt and reinforce appropriate behaviors will help the child generalize newly learned skills across settings and situations. Research has shown that parents who have received training from practitioners can successfully teach significant others how to implement behavioral strategies (Kuhn et al., 2003; Neef, 1995; Symon, 2005).

Teaching Parents to Be Intervention Agents: Part 2

Ms. Foster discusses with Nathan's parents a behavioral procedure that may be effective for changing Nathan's behavior. "Differential reinforcement is when you reinforce Nathan's appropriate behavior while ignoring his inappropriate behavior. So, when you see Nathan playing with his toys or using materials appropriately, you should give him a lot of attention and praise. You might say something like, 'What a great picture you're drawing, I like how you're sitting there working so nicely!' But when you see Nathan throwing or deliberately breaking his crayons, you should ignore that behavior. Pretend you don't even see it. Now when you start to ignore his inappropriate behavior, it might increase at first. But if you're consistent with the intervention, his inappropriate behavior should begin decreasing."

Ms. Foster practices the differential reinforcement procedure with Mom, Dad, and Grandma through modeling and role playing. Ms. Foster role-plays the child's behavior after having modeled differential reinforcement, and Mom, Dad, and Grandma all practice ignoring inappropriate behavior and reinforcing appropriate behavior.

Ms. Foster schedules the first training session with Mom and Dad for an evening. She models the procedure one time with Nathan and then Mom steps in. After this, Dad practices. Nathan is given a break in which he receives the video game that he was working for during the session. Ms. Foster then sits with Mom and Dad to give them feedback (e.g., "I like

how you didn't react when Nathan got upset and smacked the table. You remembered to praise him when he followed your directions, and then gave him a big hug when he finished his work!").

After a few weeks have passed, Ms. Foster follows up with Mom and Dad. They report that they are feeling more comfortable implementing the intervention, and they are seeing decreases in Nathan's destructive behavior. "But he can still be pretty destructive sometimes," says Dad. During this meeting, Ms. Foster provides the Davises with graphic display of the data they had been recording (see Figure 2).

Ms. Foster explains, "If you look at this graph you can get a more accurate picture of the frequency of Nathan's behavior. The first four data points are Nathan's destructive behavior before we began the intervention. So, he engaged in destructive behavior about 20 times each night before the intervention. The dotted line shows when you started the intervention. Look what happened during the first few sessions of intervention."

"His behavior got a little worse at first," Mom said.

"But after that," Dad said, "Nathan's destructive behavior steadily went down. Last night it was only 7 times. I guess that's a lot of progress in just a couple of weeks." Ms. Foster and the Davises continue their discussion about how well the intervention is working, the importance of continuing the intervention consistently, and whether or not they think the intervention should be modified.

It should be noted that collaborating with parents may not always result in expected, desirable outcomes. The amount of time and effort it takes to collaboratively plan and implement a behavioral intervention will vary across families depending on the severity of the problem behavior and the consistency with which parents implement interventions. Parents will differ in

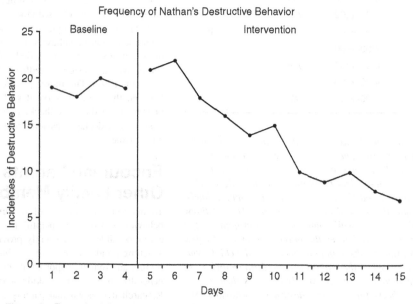

Figure 2 Example of Graphic Display of Data

their knowledge about behavioral strategies, their literacy levels, and their enthusiasm for participating in behavior change interventions. Practitioners should consider the diversity of the parents they work with when providing training. For example, if parents have difficulties with reading or if English is not their first language, it may be effective to provide in vivo modeling and video clips rather than only written guidelines when teaching them how to implement a certain behavior strategy. Practitioners working with parents should be aware of any accommodations the parents may need to effectively implement a behavior change program. If an intervention is not working, the practitioner should maintain open communication with the parents to determine the reasons and to modify the plan to ensure success.

Helping Parents Maintain and Extend Their Involvement in Behavioral Interventions

When parents are regarded as valuable members of the collaborative team, they are more likely to work effectively with practitioners. Practitioners should encourage parents to be collaborative decision makers. In addition, they should share information and ownership with parents, demonstrate mutual respect, and communicate clearly in order to increase effectiveness of parent-delivered interventions (Dunlap, Newton, Fox, Benito, & Vaughn, 2001). Practitioners should consider parents as equal partners throughout the development and implementation of behavioral interventions.

Practitioners should consider parents as equal partners throughout the development and implementation of behavioral interventions.

To maintain parents' involvement over time, practitioners should always be sensitive to the family's needs and remain flexible (Brookman-Frazee, 2004). For example, parents may feel more comfortable when training is provided at their home rather than in a public training center (Ingersoll & Dvortcsak, 2006). Parents may also need to arrange meetings at night or on weekends because of their work schedules. Behavioral interventions that are incorporated effectively into the existing family ecology will increase successful parent involvement and result in generalized outcomes (Lucyshyn et al., 2002).

To help parents continue to be involved in the behavior intervention for their child, it may also be helpful to offer parents the opportunity to join a supportive group. Support groups may motivate parents and help them overcome obstacles. One obstacle might be feelings of isolation (Stahmer & Gist, 2001). In support groups, parents may share similar difficulties related to their children's behavioral problems, exchange useful information, and provide emotional support to one another.

Figure 3 Web Sites for Parents of Children with Challenging Behaviors

- **Children and Adults with AD/HD (CHADD)**
  www.chadd.org/AM/Template.cim?Section=Especially_For_Parents

  CHADD is a nonprofit, membership organization that supports individuals with AD/HD, their families, and professionals working with them. CHADD provides various materials such as newsletters, magazines, and other publications dealing with AD/HD-related issues.

- **National Association of School Psychologists**
  www.nasponline.org/families/index.aspx

  Parents can obtain helpful information about effective practices to promote children's positive behaviors.

- **National Resource Center on AD/HD**
  www.help4adhd.org/en/treatment/behavioral

  Introduces information necessary for improving the quality of life of children and adolescents with AD/HD, such as behavior modification programs, parenting, and education.

- **OSEP Technical Assistance Center on Positive Behavioral Interventions and Supports (PBIS)**
  www.pbis.org/family/default.aspx

  Information and materials for parental involvement with individualized positive behavior support plans for children, including tools, videos, and presentations.

- **Technical Assistance Center on Social Emotional Intervention for Young Children (TACSEI)**
  www.challengingbehavior.org/do/resources.htm

  Provides professionals and parents with a variety of web resources (e.g., training materials, workshop information, consultant location, research outcomes) to address social and emotional difficulties and challenging behaviors of children with disabilities.

In addition, providing information and resources (e.g., see Figure 3) related to addressing challenging behaviors or family needs can help parents continue to expand their application of effective behavioral interventions. Such information about diagnostic issues, evaluation of alternative treatments, community resources, and parents' rights may serve to enhance parents' knowledge and enable them to be more competent as intervention providers (Stahmer & Gist, 2001).

Helping Parents Maintain and Extend Their Involvement in Behavioral Intervention

During follow-up visits, Ms. Foster finds that things are generally going well. She shares that recently a parent support group was organized that meets on Saturday mornings. The Davises say this may be of interest to them so she provides a brochure about the program. "A friend of mine attends this group every Saturday and they have become quite a tight knit group. This has been helpful for her, because she felt that she was sometimes burdening friends and family with conversations about her child. Now, she and the other parents meet in a relaxed and nonjudgmental environment to discuss whatever is on their minds."

Conclusion

Parents have the potential to be effective agents of behavior change when they have opportunities to work with practitioners in planning and providing interventions. Practitioners should regard the parent-practitioner partnership as critical and indispensable in working with children. To create an effective partnership, practitioners should be aware of the strengths and needs of each family and assist parents to take an active role in behavioral interventions by helping them understand the behavioral approach, including them in the process of planning and implementing an intervention, and encouraging them to continuously use the intervention.

As parents collaborate with practitioners, they recognize the effectiveness of the behavioral approach, the nature and the extent of their child's challenging behaviors, and how to effectively change their child's behavior. In addition, parents can serve as trainers who teach significant others to implement effective interventions. Parents' participation throughout the intervention process is likely to result in improved outcomes for their children and continuing participation.

References

Brookman-Frazee, L. (2004). Using parent/clinician partnerships in parent education programs for children with autism. *Journal of Positive Behavior Interventions, 6*, 195–213.

Dunlap, G., Newton, J. S., Fox, L., Benito, N., & Vaughn, B. (2001). Family involvement in functional assessment and positive behavior support. *Focus on Autism and Other Developmental Disabilities, 16*, 215–221.

Fox, L., Benito, N., & Dunlap, G. (2002). Early intervention with families of young children with autism and behavior problems. In J. M. Lucyshyn, G. Dunlap, & R. W. Albin (Eds.), *Family and positive behavior support: Addressing problem behavior in family contexts* (pp. 251–266). Baltimore, MD: Paul H. Brookes.

Heward, W. L. (2009). *Exceptional children* (9th ed.). Upper Saddle River, NJ: Pearson.

Ingersoll, B., & Dvortcsak, A. (2006). Including parent training in the early childhood special education curriculum for children with autism spectrum disorders. *Journal of Positive Behavior Interventions, 8*, 79–87.

Koegel, R. L., Koegel, L. K., & Schreibman, L. (1991). Assessing and training parents in teaching pivotal behaviors. In R. J. Prinz (Ed.), *Advances in behavioral assessment of children and families: A research annual,* (Vol. 5, pp. 65–82). Bristol, PA: Jessica Kingsley.

Kuhn. S. A. C, Lerman, D. C.. & Vorndran, C. M. (2003). Pyramidal training for families of children with problem behavior. *Journal of Applied Behavior Analysis, 36*, 77–88.

Lucyshyn, J. M., Blumberg, E. R., & Kayser, A. T. (2000). Improving the quality of support to families of children with severe behavior problems in the first decade of the new millennium. *Journal of Positive Behavior Interventions, 2*, 113–115.

Lucyshyn, J. M., Horner, R. H., Dunlap, G., Albin, R. W., & Ben, K. R. (2002). Positive behavior support with families. In J. M. Lucyshyn, G. Dunlap, & R. W. Albin (Eds.), *Family and positive behavior support: Addressing problem behavior in family contexts* (pp. 3–43). Baltimore, MD: Paul H. Brookes.

Mirenda, P., MacGregor, T., & Kelly-Keough, S. (2002). Teaching communication skills for behavioral support in the context of family life. In J. M. Lucyshyn, G. Dunlap, & R. W. Albin (Eds.), *Family and positive behavior support: Addressing problem behavior in family contexts* (pp. 185–207). Baltimore, MD: Paul H. Brookes.

Moes, D. R., & Frea, W. D. (2000). Using family context to inform intervention planning for the treatment of a child with autism. *Journal of Positive Behavior Interventions, 2*(1), 40–46.

Neef, N. (1995). Pyramidal parent training by peers. *Journal of Applied Behavior Analysis, 28*, 333–337.

O'Shea, D. J., O'Shea, L. J., Algozzine, R., & Hammitte, D. (2001). *Families and teachers of individuals with disabilities.* Austin, TX: Pro-Ed.

Shea, T. M., & Bauer, A. M. (1985). *Parents and teachers of exceptional students: A handbook for involvement.* Newton, MA: Allyn & Bacon.

Stahmer A. C., & Gist, K. (2001). The effects of an accelerated parent education program on technique mastery and child outcome. *Journal of Positive Behavior Interventions. 3*, 75–82.

Symon, J. B. (2005). Expanding interventions for children with autism: Parents as trainers. *Journal of Positive Behavior Interventions, 7*, 159–173.

Critical Thinking

1. What are behavioral interventions?
2. Why is collaboration with parents essential to successful SPED?
3. Explain the concept of antecedent-behavior-consequence (ABC).
4. Who can serve as models for behavioral interventions?

Create Central

www.mhhe.com/createcentral

Internet References

The National Coalition for Parent Involvement in Education (NCPIE)

www.ncpie.org

Ju Hee Park, Assistant Professor, Special Education Department, Wheelock College, Boston, MA. **Sheila R. Alber-Morgan** (Ohio CEC), Associate Professor, and **Courtney Fleming** (Ohio CEC), Doctoral Student: Special Education Program, The Ohio State University, Columbus.

Correspondence concerning this article should be addressed to Sheila R. Alber-Morgan, A356 PAES Building, 305 W. 17 Ave. Columbus, OH 43210 (e-mail: morgan.651@osu.edu).

Article   Prepared by: Rebecca B. Evers, *Winthrop University*

Why Age Matters

A unique program connects grandparents with local at-risk students.

JESSICA MULHOLLAND

Learning Outcomes

After reading this article, you will be able to:

- Plan to use "grandparents" to support learning in your classroom.

Aiken, S.C., a town of 29,000 near the Georgia border, is ahead of the curve in adapting to older populations. Nearly 22% of its population is older than 65—demographically, Aiken represents what most cities and towns will look like in 2050.

What further distinguishes Aiken from other communities is its bevy of senior programs: The town has a Council on Aging that advises the mayor and City Council on senior issues, a service called Smart 911 to display pertinent information to 911 dispatchers when an elderly person calls, and the city is implementing Project Lifesaver, a service that provides people who have dementia with bracelets that continuously transmit their location via GPS technology.

Aiken also encourages seniors to stay busy and engaged. One of the ways it does this is through Foster Grandparents, a federally funded program for senior citizens 55 and older. The participants visit schools, Head Start centers, nonprofit day-cares and after-school programs to help at-risk children, says Director Toni Brunson.

"Teachers will assign [senior citizens to] children who need extra help or just a little bit of extra attention one-on-one, and they'll help that child with spelling, reading, math, things like that," she says. "If they're falling behind in class, that one-on-one attention helps get them back on track." At Head Start centers, the volunteers are assigned to children who "sometimes just need a grandma," Brunson says. "So they get one-on-one bonding time with a grandparent figure."

Foster Grandparents, which also gets funds from the National Senior Service Corporation and is sponsored in the region by the Aiken-Barnwell Community Action Commission, has been operating in Aiken since the mid-1980s.

The program has grown from about 20 volunteers in the region to 112. Senior citizens living on a limited income are eligible to receive a modest stipend. They earn 16 cents per mile driven between their homes and volunteer sites, and $2.65 per hour. They don't do it for the money, Brunson says, but many find it to be a valuable source of extra income. The money earned by the elderly volunteers is defined as a stipend, so that it cannot be taxed or reported as income should they need to apply for food stamps or government-assisted housing. "Believe it or not, they actually come to depend on the stipend check they get," which they receive every two weeks.

The key to Foster Grandparents is that it is as much about helping at-risk kids as senior citizens. "There are a lot of children in our community and everywhere who don't really have a grandparent figure in their life, and they really come to know these volunteers—they call them grandma and grandpa," Brunson says. "It's just a good thing—it makes the grandma feel good, it makes the child feel good. It's a win-win situation for the children and the senior citizens."

In addition to the stipend, all seniors receive one meal on the day they volunteer, supplemental accident and liability insurance while on duty, and a free yearly physical with a physician. "That helps a senior who may not normally go to the doctor," Brunson says. "They'll go, we pay for it and it helps them stay healthy."

The volunteers donate a minimum of 15 hours of their time a week, up to 40 hours per week. If the budget would allow it, Brunson says, they'd all likely work the maximum. "They enjoy working with the children. They feel like if they're not at the school, that they're needed there," she says. "And the children do really miss them; so do the teachers they assist."

Globally, the world's population is aging in dramatic ways. For the first time in history, people age 65 and older will outnumber children under the age of 5. Studies have shown that societal aging affects economic growth and many other issues, including the sustainability of families, the ability of states and communities to provide resources for older citizens, and even international relations.

Because programs like Foster Grandparents benefit senior citizens and at-risk kids alike, they've been embraced by other communities in South Carolina and in other states, as well. For the seniors that participate, they feel useful, says Brunson, giving them something to do to get out of the house. "It gives them a reason to get up in the morning, and they feel like they're making a difference in a child's life."

Critical Thinking

1. What makes the "grandparent" effect work?
2. How might senior citizens be used in middle and high school settings where knowledge of specific content is very important?
3. If you are a prospective administrator, what qualifications would you want the "grandparent" to have?
4. Do you think that there would be any down side to having persons who are not related to students working in schools? Or is it possible that non-relatives would be best?

Create Central

www.mhhe.com/createcentral

Internet References

Corporation for National and Community Service
www.nationalservice.gov/programs/senior-corps/foster-grandparents

---

JESSICA MULHOLLAND is the associate editor of *Governing,* and is also the associate editor of both *Government Technology* and *Public CIO* magazines.

Jessica Mulholland From *Governing,* January 2012, pp. 50–51. Copyright © 2012 by e.Republic Inc. Reprinted by permission via Wright's Media.

Unit 8

UNIT

Prepared by: Rebecca B. Evers, *Winthrop University.*

Sexual Minority Students

Over the last several years there have been widespread debates and legal actions attached to the consideration of legalizing gay marriage. At this time, 30 states have passed legislation defining marriage as only between a man and a woman, despite the numerous high-profile politicians and celebrities who have advocated for such marriages. The opponents and proponents of gay rights have engaged in very heated debates and some name-calling in public places. Persons who are in the sexual minority can often be exposed to hostility and apprehension due to their nonconformity in sexual orientation and gender identity. Our society and media may be demonstrating an increase in acceptance through positive portrayals of sexual minority persons in public venues, such as in television shows like *Modern Family* and *GLEE,* or the rise in popularity of celebrities like Ellen DeGeneres and Rachel Maddow, but we should not assume this is acceptable to everyone everywhere. Especially, we should not assume that the school experiences of students who are LGBT are as inclusive as the portrayals in the media or that they are accepted by all of their teachers and peers (Kim, Sheridan, & Holcomb, 2009).

Kim, Sheridan and Holcomb (2009) note that school personnel who are LGBT face societal and legal pressures to stay "in the closet" at school and especially in front of students. This can lead to feelings of isolation and a diminished sense of safety or belonging, which in turn can hamper their efforts to teach and mentor students. School personnel, both LGBT and straight, may sometimes feel uncomfortable mentoring students because of concerns for their own personal safety and therefore, they may ignore homophobic bullying when they witness it.

Schools reflect much of the societal debate. Sexual minority adolescents challenge educators to think about the tension between competing public opinions and serving all students. Due to conflicts that may arise within the schools, many educators may not feel comfortable for political and personal reasons, or prepared for the conversation and changes in policy and practices that are necessary if sexual minority adolescents are to be successful in our schools (Kim, Sheridan, & Holcomb, 2009).

There is some mixed news reported by the Gay, Lesbian and Straight Education Network (GLSEN, 2011). There was a steady decline in the frequency of hearing homophobic remarks from 1999 to 2011. Between 2009 and 2011, student reports of hearing these types of remarks had decreased significantly. LGBT experiences of harassment and assault showed small but significant decreases in frequencies of verbal harassment, physical harassment, and physical assault from 2009 to 2011. The best news of this report is that there has been an increase over time in the presence of LGBT-related resources and supports in schools, specifically: Gay-Straight Alliances or other student clubs that address LGBT issues in education as well as increases in school staff who support LGBT students and LGBT-related materials in school libraries. However, if we look at the key findings noted on the website referenced below, there are still too many incidents of harassment and verbal abuse occurring in our schools. The articles in this unit will offer additional information about students who identify themselves as LGBT, data regarding the barriers they face in public schools, and strategies that can help you take action to remove the barriers.

In their study of sexual orientation of minority students from diverse ethnicities, Austin, et al. found that obesity in female and male bisexual youths posed serious, long term problems for their health. These findings lead to the conclusion that appropriate interventions should be offered to eliminate stressors, such as referrals for treatment and programs to promote healthful eating and life-style habits.

Young suggests that the spike in bullying-related suicides of persons who were LGBT caused a raised awareness among educators for the critical issues of this minority group. She personally interviewed 30 youth over a four-month period to determine what might be done. In this article she shares the words of those students and summarizes their advice to adults.

In this unit of Annual Edition: Education, we take an in-depth look at bullying and sexual harassment in general. However, in the unit we included an article about bullying and harassment of students who are defined as the sexual minority. Bishop and Casida discuss the specifics of bullying and harassment of this minority group, the prevalence and characteristics of homophobia, legal ramifications, and ways to improve the school climate.

Even if schools teach tolerance, offer safe places within the school, and have vigilant faculty and staff, bullying and harassment still may exist in some shape or form. In efforts to protect students, some school districts have open, "gay-friendly" schools. These are schools where students who are LGBT may self-segregate. Pardini shares the story of one such school in Milwaukee, where students are able to be who they are in a laid back, accepting environment. As one student pointed out, "We don't do drama here." However, as Pardini explains, budget cuts are forcing these schools to cut back some programs and grades.

References

Kim, R., Sheridan, D., & Holcomb, S. (2009). *A Report on the Status of Gay, Lesbian, Bisexual and Transgender People in Education: Stepping Out of the Closet, into the Light.* Washington, D.C.: National Education Association. Retrieved from www.nea.org/home/Report-on-Status-of-GLBT.html

Gay, Lesbian and Straight Education Network (*2011*). *The 2011 National School Climate Survey: Key Findings on the Experiences of Lesbian, Gay, Bisexual and Transgender Youth in Our Nation's Schools.* Author. Retrieved from www.glsen.org/cgi-bin/iowa/all/news/record/2897.html

Article

Prepared by: Rebecca B. Evers, *Winthrop University*

Eating Disorder Symptoms and Obesity at the Intersections of Gender, Ethnicity, and Sexual Orientation In US High School Students

S. Bryn Austin, et al.

Learning Outcomes

After reading this article, you will be able to:

- Explain who sexual minority students are and the major issues they face in school.

- Discuss the key findings regarding health issues of LGBT students.

T he prevalence of childhood obesity has markedly increased in the past few decades, more than tripling in the last 30 years.[1] Obesity in adolescence is especially concerning because of the high risk of immediate- and long-term problems associated with the condition. Obese adolescents are at an elevated risk for high cholesterol, hypertension, prediabetes, bone and joint problems, and sleep apnea.[2–5] They are 20 times more likely to become obese adults,[6] increasing the odds of long-term health consequences secondary to obesity, such as type 2 diabetes, heart disease, stroke, cancer, and osteoarthritis.[7] Eating disorders and disordered weight-control behaviors, such as purging and diet pill use, represent the third most common chronic childhood illnesses, after obesity and asthma,[8] and are associated with a range of serious comorbidities, including disorders of the cardiovascular, gastrointestinal, and endocrine systems.[9] In addition, children and adolescents who are obese have been found to be at increased risk of eating disorder symptoms.[10–12]

These health problems affect individuals during crucial physiological and psychological developmental periods and disproportionately affect marginalized subgroups of youths. Numerous studies have highlighted disparities based on ethnicity,[13–17] sexual orientation,[18–22] and gender.[23–26] However, little is known about how these disparities intersect and the ways in which individuals who are members of multiple minority subgroups may be affected.

Minority stress theory posits that members of marginalized social populations are subject to health consequences as a result of experiences of stigma and discrimination associated with possessing a minority identity.[27] These stressors may have direct health consequences through chronic perturbations of biological systems or may cause psychological distress, influencing health behaviors (substance use, weight-control behaviors, sexual risk behaviors, etc.) and health care utilization. Multiple minority

Objectives. We examined purging for weight control, diet pill use, and obesity across sexual orientation identity and ethnicity groups.

Methods. Anonymous survey data were analyzed from 24 591 high school students of diverse ethnicities in the federal Youth Risk Behavioral Surveillance System Survey in 2005 and 2007. Self-reported data were gathered on gender, ethnicity, sexual orientation identity, height, weight, and purging and diet pill use in the past 30 days. We used multivariable logistic regression to estimate odds of purging, diet pill use, and obesity associated with sexual orientation identity in gender-stratified models and examined for the presence of interactions between ethnicity and sexual orientation.

Results. Lesbian, gay, and bisexual (LGB) identity was associated with substantially elevated odds of purging and diet pill use in both girls and boys (odds ratios [OR] range = 1.9 – 6.8). Bisexual girls and boys were also at elevated odds of obesity compared to same-gender heterosexuals (OR = 2.3 and 2.1, respectively).

Conclusions. Interventions to reduce eating disorders and obesity that are appropriate for LGB youths of diverse ethnicities are urgently needed. (*Am J Public Health.* 2013;103:e16–e22.)

stress theory focuses on the intersection of ethnicity, gender, and sexual orientation and proposes that lesbian, gay, and bisexual (LGB) people of color are exposed to multiple stressors that may create an additive health disadvantage.[28,29] Several population-based studies have supported the additive hypothesis, demonstrating increased prevalence of health risks among LGB people of color compared with their White LGB counterparts, including disparities in mental health disorders,[30,31] chronic health conditions,[32] adolescent suicide,[33] and obesity.[34]

The additive hypothesis of minority stress theory, however, has been scrutinized because it has not been consistently borne out. For example, other studies[35,36] found that ethnicity did not modify sexual orientation-related health disparities, and 1 study[29] found that being a member of a ethnic minority group had some protective effect on mental health among LGB individuals, specifically for adolescent girls.

We found a limited number of studies that addressed health disparities affecting LGB people of color and an even smaller number of studies that addressed adolescents and young adults.[29,33,35–37] In addition, no studies, to our knowledge, specifically examined the issue of disordered weight-control behaviors. We were aware of only 1 study that examined the prevalence of obesity among sexual minorities as associated with ethnicity; this study found that Asian Pacific Islanders had lower body mass index (BMI) and African Americans had higher BMI in a sample of lesbian and bisexual women compared with White women.[34] The aim of the present study examined how gender and ethnicity were associated with sexual orientation identity disparities in obesity and disordered weight-control behaviors in youths using data from the Youth Risk Behavior Surveillance System (YRBSS), a biennial survey conducted by the Centers for Disease Control and Prevention (CDC) in US high schools. This study was unique in its focus on disordered weight-control behaviors and obesity, 2 important adolescent health issues in LGB ethnic minority youths, who are an understudied population.

Methods

For the present study, we pooled anonymous data gathered from US high school students in 2005 and 2007 as part of the YRBSS. Four cities (Boston, Massachusetts; Chicago, Illinois; New York City, New York; and San Francisco, California) and 5 states (Delaware, Maine, Massachusetts, Vermont, and Rhode Island) administered an item on sexual orientation identity; therefore, for the present study, we analyzed data from these jurisdictions. More details about the pooling methods used and the characteristics of jurisdictions included in analyses can be found elsewhere.[38]

Measures

Students in participating high schools completed self-report surveys assessing sexual orientation identity, demographic characteristics, and health-related behaviors and exposures. An item assessing sexual orientation identity asked students to indicate which identity best described them from the options heterosexual, bisexual, lesbian or gay, or unsure.

Outcomes included purging for weight control, use of diet pills, and obesity. The YRBSS survey includes 1 item asking whether respondents engaged in self-induced vomiting or used laxatives (i.e., purging) in the past 30 days and another item asking whether they used diet pills without a doctor's orders to lose or maintain weight.[39] Each item was treated as binary. Students were asked to report their height and weight, which was then used to calculate age-and sex-specific BMI (defined as weight in kilograms divided by the square of height in meters) percentiles based on CDC guidelines; biologically implausible BMI values were also identified and set to missing per CDC guidelines.[40] Youths were then categorized as obese if their BMI was at or above the 95th percentile for their age and gender. It was shown that self-reported BMI had moderate validity in adolescents.[41]

Statistical Analysis

All descriptive analyses were carried out with SPSS (version 20; SPSS Inc, Chicago, IL), and multilevel software HLM (version 7; Scientific Software International, Lincolnwood, IL) was used to fit final multivariable models. Gender-stratified multivariable logistic regression models were used to estimate the odds of each of the 3 outcome variables (purging, diet pill use, and obesity) associated with sexual orientation identity and ethnicity, controlling for age, region, and data collection wave. Heterosexual youths served as the referent group for sexual orientation group comparisons, and White youths for ethnicity group comparisons. In additional multivariable models, we examined whether ethnicity modified associations between sexual orientation identity and the 3 outcomes by entering interaction terms into the models.

The YRBSS complex sampling design was accounted for by adjusting the relative weights and altering the effective sample size for each jurisdiction (i.e., city or state). Because data were clustered, hierarchical linear modeling was done with jurisdiction assigned at level 2 in each model. See Mustanski et al.[38] for additional information about methods used to calculate design effects and to account for intracluster correlation.

Surveys received from 28 887 youths were combined across the 9 jurisdictions and 2 waves of collection. Students were excluded if they did not provide important information for analyses (i.e., were missing covariates or outcome variables), leading to a final analytic sample of 24 591 youths (85.1% of original sample).

Results

Table 1 presents selected sociodemographic characteristics of the ethnically diverse youths included in analyses. Among girls, those identifying as a sexual minority made up more than 8% of the analytic sample, and among boys, sexual minorities made up almost 5% of the analytic sample. Mean age was 15.9 years (SD = 1.3; range = 13–18 years).

The percentage of youths engaging in purging and diet pill use are presented in Table 2 for each gender, ethnicity, and sexual orientation identity group. In general, a higher percentage of sexual minorities within each ethnicity group reported

Table 1 Sample Characteristics of US High School Students: Youth Risk Behavioral Surveillance System Survey, 2005 and 2007

Characteristics	No. (%)
Girls (n = 12 132)	
Ethnicity	
Asian-American	1357 (11.2)
African-American	3218 (26.5)
Latina	2222 (18.3)
Other ethnicity[b]	1114 (9.2)
White (Ref)	4221 (34.8)
Sexual orientation identity	
Lesbian	137 (1.1)
Bisexual	628 (5.2)
Unsure	303 (2.5)
Heterosexual (Ref)	11 064 (91.2)
Boys (n = 12 459)	
Ethnicity	
Asian-American	1714 (13.8)
African-American	2906 (23.3)
Latino	2220 (17.8)
Other ethnicity[a]	1046 (8.4)
White (Ref)	4573 (36.7)
Sexual orientation identity	
Gay	149 (1.2)
Bisexual	221 (1.8)
Unsure	268 (2.2)
Heterosexual (Ref)	11 821 (94.9)

Note. The maximum sample size was n = 24 591.

[a]Other ethnicity group includes youths who identified as Pacific Islander, American Indian, Alaskan Native, or multiple ethnicity groups.

purging and use of diet pills than did heterosexuals among both girls and boys. Within some groups, as much as a one quarter to more than one third of sexual minorities reported purging or diet pill use to control weight in the past 30 days, compared with a mean of approximately 8% of heterosexual girls and 5% of heterosexual boys across ethnicity groups. Table 2 also presents the percentages of obesity for each gender, ethnicity, and sexual orientation identity group. Among girls who were not Asian American, the percentage of obesity in heterosexuals ranged from 6% to 12% across ethnicity groups, whereas this percentage in sexual minorities ranged widely from 4% to 27%. Among boys, the percentage of obesity in bisexuals was especially elevated, ranging from 20% to 50% in Latinos, Whites, and other ethnicity groups compared with a mean of approximately 15% among heterosexuals in these groups.

Asian Americans had a lower percentage of obesity compared with other ethnicity groups among both girls and boys.

Multivariable models were fit to examine main effects for sexual orientation identity and ethnicity on eating disorder symptoms and obesity and to examine for possible interaction effects. Ethnicity did not modify sexual orientation identity associations with outcomes; therefore, results of main effects models are presented in the following and in Table 3. Sizable sexual orientation disparities in eating disorder symptoms in both girls and boys were observed. Sexual minority girls had 2 to 4 times the odds of purging and diet pill use compared with heterosexual peers, and sexual minority boys had 3 to approximately 7 times the odds of these behaviors compared with heterosexual peers. Compared with White same-gender peers, Asian American and African American girls had lower odds of purging and diet pill use, whereas African American boys had higher odds of purging, and other ethnicity boys had higher odds of both purging and diet pill use.

Sexual orientation identity disparities were also observed for obesity. Bisexual girls and boys had higher odds of obesity compared with same-gender heterosexual peers. Although Asian Americans had lower odds of obesity compared with White youths, all other youths of color, with the exception of African American boys, had higher odds of obesity than their same-gender White peers.

Discussion

Obesity and eating disorders in adolescence put young people at risk for a myriad of immediate- and long-term health problems associated with significant morbidity, disability, medical costs, and increased risk of premature death.[9,42-45] Identifying groups at elevated risk is essential to informing an effective and appropriately targeted public health response to the health burden posed by these conditions.

Findings from our study of US high school students of diverse ethnicities indicated that both female and male sexual minorities of all ethnic groups were at substantially elevated risk of disordered weight-control behaviors, in some cases as much as a 7-fold increased risk. Across ethnicity groups, as many as 1 in 3 lesbian and bisexual girls engaged in these behaviors in the past month compared with fewer than 1 in 10 heterosexual girls. Similarly, across ethnicity groups, 1 in 5 gay and bisexual boys reported disordered weight-control behaviors in the past month compared with 1 in 20 heterosexual boys. Rates of obesity were elevated in female and male bisexuals compared with their same-gender heterosexual peers.

Our findings of elevated rates of disordered weight-control behaviors among sexual minority adolescents were consistent with those from previous research.[19,21,22] Previous statewide surveys in Massachusetts and Minnesota found gay and bisexual adolescent boys had high rates of these behaviors[46,47] compared with heterosexual boys, as was also found in the Growing Up Today Study, a nationwide cohort of predominantly White youths.[19] The present study added to the literature by documenting patterns of elevated risk in sexual minority boys of diverse ethnicities living across the United States. In addition,

Table 2 Prevalence of Purging (Vomiting or Laxatives), Diet Pill Use, and Obesity in US High School Students: Youth Risk Behavioral Surveillance System Survey, 2005 and 2007

Characteristics	Total, No. (%)	Purge,[a] %	Diet Pills,[a] %	Obese,[b] %
Girls (n = 12 132)				
Asian-American				
Lesbian	12 (0.9)	...[c]	...[c]	0
Bisexual	33 (2.4)	13.9	11.8	0
Unsure	52 (3.8)	5.7	8.9	0
Heterosexual	1260 (92.9)	3.0	1.9	2.3
African-American				
Lesbian	52 (1.6)	15.2	1.4	19.2
Bisexual	156 (4.8)	6.3	6.7	26.9
Unsure	62 (1.9)	24.2	8.5	12.9
Heterosexual	2948 (91.6)	3.5	2.8	12.2
Latina				
Lesbian	22 (1.0)	26.7	44.7	4.5
Bisexual	124 (5.6)	15.1	9.1	16.9
Unsure	46 (2.2)	8.2	10.1	15.2
Heterosexual	2030 (91.5)	6.4	4.0	9.1
Other ethnicity[d]				
Lesbian	28 (2.5)	18.8	0	16.7
Bisexual	88 (7.9)	13.4	11.5	11.4
Unsure	50 (4.5)	22.2	3.3	14.0
Heterosexual	948 (85.1)	6.1	4.9	11.2
White				
Lesbian	23 (0.5)	15.2	18.4	13.0
Bisexual	227 (5.4)	18.6	14.2	14.5
Unsure	93 (2.2)	8.3	6.9	9.7
Heterosexual	3878 (91.9)	6.1	5.1	5.6
Boys (n = 12 459)				
Asian-American				
Gay	14 (0.8)	...[c]	...[c]	7.1
Bisexual	29 (1.7)	18.9	21.1	10.3
Unsure	9 (5.2)	9.1	1.4	5.6
Heterosexual	1582 (92.3)	2.1	2.9	9.3
African-American				
Gay	39 (1.3)	14.6	17.7	5.1
Bisexual	51 (1.8)	35.3	41.9	15.7
Unsure	52 (1.8)	7.2	6.5	13.5
Heterosexual	2764 (95.1)	4.8	3.5	14.8
Latino				
Gay	32 (1.4)	12.4	6.5	21.9
Bisexual	36 (1.6)	7.8	5.8	50.0
Unsure	24 (1.1)	17.8	29.6	25.0
Heterosexual	2128 (95.9)	2.8	4.1	18.1

(continued)

Characteristics	Total, No. (%)	Purge,[a] %	Diet Pills,[a] %	Obese,[b] %
	Girls (n = 12 132)			
Other ethnicity[d]				
Gay	21 (2.0)	22.2	23.1	23.8
Bisexual	29 (2.8)	30.4	20.0	48.3
Unsure	30 (2.9)	10.3	30.4	16.7
Heterosexual	966 (92.4)	3.7	4.2	16.6
White				
Gay	43 (0.9)	16.2	12.8	11.6
Bisexual	76 (1.7)	13.6	11.4	19.7
Unsure	73 (1.6)	11.1	9.0	22.9
Heterosexual	4381 (95.8)	2.1	2.9	3.7

Note. The maximum sample size was n = 24 591.

[a]Purging defined as any vomiting or use of laxatives in the past month to control weight; diet pill use defined as use of diet pills to control weight without a doctor's prescription in the past month.

[b]Obesity defined as body mass index three quarters of 95th percentile for age and sex as per percentile definitions based on guidelines from the US Centers for Disease Control and Prevention.

[c]Fewer than 10 participants responded in this category; therefore, data are not presented.

[d]Other ethnicity group includes youths who identified as Pacific Islander, American Indian, Alaskan Native, or multiple ethnicity groups.

the present study added to previous studies on adolescent girls,[19,22] by providing clear evidence that purging for weight control and diet pill use were highly prevalent among sexual minority girls of diverse ethnicities.

In relation to ethnicity, our study suggested that African American female adolescents might have some protection against engaging in vomiting or abuse of laxatives or diet pills to control weight. Previous studies showed mixed results on this point, with some finding a similar protective effect,[17,48] whereas others did not find reduced risk.[15,21,49] Our study also suggested that Asian American girls might be at decreased risk for disordered weight-control behaviors compared with Whites, consistent with previous findings from the National Latino and Asian American Study.[50] Among ethnic minority boys, our findings were consistent with previous research that showed Latino and African American boys had higher rates of disordered weight-control behaviors compared with White boys.[16,49] This trend was not found among Asian American boys, which was consistent with previous literature.[50]

Few studies have examined associations of sexual orientation with obesity in adolescents. One previous study with youths participating in the Growing Up Today Study, a cohort made up predominantly of White youths, demonstrated that sexual orientation minority girls had a higher BMI than heterosexual girls, whereas among boys the reverse was found, with heterosexual boys having higher BMI than gay boys.[18] For girls, the present findings differed from the previous study, in that elevated odds of obesity were found only for bisexuals and not lesbians. For boys, results from the present study also differed from previous findings, in that gay boys did not differ from heterosexuals, whereas bisexual boys had 2 times the odds of obesity compared with heterosexual peers.

A number of studies have shown elevated rates of obesity among ethnic minority adolescents,[13-17] especially in African American and Latina girls compared with their White same-gender peers. Our findings were consistent with these studies, demonstrating an increased notable risk of obesity among African American and Latina girls. Our results were also consistent with those of previous research, which found Asian American youths were at lower risk of obesity compared with White youths.[14,51]

The present study did not find support for the additive hypothesis of multiple minority stress theory, as sexual orientation-by-ethnicity interactions were not found to be significant in multivariable regression models. This null finding might have been because of insufficient statistical power; however, prevalence estimates for outcomes presented in Table 2 did not suggest any consistent patterns of additivity. Contemporary approaches to intersectionality research recommend studying the risk associated with the unique experiences of being LGB people of color (e.g., the experience of being Asian American, bisexual, and female), rather than assuming that the experience was merely the sum of the risk of being a sexual minority in addition to an ethnic minority.[52-54] Such research requires collecting data on the processes and contexts that generate unique risks and protections for individuals with LGB people of color identities. For example, a few studies found that gay and bisexual males who were an ethnic minority, especially Latino, might be at particularly elevated risk for mental health problems because of family rejection.[28,37,55]

Limitations

Our study had several limitations that should be considered. Although our analytic sample was very large, we still might

Table 3 Odds of Purging, Diet Pill Use, and Obesity Associated With Ethnicity and Sexual Orientation Identity in US High School Students: Youth Risk Behavioral Surveillance System Survey, 2005 and 2007

	Purging,[a] OR (95% CI)	Diet Pill Use,[a] OR (95% CI)	Obese,[b] OR (95% CI)
		Girls	
Age, y	1.02 (0.96, 1.10)	1.16* (1.07, 1.26)	0.99 (0.93, 1.05)
Ethnicity			
Asian-American	0.42* (0.27, 0.65)	0.46* (0.27, 0.79)	0.45* (0.29, 0.68)
African-American	0.59* (0.45, 0.77)	0.58* (0.43, 0.80)	2.59* (2.14, 3.14)
Latina	0.92 (0.79, 1.20)	0.89 (0.65, 1.22)	1.90* (1.51, 2.41)
Other ethnicity[c]	0.93 (0.72, 1.21)	0.94 (0.67, 1.32)	2.16* (1.73, 2.70)
White (Ref)	1.0	1.0	1.0
Sexual orientation identity			
Lesbian	3.95* (2.26, 6.89)	4.00* (2.11, 7.58)	1.50 (0.81, 2.76)
Bisexual	3.23* (2.52, 4.16)	3.06* (2.29, 4.11)	2.25* (1.75, 2.88)
Unsure	2.55* (1.77, 3.73)	1.91* (1.09, 3.35)	1.41 (0.88, 2.24)
Heterosexual (Ref)	1.0	1.0	1.0
		Boys	
Age, y	1.04 (0.97, 1.11)	1.15 (1.05, 1.27)	0.97 (0.93, 1.01)
Ethnicity			
Asian-American	0.77 (0.52, 1.14)	0.84 (0.51, 1.39)	0.66* (0.53, 0.83)
African-American	1.60* (1.26, 2.03)	1.16 (0.84, 1.61)	1.16 (0.98, 1.36)
Latino	1.28 (0.96, 1.70)	1.21 (0.84, 1.75)	1.61* (1.35, 1.91)
Other ethnicity[c]	1.54* (1.19, 2.01)	1.49* (1.06, 2.09)	1.41* (1.18, 1.68)
White (Ref)	1.0	1.0	1.0
Sexual orientation identity			
Gay	5.21* (3.47, 7.82)	4.33* (2.72, 6.91)	0.87 (0.53, 1.41)
Bisexual	6.16* (4.09, 9.26)	6.77* (4.20, 10.91)	2.10* (1.43, 3.07)
Unsure	3.76* (2.51, 5.65)	3.00* (1.71, 5.29)	1.21 (0.84, 1.74)
Heterosexual (Ref)	1.0	1.0	1.0

Note. CI = confidence interval; OR = odds ratio. Models are gender-stratified and control for age, ethnicity, sexual orientation, region, and data collection wave. The maximum sample size was n = 24 591.

[a] Purging defined as any vomiting or use of laxatives in the past month to control weight; diet pill use defined as use of diet pills to control weight without a doctor's prescription in the past month.

[b] Obese defined as body mass index of three quarters of 95th percentile for age and sex based on guidelines from the US Centers for Disease Control and Prevention.

[c] Other ethnicity group includes youths who identified as Pacific Islander, American Indian, Alaskan Native, or multiple ethnicity groups.

*P < .05.

not have had sufficient statistical power to detect sexual-orientation- by-ethnicity interactions or to detect a possible modest increased odds of obesity for lesbians compared with heterosexual peers. Generalizability of findings was limited to the jurisdictions across the country that provided data. Our findings relied on self-reported height and weight. Studies showed that although self-reported height and weight are highly correlated with measured height and weight, adolescents tend to overreport their height and underreport their weight. In particular, some studies found that males and non-Hispanic Whites were

more likely to overreport height and females were more likely to underreport weight.[39,56,57] Importantly, another study of adolescents and young adults found no evidence that sexual orientation modified bias in self-reported BMI among females, although gay males were found to underreport BMI to a greater degree than were heterosexual males.[58] The YRBSS provided little information on important factors that might help to explain disparities in disordered weight-control behaviors and obesity, such as socioeconomic status, harassment and violence victimization, respondents' family and social environment, and psychological health.[8,59,60] The use of identity to classify sexual orientation hindered our ability to examine the subset of sexual minorities who had same- or both-gender attractions or sexual partners but did not identify as bisexual, gay, or lesbian. The YRBSS did not assess several important indicators of eating disorders, such as fasting and psychological symptoms; therefore, our analyses likely underestimated the prevalence of eating disorder symptoms in the population. Our dichotomous measures of any purging and diet pill use in the past 30 days did not allow us to examine symptom severity, which also might differ by sexual orientation identity and ethnicity.

Conclusions

Eating disorders and obesity are serious conditions with short- and long-term implications for comorbid disease risk, medical and psychiatric treatment costs, quality of life, and longevity.[9,42–45] In the present study, sizable disparities in disordered weight control behaviors adversely affecting all sexual minority groups of both genders were found for self-induced vomiting and abuse of laxatives and diet pills. Because of minimal regulation on the sale of laxatives and diet pills in the United States,[61] vulnerable and marginalized youths, such as sexual minorities and others, have largely unfettered access to purchase these products, which are then too often abused in dangerous attempts to control weight. As done with regard to other abused substances, such as alcohol and tobacco, public health professionals and policymakers need to step up efforts to protect minors from industries that currently profit from the abuse of their products by vulnerable youths.[61] The findings of the present study also highlighted the serious issue of obesity in female and male bisexual youths. Obesity in adolescence is strongly associated with a myriad immediate- and long-term adverse consequences.[6,7] Health and other professionals working with sexual minority youths need to establish mechanisms to screen for symptoms of eating disorders so that affected youths can be referred for treatment and need to develop programs to promote healthful weight-control behaviors in sexual minorities of all ethnicities and in both girls and boys. In addition, interventions that are appropriate for sexual orientation minority youths of diverse ethnicities are urgently needed to eliminate stressors and other factors contributing to these disparities.

References

1. Ogden CL, Carroll MD, Kit BK, Flegal KM. Prevalence of obesity and trends in body mass index among US children and adolescents, 1999–2010. *JAMA*. 2012;307 (5):483–490.

2. Freedman DS, Zuguo M, Srinivasan SR, Berenson GS, Dietz WH. Cardiovascular risk factors and excess adiposity among overweight children and adolescents: the Bogalusa Heart Study. *J Pediatr*. 2007;150(1):12–17.

3. Li C, Ford ES, Zhao G, Mokdad AH. Prevalence of pre-diabetes and its association with clustering of cardiometabolic risk factors and hyperinsulinemia among US adolescents: NHANES 2005–2006. *Diabetes Care*. 2009;32(2):342–347.

4. Daniels SR, Arnett DK, Eckel RH, et al. Overweight in children and adolescents: pathophysiology, consequences, prevention, and treatment. *Circulation*. 2005; 111(15):1999–2012.

5. Dietz WH. Overweight in childhood and adolescence. *N Engl J Med*. 2004;350(9):855–857.

6. Whitaker RC, Wright JA, Pepe MS, et al. Predicting obesity in young adulthood from childhood and parental obesity. *N Engl J Med*. 1997;337(13):869–873.

7. Office of the Surgeon General. *The Surgeon General's Vision for a Healthy and Fit Nation*. Rockville, MD: U.S. Department of Health and Human Services; 2010.

8. Croll J, Neumark-Sztainer D, Story M, Ireland M. Prevalence and risk and protective factors related to disordered eating behaviors among adolescents: relationship to gender and ethnicity. *J Adolesc Health*. 2002;31(2):166–175.

9. Crow S. Medical complications of eating disorders. In: Wonderlich S, Mitchell J, de Zwaan M, Steiger H, eds *Eating Disorders Review, Part 1*. Abingdon, UK: Radcliffe Publishing Ltd.; 2005:127–136.

10. Haines J, Kleinman KP, Rifas-Shiman S, Field AE, Austin SB. Examination of shared risk and protective factors for weight-related disorders in adolescents. *Arch Pediatr Adolesc Med*. 2010;164(4):336–343.

11. Neumark-Sztainer DR, Wall MM, Haines JI, Story MT, Sherwood NE, van den Berg PA. Shared risk and protective factors for overweight and disordered eating in adolescents. *Am J Prev Med*. 2007;33(5):359–369.

12. Goldschmidt AB, Aspen VP, Sinton MM, Tanofsky-Kraff M, Wilfley DE. Disordered eating attitudes and behaviors in overweight youth. *Obesity (Silver Spring)*. 2008;16(2):257–264.

13. Scharoun-Lee M, Kaufman JS, Popkin BM, Gordon-Larsen P. Obesity, race/ethnicity and life course socioeconomic status across the transition from adolescence to adulthood. *J Epidemiol Community Health*. 2009;63(2):133–139.

14. Yates A, Edman J, Aruguete M. Ethnic differences in BMI and body/self-dissatisfaction among Whites, Asian subgroups, Pacific Islanders, and African-Americans. *J Adolesc Health*. 2004;34(4):300–307.

15. Austin SB, Spadano-Gasbarro J, Greaney ML, et al. Disordered weight control behaviors in early adolescent boys and girls of color: an under-recognized factor in the epidemic of childhood overweight. *J Adolesc Health*. 2011;48(1):109–112.

16. Johnson WG, Rohan KJ, Kirk AA. Prevalence and correlates of binge eating in white and African American adolescents. *Eat Behav*. 2002;3(2):179–189.

17. Neumark-Sztainer D, Croll J, Story M, Hannan PJ, French SA, Perry C. Ethnic/racial differences in weight-related concerns and behaviors among adolescent girls and boys: findings from Project EAT. *J Psychosom Res*. 2002;53(5):963–974.

18. Austin SB, Ziyadeh NJ, Corliss HL, et al. Sexual orientation disparities in weight status in adolescence: findings from a prospective study. *Obesity (Silver Spring)*. 2009;17(9):1776–1782.

19. Austin SB, Ziyadeh NJ, Corliss HL, et al. Sexual orientation disparities in purging and binge eating from early to late adolescence. *J Adolesc Health*. 2009;45(3): 238–245.

20. Austin SB, Ziyadeh N, Kahn JA, Camargo CA Jr, Colditz GA, Field AE. Sexual orientation, weight concerns, and eating-disordered behaviors in adolescent girls and boys. *J Am Acad Child Adolesc Psychiatry*. 2004;43(9):1115–1123.

21. French SA, Story M, Remafedi G, Resnick MD, Blum RW. Sexual orientation and prevalence of body dissatisfaction and eating disordered behaviors: a population-based study of adolescents. *Int J Eat Disord*. 1996;19(2):119–126.

22. Wichstrøm L. Sexual orientation as a risk factor for bulimic symptoms. *Int J Eat Disord*. 2006;39(6):448–453.

23. Darcy AM, Doyle AC, Lock J, Peebles R, Doyle P, Le Grange D. The eating disorders examination in adolescent males with

anorexia nervosa: how does it compare to adolescent females? *Int J Eat Disord.* 2012;45(1):110–114.

24. Dominé F, Berchtold A, Akré C, Michaud PA, Suris JC. Disordered eating behaviors: what about boys? *J Adolesc Health.* 2009;44(2):111–117.

25. Farrow JA. The adolescent male with an eating disorder. *Pediatr Ann.* 1992;21(11):769–774.

26. Saewyc EM, Bearinger LH, Heinz PA, Blum RW, Resnick MD. Gender differences in health and risk behaviors among bisexual and homosexual adolescents. *J Adolesc Health.* 1998;23(3):181–188.

27. Meyer IH. Prejudice, social stress, and mental health in lesbian, gay, and bisexual populations: conceptual issues and research evidence. *Psychol Bull.* 2003;129 (5):674–697.

28. Balsam KF, Molina Y, Beadnell B, Simoni J, Walters K. Measuring multiple minority stress: the LGBT People of Color Microaggressions Scale. *Cultur Divers Ethnic Minor Psychol.* 2011;17(2):163–174.

29. Consolacion TB, Russell ST, Sue S. Sex, race/ethnicity, and romantic attractions: multiple minority status adolescents and mental health. *Cultur Divers Ethnic Minor Psychol.* 2004;10(3):200–214.

30. Kim H-J, Fredriksen-Goldsen KI. Hispanic lesbians and bisexual women at heightened risk of health disparities. *Am J Public Health.* 2012;102(1):e9–e15.

31. Cochran SD, Mays VM, Ortega AN, Alegria M, Takeuchi D. Mental health and substance use disorders among Latino and Asian American lesbian, gay, and bisexual adults. *J Consult Clin Psychol.* 2007;75(5):785–794.

32. Mays VM, Yancey AK, Cochran SD, Weber M, Fielding JE. Heterogeneity of health disparities among African American, Hispanic, and Asian American women: unrecognized influences of sexual orientation. *Am J Public Health.* 2002;92(4):632–639.

33. O'Donnell S, Meyer IH, Schwartz S. Increased risk of suicide attempts among Black and Latino lesbians, gay men, and bisexuals. *Am J Public Health.* 2011;101 (6):1055–1059.

34. Yancey AK, Cochran SD, Corliss HL, Mays VM. Correlates of overweight and obesity among lesbian and bisexual women. *Prev Med.* 2003;36(6):676–683.

35. Kertzner RM, Meyer IH, Frost DM, Stirratt MJ. Social and psychological well-being in lesbians, gay men, and bisexuals: the effects of race, gender, age, and sexual identity. *Am J Orthopsychiatry.* 2009;79(4):500–510.

36. Mustanski BS, Garofalo R, Emerson EM. Mental health disorders, psychological distress, and suicidality in a diverse sample of lesbian, gay, bisexual, and transgender youths. *Am J Public Health.* 2010;100(12):2426–2432.

37. Ryan C, Huebner D, Diaz RM, Sanchez J. Family rejection as a predictor of negative health outcomes in white and Latino lesbian, gay, and bisexual young adults. *Pediatrics.* 2009;123(1):346–352.

38. Mustanski B, Van Wagenen A, Birkett M, Eyster S, Corliss H. Identifying sexual orientation health disparities in adolescents:methodological approach for analysis of a pooled YRBS dataset. *Am J Public Health.* 2012.

39. Brener ND, Mcmanus T, Galuska DA, Lowry R, Wechsler H. Reliability and validity of self-reported height and weight among high school students. *J Adolesc Health.* 2003;32(4):281–287.

40. Centers for Disease Control and Prevention. Growth charts. Available at: www.cdc.gov/growthcharts. Accessed on December 3, 2012.

41. Sherry B, Jefferds ME, Grummer-Strawn LM. Accuracy of adolescent self-report of height and weight in assessing overweight status: a literature review. *Arch Pediatr Adolesc Med.* 2007;161(12):1154–1161.

42. Crow S, Peterson CB. The economic and social burden of eating disorders: a review. In: Maj M, Halmi K, Lopez-Ibor JJ, Sartorius N, eds *Eating Disorders.* Hoboken, NJ: John Wiley & Sons, Ltd; 2003:383–396.

43. Franko DL, Keel PK. Suicidality in eating disorders: occurrence, correlates, and clinical implications. *Clin Psychol Rev.* 2006;26(6):769–782.

44. Jia H, Lubetkin EI. The impact of obesity on health-related quality-of-life in the general adult U.S. population. *J Public Health.* 2005;27(2):156–164.

45. Mokdad AH, Ford ES, Bowman BA, et al. Prevalence of obesity, diabetes, and obesity-related health risk factors, 2001. *JAMA.* 2003;289(1):76–79.

46. Ackard DM, Fedio G, Neumark-Sztainer D, Britt HR. Factors associated with disordered eating among sexually active adolescent males: gender and number of sexual partners. *Psychosom Med.* 2008;70(2):232–238.

47. Massachusetts Department of Education. *1999 Youth Risk Behavior Survey.* Malden, MA: Massachusetts Department of Education; 2000.

48. Chao YM, Pisetsky EM, Dierker LC, et al. Ethnic differences in weight control practices among U.S. adolescents from 1995 to 2005. *Int J Eat Disord.* 2008;41(2):124–133.

49. Field AE, Colditz GA, Peterson KE. Racial/ethnic and gender differences in concern with weight and in bulimic behaviors among adolescents. *Obes Res.* 1997;5 (5):447–454.

50. Nicdao EG, Hong S, Takeuchi DT. Prevalence and correlates of eating disorders among Asian Americans: results from the National Latino and Asian American Study. *Int J Eat Disord.* 2007;40(suppl):S22–S26.

51. Shabbir S, Swan D, Wang MC, Shih M, Simon PA. Asians and Pacific Islanders and the growing childhood obesity epidemic. *Ethn Dis.* 2010;20(2):129–135.

52. Bowleg L. When black + lesbian + woman ≠ black lesbian woman: the methodological challenges of qualitative and quantitative intersectionality research. *Sex Roles.* 2008;59(5–6):312–325.

53. Collins PH. It's all in the family: intersections of gender, race, and nation. *Hypatia.* 1998;13(3):62–82.

54. Weber L, Parra-Medina D. Intersectionality and women's health: charting a path to eliminating health disparities. *Advances Gend Res.* 2003;7:181–230.

55. Díaz RM, Ayala G, Bein E, Henne J, Marin BV. The impact of homophobia, poverty, and racism on the mental health of gay and bisexual Latino men: findings from 3 US cities. *Am J Public Health.* 2001;91(6): 927–932.

56. Elgar FJ, Roberts C, Tudor-Smith C, Moore L. Validity of self-reported height and weight and predictors of bias in adolescents. *J Adolesc Health.* 2005;37(5): 371–375.

57. Himes JH, Hannan P, Wall M, Newmark-Sztainer D. Factors associated with errors in self-reports of stature, weight, and body mass index in Minnesota adolescents. *Ann Epidemiol.* 2005;15(4):272–278.

58. Richmond TK, Walls CE, Austin SB. Sexual orientation and bias in self-reported body mass index. *Obesity (Silver Spring).* 2012;20(8):1703–1709.

59. Gordon-Larsen P, Nelson M, Page P, Popkin BM. Inequality in the built environment underlies key health disparities in physical activity and obesity. *Pediatrics.* 2006;117(2):417–424.

60. Swanson SA, Crow SJ, Le Grange D, Swendsen J, Merikangas KR. Prevalence and correlates of eating disorders in adolescents. *Arch Gen Psychiatry.* 2011;68 (7):714–723.

61. Pomeranz JL, Taylor L, Austin SB. Over-the-counter and out-of-control: legal strategies to protect youth from abusing products for weight control. *Am J Public Health.* 2012 (Epub ahead of print).

Critical Thinking

1. Explain why this information is important to educational professionals?

2. Design two interventions that could be implemented in a school setting to alleviate or eliminate eating disorders or obesity for sexually minority students.

Create Central

www.mhhe.com/createcentral

Internet References

Safe Schools
www.safeschoolscoalition.org/
LGTB Youth Organizations
http://brandonshire.com/lgbt-youth-organizations/

S. Bryn Austin and Jerel P. Cabo are with the Division of Adolescent and Young Adult Medicine at Boston Children's Hospital, Boston, MA, and the Department of Pediatrics of Harvard Medical School, Boston. S. Bryn Austin is also with the Department of Society, Human Development, and Health, Harvard School of Public Health, Boston. Lauren A. Nelson is with Department of Pediatrics, University of California San Francisco Medical Center, San Francisco, Michelle A. Birkett is with Department of Medical Social Sciences, Northwestern University, Chicago, IL. Bethany Everett is with Department of Sociology, University of Illinois at Chicago.

Correspondence should be sent to S. Bryn Austin, ScD, Division of Adolescent and Young Adult Medicine, Boston Children's Hospital, 300 Longwood Ave., Boston, MA 02115 (e-mail: bryn.austin@childrens

.harvard.edu). Reprints can be ordered at www.ajph.org by clicking the "Reprints" link. This article was accepted November 8, 2012.

Contributors—S. B. Austin was responsible for study conceptualization, data analysis and interpretation, and article preparation. M. A. Birkett was responsible for data analysis and interpretation, and article preparation. L. A. Nelson, J. P. Calzo, and B. Everett were responsible for data interpretation and article preparation.

Acknowledgments—This project was supported by the Eunice Kennedy Shriver National Institute of Child Health and Human Development (Award Number R21HD051178) and by the IMPACT LGBT Health and Development Program at Northwestern University. Assistance from the Centers for Disease Control and Prevention (CDC) Division of Adolescent and School Health and the work of the state and local health and education departments who conduct the Youth Risk Behavior Surveys made the project possible. S. B. Austin is supported by the Leadership Education in Adolescent Health project, Maternal and Child Health Bureau (HRSA grant 6T71-MC00009). J. P. Calzo is supported by National Research Service Award F32HD066792, and B. Everett is supported by grant R03 HD062597, both from the Eunice Kennedy Shriver National Institute of Child Health and Human Development.

The authors would like to thank Annabel Chang for her help with preparing the article, and the thousands of students and school staff across the country who made this study possible.

Note—The content is solely the responsibility of the authors and does not necessarily represent the official views of the National Institutes of Health, the CDC, or any agencies involved in collecting the data.

Human Participant Protection—Protocol approval was not necessary because de-identified data were obtained from secondary sources. Data use agreements were obtained from Vermont Department of Health and the Rhode Island Department of Health, which were the only 2 state departments of health that required these agreements for access to Youth Risk Behavior Surveillance System data.

Article

Prepared by: Rebecca B. Evers, *Winthrop University*

LGBT Students Want Educators to Speak Up for Them

Learning for all depends on safety for all students.

ABE LOUISE YOUNG

Learning Outcomes

After reading this article, you will be able to:

- Consider the impact and repercussions of establishing a gay alliance club in your school.

In a school of 1,000 students, up to 100 will be gay, lesbian, or bisexual; 10 will be transgender; and one will be intersex (biologically neither male nor female). If their lives are average, 87 of them will be verbally harassed, 40 of them will be physically harassed, and 19 will be physically assaulted in the next year because of their sexual orientation or gender expression. Sixty-two will feel mostly unsafe going to school. Thirty will harm themselves in what may be suicide attempts. Their academics will suffer because social and emotional needs go hand in hand with educational needs, and nervous students don't learn easily.

The youth make clear that it's not being LGBT that causes these problems. About as many people are born queer in the world as people who are born lefthanded. The problems are the outcome of intolerant actions and speech by peers, parents, teachers, clergy, and strangers. Bullying is a symptom of the culture. An informed educator can use this moment to deeply engage students in inquiry.

Changing a school's climate can seem as impossible as changing the direction of the tides. But educators must take the temperature of a school climate, map a route, establish rules, and hand out safety gear. We know that the values, actions, and atmosphere of a school are lived first by students, in their conversations. Their talk moves the current and sets the compass spinning. Their energy is the gravity that moves the tides.

When a spike in bullying-related suicides of lesbian, gay, bisexual, transgender, and queer students took place in fall 2010, many educators awakened to the need for profoundly new bearings. How could they guide this conversation? What Kids Can Do, Inc., commissioned a study to talk with LGBT students from across the nation to learn what they would say to educators about how to improve the atmosphere in schools for LGBT students.

I interviewed 30 youth over four months, some in person and some by telephone, and learned while listening to them that educators need to enter the conversations of students. Not just listen in, or overhear the lunchroom roar—but position themselves as eager learners and conversation partners inside and outside of classrooms. Here is some inside talk from middle, junior high, and high school LGBT students on how educators can protect and respect them. You may be surprised by their suggestions. If you're already an expert at supporting this population, consider these suggestions and comments an entrée to discussion with other colleagues. At any rate, the students and I hope to get folks talking.

Some students elected to choose pseudonyms; others wanted to be fully named. We settled on using first names and a few noms de plume.

Intervene when you hear the word "gay" used as a put-down, even if it's in jest.

When youth feel safe and protected by an adult at school, it can make the difference between dropping out or graduating. Students learn more, make better grades, and have enhanced emotional well-being when the adults in their schools stand up for their right to learn free of verbal and physical harassment.

When dealing with prejudicial comments in the classroom, preserve the self-respect of those making comments as well as those receiving them. *First*, call an immediate time-out to stop the behavior or speech. *Second*, educate students about why the comments are out of line. *Third*, offer them an opportunity to apologize, ask questions, or otherwise make amends. This three-tier approach creates the best potential for positive change. In the case of students who continue to make hurtful comments, offer them clear consequences of escalating severity.

Sam: Teachers have the right to say, "We will not tolerate this. You need to stop."

Amanda: I think that they should make it a policy—intervening at least. Even though some people might not agree with being gay, it's like their words are still hurting somebody and it's putting somebody in the classroom, you don't know who it could be, in an unsafe feeling.

Dawson: My freshman year in high school was one I won't forget. A peer in class started saying, "That's nasty, gays are nasty." The teacher said to him, "That is not OK. Don't do it again." And he never bothered me after that day!

Examine language in the classroom, and how the meaning of a word changes in different contexts.

In the 2005 Gay, Lesbian, and Straight Education Network's (GLSEN) National School Climate Survey, three-quarters of the high school students surveyed said they heard derogatory and homophobic remarks "frequently" or "often" at school, and 90% heard the term "gay" used generally to imply someone is stupid or worthless.

In the 2004 GLSEN National School Climate Survey, 83% of LGBT students reported that school personnel "never" or "only sometimes" intervened when homophobic remarks were made in their presence.

Marcela: I think it would help if we had a way to name it when somebody says "gay" in a mean way, as opposed to just describing someone. Like, "the bad 'gay'." Or "the gross 'gay'." As opposed to "the cool 'gay'" which is when you are being yourself and you are gay. Because otherwise, you are going to ban a word that also means good things.

Amanda: I feel that racist speech would be reacted to much more forcefully than anti-gay speech at my school. It would be a really big deal. Whereas this—how people talk about queers— gets more like a mild warning, or it is ignored completely.

Recognize that straight youth also suffer in an anti-LGBT climate.

For every lesbian, gay, bisexual or gender nonconforming youth who is bullied, four straight students who are perceived to be nonstraight are bullied, according to the National Mental Health Association's survey, What Does Gay Mean? (2002). That figure alone should give us pause. A climate in which intolerance of any kind flourishes puts undue pressure on all students. The choice is stark: Either hide one's own differences, or risk standing up against peers in conflict. Increasingly, students are incredulous when teachers stay neutral.

Wilfrido: I know a lot of gay people. But I have a lot of friends who are straight as well. They always make fun of my gay

friends, which is kind of . . . not cool. I always kind of go away from that. . . . People would tease a particularly effeminate guy in our grade who is actually straight. I called a class meeting and called everyone out on it, and it pretty much stopped.

Deshaun: I have to stand up for my people when people start calling them out. And when the teacher says nothing, I'm like, "Miss? What? Are you ignoring this mess? Someone is being stepped on here for who they are and that is not right."

Amanda: I think it should definitely be brought to the attention of students how many kids around the world have committed suicide or attempted suicide because of how they were treated. I'm not saying everyone's mind should be changed, and it's just gonna be OK, the world's gonna be peachy— it's not. You can't change everyone's mind, but you can definitely put it out there that there are consequences to actions.

Annie: Teachers need to step up! By making sure that this type of hate language—or all hate language—isn't accepted in the classroom. Even if they don't hear it, if a student comes up to them or somebody puts a note on their desk or something . . . just make sure that it's just not accepted.

Reframe the conversation. Identify LGBT-issues as one of the important 20th-century social movements leading to greater human and civil rights.

It's one thing to say, "don't bully the gay kids." But it's another thing to tell students, "You can be a leader, you can support your friends, and you can stand up for the rights of others anywhere you go." Most youth are looking for opportunities to make a better world, and want to be involved in things that matter.

Adrian: To solve the bullying of students inside schools, we, as a country and a society, have to make changes. LGBT rights are human rights, and there needs to be social reform as to how the LGBT community is seen.

Alex H: I am the only openly out person (at my school), and I am one of the most genuinely joyous people on campus.

Eddie: I would still love to see teachers state they will not tolerate "faggot" just as they wouldn't tolerate the N-word. I constantly hear people use the word faggot, and I will tell them, "That's not cool, educate yourself!"

Marcus: "I want my teachers to teach about people of color and other cultures. And about gay and lesbian people and about women and the prejudices people have faced, and like, how they overcame them, something I haven't seen before.

Alex B: The school needs programs that teach openness starting in the 1st or 2nd grade about other sexualities and it being OK, so students do not develop that, "it's different and bad" mindset.

Eddie: I feel the school tries not to address the elephant in the room, but this year has been revolutionary. The kids have taken the gay rights movement into their own hands.

Ensuring physical and emotional safety for LGBT students is an excellent starting place—but educators can be far more ambitious in envisioning an end goal. With these student voices in mind, I ask what gifts can LGBT students bring to the classroom? How can their perspectives and different vantage points move a school community forward?

Don't worry if you're new to the subject—or if it already looks like your school has a problem. Let students hear that you're willing to listen and will act to protect and respect them. They'll teach you anything you need to know.

Reference

National Mental Health Association. (2002). *What Does Gay Mean?* www.nmha.org/go/what-does-gay-mean

Critical Thinking

1. Some students may feel that their teachers are not supportive. In some cases, they may even feel that the teachers themselves are the actual bullies. Are you aware of teachers ignoring or even engaging in bullish behavior toward students who are LGBT? Share one of those in class discussion.

2. Offer one or two reasons why teachers do not intervene or engage in bullying themselves.

3. Does this bullying of persons who are LGBT continue into post-secondary settings, college or work setting?

Create Central

www.mhhe.com/createcentral

Internet References

GLSEN: Gay, Lesbian and Straight Education Network
www.glsen.org

ABE LOUISE YOUNG (abelouiseyoung@gmail.com) is an independent educator and consultant in Austin, Texas, and author of *Queer Youth Advice for Educators: How to Respect and Protect Your Lesbian, Gay, Bisexual, and Transgender Students* (Next Generation, 2011).

Article   Prepared by: Rebecca B. Evers, *Winthrop University*

Preventing Bullying and Harassment of Sexual Minority Students in Schools

HOLLY N. BISHOP AND HEATHER CASIDA

Learning Outcomes

After reading this article, you will be able to:

- Discuss the psychological repercussions of bullying on sexual minority students. How might having a program or club available to students lessen those repercussions?

Often, when the term *bullying* comes up in a conversation, a vision of a large, tough child picking on a smaller, weaker child comes to mind. The common perception of a bully is a single individual or a group of so-called mini-mafia bullies who are feared and loathed by most in the school. This view of bullying leaves out the everyday persistent bullying that happens in schools among a variety of students. Constant verbal abuse, talking down to others, and ridicule are commonplace among many school-aged children. Teasing and verbal harassment are often stopped by teachers when noticed. Unfortunately, in this age of technology, many students avoid teacher intervention by texting or using common Internet websites such as Facebook or MySpace for cyberbullying, resulting in devastating consequences (Cook 2005; Kite, Gable, and Filippelli 2010). While it is almost impossible for teachers and school administrators to police all forms of bullying, one type of bullying often causes ambivalence among teachers resulting in its perpetuation (Anagnostopoulos et al. 2009): the harassment of sexual minority students (gay, lesbian, or bisexual) and students who are perceived by others as being sexual minorities. Words such as *gay, lesbian,* and *faggot* are inappropriately used as put-down and are directed toward sexual minority students or perceived sexual minority students. Use of these commonly unacceptable terms in schools is often unnoticed or ignored by adults (Smith 1998). Estimates show that 6.6% of teenage girls and 8.4% of teenage boys report homosexual or bisexual attraction (Narring, Stronski Huwiler, and Michaud 2003), and 5–6% of youth identify as gay, lesbian, or bisexual; this is as many as two million students or more who are dealing with sexual identity issues (Swearer, Turner, and Givens 2008). These children, along with those who are questioning their sexuality or who are perceived by others as being gay or lesbian, deserve protection from bullying and verbal abuse.

No matter the motive, bullying can damage the psychological well-being of students (Rivers and Noret 2008). Boys who are bullied by being called "gay" for either being gay or being perceived to be gay are at a greater risk of psychological distress as well as more physical and verbal abuse than students bullied for other reasons (Swearer, Turner, and Givens 2008). Because of societal pressures and belief systems, being a gay male is often difficult for young boys to accept about themselves (Rivers and Noret 2008) and difficult for others to accept as well. Bullying of these young men must be stopped in order to provide an appropriate, nonthreatening educational setting where the focus is learning rather than fear, self-hatred, and physical and mental anguish.

Effects on Bullied Students

Degrading words such as fag, queer, dyke, homo, and gay are used on a regular basis at schools in the United States. As many as 98% of adolescents reported having heard such words at school and 51% reported hearing them on a daily basis (International Communications Research 2002; Rivers and Noret 2008). Two-thirds of students who identify as being gay, lesbian, or bisexual (GLB) report being victimized (California Safe Schools Coalition and 4-H Center for Youth Development 2004; Rivers and Noret, 2008). This number does not include students who do not identify as being GLB, yet, because of the way they look or act, are bullied because of others' perceptions of their sexuality. With the commonality of the degrading of sexual minorities in school, it should come as no surprise that bullied sexual minority or perceived sexual minority students often do poorly in school (Gibson 1994).

While bullying of any type is painful and detrimental to students, many studies have revealed the seriousness of bullying pertaining to sexual minority students or those who are perceived to be sexual minorities regardless of their actual sexual orientation. Sexual minority youth face both physical and verbal abuse along with rejection by friends and family (Gibson 1994). Many experience family violence (Ortiz-Hernandez, Gomez Tollo, and Valdes 2009) and, in some cases, are disowned by their families (Gibson 1994). Add to that bullying at school, and many of these students have no peace in their lives. Bullying because of sexual orientation often manifests with physical problems linked to anxiety as well as loss of interest in school or friends (Davis 2006). Students who are bullied because of sexual orientation are more likely to drink alone, which has been shown to correlate with loneliness (Rivers and Noret 2008). Gibson (1994) also found that these students are often isolated and withdrawn for fear of the consequences of being homosexual. These young people are at a higher risk for psychosocial problems such as drug and alcohol abuse and depression (Gibson 1994), and they were found to smoke six or more cigarettes per day on average (Ortiz-Hernandez, Gomez Tollo, & Valdes 2009). In addition to an unhealthy lifestyle, many have relationship problems (Gibson 1994), which may limit the support they find in their lives. These all increase the risk for suicidal feelings (Gibson 1994). "Gay youth are 2 to 3 times more likely to attempt suicide than other young people. They may comprise up to 30% of completed suicides annually" (Gibson 1994, 15).

Stopping the bullying of sexual minority students is crucial. Dealing with one's own homosexuality can be difficult. Many sexual minority students report worrying about being gay or lesbian (Rivers and Noret 2008), but if the students are in a supportive atmosphere, the likelihood of many of the negative effects can be avoided. Bullying is a major factor in determining many of the negative effects students must bear, and the results are alarming. Bullied sexual minority students are more likely to get C grades in school, skip school, and engage in health-risk behaviors such as drinking and driving and substance abuse than nonbullied sexual minority students (Rivers and Noret 2008). A negative effect of bullying includes physical harm or perceived physical harm. Because of this, bullied sexual minority students are four times more likely to carry weapons to school and six times more likely to be hurt or threatened by someone with a weapon than nonbullied sexual minority students (Rivers and Noret 2008). More than half (53%) of bullied American sexual minority youth reported contemplating or attempting suicide or self-harm as a direct result of bullying (Rivers and Noret 2008).

The most common victims of bullying and homophobic victimization have been reported to be students who are questioning their sexuality—even more so than students who report being gay, lesbian, or bisexual (Birkett, Espelage, and Koenig 2009). About 5% of teenagers in the United States have been found to be unsure about their sexual identity (Narring, Stronski Huwiler, and Michaud 2003). This large group of questioning students also report having the greatest tendency for drug use, feelings of depression, suicidal thoughts, and truancy compared to both heterosexual students and students who consider themselves to be lesbian, gay, or bisexual (Birkett, Espelage, and Koenig 2009). One hypothesis for this is that the students who report being gay, lesbian, or bisexual have the support of each other (Espelage et al. 2008). If this is indeed the case, the need and importance of an accepting, supportive environment for questioning and homosexual students is crucial to lessen bullying, harassment, and all the negative effects that result from such abuse. Unfortunately, some studies suggest that the bullying, harassment, and victimization of sexual

minority students is increasing (Hunt and Jensen 2007; Rivers and Noret 2008), and schools are at the forefront of turning this trend around.

Homophobia, Bullying, and Schools at Risk

Homophobia is the greatest enemy of sexual minorities. The United States is often described as a Christian nation. Unfortunately, theologically conservative religion has been shown to be a strong predictor in homophobia (Finlay and Walther 2003; Morrison and Morrison 2002; Schulte and Battle 2004). Although research has found that males typically display more homophobia than females (Berkman and Zinberg 1997; Eagly et al. 2004; Whitley and Kite 1995), religiousness is more of an indicator of homophobia than gender (Roisk, Griffith, and Cruz 2007). Some conservative Christians feel that Western civilization, Christianity, and school children are threatened by any perceived promotion of homosexuality (Lugg 1998). The so-called religious right's battle against tolerance and acceptance of sexual minorities stigmatizes them as being homophobic. The term *homophobia* will likely make reference to conservative religious communities in the future because they may become the only identifiable group to continue holding negative views toward the gay and lesbian community (Roisk, Griffith, and Cruz 2007). The idea of homosexuals having access to children in order to recruit them has caused many right-wing Christian activists to promote homophobic attitudes and legislation, including banning homosexuals from teaching and overturning ordinances protecting homosexuals from discrimination (Lugg 1998). Some even go so far as to believe that anything that shows any tolerance of homosexuality is part of a recruitment effort by pro-gay activists (Lugg 1998). The impact of those with conservative religious values on schools and children is enormous. "Homophobia and bullying are intimately linked. Homophobic bullying represents the physical policing of those perceived not to subscribe in some manner to the heteronormative ideology and agenda" (Stanley 2007, 5). If homophobia is at the root of bullying and hostility toward sexual minority students, and homophobia is itself rooted in the religious values of much of society, then it will be difficult for the pendulum to swing to change these values to be more accepting of sexual minorities.

School staff members were found to have mixed feelings about how, or if, they should deal with bullying toward gay and lesbian students (Anagnostopoulos et al. 2009). This may be attributed to their own religious beliefs about homosexuality or to their fear of repercussion from parents or administrators with homophobic attitudes. Students are harassed and bullied for not acting or dressing like a typical boy or girl as stereotyped by society; basically, for not fitting in (Cook 2005). The push for heteronormativity in schools causes both sexual minority students and faculty to try to pass as heterosexual to fit in (Lugg 2006). Lugg (2006) also refers to public school administrators' roles as functioning as "sexuality and gender police" (42) who are required to enforce social and legal norms, including oppressing outward or perceived homosexual behavior among students. Homosexual teachers and administrators also enforce these norms that encourage socially acceptable heterosexual behavior while remaining closeted themselves (Lugg 2006). Pressure from conservative religious communities is placed on district administrators to enforce these socially acceptable heterosexual norms with little regard for their effects on sexual minority students.

School districts in regions where conservative religion has its roots are at greater risk for bullying and harassment of sexual minority students because of the higher rates of homophobia directly linked to theologically conservative religion (Finlay and Walther 2003; Morrison and Morrison 2002; Schulte and Battle 2004). This is also demonstrated by there being a 10% higher incidence of bullying of sexual minority students in faith-oriented schools than public schools (Hunt and Jensen 2007; Rivers and Noret 2008). Contrary to the idea of smaller schools being less gay-friendly, school district size and ratios of students to personnel have little to do with hostility toward sexual minority students (Kosciw, Greytak, & Diaz, 2009). However, sexual minority youth in rural communities and areas where adults have lower levels of education often face particularly hostile environments (Kosciw, Greytak, and Diaz 2009). School administrators and faculty in these environments need to be particularly mindful of the hardships with which sexual minority students, questioning students, and students who are perceived to be sexual minorities are dealing.

Legal Ramifications

Sexual minority students are resisting attempts by schools to regulate sexual orientation and gender expression (Meyer and Stader 2009). The number of legal complaints against school districts by sexual minority youth for harassment and access to extracurricular activities has increased significantly in recent years (Meyer and Stader 2009). Legal redress is said to be one of the most prominently used methods for the sexual minority community to fight oppression both in schools and in their personal lives (Stanley 2007). School administrators and faculty should be aware of the consequences of not protecting sexual minority or perceived sexual minority students from bullying and harassment.

Gay, lesbian, and bisexual youth who challenge the system and pick legal battles with their school districts are having a significant impact on the dismantling of heteronormative standards commonly implemented in school districts, and courts are siding with the students who file complaints (Meyer and Stader 2009). In the case of *Nabozny v. Pollesny, Davis, Blanert,* et al. (1996), a student reported harassment and abuse from other students because of his homosexuality. The court found that the defendants failed to protect him based on his sexual orientation, which violated his Fourteenth Amendment right to equal protection. Since then, many school districts have implemented stricter policies against harassment. Even if a district has a zero-tolerance policy for harassment, the district must enforce the policy or risk litigation. In the case of *L. G. v. Toms River Regional School Board of Education* (2007), a woman sued her son's school district for emotional distress resulting from harassment from other students for his perceived sexual

orientation. The district was found liable for failure to take corrective action to reinforce the zero-tolerance policy. The court found that school districts must administer reasonable preventive and remedial actions to protect students from harassment. The case of Constance McMillen (*McMillen v. Itawamba County School District,* 2010) made national news when McMillen sued the Itawamba County School District in Mississippi for discrimination when she was told she could neither bring her girlfriend to prom nor wear a tuxedo. The judge in the case ruled for McMillen, judging that her First Amendment rights had been violated. The district claimed no wrongdoing and settled for $35,000 to end the lawsuit and agreed to implement a nondiscrimination policy that includes sexual orientation (Joyner 2010).

Students who take a stand against school districts that do not protect their rights are improving their own school experiences while setting precedence for all sexual minorities that harassment and abuse will not be tolerated (Meyer and Stader 2009). Sexual minority students are being supported by the courts when it comes to harassment. School districts need to be aware of their obligation to protect all students because all students have the right to equal protection under the Constitution of the United States. Schools that do not offer such protection are in danger of legal recourse.

Ways to Improve the School Setting for Sexual Minority Students

In order to set a tone of acceptance for all students and reduce bullying and harassment based on real or perceived sexual orientation, districts should approve a strong antiharassment policy specifically protecting sexual minorities. A strong policy in place acts as a statement of expectations of how students are to behave, and it leads to an improvement in the school climate (Cook 2005). A positive school climate can result in a reduction in homophobic teasing (Birkett, Espelage, and Koenig 2009) and set the stage for an improved learning environment for all students.

Faculty, staff, and the student body should be educated about the realities and myths associated with sexual orientation (Poland 2010) as well as the results of harassment. Sexual minority students are more likely than other students to ask for support from school staff members (Rivers and Noret 2008), so school faculty and administration should be prepared to show acceptance to these students as well as be ready to step in to stop or prevent harassment. According to Davis (2006), the most important thing teachers and administrators can do is to listen when students ask for help. They should not view sexual minority students as damaged or vulnerable, but, rather, as individuals (Rivers and Noret 2008) and treat them with the same respect they would show any student. Special attention should be paid to students who are questioning their sexuality because they are at greater risk of negative outcomes, such as depression, drug use, and bullying, than either homosexual or heterosexual youth (Birkett, Espelage, and Koenig 2009). A positive school environment and strong parental support have been found to actually shield sexual minority and questioning students from depression and drug use (Espelage et al. 2008). Support from family members is very important in the coming-out process (Rivers and Noret 2008; Willoughby, Malik, and Lindahl 2006), and support at school reinforces this by allowing students to feel comfortable with who they are. School staff should not focus on the negatives associated with sexual minority students or they might actually promote the self-destructive behaviors that are trying to be stopped (Rivers and Noret 2008; Savin-Williams 2005). Instead, they should work to create a positive school climate where differences are accepted and diversity is valued.

Clubs such as gay-straight alliances should be made available to students (Poland 2010) to offer support and educate the student body. The purpose of gay-straight alliances is to make schools safer by specifically addressing homophobic or anti-gay, lesbian, bisexual, or transgender behavior (Gay, Lesbian, and Straight Education Network 2010). The Gay, Lesbian, and Straight Education Network (GLSEN) has now started more than 4,000 gay-straight alliances (Gay, Lesbian, and Straight Education Network 2010), up from 100 in 1997 (Cook 2005). Because of support at home, from schools, and in the media, teenagers today are more open-minded than older generations. Teenagers are more likely to support same-sex marriages and gay adoptions than the general public, and gay teens in some schools and regions of the country often feel good about their sexuality and find that most of their classmates do not care about their sexuality all that much (Cook 2005). Support from teachers, administrators, and other students promotes positive thinking, self-confidence, and a reduction in bullying and harassment that is at the very root of so many problems faced by sexual minority students.

Conclusions

Bullying and harassment of sexual minority students or those perceived to be sexual minorities leads to mental and physical anguish. School performance suffers, unhealthy habits are formed, and suicide could result. Schools in areas with a conservative religious culture should be aware of the possibility of increased homophobia, which is directly linked to bullying and harassment of students who are or who are perceived to be homosexuals.

School districts and personnel are being held responsible in the courts for protecting these students from harassment and must offer them the same opportunities as other students. To provide a safe, accepting learning environment for all students, school districts are creating and enforcing zero-tolerance policies specifically addressing sexual orientation. Districts can further create a positive learning environment by educating the faculty and staff about sexual minority students, the challenges they face, and the consequences many endure. Clubs such as gay-straight alliances further increase a positive school climate. The results of these efforts will not only prevent litigation against districts but also promote diversity, inclusion, and improve the lives of many of the student body.

References

Anagnostopoulos, D., N. Buchanan, C. Pereira, and L. Lichty. 2009. School staff responses to gender-based bullying as moral interpretation: An exploratory study. *Educational Policy* 23 (4): 519–53.

Berkman, C. S., and G. Zinberg. 1997. Homophobia and heterosexism in social workers. *Social Work* 42: 319–32.

Birkett, M., D. Espelage, and B. Koenig. 2009. LGB and questioning students in schools: The moderating effects of homophobic bullying and school climate on negative outcomes. *Journal of Youth and Adolescence* 38 (7): 989–1000.

California Safe Schools Coalition and 4-H Center for Youth Development, University of California, Davis. 2004. *Consequences of harassment based on actual or perceived sexual orientation and gender nonconformity and steps to making schools safer.* San Francisco: California Safe Schools Coalition and 4-H Center for Youth Development, University of California, Davis.

Cook, G. 2005. Up front: News, views, and trends you should watch; A new study shows the prevalence of bullying and harassment at school. *American School Board Journal* 192 (12): 4–6.

Davis, C. 2006. School's out for bullying. *Nursing Standard* 20 (21): 24–25.

Eagly, A. H., A. B. Diekman, M. C. Johannesen-Schmidt, and A. M. Koenig. 2004. Gender gaps in sociopolitical attitudes: A social psychological analysis. *Journal of Personality and Social Psychology* 87: 796–816.

Espelage, D. L., S. R. Aragon, M. Birkett, and B. W. Koenig. 2008. Homophobic teasing, psychological outcomes, and sexual orientation among high school students: What influence do parents and schools have? *School Psychology Review* 37 (2): 202–16.

Finlay, B., and C. S. Walther. 2003. The relation of religious affiliation, service attendance, and other factors to homophobic attitudes among university students. *Review of Religious Research* 44: 370–93.

Gay, Lesbian, and Straight Education Network (GLSEN). 2010. *About gay-straight alliances (GSA's).* www.glsen.org/cgi-bin/iowa/all/library/record/2342.html?state=what. (accessed July 23, 2010).

Gibson, P. 1994. Gay male and lesbian youth suicide. In *Death by denial: Studies of suicide in gay and lesbian teenagers,* ed. G. Remafedi, 15–68. Boston: Alyson.

Hunt, R., and J. Jensen. 2007. *The school report: The experiences of young gay people in Britain's schools.* London: Stonewall.

International Communications Research. 2002. *What does gay mean? Teen survey.* Alexandria, VA: National Mental Health Association.

Joyner, C. 2010. Miss. school settles lesbian prom-date case. *USA Today,* July 20. www.usatoday.com/news/nation/2010-07-20-lesbian-prom-lawsuit_N.htm.

Kite, S., R. Gable, and L. Filippelli. 2010. Assessing middle school students' knowledge of conduct and consequences and their behaviors regarding the use of social networking sites. *Clearing House* 83 (5): 158–63.

Kosciw, J., E. Greytak, and E. Diaz. 2009. Who, what, where, when, and why: Demographic and ecological factors contributing to hostile school climate for lesbian, gay, bisexual, and transgender youth. *Journal of Youth and Adolescence* 38 (7): 976–88.

L. G. v. Toms River Regional School Board of Education, 189 N.J. 381; 915 A. 2d 535, (2007) (LEXIS 184).

Lugg, C. A. 1998. The religious right and public education: The paranoid politics of homophobia. *Educational Policy* 12 (3): 267–83.

Lugg, C. A. 2006. Thinking about sodomy: Public schools, legal panopticons, and queers. *Educational Policy* 20 (1): 35–58.

McMillen v. Itawamba County School District No. 1, 10CV61-D-D, United States District Court for the Northern District of Mississippi, Eastern Division (United States Dist. filed March 23, 2010) (LEXIS 27589).

Meyer, E. J., and D. Stader. 2009. Queer youth and the culture wars: From classroom to courtroom in Australia, Canada, and the United States. *Journal of LGBT Youth* 6 (2/3): 135–54.

Morrison, M. A., and T. G. Morrison. 2002. Development and validation of a scale measuring modern prejudices toward gay men and lesbian women. *Journal of Homosexuality* 43: 15–37.

Nabozny v. Pollesny, Davis, Blanert, et al., 92 F.3d 446 (United States App. 7th Cir. July 31, 1996).

Narring, F., S. M. Stronski Huwiler, and P. A. Michaud. 2003. Prevalence and dimensions of sexual orientation in Swiss adolescents: a cross-sectional survey of 16 to 20-year-old students. *Acta Paediatrica* 92: 233–39.

Ortiz-Hernandez, L., B. Gomez Tello, and J. Valdes. 2009. The association of sexual orientation with self-rated health, and cigarette and alcohol use in Mexican adolescents and youths. *Social Science and Medicine* 69 (1): 85–93.

Poland, S. 2010. LGBT students need support at school. *District Administration* 46 (1): 44.

Rivers, I., and N. Noret. 2008. Well-being among same-sex- and opposite-sex-attracted youth at school. *School Psychology Review* 37 (2): 174–86.

Roisk, C. H., L. K. Griffith, and Z. Cruz. 2007. Homophobia and conservative religion: Toward a more nuanced understanding. *American Psychological Association* 77 (1): 10–19.

Savin-Williams, R. C. 2005. *The new gay teenager.* Cambridge, MA: Harvard University Press.

Schulte, L. J., and J. Battle. 2004. The relative importance of ethnicity and religion in predicting attitudes towards gays and lesbians. *Journal of Homosexuality* 47: 127–41.

Smith, G. 1998. The ideology of "fag": The school experience of gay students. *Sociological Quarterly* 39 (2): 309–35.

Stanley, N. 2007. Preface: "Anything you can do": Proposals for lesbian and gay art education. *International Journal of Art and Design Education* 26 (1): 2–9.

Swearer, S. M., R. K. Turner, and J. E. Givens. 2008. "You're so gay!": Do different forms of bullying matter for adolescent males? *School Psychology Review* 37 (2): 160–73.

Whitley, B. E., and M. E. Kite. 1995. Sex differences in attitudes toward homosexuality: A comment on Oliver and Hyde (1993). *Psychological Bulletin* 117: 146–54.

Willoughby, B., N. Malik, and K. Lindahl. 2006. Parental reactions to their sons' sexual orientation disclosures: The roles of family cohesion, adaptability, and parenting style. *Psychology of Men and Masculinity* 7: 14–26.

Critical Thinking

1. Bishop and Casida summarize three court cases that settled in favor of the student. The courts cited the First and Fourteenth Amendments and a school's Zero-tolerance policy. Explain how the amendments and school policy apply to bullying.

2. The authors note that family support is very important in the coming-out process. Using the websites provided in this unit or that you find in a Google search, construct a handout that school personnel might give to family members who want to be supportive. The handout should contain specific actions for providing support.

3. Find out what local schools are doing to avoid violating the rights of students who are LGBT.

4. If local schools have clubs such as the gay-straight alliances, find out how those groups are supporting students and working to prevent bullying.

Create Central

www.mhhe.com/createcentral

Internet References

What Kids Can Do
 www.whatkidscando.org/publications/pdfs/QueerYouthAdvice.pdf

HOLLY N. BISHOP and **HEATHER CASIDA** are both graduate students in the Department of Educational Leadership and Policy Studies at the University of Texas Arlington.

Article   Prepared by: Rebecca B. Evers, *Winthrop University.*

Having Allies Makes a Difference

**One of the nation's only schools created specifically to be
gay-friendly has made the difficult teenage years easier
for a population of students who often struggle.**

Priscilla Pardini

Learning Outcomes

After reading this article, you will be able to:

- Explain why having allies in a gay-friendly school is important for the well-being and support of students who are LGBT.

W alk in the front door of Milwaukee's gay-friendly Alliance School and at first it doesn't seem all that different from many big-city high schools. Metal lockers line the hallways of the old cinderblock building, once home to a city recreation program. Interspersed with the lockers are colorful student artwork and fliers taped to the walls and classroom doors. Before and after school and during passing periods, students crowd the hallways, jostling and calling out loudly to each other, even as others make little to no eye contact. Teachers threading their way through answer questions about homework and order kids to class. Students drift into the office asking for bus passes. Lockers, one after another, slam shut.

But, look and listen more closely, and the unique characteristics of Alliance emerge. Its vibe: laid-back but edgy. No bells signal the beginning and end of class periods. Students talk freely on their cell phones and address teachers by their first names. But many of the flyers and wall posters carry messages urging "peace" and "respect." Some students seem wary of a visitor in the building, with more than one asking, "Are you a sub?" And even by the almost anything goes sartorial standard of today's high school, many Alliance students stand out for their wildly flamboyant, unconventional style. To be sure, plenty of boys are wearing jeans, some carrying skateboards or basketballs under their arms. But it's not unusual to see them talking to other males wearing multiple earrings and dramatic, perfectly applied eye makeup. Some girls are dressed as if for a fashion show runway, wearing three-inch heels and glittery tops. Others express themselves through rainbow-hued hair, multiple body piercings, or a long, black trench coat.

Teachers eventually clear the halls, curbing off-color and rude comments. And students know that once they get to class, cell phones must be silenced and used only to take emergency calls. Yes, there are rules. But, on a day last fall when a substitute teacher ordered a student out of her classroom for refusing to take off his hat, regular staff members rolled their eyes at what was clearly viewed as an overreaction. "Why would I waste my time worrying about students wearing hats in class given the problems they're facing, the issues they're dealing with?" asked English teacher Paul Moore, one of the school's founding teachers. "What we need to be doing is establishing relationships with these kids and making sure they feel safe and accepted. Only then can we can expect them to be in a position to learn."

> **What they need is a place to be safe from physical abuse and psychological trauma while they explore who they think they are, and get a chance to grow, in peace, at their own rate.**
>
> — Paul Moore, English and social studies teacher

A Safe Haven

Moore and his colleagues at Alliance face the daunting task of meeting the social/emotional *and* academic needs of a group of students whose sexual orientation puts them in what some say is society's last unprotected class. The school opened in 2005 as a teacher-led charter school operating under the auspices of the Milwaukee Public Schools. The school's lead teacher is Tina Owen, a former MPS instructor whose vision shaped Alliance as a safe haven for students who had been bullied or discriminated against not only because of their sexual orientation, but also their beliefs, abilities, or appearance.

Several students transferred to Alliance after being bullied at their neighborhood schools for their conservative Christian views, and some academically oriented students taunted for being nerdy enrolled at Alliance seeking the chance to study in peace. Still other students say they were driven out of their neighborhood schools by unrelenting criticism of their weight, clothing choices, or body odor.

When it opened, Alliance was one of only two high schools in the country (the other, New York City's Harvey Milk High School) explicitly designated as gay-friendly. Four years later, it was expanded to include grades six through eight, making it the first and only such school in the country to serve middle school students.

Alliance is small—it has 172 students, 12 full-time, and six part-time faculty and staff. Last year's graduating class was made up of just 21 students. Like most urban schools, Alliance also is diverse in terms of race, family income, and special education eligibility. About 40% of its students are black, 31% are white, 24% are Hispanic, and 5% are Asian. Almost 77% are eligible for free- or reduced-priced lunch, 25% are homeless or in foster care, and close to one-third qualify for special education.

Still, Alliance is primarily known as Milwaukee's "gay school," with about half of the student body identifying as gay, lesbian, bisexual, or transgender. They come to Alliance from all over the city, its suburbs, and from rural communities as far as 50 miles away.

"Once you're explicitly gay-friendly and say that, it sets up a certain level of expectation," Owen said.

But she points out that the school's mission is broader. "We're not looking only through the lens of gender," she said. "That's just one piece of who we are as humans. At other schools, if you don't fit in this box or that box, you're harassed, kicked around, pushed out. Here, it doesn't matter. We promise all our students the same level of safety and acceptance we promise the LGBT students."

To that end, Alliance's curriculum is designed to address the issue of bullying with restorative justice practices and community-building activities. Its Restorative Justice class, a popular elective course for upperclassmen taught by Heather Sattler, trains students to participate in Peacemaking Circles, a technique derived from Native American traditions and steeped in ritual, that are used to resolve conflicts, promote honest communication, and develop positive relationships. During an intense circle session convened by Sattler and Beth Wellinghoff last fall in an English class they coteach, they asked each student to tell of a significant change in his or her life. They shared experiences that were overwhelmingly personal and often tragic. One girl revealed that at the age of six she had been blamed by family members for the accidental death of her baby sister. Another, who admitted that for years she had considered committing suicide, said she now felt she had to go on living in order to care for her cancer-stricken mother. "It's a nonjudgmental way to tap into what the kids are about and to begin to develop trust," said Sattler of the circle process.

Culture of Acceptance

Jasmin Price, 16, is one of several dozen students who on most days end up eating lunch in Moore's classroom, a huge space dominated at one end by an elevated stage. Some join Moore for a round of the card game Magic; others play Dungeons & Dragons. A third group of kids settles in on the old couch and easy chairs scattered around the stage to play a video game.

Jasmin, a relative newcomer, sits nearby watching, a book open on her lap. Her path to Alliance, which began in 5th grade, is heartbreakingly typical of that reported by many of her peers. Raised in a mostly upscale Milwaukee suburb 20 miles from the city, she loved elementary school.

"But middle school was horrible," she said. "If you didn't have a lot of money and weren't a real girly girl, you'd get picked on. It was constant. And I'd get so anxious I'd make myself sick, which meant I'd miss school, which would make me even more anxious."

Jasmin, whose mother is gay, describes herself as bisexual. She begged to be homeschooled, but, because that wasn't an option, she bounced around to a few other traditional schools before happily landing at Alliance last September.

"After just four weeks here, I'm already more comfortable than I've been since 5th grade," she said. "It's really different, in a good way. Everyone here knows what it's like to be bullied or harassed just for being yourself. So we don't pick on each other. We may not all be best friends, but we treat each other like human beings."

Sommer Kersten, 17, describes herself as pansexual. She said she has a "boyfriend" who is a girl. "I don't care about people's gender," Sommer said. "I have my own taste, but I accept that there are many gender options." At her former school she was routinely called a "dyke"—when she wasn't being ignored. "Here, I felt real comfortable right away. I noticed there were some people who liked the same things as me—like the piercings. And I wasn't the only one with exotic hair."

According to Domonic Exum, 19, the culture at Alliance is based on the premise that "You get along with everyone, and everyone gets along with you." At his former high school, he said, "Kids would start out arguing about petty stuff. There would be a lot of 'He said . . . ' and 'She said . . . ' By the end of the day, it would have escalated to the point where the police were called, and the school was put on lockdown. Here, we're more mellow. New kids sometimes come with an attitude, but by the time they're four weeks in, they get the message: We don't do the drama stuff here."

An At-Risk Population

Because so many of Alliance's students are considered at risk of dropping out of school before graduating, the school operates on a four-days-a-week, year-round schedule. The block schedule enables students to take just four, 100-minute classes each day.

Going to school year round not only helps combat the so-called summer brain drain that affects many low-income and minority students, but also aims to counteract an even more alarming reality: higher-than-average national suicide rates for students who are homeless, in foster care, or who identify as transgender. "Many of them don't have the ongoing support they need outside of school," Owen said.

As a charter school, Alliance also has the flexibility to set aside Tuesdays for staff professional development; students don't report to school, but instead are expected to spend the day working to complete a 60-hour community service requirement for which they receive one-half course credit, and a required online course. Among the students' online class options: credit recovery classes, remedial education classes designed to boost math or English skills, Advanced Placement classes, or electives such as Art History or Digital Art. Some students also spend Tuesdays working at part-time jobs. Giving students so much flexibility in their schedule, Owen said, helps them learn how to manage "freedom with responsibility."

Students say the culture at Alliance and the way classes are structured make it easier for them to concentrate on their schoolwork. "I remember I used to try to buckle down in my classes, but there was so much stress, and I was so depressed or angry that I ended up cutting school a lot," Sommer said. "Here, I go every day, the teachers are easygoing, and I only have four classes to deal with at a time."

Meeting Academic Needs

Yet, despite such accolades, huge challenges persist. Owen is so concerned about the 10% of Alliance students who are transgender that she's made their academic needs one of the issues she's focusing on this year. Although she says transgender students are well accepted, many of them struggle to achieve. The transgender community, she wrote in her annual mission statement, is "particularly vulnerable to street crime, homelessness, sexual assault, and discrimination. The sense of hopelessness that many of these young people feel is devastating, and this has a measurable effect on their achievement."

But teachers also struggle to meet the academic needs of the school's less emotionally vulnerable students. Due to Alliance's small size, the number of course offerings is limited. With the exception of 9th-grade English and math, classes are taught in mixed grade-level settings where student ability varies widely. In fact, because Alliance offers a full-inclusion special education program, some students are reading at only the 4th- or 5th-grade level. Beyond that, many average or above-average students come to Alliance after spending years in hostile environments where they languished academically, severely underachieving and developing bad habits.

One day last fall in teacher Chris Gruntzel's Advanced Algebra class, Gruntzel had a group of eager students in the palm of his hand as he taught a lesson on root-mean-square error. Yet as he explained how the concept measures differences between values predicted by a mathematical model, Gruntzel was interrupted by students arriving late to class and later was forced to slow the pace of the lesson to attend to several students who clearly were lost.

Asked if psychological support trumped intellectual rigor, Sattler said that while social justice issues permeate her teaching, and that teacher-student relationships are critical to Alliance's mission, "I don't coddle students when it comes to academics." Indeed, the first of "The Six Agreements" drawn up by Alliance's inaugural class and posted on a bulletin board in Sattler's classroom states that "Schoolwork comes first."

Owen, who teaches online Spanish and physical education classes, said that's the norm. "I don't think academics take a backseat here," she said. "We're tough. You don't do the work, you're going to fail." Nonetheless, she conceded, "It does sometimes take awhile to get students where we want them to be. But we're patient. We don't give up. We don't get angry. We just keep pulling them forward."

But, said Moore, "It's especially challenging to find ways to offer the smart kids the level of rigor they need." He routinely supplements their required reading lists, asks them in-class discussion questions designed to promote higher-level thinking, and sets increasingly higher standards when it comes to their written work. Gruntzel is in the process of building a sequence of math courses designed to offer Alliance's brightest students more rigor.

Standardized test data, at first glance, is not encouraging. Last year, according to the Wisconsin Department of Public Instruction, only 33% of Alliance 10th graders scored at the proficient or advanced level in reading; 25% did so in math. In both cases, that was lower than the district average, landing Alliance on the list of Schools Identified for Improvement for the second time in three years. But Owen points out that only 24 10th graders took the test last year, including eight special education students. "Given the sample's small size and its makeup, it's hard to see the scores as meaningful," she said.

Owen prefers to look for evidence of success in other measures, such as Alliance's mobility rate, which has decreased from 60% in 2005 to 17% this year, and its attendance rate, which over the same period has jumped from 66% to 91%. And she points with special pride to the fact that 15 of the 21 students in the 2012 graduating class are now in college or other postsecondary schools.

Ana Jimenez, 19, is one of those students. A freshman at Milwaukee's Alverno College, she vividly recalls years of bullying, family problems, and depression that nearly derailed her. At Alliance, she "became part of a family," she said, and transitioned from "a girl who looked and felt angry all the time" to the school's prom queen and talent show winner. She also won Alliance's Toccara Wilson Award, named in memory of one of the school's founders and awarded to the student who best represents, over four years, the ideals to which Alliance aspires. "I still can't believe it. This school saved my life," Ana said.

Spreading the Word

A spate of positive national publicity, not to mention several awards, have helped boost Alliance's reputation. *Time, U.S. News & World Report,* and *People* magazines, as well as ABC News, all have showcased its program. The school also was honored with the Wisconsin Charter Schools Association's 2011 Charter School of the Year Platinum Award and, last January, the Fair Wisconsin Organization of the Year Award.

In August, Owen learned that the school had received a $125,000 grant from Wisconsin's Department of Public Instruction.

Owen said the grant money will be used to underwrite anti-bullying workshops and restorative justice training sessions that Alliance staff and students will put on at other area secondary schools, universities, and community agencies. Plans also call for creating a video and summer training programs, and developing visitation days when the school will be opened to those interested in learning more about how to replicate the Alliance model.

Yet even the positive press, the awards, and the grant money couldn't stop state budget cuts that have forced Alliance to begin phasing out its middle school program. This year, its 6th grade was eliminated; by the 2014–15 school year, it will serve only high schoolers. "It's a shame," Owen said. "There are so many middle school kids who really need to be in this kind of an environment."

Despite the setback, Owen and her staff know Alliance continues to meet the profound needs of a subset of students whose very lives, in some cases, depend on its continued existence. They have become adept at responding to the often-heard criticism that Alliance's model provides nothing more than a temporary respite, a Band-Aid for students who would be better served by learning how to stand up and face—rather than be sheltered from—the abuse bound to be heaped on those living on what many still consider the fringe of society.

"What they need," Moore said, "is a place to be safe from physical abuse and psychological trauma while they explore who they think they are, and get a chance to grow, in peace, at their own rate. Sure, they'll face discrimination, but it's a whole different ballgame once you're 17 or 18 and a more confident person than it is when you're just 13 or 14."

Sommer said she's contemplated the hard reality of taking her place in the real world. "Sure, I'll have to deal with it. And I will. But for now, here, I can just be myself."

Critical Thinking

1. Overtly gay-friendly schools are controversial, even in the gay rights community. Pick a side, either for or opposing. Prepare to debate the issue. Use information from the other articles in this unit and information from the websites at the beginning of the unit for more information.

2. Do you know of gay-friendly schools in your area? If so, research the local response to the school. Perhaps you could interview someone at the school, such as a teacher, administrator, or student. Other persons to consider could be a parent, a neighbor who lives near the school, or a local school district official.

Create Central

www.mhhe.com/createcentral

Internet References

Parents, Families, and Friends of Lesbians and Gays (PFLAG)
www.pflag.org

Priscilla Pardini is a freelance education writer in suburban Milwaukee, Wisc.

Pardini, Priscilla. From *Phi Delta Kappan*, vol. 94, no. 5, February 2013, pp. 14–20. Reprinted with permission of Phi Delta Kappa International. All rights reserved. www.pdkintl.org

Unit 9

UNIT

Prepared by: Rebecca B. Evers, *Winthrop University*

Bullying Continues to Be a Serious Problem

Here are a few reasons why this edition of *Annual Edtions: Education* has a dedicated unit on bullying this year:

- Almost one-third of students (12 to 18) report being bullied at school (Bullying Statistics, 2010).
- There are about 282,000 students that are reportedly attacked in high schools throughout the nation each month (Bullying Statistics, 2010).
- About one in ten students drop out or change schools due to repeated bullying (Bullying Statistics, 2010).
- As many as an estimated 160,000 children miss school every day because they fear being bullied (Bullying Statistics, 2010).
- One in five teens reports being cyber-bullied, but only one in ten will tell their parents they have been cyber-bullied (Cyber Bully Statistics, 2010).
- Victims of cyber-bullying are more likely to have a low self-esteem and to consider suicide (Cyber Bully Statistics, 2010).
- Nearly half (48%) of students experienced some form of sexual harassment in 2010–2011 (AAUW, 2011).
- Approximately one-third (30%) of students experienced some form of cyber-sexual harassment (AAUW, 2011).
- Sixty percent of students with disabilities reported being bullied (AbilityPath.org, 2011).
- Eighty-five percent of children with learning disabilities are bullied at school (AbilityPath.org, 2011).
- Sixty percent of children with learning disabilities have been physically attacked (AbilityPath.org, 2011).

Creating caring communities of learners seems impossible if we look carefully at the statistics above, or if we are aware of news of reported bullying cases that end in the victims' death. Then we have the popular television programs such as *GLEE* with recurring cases of bullying but no evidence of adult intervention. Why do adults allow bullying to occur? Most will admit they see the problem but do not think adults should intervene. Others either say it is the victim's fault, they just do not know what to do, or a very few are personally afraid of the bullies. The first and best step is to understand the truth of what is happening. Have you heard that teasing and bullying is a natural part of growing up and that as students grow and mature, the bullying will decrease? Do you think that girls are just gossips and not really mean or physical? Has someone told you that if the victims would just change the way they act or dress, the bullying will stop? As bullying has become more apparent and been perceived as a growing national problem of endemic proportions,

experts began offering advice to victims and solutions to schools and parents. However, for every solution or response given, there is an expert who suggests the opposite actions should be taken. The articles in this unit will challenge you to think about bullying from several perspectives.

Even though sexual harassment is often thought to be a form of bullying it is not. Each of these actions has a specific definition and is regulated by a different law. Also, sexual harassment is an especially serious problem because it may have worse long-term effects. The article by Munsey provides an overview and suggests some actions. Including this article allows us to open the conversation about this specific form of harassment to add to your awareness of the issues. To begin, here is the definition:

> Sexual harassment is unwelcome conduct of a sexual nature, which can include unwelcome sexual advances, requests for sexual favors, or other verbal, nonverbal, or physical conduct of a sexual nature. (U.S. Department of Education Office of Civil Rights, 2008).

The American Association of University Women conducted a survey, *Crossing the Line*, during May and June of 2011, of 1,965 students in grades 7–12. They concluded that sexual harassment is a widespread problem in middle and high schools. Sexually harassed students reported having trouble studying, not wanting to go to school, and feeling sick to their stomach. Some students stayed home from school, others skipped classes, dropped extra activities, and some changed schools. Girls were especially negatively affected because they faced a higher rate of sexual harassment than boys did, including the most physical forms of sexual harassment. In addition, more than one-third of girls (36%) and nearly one-quarter of boys (24%) experienced some type of cyber-sexual harassment through text messages, e-mail, Facebook, or other electronic means (AAUW, 2011). Finally, we should be aware that the Supreme Court decision in *Davis v. Monroe County Board of Education* (1999) determined that repeated sexual harassment which affects a child's grades or makes a child afraid to enter the school denies that student's right to equal protection in school programs under Title IX.

In the U.S., only a few studies have been conducted on bullying and developmental disabilities. All reported that children with disabilities were two to three times more likely to be bullied than their nondisabled peers. Further, researchers (AbilityPath.org, 2011) have concluded that children with special needs are bullied more because:

- They may have a low frustration tolerance.
- Students with developmental disabilities may have difficulty paying attention to more than one piece of information, which may cause them to stay "stuck" in a conversation.
- Children with motor difficulties are often made fun of on the playground and in class because they are unable to perform age-appropriate motor skills.
- They often have assistive technology devices that other students do not understand and so other students think they are "weird."
- Students with physical impairments may be viewed as weak and precipitate both physical and verbal abuse.

As studies have shown that students with visible and invisible disabilities are subject to more bullying than their peers, we should consider whether we are providing students with disabilities the skills they need to protect themselves. Raskauskas and Modell recommend that any anti-bullying programs used by schools can and should be modified to include students with disabilities.

Porter proposes a shift in the definition of bullying and asserts that the labels we use to describe the persons who are associated with bullying are harmful to making any permanent or significant change in the occurrence of such incidences. In fact, Porter suggests how we label and seek to prevent bullying may not be helpful at all. In a discussion of adolescent brain development, she explains how behaviors now determined to be bullying may in fact simply be missteps as students grow to maturity.

References

American Associations of University Women. (2011). *Crossing the Line*. Author. Retrieved from www.aauw.org/learn/research/crossingtheline.cfm

AbilityPath.org. (2011). *Walk a Mile in Their Shoes*. Author. Retrieved from www.abilitypath.org/areas-of-development/learning—schools/bullying/articles/walk-a-mile-in-their-shoes.pdf

Bullying Statistics. (2010). Bullying statistics 2010 [data set]. Retrieved from www.bullyingstatistics.org/content/bullying-statistics-2010.html

Cyber Bully Statistics (2010) Cyber Bully statistics 2010 (data set). Retrieved from www.bullyingstatistics.org/content/cyber-bullying-statistics.html

Hinjuda, S. & Patchin, J. W. (2010). *Cyberbullying fact sheet: Identification, prevention, and response*. Cyberbullying Research Center. Retrieved from www.cyberbullying.us/Cyberbullying_Identification_Prevention_Response_Fact_Sheet.pdf

U.S. Department of Education Office of Civil Rights (2008). *Sexual Harassment: It's not Academic*. Author. Retrieved from www2.ed.gov/about/offices/list/ocr/docs/ocrshpam.pdf

Article Prepared by: Rebecca B. Evers, *Winthrop University*

Hostile Hallways

It's not as common as run-of-the-mill bullying, but sexual harassment in schools may have worse long-term effects, research suggests.

CHRISTOPHER MUNSEY

Learning Outcomes

After reading this article, you will be able to:

- Hypothesize why bullying is so difficult to stop.
- Conduct a survey to learn how much bullying and/or sexual harassment is present in your school.

B ullying has received intense national attention in recent years. But psychologists say there's an equally serious problem in schools that's not drawing nearly as much attention: sexual harassment.

A troubling 44% of female and 27% of male middle and high school students report experiencing unwanted sexual touching from another student, according to a 2009 Center for Research on Women report. What's more, only 16% of students who had been harassed by a fellow student reported it, says report author, psychologist Lynda Sagrestano, PhD, of the University of Memphis.

It may not be as common as bullying, but school-based sexual harassment may be even worse for students' health and school outcomes, according to a study published in 2008 in the journal *Sex Roles*.

"Sexual harassment, more so than bullying, diminishes students' trust of teachers. . . . Sexually harassed students are much more alienated from school than bullied students in terms of thinking about quitting or transferring schools or skipping school," says James Gruber, PhD, a sociology professor at the University of Michigan-Dearborn.

Yet, despite the seriousness of school-based sexual harassment, most schools do not have an administrator trained to investigate sexual harassment complaints and educate teachers and students about how to intervene, says Dorothy Espelage, PhD, a professor of psychology with the department of educational psychology at the University of Illinois at Urbana-Champaign.

"We need more research, we need a better curriculum, and we need to start talking to kids about sexual harassment," she says.

A Toxic Environment

Sexual harassment in the school environment can lead to a constellation of ill effects for students, says Linda L. Collinsworth, PhD, an associate professor of psychology at Millikin University in Decatur, Ill. In a 2008 study of 569 students from seven Midwestern high schools that appeared in *Psychology of Women Quarterly*, Collinsworth and her colleagues found that girls who had been upset by one or more incidents of sexual harassment across a wide range of harassing behaviors reported signs of depression and anxiety.

Both boys and girls who perceived their school as tolerating sexual harassment reported more symptoms of depression, Collinsworth says.

"It's like second-hand smoke," says Collinsworth. "If you're in this environment where there's this tolerance of sexual harassment, it has this effect on you, even if you're not harassed."

Lesbian, gay, bisexual and questioning students are especially at risk for sexual harassment, according to the survey of 522 middle school and high school students published by Gruber in 2008. He and co-author Susan Fineran, PhD, of the University of Southern Maine, found that 71% of LGBQ students had experienced sexual harassment in the last year, compared with 35% of students overall. "Maybe the real victims are LGBQ students," Gruber says. "They not only report much higher levels of bullying and sexual harassment, but the harm is significantly greater, both in terms of health outcomes and school outcomes."

What Can Be Done

Psychologists and other researchers who study sexual harassment in schools say that key steps to address it include:

- **Educating educators.** Teachers and school administrators need more training on how to respond to sexual harassment and its negative consequences, says Nan Stein, EdD, a senior research scientist at the Wellesley Centers for Women.

Preventing Sexual Assault in College

In April 2011, when Vice President Joseph Biden and Secretary of Education Arne Duncan announced the release of federal guidance on preventing sexual violence on college campuses, they cited a prevention program designed by psychologist Victoria Banyard, PhD, and her colleagues at the University of New Hampshire as a model for other colleges and universities across the country.

Banyard's "Bringing in the Bystander" program teaches both men and women how to prevent sexual violence through an hourlong skill-building educational session that covers how to intervene in scenarios that could culminate in sexual assault. The effort includes a campus-based social marketing campaign to build community awareness.

On a college campus, that might mean noticing if someone who's had too much to drink is being led away from the party by a fellow party-goer. In that case, steering the pair back to the party and making sure the woman's friends are watching out for her could help prevent a possible assault, Banyard says.

In more extreme situations, concerned bystanders might need to request assistance from a resident adviser or the campus police, she says.

"We're trying to teach people safe tools that might make them more likely to step in and help out, in situations across the continuum of sexual violence," Banyard says.

The program also teaches students how to support a friend who reports being assaulted. It helps victims heal if they hear "It's not your fault" and "I believe you" instead of the blame they often receive from family and friends, Banyard says.

About one in three women and one in five men will have a friend tell them about an unwanted sexual experience, she says.

—C. MUNSEY

- **Teaching students.** Educators should add class modules teaching students how to spot harassment and the steps for filing a complaint. Schools also need to encourage students to report sexual harassment to a trusted network of specially trained school officials, and stress that they will not face negative repercussions or retribution, Stein says.
- **Enforcing consequences for offenders and supporting victims.** Some school systems, such as the Austin Independent School District in Texas, allow students to file for a "stay away" order that requires an offender to avoid contact with the victim on school grounds. And through a program called Expect Respect, victims of sexual harassment are offered individual counseling and an invitation to a school-sponsored support group.

Critical Thinking

1. What is the difference between bullying and sexual harassment? If you are not clear on the difference, visit the website (provided at the beginning of this unit) for the American Association of University Women's research report, *Crossing the Line*.

2. Check with a local school or district official for information on bullying and sexual harassment. Do they collect data for both or just for bullying with no differential for harassment?

3. The *Bringing in the Bystander* program at the University of New Hampshire addresses harassment at the college level. Which of their activities might be used to address harassment in middle and high schools?

Create Central

www.mhhe.com/createcentral

Internet References

Olweus Bullying Prevention Program
www.violencepreventionworks.org/
American Association of University Women
www.aauw.org/learn/research/crossingtheline.cfm

CHRISTOPHER MUNSEY is a staff writer for *Monitor on Psychology*.

Article   Prepared by: Rebecca B. Evers, *Winthrop University*

Modifying Anti-Bullying Programs to Include Students with Disabilities

Juliana Raskauskas and Scott Modell

Learning Outcomes

After reading this article, you will be able to:

- Conduct a survey to learn how much bullying and/or sexual harassment is present in your school.

- Design a plan to make your school a safe place.

Most of us have seen or experienced bullying at some point in our schooling and we know that some students are more at risk of being targeted. *Bullying* is defined as any aggressive behavior with the intent to harm that involves a real or perceived power imbalance (Olweus, 1993). Bullying is identified as one of the most predominant problems faced by children in the United States education system (Cantu & Heumann, 2000), as well as one of the most significant health risks to children (Cantu & Heumann, 2000; Espelage & Swearer, 2003; Rigby, Smith, & Pepler, 2004). Exactly how prevalent this issue is among students with disabilities is unclear because research focusing on this cohort is limited. However, most experts agree that children with disabilities are harassed by peers at higher rates than their peers without disabilities (Modell, 2005; Modell, Mak, & Jackson, 2004; Rose, Espelage, Stein, & Elliot, 2009; Sullivan & Knutson, 2000). Bullying can have a profound impact on students' performance, emotional health, and ability to reach their potential (e.g. Espelage & Swearer, 2003). Victimization can hinder a student's capacity to learn in the school environment and can interfere with the ability of students with disabilities to receive the education critical to their advancement.

Bullying and Students with Disabilities

Section 504 of the Rehabilitation Act of 1975, the Individuals With Disabilities Education Act, and the Americans with Disabilities Act of 1990 require schools to provide equal educational opportunity to all students. This responsibility includes the right to learn in a safe and supportive environment. The limited research on bullying among students with disabilities shows that they have a greater likelihood of being bullied than their classmates without disabilities (Pivik, McComas, & LaFlamme, 2002; Rose et al., 2009; Saylor & Leach, 2009; Whitney, Smith, & Thompson, 1994). Children who are victimized or rejected by their peers are more likely to display physical, behavioral, developmental, and learning disabilities than matched control groups (Doren, Bullis, & Benz, 1996; Marini, Fairbairn, & Zuber, 2001). Morrison and Furlong (1994) examined violence at school with 554 high school students, of whom 30 were students with special needs. They found that students in special day classes were victimized more often than those in more inclusive settings (Kaukiainen et al., 2002; Morrison & Furlong, 1994). This outcome may be because isolation from the general education students can limit opportunities to learn social skills (Mishna, 2003) and develop a protective group of peers (Morrison & Furlong, 1994; Whitney et al., 1994).

> **Bullying is identified as one of the most predominant problems faced by children in the United States education system . . ., as well as one of the most significant health risks to children.**

Saylor and Leach (2009) recently examined bullying among students with disabilities and matched general education students who were part of the Peer EXPRESS Inclusion Program. Of the 48 participants, students with disabilities were significantly more likely than those without disabilities to report being bullied and were more anxious about the possibility of being harassed.

Whereas some studies have examined the relative risk of students with disabilities, others have compared different categories of special needs. In one convenience sample, over 50% of students diagnosed as having learning disabilities, intellectual disabilities, speech-language disability, or autism reported that they had been teased, harassed, stolen from, hit, or beaten up by peers at school (Doren et al., 1996). Whitney and colleagues (1994) found with 93 students with disabilities (matched with peers in their inclusion classroom) that 55% of students with mild learning disabilities and 78% of students with moderate learning disabilities experienced bullying, compared to only 25% of their matched peers.

Although studies, in general, have not compared bullying of students diagnosed with different disabilities, children with learning disabilities have been found to be more likely to be identified by peers as victims of bullying than those without learning disabilities (Baumeister, Storch, & Geffken, 2008; Humphrey, Storch, & Geffken, 2007; Nabuzoka, 2003; Nabuzoka & Smith, 1993). In Whitney et al.'s (1994) study, 67% of children with learning disabilities reported being victimized by peers through name calling, taunting, mimicking, kicking, punching, and spitting, as compared to only 25% of peers without disabilities (Whitney et al., 1994). As many as 20% more students with language impairments may be bullied than their peers (Davis, Howell, & Cooke, 2002; Knox & Conti-Ramsden, 2003). Similarly, students with attention deficit hyperactivity disorder (Humphrey et al., 2007) and learning disabilities (Baumeister et al., 2008) are at higher risk and report higher incidences of bullying than students without learning or attention problems.

Most of the research on bullying relating to students with disabilities has focused on students with disabilities who are high functioning. Prior studies have not included students with more moderate and severe disabilities. School districts vary in how they classify and place students with disabilities; in any given school there may be several types of classrooms serving students with disabilities. Our focus in this article is on students classified as having either mild/moderate disabilities (based on their placement in a mild/moderate class) or moderate/severe disabilities (based on their placement in a moderate/severe class). Classes that serve students with mild/moderate disabilities generally include students with developmental or intellectual disabilities whose functional levels may require an educational setting that is more restrictive than the general population. However, it is very common for these students to spend part of their school day in general education classes, based on their functional level and educational needs.

Modifying Anti-Bullying Programs to Include Students With Disabilities

Key to the success of any anti-bullying program is a "whole-school" approach (Dake, Price, Telljohann, & Funk, 2003; Olweus, 1993; Rigby et al., 2004). This approach creates a supportive school atmosphere, where children feel safe to report and are assured that staff care and will respond to reports of bullying or maltreatment. The whole-school approach involves educating and involving everyone affiliated with the school about bullying and their roles in changing the culture. The three areas that are commonly addressed for all stakeholders are:

- Awareness building.
- Efficacy building.
- Skill building.

All staff, faculty, and students—as well as parents and other community members—need to be included in this process, including those students traditionally overlooked in bullying programs (e.g., students with disabilities; Heinrichs, 2003). The inclusion of students with disabilities in bullying programs is critical in order to truly address the "whole school," yet they have not been included in many programs or research studies to this point. In order to fully include students with disabilities, educators and administrators may need to modify existing antibullying programs, which in practice means modifying the program's (a) needs assessment, (b) components, and (c) delivery method (see Table 1).

Needs Assessment Modifications

Most existing anti-bullying programs start with a needs assessment or survey of bullying. To include students with mild/moderate or moderate/severe disabilities, the survey can be modified to collect the same information as for general education students. The needs assessment portion of the program should provide the questions in such a format that each group can participate and report accurately on their experiences with bullying at school.

Olweus's Bully/Victim Questionnaire (1996) is one of the most commonly used forms among general education populations. The Bully/Victim Questionnaire is an anonymous self-report questionnaire and includes exposure to physical, verbal, indirect, racial, and sexual forms of bullying, as well as where bullying occurs and the extent to which teachers, peers, and parents are informed about and respond to bullying. Frequency is reported on the 5-point scale identified by Solberg and Olweus (2003; i.e., 1 = not at all, 2 = only once or twice, 3 = three to four times, 4 = once a week, 5 = several times a week). Before distributing the survey, it's important to provide students with a definition of bullying to make sure that they understand the definition.

Although the same content should be used for the survey instrument across the entire student population, the delivery protocols may need to be modified to be appropriate for different types of students. First, because all individuals with disabilities fall across a spectrum in terms of severity and type of disability, the interview method should vary based on the needs of the student in order to obtain accurate responses. For example, it may be helpful to use overheads and read the survey out loud, or to use multiple proctors to administer the survey and make sure students are clear on the questions. Second, research suggests that children with intellectual disabilities can respond truthfully and accurately to items about their own experiences; however, because they are significantly more suggestible (Henry & Gudjonsson, 1999), interview questions should be presented in a nonleading manner using neutral verbal and nonverbal language. Third, students who are nonverbal or have limited/unintelligible speech should be interviewed using alternate formats that facilitate accurate responses. It is important to take into account whether students understand the items being presented and to be aware of any perceived power imbalance with teachers or researchers (Snelgrove, 2005).

Table 1   Modifying Anti-Bullying Program Components

Program component	Modifications
Needs assessment	Make sure definition of bullying is understood by students before beginning assessment.
	Tailor interview process to match level of understanding.
	Use neutral verbal and nonverbal language.
	Provide alternate methods of response.
Program content	Distribute bullying information so everyone (students and staff) have the same understanding of what it is.
	Educate all on the effects of both bullying and being bullied.
	Train staff working with students with disabilities on how to recognize and to respond to problem behaviors.
	Assess/modify existing disability harassment policies to ensure effectiveness for a spectrum of disabilities.
	Provide training for students on tolerance, empathy, respect, and responses to bullying.
	Take into account language and communication difficulties and provide multiple ways to report bullying.
	Match bullying content and training with positive behavior support.
Delivery method	Add additional examples into content.
	Provide concrete examples that incorporate a wide range of contexts.
	Allow more repetition of concepts.
	Provide opportunities to practice identifying, responding to, and reporting bullying.
	Make materials available in accessible ways (i.e., large print, audio recordings, Braille).
	Individualize to the needs of the students in your class.

Anti-Bullying Program Resources

Second Step: Skills for Social and Academic Success (Committee for Children, 2011; www.cfchildren.org/)

The Bully Around the Corner: Changing Brains—Changing Behaviour (Halstead, 2006), available from Brain Power Learning Group (www.brainpowerlearning.com/ALLABOUTBLJLLIES.html)

PATHS® (Promoting Alternative Thinking Strategies) Program (based on Kushé & Greenberg, 1994; curriculum available from Channing & Bete, www.channing-bete.com/prevention-programs/paths/paths.html)

Steps to Respect: A Bullying Prevention Program (Committee for Children, 2001, 2005; www.cfchildren.org/programs/str/overview/)

PeaceBuilders (www.peacebuilders.com/)

Olweus Bullying Prevention Program (www.clemson.edu/olweus/; www.olweus.org/public/index.page)

Program Components Modifications

The goal of any anti-bullying program (see box, "Anti-Bullying Program Resources") is to increase safety in the school environment. To make these programs useful for students with disabilities they should include the components identified in Cantu and Heumann's (2000) report focusing on preventing and responding to bullying and harassment occurring to children and youth with disabilities. These components include:

- A campus environment that is aware of disability concerns and sensitive to bullying and harassment.
- Whole-school approach where parents, students, employees, and community members are encouraged to discuss disability bullying and to report it.
- Publicized statements and procedures for handling bullying and harassment complaints.
- Appropriate, up-to-date, and timely training for staff and students to recognize and handle potential bullying and harassment.
- Counseling services for those who have been harassed and those who have been responsible for the harassment of others.
- Monitoring programs to follow up on resolved issues of harassment and bullying.
- Regular assessment and modification of existing disability harassment policies and procedures to ensure effectiveness.

These components should be incorporated into the anti-bullying program stages (i.e., awareness building, efficacy building, and skill building). In addition, schools need to respond to the needs of students with disabilities in each of these areas.

Awareness Building. Awareness building starts with creating a campus environment that is aware of disability needs and sensitive to bullying, through education. Raising awareness by

---

What Are the Essential Issues Surrounding Bullying?

- In bullying, a power dynamic exists such that one person feels less powerful than others. Any anti-bullying program should include training in how to regain power—through direct instruction, video instruction, and integrative activities.
- The anti-bullying program should include training on the importance of respecting others, accepting differences, and building empathy. Training should include components in tolerance, empathy, and respect.
- Everyone in the school shares responsibility for building a safe environment. Bystanders should be empowered

to report bullying and harassment they observe and provide assistance to victims, who often feel helpless. Also, the program should encourage children not to watch or join in these activities when they occur.
- It's important to break down the culture of silence that surrounds bullying. Being bullied over time often depends on victims and bystanders staying quiet about it. Good training programs seek to break down this culture of silence by teaching students that they should get help for themselves and others, how to get help, and what will happen when they report.

---

teaching the definition of bullying to both students and staff is key. Students with certain communication or processing disabilities may need to have the bullying definition explained in terms of concrete behaviors rather than relational terms. For example, for students with intellectual disabilities the teacher might explain that bullying is when someone is mean to you, they make you feel bad or hurt you, and you want them to stop. One might even go further to specify that it includes when someone hits you, pushes you, takes your stuff, or calls you names, and describe the specific behaviors involved.

Teaching everyone about the potential effects of involvement in harassment/violence lays the groundwork for efficacy building. Staff working with students with disabilities may need special training on how to recognize and respond to maladaptive behavior. This training should review the frequency, characteristics, and consequences of bullying identified in the needs assessment by students with intellectual disabilities. The training should target specific examples of those areas of greatest concern.

Efficacy Building. Efficacy here refers to the ability of students and staff to recognize and act to stop bullying. In many cases, efficacy starts with a clearly written anti-bullying policy. Policies establish a definition of bullying, reporting procedures, and consequences—and make these known to all stakeholders. Parents, students, employees, and community members should be informed of the policies and encouraged to discuss disability harassment and report it. Increases in reporting may occur as a consequence of clear and widely disseminated policies, so schools also need a monitoring system in place to follow up on unresolved issues of harassment and bullying. Provisions to regularly assess and modify existing disability harassment policies and procedures ensure effectiveness for all students.

Training for key stakeholders (e.g., students, parents, teachers, aides, administrators, yard duty, food service, transportation, security/safety officers) forms the basis for cultivating self-efficacy among those in a position to witness and report victimization. Training program components should include strategies for all stakeholders so they feel confident to take action against bullying. A basic understanding of underlying issues common to bullying is also needed to intervene effectively (see box, "What Are the Essential Issues Surrounding Bullying?").

Many students who are the targets of bullies believe that telling an adult, including parents, will not help, or might possibly make matters worse (Heinrichs, 2003; Newman & Murray, 2005). This belief is particularly salient for students with communication disorders who cannot effectively communicate a bullying event. As such, students with limited or no verbal communication are more likely to be victims of bullying: they are perfect targets who cannot "tell on" the bully. Research indicates that creating an environment in which students feel that their voice will be heard has a significant impact on reducing bullying (Rigby et al., 2004). Encouraging student self-efficacy includes both properly preparing staff to take appropriate action and also communicating to students that if they seek help their concerns will be recognized and handled in a safe and appropriate manner.

Skill Building. Providing appropriate, up-to-date, and timely preparation to staff and students to recognize and handle potential bullying and harassment is critical to a successful program. Direct training includes individual and institutional responses that have been found to reduce bullying. Prosocial skills should be emphasized. Many schools emphasize positive behavioral support as a way of managing student behavior in the classroom. Additionally, it is important to provide assistance to staff so they can use the techniques they are currently implementing to respond to bullying and harassment in ways that are supportive (e.g., reports are being taken seriously) and do not make the situation worse. Students with communication difficulties need to learn strategies for being able to report instances of bullying, harassment, and molestation. The training should also emphasize the importance of following up with students who do report and providing support and education for both bullies and victims.

Delivery Modifications

Much of the content of an anti-bullying program can be delivered to students with disabilities using the same existing modifications that teachers (both general education and special education) already use to deliver academic program content. However, some students with disabilities may need additional modifications in the delivery of anti-bullying program components. To address a broad range of needs among students with disabilities, provide additional examples of the program components; this will allow for more repetition and opportunities to practice identifying, responding to, and reporting instances of bullying and harassment. Some modifications that may be made to make program components most useful for students with disabilities include

- For students who are blind or have low vision, provide printed materials in Braille and/or with enlarged type.
- For students with intellectual disabilities, use specific examples when discussing concepts such as raising awareness of bullying and harassment.
- For students with intellectual disabilities, use a broad range of examples and scenarios when presenting program concepts; this increases the likelihood that skills will generalize across multiple contexts (e.g., across setting, people, etc.).

It is difficult to predict the needs of every student. As such, any antibullying program should be designed to offer teachers flexibility in the selection and delivery of content. These ideas allow teachers to individualize the curriculum as they deem appropriate to ensure content acquisition of all students.

Final Thoughts

Students with disabilities have the right to learn in a safe environment. Existing anti-bullying programs have largely ignored students with disabilities as being key stakeholders in the whole-school approach. However, existing programs can easily be modified to include students with disabilities in needs assessment, program components, and delivery of the program content. This information can be helpful to schools that are looking for ways to reduce bullying among students with disabilities.

References

Baumeister, A. L., Storch, E. A., & Geffken, G. R. (2008). Peer victimization in children with learning disabilities. *Child and Adolescent Social Work, 25,* 11–23. doi: 10.1007/s 10560-007-0109-6

Cantu, N. V., & Heumann, J. E. (2000). *Memorandum on harassment based on disability.* (Clearinghouse Report No. EC308035). Washington, DC: United States Department of Education. (ERIC Document Reproduction Service no. ED445431)

Dake, J., Price, J., Telljohann, S., & Funk, J. (2003). Teacher perceptions and practices regarding school bullying prevention. *Journal of School Health, 73,* 347–355. doi:10.1111/j.1746-1561.2003.tb04191.x

Davis, S., Howell, P., & Cooke, F. (2002). Sociodynamic relationships between children who stutter and their non-stuttering classmates. *Journal of Child Psychology and Psychiatry, 43,* 939–947. doi: 10.1111/1469-7610.00093

Doren, B., Bullis, M., & Benz, M. (1996). Predictors of victimization experiences of adolescents with disabilities in transition. *Exceptional Children, 63,* 7–18.

Espelage, D. L., & Swearer, S. M. (2003). Research on school bullying and victimization: What have we learned and where do we go from here? *School Psychology Review, 12,* 365–383.

Heinrichs, R. (2003). A whole-school approach to bullying: Special considerations for children with exceptionalities. *Intervention in School and Clinic, 38,* 195–204. doi:10.1177/105345120303800401

Henry, L., & Gudjonsson, G., (1999). Eyewitness memory and suggestibility in children with mental retardation. *American Journal on Mental Retardation 104,* 491–508. doi:10.1352/0895-8017(1999)104 <0491:EMASIC>2.0.CO;2

Humphrey, J. L., Storch, E. A., & Geffken, G. R. (2007). Peer victimization in children with attention-deficit hyperactivity disorder. *Journal of Child Health Care, 11,* 248–260. doi: 10.1177/1367493507079571

Kaukiainen, A., Salmivalli, C, Lagerspetz, K., Tamminen, M., Vauras, M., Maki, H., & Poskiparta, E. (2002). Learning difficulties, social intelligence, and self-concept: Connections to bully-victim problems. *Scandinavian Journal of Psychology. 43,* 269–278. doi:10.1111/1467-9450.00295

Knox, E., & Conti-Ramsden, G. (2003). Bullying risks of 11-year-old children with specific language impairment: Does school placement matter? *International Journal of Language & Communication Disorders, 38,* 1–12. doi: 10.1080/13682820304817

Marini, Z., Fairbaim, L, & Zuber, R. (2001). Peer harassment in individuals with developmental disabilities: Towards the development of a multi-dimensional bullying identification model. *Developmental Disabilities Bulletin, 29,* 170–195.

Mishna, F. (2003). Learning disabilities and bullying: Double jeopardy. *Journal of Learning Disabilities, 36,* 336–347. doi: 10.1177/00222194030360040501

Modell, S. (2005, February–March). *Disability abuse: Rape, sexual and physical assault—What can be done?* Paper presented at the 21st Annual Pacific Rim Conference, Honolulu, HI.

Modell, S., Mak, S., & Jackson, I. (2004, March). *My greatest fears: Rape, physical abuse, and neglect. What every parent needs to know. Perspectives from the parent, district attorney, and educator.* Paper presented at the 20th Annual Pacific Rim 2004 Conference, Honolulu, HI.

Morrison, G. M., & Furlong, M. (1994). Factors associated with the experience of school violence among general education, leadership class, opportunity class, and special day class pupils. *Education and Treatment of Children, 17,* 356–371.

Nabuzoka, D. (2003). Teacher ratings and peer nominations of bullying and other behavior of children with and without learning difficulties. *Educational Psychology, 23,* 307–321. doi:10.1080/0144341032000060147

Nabuzoka, D., & Smith, P. K. (1993). Sociometric status and social behavior of children with and without learning difficulties. *Journal of Child Psychology and Psychiatry, 34,* 1435–1448. doi:10.1111/j.1469-7610.1993. tb02101.x

Newman, R. S., & Murray, B. J. (2005). How students and teachers view the seriousness of peer harassment: When is it appropriate to seek help? *Journal of Educational Psychology, 97,* 347–365. doi: 10.1037/0022-0663.97.3.347

Olweus, D. (1993). *Bullying at school: What we know and what we can do.* Cambridge, MA: Blackwell.

Olweus, D. (1996). *The revised Olweus bully/victim questionnaire for students.* Bergen, Norway: University of Bergen.

Pivik, J., McComas, J., & LaFlamme, M. (2002). Barriers and facilitators to inclusive education. *Exceptional Children, 69,* 97–107.

Rigby, K., Smith, P., & Pepler, D. (2004). Working to prevent school bullying: Key issues. In P. Smith, D. Pepler, & K. Rigby (Eds.), *Bullying in schools* (pp. 1–12). Cambridge, England: Cambridge University Press.

Rose, C. A., Espelage, D. L., Stein, N. D., & Elliot, J. M. (2009, April). *Bullying and victimization among students in special education and general education curricula.* Paper presented at American Educational Research Association annual meeting, San Diego, California.

Saylor, C. F., & Leach, J. B. (2009). Perceived bullying and social support in students accessing special inclusion programming. *Journal of Developmental and Physical Disabilities, 21,* 69–80. doi:10.1007/s10882-008-9126-4

Snelgrove, S. (2005). Bad, mad and sad: Developing a methodology of inclusion and pedagogy for researching students with intellectual disabilities. *International Journal of Inclusive Education, 9,* 313–329. doi:10.1080/13603110500082236

Solberg, M. E., & Olweus, D. (2003). Prevalence estimation of school bullying with the Olweus bully/victims questionnaire. *Aggressive Behavior, 29,* 239–268. doi:10.1002/ab.10047

Sullivan, P. M., & Knutson, J. F. (2000). Maltreatment and disabilities: A population-based epidemiological study. *Child Abuse & Neglect, 24,* 1257–1273. doi:10.1016/ S0145-2134(00)00190-3

Whitney, I., Smith, P. K., & Thompson, D. (1994). Bullying and children with special needs. In P. K. Smith & S. Sharp (Eds.), *School bullying: Insights and perspectives* (pp. 213–240). London, England: Routledge.

Critical Thinking

1. Who are the students who are most often targets of bullies? Does this data surprise you?

2. Review the Essential Issues list in the article. Look for other articles in this Annual Edition that address those or similar issues. Compare the essential issues from all of these articles. Which are the most repeated issues? What does this mean for you as a teacher or administrator?

3. How can teachers and others help students with disabilities handle bullying when some students with disabilities may not understand what is happening?

Create Central

www.mhhe.com/createcentral

Internet References

Office of Safe and Drug-Free Schools
www2.ed.gov/about/offices/list/osdfs/index.html

Second Skills for Social and Academic Success
www.cfchildren.org//overview/

JULIANA RASKAUSKAS, *Assistant Professor, Department of Child Development, College of Education; and* **SCOTT MODELL** *(California CEC), Professor and Director, Autism Center for Excellence, Department of Kinesiology & Health Science, California State University, Sacramento.*

Raskauskas, Juliana and Modell, Scott. From *Teaching Exceptional Children,* vol. 44, no. 1, 2011, pp. 60, 62–67. Copyright © 2011 by Council for Exceptional Children. Reprinted by permission via Copyright Clearance Center. www.cec.csped.org

Article   Prepared by: Rebecca B. Evers, *Winthrop University.*

Why Our Approach to Bullying Is Bad for Kids

Safe schools—for a safer world.

SUSAN PORTER

Learning Outcomes

After reading this article, you will be able to:

- Debate the positive and negative issues associated with how we define and label incidences of bullying.

It's hard to avoid the topic of bullying these days. From parents chatting about it on the soccer field sidelines, to op-ed pieces calling for police presence on school campuses, to the President and First Lady hosting webcasts on the subject—just about everyone with a soapbox, real or virtual, is talking about how to deal with the bullying scourge that is sweeping the nation's schools. And, boy, is it bad.

The next time you've got a spare moment, Google "statistics on bullying" and see for yourself. When I last looked, this is what popped up:

- One in five kids is bullied.
- Twenty-three percent of students say they have been bullied several times.
- One in four kids is bullied.
- Fifty percent of kids are bullied, and 10 percent are bullied on a regular basis.
- Seventy-four percent of 8- to 11-year-olds said teasing and bullying occurs at their schools.
- Seventy-seven percent of students say they've been bullied recently.
- It is estimated that more than half [emphasis added] of school bullying incidents are never reported.

Despite the fact that the statistics are wildly inconsistent, even the lowest percentages are scary, and they suggest that our kids aren't safe in schools because they're hurting one another at alarmingly high rates. At best, the data suggest that we've got a serious problem on our hands.

Or do we?

Parents often ask me what's behind the rise of bullying among children, and whether or not kids today are different from those of previous generations. As a school counselor, with almost 25 years of experience, I tell parents that kids haven't changed much over the years, but something significant has changed recently, and that's how our culture thinks about, talks about, and deals with aggressive childhood behavior. And the change is profound.

A Shift in Definition

A few years ago, a K-12 school asked me to consult on the subject of bullying. This was about the time many schools were implementing "Zero Tolerance Anti-Bullying" policies. In preparation for my presentation, I researched the topic by reviewing local and regional policies on bullying, and articles in the professional literature. I was stunned by what I learned.

First, I discovered that bullying was everywhere. The statistics were as disturbing and wide-ranging then as they are today. Admittedly, I was shocked. Here I was, a school counselor with years of experience as both a mental health clinician in schools and a consultant to schools, and somehow I had missed all of this. Of course, I had dealt with cases of bullying in my own work, but the sweeping nature of the phenomenon, as suggested by my research, had eluded me. The ground under my professional feet started to shake. As I digested the information I felt horrible. How could I have been so blind?

But then, as I researched further, I learned another important thing about bullying. According to the many definitions I read, the term had come to include not only the classic forms of harassment between children, behaviors such as shaking down a kid for lunch money, beating up a smaller kid in the schoolyard, or repeated hate speech. Now, it also included behaviors such as social exclusion, name-calling, teasing, sarcasm, and being unfriendly. I also noted a corresponding shift in the telltale signs expressed by the victims of bullying, which in addition to extreme symptoms, such as school phobia and depression, now included symptoms such as feeling upset and being sad.

As I considered all of this, I realized what I'd missed in my work was not a rise in incidents of classic bullying, but rather the creeping expansion of the definition of bullying, which according to the average anti-bullying policy was now a catchall term for the routine—albeit nasty—selfishness, meanness, and other social misfires that characterize childhood and adolescence. I call this the expanded definition of bullying.

As I completed my research, I sensed that this expanded definition of bullying was doing more than just attempting to protect kids. It was also making a lot of normal childhood behaviors seem pathological and dangerous. Many of the behaviors described in the bullying literature were almost inevitable, given brain development, but this didn't seem to matter. What mattered instead was setting unrealistic guidelines for children's behavior in the hopes of preventing them from feeling pain. Lost, it seemed, was the intention of helping kids learn from their mistakes and developing resilience in the face of adversity.

The Preadolescent and Adolescent Brains and Development

The preadolescent and adolescent brains can be characterized in many ways, the most important of which, when it comes to the expanded definition of bullying, is that they are not yet fully developed. And the most important part of the brain that has not yet developed is the prefrontal cortex, the part of the brain that deals with functions such as impulse control, judgment, and empathy. These functions are often referred to as executive functions, and researchers believe we continue to develop these functions well into our twenties.

This means children, even older teenagers, have brains that are not yet capable of being consistently in control of themselves, even when they try really, really hard. As children age, however, the executive functions start to kick in more predictably, and therefore older teenagers can be entrusted, for example, to drive a car or babysit a younger child or do their homework without a nightly battle. That said, the key is consistency, and even the best-behaved and seemingly mature teenager can have lapses in judgment and behave without the benefit of fully formed executive functions.

If you consider the expanded definition of bullying in light of brain development, and think about behaviors such as teasing, name-calling, and social exclusion, you can see why kids and teenagers might exhibit these behaviors, given the fact that their brains simply aren't fully formed yet. Being polite, keeping their hands to themselves, not saying everything that pops into their heads, staying on task, and being thoughtful—these are the things kids work on every day, and their brains won't master these tasks for years. The brain constantly makes mistakes as it develops these capacities, and often these mistakes come at the expense of another person's feelings.

Add to this various aspects of development, such as the marked self-consciousness that characterizes adolescence, and you have a recipe for insensitive behavior. When kids walk down school hallways, they aren't thinking about other people's feelings; they're thinking me, me, me. This is normal. But this leaves them vulnerable to making big mistakes when it comes to attending to the needs of others, and acting with these needs in mind.

So, regardless of what we'd like, we can't expect kids to sail through childhood and adolescence without blundering—especially given that the average adolescent brain, still under construction, is hardwired to behave in ways that are irritating and selfish at times. This explains, in part, the prevalence of bullying (the expanded version) these days.

There are other reasons why the milder bullying behaviors are rampant (and always have been), and why we can't eradicate them.

First, brains at this age are prone to misinterpreting facial cues, a fact that has huge implications when it comes to social interactions. For example, the teenage brain might interpret a classmate's frown to mean, "She really hates me! She doesn't want to be my friend," when, in fact, it probably means something completely different. A missed cue of this kind, coupled with the self-absorption of the age, can turn a non-situation into an emotional drama, as the teenager imagines her classmate's expression to be both (A) extremely negative, and (B) necessarily about her.

Second, brains at this stage tend to respond very emotionally to social situations. For example, Cathy looks at Susie the wrong way. Unlike an adult, Susie isn't unaffected by Cathy's expression, or simply annoyed by it. Susie takes it personally. She may feel overwrought. This is especially true if Susie believes Cathy's expression indicates that she (Cathy) wishes to exclude her (Susie). Research has shown that the threat of social exclusion is one of the scariest things for a pre-teen girl's brain to deal with, so Susie's response to Cathy's expression could conceivably cause Susie's brain to initiate a fight-or-flight response, sending Susie on an emotional roller-coaster ride that terrifies her.

An important point to understand about a situation like Susie's is that her reactions and feelings are real to her, but that doesn't mean they are an accurate gauge of the outside situation. Our current approach to bullying places so much emphasis on a child's inner experience that I often deal with children (supported by their parents) who believe that their feelings are facts. In today's social climate, Susie's very real, albeit internal and emotional response to Cathy's frown can be sufficient evidence to Susie that Cathy has done something really bad. And, if Susie claimed that Cathy had repeatedly acted this way, and if Susie had some very wounded feelings as evidence, then Cathy could be in big trouble. At the very least, she'd probably get a stern talking-to from a teacher or school administrator. And for what, making a face? But with our expanded definition of bullying, Susie's pain is the trump card.

Finally, bullying is widespread because kids at this age tend to see the world in black and white terms. Their brains are just developing the capacity for abstract thought, and while they may have glimpses of it here and there, for the most part, and especially when it comes to social situations, the world to them is pretty cut and dried. As such, there is little room for a nuanced interpretation of painful situations, so a perceived social attack is usually interpreted in dire terms.

Unfortunately, in our desire to protect perceived victims, we downplay or ignore these essential truths about development such that, over the past decade or so, we have succeeded in redefining many unpleasant childhood behaviors as bullying, and thus the epidemic. With this expanded definition of bullying in place, the average child, behaving in an average way, is statistically likely to be branded a bully at some point, and to become a victim of bullying—and this troubles me.

None of this means that we should ignore children's bad behavior or pain. But our current approach to bullying, which superimposes on the childhood brain an adult-like capacity for intent and self-control, gives little encouragement for growth and change. It also ignores children's capacity for resilience, and it does both through its use of labels.

Fixed Mindsets and the Problem with Labels

Labels are everywhere when it comes to bullying, and they are an important part of how anti-bullying rhetoric aims to educate kids about aggression. Go to any anti-bullying website, or review anti-bullying curricula, and you will see what I mean. The labels are ubiquitous: active bully, passive bully, lieutenant, henchman, bystander, ally, hero, and, of course, victim. They constitute the dramatis personae of the bully play. In learning about bullying, students are instructed to identify the players, imagine what roles they play, and clearly distinguish between the wrongdoer and the wronged. It's all fixed, perhaps in an effort to simplify what is usually an inherently complicated situation. And with these labels, the painful dynamics that occur among children become carved in stone.

By now, most educators are familiar with the work of Stanford University psychologist Carol Dweck. In *Mindset: The New Psychology of Success*, she describes the two lenses through which we make sense of the world: the fixed mindset and the growth mindset. The fixed mindset is characterized by a belief that personality and intelligence are static qualities, and that they can't be developed. A growth mindset, on the other hand, is characterized by a belief that these qualities can change and develop, and that effort leads to learning and therefore growth.

Our approach to bullying is problematic, if for no other reason, because it provides kids (and adults) with little conceptual room to maneuver. When a child misbehaves and is labeled a bully, the label declares something about his character, not just about his behavior. For adults, the bully label affixed to a child sticks in our minds, and encourages us to view the child's behavior—past, present, and future—through this lens. If we consider that children don't develop the capacity for abstract thought until early adolescence (if then), we see how problematic labels are. Children can't see beyond the concrete, so they

will take labels like bully or victim and run with them, usually to their own detriment. But adults should know better. Our goal is to facilitate growth and change.

I encourage readers to carefully examine their own schools' and states' anti-bullying policies and curricula to bring this point home. I have yet to come across a policy that approaches the issue of problematic childhood and adolescent behavior from a growth mindset. These policies, in their presumed effort to protect kids and shape behavior, do little more than make us view children and their behavior in a fixed framework. The formulaic ways in which aggression among kids is described, and a general indifference to context through the use of easy-to-apply labels, let us off the hook for approaching problematic situations between children with compassion for all parties involved.

The use of labels, and the accompanying fixed mindset they engender, does nothing to help us help kids. Children need us to understand their social lives and behavior in dynamic, not static, terms, and to separate their behavior from their characters. Children should be allowed to make mistakes, and these mistakes, even if egregious, should not result in the children receiving labels that limit our ability (and possibly our desire) to help them develop into responsible adults.

But labels aren't bad for just the bullies; they're bad for the victims, too. Remember, mindsets are about whether we see the world through fixed or growth lenses, and the victim label is as fixed and inflexible as the bully one. Both discourage self-exploration and faith in change. The bully has no incentive to change as long as the adults (and children) around him see him in wholly negative terms, while the victim has no incentive to develop resilience if he is continually identified with and reminded of his wounds. In my experience, victims are often the biggest losers when it comes to labeling because, as victims, they are encouraged to identify with their vulnerability, and as a result, their sense of agency often derives from their feelings of helplessness and pain.

The other labels used in the bully rhetoric—such as bystander, ally, and hero—are also problematic. For starters, they give children, and especially young children, the incorrect impression that they are responsible for preventing other people's pain. In addition, they lead children to believe that they must be vigilant at all times, and know when and how to intervene in complex social situations. Sure, kids should be encouraged to help out other kids, but it is neither their role nor their duty to assume this much responsibility for situations beyond their control, and yet this is the impression our use of labels gives them.

If nothing else, we should abandon labels and the fixed mindset around bullying because they alienate parents, and we need to work closely with parents if we want to help children change their behavior. I routinely tell parents to stop listening if someone (let's say a teacher or another parent) calls their child a bully. Why? Because when adults use the term bully, they have stopped seeing a child's potential, and they aren't focused on helping that child grow. Using the term bully is an easy way out, and it allows adults to avoid the very hard work of helping children change their behavior. This is not just an issue

---

Code of Conduct for XYZ Academy

Middle School (or High School) is a time of tremendous physical, psychological, and emotional growth and change, and the expectations for XYZ Academy students reflect the capabilities of adolescents (or children) at this developmental stage and the aspirations the community has for them.

All XYZ Academy students are expected to behave in ways that support the well-being, health, and safety of themselves and others. To this end, students should be respectful in their interactions and relationships and learn to recognize how their actions, including their speech, affect others. XYZ students should aim to be courteous, kind, and inclusive, and accept constructive feedback and criticism as being essential parts of learning and membership within the community.

As an educational community, XYZ recognizes that social-emotional development, as any other subject, takes time to master, and involves mistakes and missteps. As such, adults are charged to help students reflect upon their behavioral choices, especially when these choices hurt or deny the rights of others. In cases of severe or repeated negative behavior that falls short of expected conduct, disciplinary action may be taken.

---

of semantics, as any parent of an accused child can attest. It's about believing in growth or not.

An Alternative Approach

In order to do right by our students, we must first understand brain and psychological development and set reasonable expectations for student behavior. We must recognize that the brain doesn't fully develop for years, and that it makes plenty of mistakes along the way, whether in mathematics or history or relationships. We succeed as educators when we help students solve academic problems. Likewise, we succeed when we help students solve behavioral problems. And just as we avoid labels when it comes to students as academic learners, we should avoid labels when it comes to students as social-emotional learners.

We must also abandon the conceptual frameworks and rhetoric that encourage us to understand childhood aggression in simple and formulaic ways, and we should adopt policies that reflect a growth mindset. To this end, I have included a Code of Conduct statement that approaches behavior and expectations from a growth mindset. You will note that it does not specify certain behaviors or reactions to behaviors, as do most anti-bullying policies. It is aspirational, open-ended, and doesn't dictate how a school should respond to complex social situations among students.

As educators, it is our job to lead the way. When we stop seeing the potential for growth and change in children, it's time for us to retire.

Critical Thinking

1. Porter holds what may be considered a controversial view on bullying. Do you agree or disagree with her new definition and primary concerns about bullying? Justify your answer with at least three reasons.

2. Think back to your childhood, particularly during "tween" years. What bullying label would you give yourself? At what point in your life did that label no longer apply to you? Now, describe how and why your behavior changed. Does your experience support or deny Porter's assertions?

Create Central

www.mhhe.com/createcentral

Internet References

Wrightslaw on Bullying
    www.wrightslaw.com/blog/?tag=bullying

Susan Porter is dean of students at The Branson School (California). Her book, *Bully Nation: Why America's Approach to Bullying Is Bad for Everyone,* is scheduled to be released by Paragon Press in the spring of 2013.
